Enemy in the Promised Land

ENEMY IN THE PROMISED LAND

SANA HASAN

An Egyptian Woman's
Journey into Israel

SCHOCKEN BOOKS
NEW YORK

All rights reserved under International and Pan-American
Copyright Conventions. Published in the United States
by Pantheon Books, a division of Random House, Inc.,
New York, and simultaneously in Canada by Random
House of Canada Limited, Toronto. Originally published
in hardcover by Pantheon Books, a division of
Random House, Inc.

Library of Congress Cataloging-in-Publication Data

Hasan, Sana.
Enemy in the promised land.
1. Israel—Description and travel.   2. Hasan, Sana.
3. Jewish-Arab relations—1973–   .   I. Title.
DS107.4.H3438   1987   915.694′0454
86-42623
ISBN 0-394-52765-8
ISBN 0-8052-0853-4

Manufactured in the United States of America

Book design by Guenet Abraham

First Schocken Edition

For Monica,
without whom this book would not have been.
And
for Harvard University,
my second home
during five years of exile.

CONTENTS

Preface

THROUGHOUT MY STAY IN ISRAEL I kept a diary in which, every night, I wrote down what had happened to me during the day. Sometimes, after meeting someone who had an interesting life story or point of view, I would ask if I might meet him or her again in order to hear the story once more and record it. In those instances where there was no tape recording I have recreated the conversation to the best of my ability, through the use of my diary, or, as in the episodes from my childhood, from my best memory. In the case of politicians or official spokesmen for a community, I would take a tape recorder along if it was a meeting I had requested myself. But if I was invited by them for lunch, dinner, or tea—as in the cases of Golda Meir, Menachem Begin, or Shimon Peres, to name a few examples—I judged it impolite to show up with a recorder in hand, and contented myself with noting what they had told me in my diary after I returned home.

In writing this book (which I did some years after my trip) I disguised the identities of all the people in it, with the exception of well-known public figures, by changing their names and sometimes their appearances, and wherever possible, their locations as well. In addition, I changed the names of anyone related to them. Similarly, during my trip, I had sometimes had to conceal my own identity from people who now appear in this book, in order to act as a participant-observer. Finally, in grouping things thematically into chapters, it has been necessary in some cases to alter locations, change chronologies, and telescope events. None of this, however, in any way alters the truth of the story.

In Israel the number of people I am indebted to is legion. I would like to thank all the cabinet ministers past and present who so generously gave their time, and to assure them that any criticism I might have made of their views and policies in no way diminishes the appreciation I feel for their having consented to meet me. These include the late Golda Meir and the late Moshe Dayan; Menachem Begin, Shimon Peres, Yitzhak Rabin, Ezer Weitzman, Chaim Bar-lev, Ariel Sharon, Abraham Shapiro, Yitzhak Navon, Victor Shemtov, Amnon Rubinstein, Shlomo Hillel, Moshe Kol, and Abba Eban. Mr. Eban helped me get a visa to Israel, for which I am deeply grateful. I would like to thank Ambassador Simcha Dinitz, Moshe Ben-Meir, Chaim Shur, and Knesset members Ehud Olmert, Geula Cohen, Moshe Una, Shulamit Aloni, Lova Eliav, Matti Peled, Meir Pail, Ran Cohen, and Tewfik Toubi, who enabled me to learn about Israel's entire political spectrum.

I am grateful to General Israel Tal for the many meetings at his house and mine, during which he expounded to me candidly on strategic and tactical military issues related to Israel's defense; to him I owe any ability to distinguish between Israel's genuine security concerns and its professed ones. Mayor Teddy Kollek of Jerusalem was so generous as to invite me to live in Mishkenot Sha'ananim, and Annie Ohayon, the receptionist of Mishkenot Sha'ananim, was gracious and helpful throughout my stay. I thank Mayor Shlomo Lahat of Tel Aviv for inviting me to stay at the Grand Beach Hotel. Yoav (fictitious name) made my stay in Israel infinitely more convenient by offering me the use of his Tel Aviv apartment, and I am grateful as well to Theo Klein for offering me the use of his Jaffa apartment, and Shoshana Ellings for offering me the use of her Haifa apartment. Ambassador Mordechai Gazit provided help of all kinds—from setting up the interview with then Prime Minister Yitzhak Rabin to arranging my return flight to America—and El Al public-relations manager Arnold Sherman offered me a free round trip to Paris to visit my parents. I am indebted to them both.

I would like to thank all those Israelis who appear in this book, as well as those who opened their homes and hearts to me (especially Dr. Eddy Kaufman, Katy Katz, and Tami Litani) as well as the kibbutzniks —particularly Chava Shafir and Yankele Yoav—who, as I traveled back and forth between the kibbutzim and the cities, translated for me from Hebrew at the beginning of my stay and helped me in every conceivable way.

Many people who contributed to my understanding of Israel do not appear in this book. I owe much of my understanding of Israel's religious life to Rabbi Adin Steinsaltz, who sat up late into the nights with me explaining Jewish law; to Rabbi Posner of Kfar Chabad, who had me as an overnight guest, and opened a window for me onto the world of Chasidism; and to Rabbi Goldstein, who gave me a rare insight into yeshiva life by inviting me to the Diaspora Yeshiva, which he runs.

For contributing to my understanding of the secular side of Israel, I thank novelists Amos Oz and Chaim Guri, Professor Shimon Shamir, Dr. Israel Katz, journalists Uri Avneri and Amos Kenan, and playwright Yehoshua Sobol, whose wonderful plays were an invaluable source of insights on everything from the problems of the early communal settlements in Palestine to those of Oriental Jews today. My special thanks go to television producer Ram Levy, who took me to many Arab-Israeli villages and showed me his excellent documentaries on the Palestinian and Oriental Jews, adding much to my knowledge of these ethnic communities in Israel, and to director Nola Chilton, who gave up her days off to drive me about the country and staged for me her moving play on war widows. The poet Natan Yonatan and his wife, Zfira, shared with me their grief as bereaved parents, as did General Zorea and his wife, Chaim Shur and his wife, and Ruth Lies; and Avraham Kochavi of Kibbutz Yad-Mordechai and Rabbi Lau of Tel Aviv were kind enough to tell me their memories of Auschwitz, where their families were destroyed. I deeply appreciate the effort they made even at the cost of their pain. I also thank Surika Braverman of Kibbutz Shamir, who gave me a glimpse into her life as a woman partisan who parachuted, along with Hana Senesh, behind enemy lines in Europe during World War II; and Antek Zukerman and his wife of Kibbutz Lochamei Hagetaot, who spent days describing to me their lives as partisans in the uprising against the Nazis in the Warsaw Ghetto. Finally, I am grateful to two people who gave me a chance to hear about the occupation of Arab territories from the point of view of the occupier: Shlomo Gazit, military administrator of the West Bank, who presented to me the "official line," and Meron Benvenisti, deputy mayor in charge of the Palestinians of Jerusalem, who gave a very forthright account of the complex moral issues facing an administrator who feels ill at ease in the role of occupier.

In the occupied territories I owe much to the many Palestinians who offered me the hospitality of their homes, and who elucidated for me their problems and shared with me their pain. I am particularly grateful to Mr. Khalidi of Arab Jerusalem, and the el Misris of Nablus. To Dr. Haidar el Shafei of the Gaza Strip I owe yet another perspective, that of Palestinian life under the Egyptian adminstration. My special thanks go to the journalist Jamil Hamad of Bethlehem, who more than anyone else helped me to develop a feel for the indignities of occupation. I am greatly indebted to Adel (ficticious name) of Jericho for sharing with me his very moving experience as a PLO suspect under torture in an Israeli prison. My thanks, finally, to the many Palestinian workers who allowed me to interview them. Though I have chosen to limit myself to the Palestinians within Israel proper in this book, because I believe the Palestinians in the occupied territories deserve a book of their own, the latters' experience has shed light on much that is dealt with in this book, for it is clearly impossible to treat Israeli themes without touching on the other side of the equation—the Palestinians.

In the United States, my special thanks go to my friend Arlette, who offered me the hospitality of her New York apartment whenever I had to fly in for work on the book; to my editor Sara Blackburn, who strove to give shape to a vast, incoherent mass of material; to Natalie Chapman, the copyeditor; and to my agent Julian Bach, who was so generous with his time and money.

Here, in the city of Vienna, I one day tore myself loose from the entire circle of my life, from all my acquaintances and all my friends, and, as a lonely man, stood up for what I considered right. I do not feel a need for a majority. I need only to be in harmony with my own conviction.

Then I am content even if no dog accepts a piece of bread from me.

Theodor Herzl

PART ONE

1

The Tower of Babel

Pitch dark. The roar builds. A tiny particle detaches itself from the earth and soars up, intent on its solitary course. The voyage has begun.

This was it. I was sure of it now. There was that sharp pain in my elbows—an old, familiar symptom of fear. Up to the moment when the door of the plane closed behind me with irrevocable finality, going to Israel had been flirtation with danger: secret visits to the Israeli consulate, hushed conversations with close friends in Cambridge cafés; I knew all along that I could still back out of it—even after having obtained the visa, even after having purchased my ticket. But now I had gone too far to retreat.

A blinding flash of light slashed the sky. For some time, the airplane struggled upward, trying to hoist itself over the somber clouds. Then, as if resigned to its fate, it pitched ahead into the night. I pressed my forehead against the window, trying to pierce through the darkness outside. My eyes roamed about in search of land. There were no frontiers here, only the sky, spread out like a veil. I remembered the maps in my geography books. They were always shaded black and labeled "Occupied Palestine."

Nothing was ever said about developments on Palestinian soil since gangs of "marauders" had "stolen" it with the help of Great Britain, the United States, and other imperialist countries. Furthermore, all the pages about Israel were missing from the *World Economic Handbook* on the shelf of our school library. The same treatment was meted out to the venerable *Encyclopaedia Britannica*.

In sixth grade, our civics textbook, which bore the Arabic epigraph *"Al ilm nur"* ("Learning is light"), taught us all we needed to know on the subject of Israel. Palestine was an Arab nation that should have lived

3

a prosperous and good life, but evil people had pounced on its land, seized its homes, and indiscriminately butchered innocent civilians.

Just in case we had missed it, our reading and poetry book reiterated the point:

> Rise in vengeance!
> Crush the heads of the marauders!
> Make out of Palestine a fatherland for the Arabs,
> And a graveyard for the Jews.

And our homework lent the subject the implacable logic of grammar:

> The following words are in the accusative. Indicate the reason for this:

> We will not forget the *land* of Palestine.
> We will expel the *usurper* from our land.

> The words underlined in the following sentences are in the nominative. Indicate the reason for this:

> The *battle* for the sake of Palestine is a duty.
> The *Arabs* will drive the Jews out of Palestine.

Very early on, my fear of these "evil people" turned into a forbidden attraction. I often daydreamed about crossing the Egyptian border into Israel with the same yearning nineteenth-century adventurers must have felt at the thought of exploring darkest Africa.

I would make the escape while my parents slept. I modeled my adventure on the heroic feats of the prisoner of Zenda. Like him, I possessed all the physical prowess necessary for the exploit. I would knot my bedsheets together and, in a remarkable display of agility, lower myself out the window, gliding down the improvised rope. Then I would steal away in the night, heading for my cousin Nadia's house. Once I had climbed over the railing that surrounded her garden, I would creep forward, concealing myself behind the eucalyptus trees. Three pebbles aimed at her window would wake her up. She would jump onto the terrace in front of her bedroom, and we would flee together in search of Ali, the Bedouin boy with slippers made of palm leaves, who brought our pitas every morning. Ali lived in a desert encampment, by the Great Pyramids of Giza. Once we had reached it, I would sound a low whistle and he would appear instantly with his camel. Our caravan would journey for many days and many nights across the desert. We would sleep in the holes we had scooped out in the warm sand, drink goat milk, and eat a pastry that Ali made by deftly rolling flour and dates together with the palms of his hands and then cooking it over a fire. Ali would drop us off at the Israeli border, and from there on we would roam on our own.

Here the picture became hazy. In those childhood flights of fantasy the enemy did not have a human form. The dark, menacing region called Israel was populated only by the mythical monsters of my picture books, until I met Dany.

Along with other members of the Egyptian and European upper class in Cairo, my family often spent summers in Bad Gastein, an Austrian mountain spa. Although my parents could not find enough praises to lavish on the resort—they professed it worked wonders with their rheumatism—boredom was what it inspired in me. The average age of the clients at our hotel, Der Kaiserhof, was sixty. There were only a handful of children, and for these unfortunates little entertainment existed outside of sedate walks with their families.

Day in and day out, the same schedule reigned. In the morning, the older people took the waters, returned, and then rested in their rooms until noon. After lunch they napped, and in the afternoon the whole family would go to one of the many terraces or cafés for tea. While the children fidgeted in their chairs, the grown-ups gossiped. Then came the time for a walk in the woods before sunset. This was followed by supper, after which the men retired to the billiard room and the women played cards, leaving the children to their own devices until bedtime. In my case, this meant making the rounds of the hotel lobby in search of old ladies whom I might inveigle into a game of gin rummy or poker. Since I was not allowed to play for cash, we used candies. At the end of the game, I almost invariably walked away with a large booty. This dreary routine was broken once a month by a magician, who entertained the children in the hotel lobby with a sad show of tricks and ventriloquy.

But one afternoon, while my parents napped and I was out on the terrace absorbed in my favorite comic book, *Max und Moritz* (whose pranks were for me such a source of inspiration that Mother had threatened more than once to ban the series), my routine was irrevocably altered by the arrival of an Israeli family—the first I had ever set eyes on. Yes, that was unmistakably what they were, for I had heard the woman tell the receptionist, "*Ach! Es war so furchtbar heiss in Tel Aviv. Ganz schrecklich!*" ("Ach! It was so dreadfully hot in Tel Aviv. Just awful!").

I sat entranced, taking in every detail of their appearance. The elderly lady wore an exotic straw hat studded with wine-colored berries. Her spangled dress of navy silk set off her beige gloves and matching alligator handbag. She looked so frail, with her diminutive frame, birdlike profile, and watery blue eyes, that I could not help being reminded of my collection of dried butterflies, which crumbled to pieces if they were handled indelicately. Her husband, decked out in his stiffly starched shirt, bow tie, red-suspendered trousers, puttees, ankle-high shoes, and ivory-handled black cane, could have been straight out of a Charlie Chaplin movie. He was a man of medium height with splendid, upward-curling white whiskers, and his hair, parted down the middle, looped around the sides of his forehead. Their grandson, Dany, was eleven and plump: a headful of red curls, a round nose, and hundreds upon hundreds of freckles.

From that day on, posting myself on the terrace after lunch, I would wait for their appearance as one awaited the arrival of creatures from Mars. The Israelis would always have their coffee there and then sit and read the papers. I scrutinized them from a safe distance with the same curiosity each day—almost surprised to discover that they possessed eyes, noses, feet. I had always known, of course, that Israelis existed, but until then they had just been an abstraction. Now I could watch them, as one watched a pornographic performance that is at once forbidden, repulsive, and terribly attractive. I was shocked to see the hated enemies joking, laughing, and drinking coffee with such carefree levity, totally oblivious to their own evil, and I was offended by the courtesy shown them by the hotel waiters. How could they be so indifferent to the harm these people had done us?

Of Austrian origin, the couple spoke German most of the time, but occasionally, when addressing the little boy, they used Hebrew. I would listen to these demonic Hebraic sounds transfixed, as if I were catching the cackle of witches at a distance. Each note screeched through the air. I latched onto every syllable, desperately trying to decode the magic formula yet afraid to draw too near lest I should fall under its spell.

Three weeks of such observation emboldened me. One day, no longer able to contain my curiosity, I ventured to talk to them. I approached their table with a pounding heart, and after a moment of silence, in which I struggled to force the voice out of my throat, I asked the lady in German what time it was. I was trembling so much that I fled without waiting for the answer, but even as I ran off, I was flushed with pride at the thought of this act, which in my eyes was nothing short of heroic. I was seven, and it seemed to me as though I had stuck my head into a lion's mouth. I had emerged! I had survived!

Encouraged by my first success, I grew even more intrepid. I accosted the little boy one day and asked him if he wanted to go berry picking with me in the woods. From then on, we became inseparable. We climbed trees, fed squirrels, picked edelweiss, and went on long hikes. Once, at Dany's suggestion, we hid behind the heavy velvet curtains in the billiard room and played you-show-me-and-I'll-show-you. It was the first time I had seen anything like that.

But our friendship, to which I believed my parents were still oblivious, was to be of short duration. One day we were playing hide-and-seek in the woods. It was Dany's turn to hide, and I was leaning against a tree, arm over my eyes, counting "eighteen, nineteen, twenty." I turned. But instead of Dany, I saw Mother storming downhill toward me. I was cornered. Dany was nowhere in sight. I stood alone, face to face with her.

"What are you doing here?" she asked dryly.

"I was only playing . . ."

"You've no business talking to Israelis!" she retorted, her voice ringing with indignation.

"But Mother, I was only—"

Without giving me a chance to finish, she grabbed my arm, menacingly intoning, "Our children don't talk to Zionists," and dragged me off.

It was my first encounter with the term *Zionists*. I had always known the word *Israel* to connote evil. Because of the very way it was pronounced in Arabic—*Isssraeeel*—I had been forced to conclude almost from infancy that we were not moved by any great sentiment of benevolence toward that nation. Its sound so resembled the hiss of snakes in the Tarzan movies I had seen that I automatically associated it with something sinister. But "Zionist," "Zionist"—this echoed through me all the way up to the hotel. I did not comprehend it, but it held for me the allure of the forbidden.

Once back in the hotel, I was privy to Mother's long list of all-too-familiar recriminations. Why couldn't I be more like my sister and brother? I had always been a troublemaker, "like Gamal Abdel Nassar." From the day I was born, no, even before that, I had given my poor mother no peace. Hadn't I troubled her pregnancy by furiously kicking her in the stomach, and wasn't I the only one of her children to have given her such labor pains that she needed a cesarean? And so on.

She had always suspected that the problems I caused her later in life had something to do with my birth being a "mistake" in the first place. They had planned only two children, and when "it" happened, Mother, acting on a friend's counsel, had resorted to cod-liver oil followed by hot showers, but she had not aborted. When I was only eight months old, Miss Boden, my English nanny, said, "She's a bad egg, madam, there's plenty of trouble in store for you in the future." It may have been the loss of my hair, brought on by a spell of eczema, that had inspired my nanny to liken my head to an egg, but Mother was not amused and had her fired. Later, however, she came to see that the nanny had been right all along. When I was five, Mother placed me in the Mère de Dieu, a French Catholic school in Cairo that she and her sisters had attended. In her view, only a Catholic education would tame my incorrigible nature. A month after my enrollment, the sister called Mother in for "a serious talk." She complained about my bad "American manners." I would clutch her veil, shrieking, "I want an apple! Give me an apple," and one night, goaded by my curiosity to see if the sisters undressed before going to bed, I had had the audacity to hide behind the curtains surrounding her cubicle in order to spy on her when she turned in. It was in vain that Mother supplicated the sister: "*Pardonnez-lui, ma soeur, comme Jésus a pardonné aux pécheurs. Il faut la comprendre, cette petite a un tempérament nerveux parce qu'elle est asthmatique*" ("Forgive her, Sister, as Jesus forgave the sinners. You must understand her, this girl has a nervous disposition because she is asthmatic"). Such arguments carried little weight with the sister, and when, at the end of the year, I was caught redhanded with eight rulers I had filched from my classmates' schoolbags, she expelled me. In the next school, the Sacré Coeur, I lasted a few months longer. But Mother was soon informed that I was lazy, disobedient, and disrespectful of authority. Punishments were of no avail in my case; in fact, I seemed to enjoy them. Had I not retaliated for having been deprived of my Sunday outing three weeks in a row by watering the first-floor classroom with the garden hose?

The only solution was to keep me at home and get me private tutors, Mother was advised. "She is not the daughter of King Farouk, you know," was her peeved reply. Besides, I was too much to handle, so off I went to the Deutsche Evangelische Schule at the suggestion of an aunt who was a great believer in German discipline. That lasted a few months. Next came the English Girls' College in Alexandria. Within two years, on the headmistress's recommendation, Mother had resigned herself to sending me to England to attend a school for children with "special problems." My conduct left her little choice. Inspired by a Western, I had slashed my arm and a friend's arm with a penknife, mixing our blood together to cement our "Apache brotherhood." My numerous attempts to run away from school had compelled the authorities to install iron grills on all the first-floor windows and to replace the fence that surrounded the hockey field with a brick wall.

Sometime thereafter, on a friend's dare, I almost broke my neck climbing down the tile roof three floors above the marble patio of the courtyard, and Mother was notified that I would have to leave at the end of the school year. Fortunately, a small miracle intervened: The Suez War broke out, and it was the headmistress of the English Girls' College who was kicked out of the country instead, along with all the other British nationals.

After completing this long inventory of my sins, Mother warned me that if she ever caught me talking to Dany again, it would mean a week without ice cream. I was spared the agonizing choice because Dany and his family left Bad Gastein shortly thereafter.

It was not until my adolescence that I was to have Jewish friends again, this time Egyptian Jews. I had of course mingled with Jews when I was a little girl in primary school, but I was totally oblivious to their Jewish identity. Only much later did I realize that Mrs. Hazan, the math teacher who invited me to her house to eat huge bowls of strawberries with whipped cream and always stuck up for me at the staff meetings, was an English Jew, and that my classmate Alice Benzakim, who tidied my desk for me and left me little bars of Bazooka bubble gum, was an Italian Jew.

At the age of fourteen I entered a group that was exclusively Jewish. In Egypt one "entered," or rather, was admitted into, a group the way one joined a religious sect. Not only were the exigencies of group loyalty and solidarity as stringent, but one was together from morning till night. One studied *en groupe*, went to the movies, the club, dances, and excursions *en groupe*—in fact, even the most emancipated of families would not allow their daughters to go out with a boy unless she was *en groupe*. The group was in their eyes a substitute for a chaperon, and the possibility that it might break up into couples the moment it left the parental parlor never so much as crossed their minds.

My parents regarded the fact that any new friend I brought home in those days invariably turned out to be Jewish as just another one of my eccentricities. They kidded about it with my relatives, and though their jokes implied no ill will toward Jews, they occasionally hinted that it might be "healthier" if my acquaintances were more varied.

Yet somehow it had never occurred to me to equate Jews like my boyfriend, Halfon, or my best friend, Arlette, with "those people over there." Jews and Zionists were two different species: Jews were familiar and friendly, while Zionists were a menace lurking beyond the border. I had been told repeatedly that the Zionists had *tabg tani* ("a different nature"), and I accepted this as an article of faith, perhaps because it was so difficult to see any similarity between the villains in my school textbooks and my Jewish friends, and perhaps because I never talked about Zionists with them, which would have been as tactless as reminding them of criminal relatives. Or was it my total ignorance of the Holocaust that made it impossible for me to grasp the visceral identification of Jews with Israel? Whatever the reason, I was shocked to discover later on, when I went to Harvard, that most of my Jewish friends' parents, who had since emigrated to the United States, were now openly Zionist, and that the neat division I always thought existed between these "nice" people and "those evil people over there" was only a fiction.

Although I went on loathing Zionism right through my adolescence, these friendships must have had some influence, albeit indirect, on my first attempt to visit Israel in 1967. While the '56 war had scarcely affected me, since I was a child at the time, the '67 war, with its horrible death toll, had troubled me greatly. It was in June of that year that I first broached the subject of going to Israel to my parents.

That day, I had hurried home for lunch earlier than usual (my father was a fanatic about punctuality). During the summer we ate on a glassed-in veranda adjacent to the reception rooms furnished with the Louis XV brocade armchairs that had been the rage of the Cairene aristocracy in the first half of the century and as such were part of Mother's dowry.

Our apartment, on the exclusive residential island of Zamalek, had one of the finest views in Cairo. Our veranda overlooked the Nile. On a crisp, cool day, one could hear the palm trees swish in the breeze, their branches brushing against the window panes. Behind them, the simple, lean hulls of feluccas glided gracefully over the water. White sails dipped and rose in the wind. Sometimes a flock of birds would hover overhead with outstretched wings flashing and gleaming in the sunlight.

It was not by mere coincidence that my family lived on an island—a situation I always saw as an apt metaphor for our social insularity.

Two bridges linked the small island of Zamalek to the mainland. One of them, the Boulak, which our chauffeur had instructions to avoid, led to the poor section of town. There life had hardly ever changed. The alleyways teemed with street vendors: wizened, bleary-eyed men in *kaffiyehs*, carting *sus*, a licorice syrup; little boys with pinched cheeks and bad teeth peddling sugar cane; black-veiled women balancing urns of buffalo milk on their heads.

It was a world we hardly knew outside of the organ grinders who came to beg for money under our windows. Father would toss them a coin, in exchange for which their monkeys would perform a few grateful somersaults. And Mother would shake her head, saying, *"C'est une honte! Le gouvernement devrait ramasser ces espèces et les mettre hors de vue"* ("It's a shame! The government should collect those specimens and put them out of sight"). Only on Sham el Nessim (literally, "Inhaling the Breeze"), a celebration of spring dating back to the Pharoahs, who commemorated it by sacrificing the fairest virgins to the Nile, were the poor brazen enough to cross into our neighborhood. Their children swarmed across the bridge clad in rakish purple and orange tulles, the new frocks they had received for the occasion, and we would stand on the veranda, tittering and pointing fingers at their "vulgar rags."

On Sham el Nessim we stayed indoors. There would be no question of our eating out on the veranda because of the reek of *fissich*, a pickled fish consumed in honor of the feast, which wafted in from the public garden down the street. At sunset, when the poor began streaming back toward the Boulak Bridge, a handful of them would occasionally linger for a short while. Seating themselves along the banks of the Nile, they would look up at our apartments and observe our privileged lives, rendered even more splendid by the dazzling light of the crystal chandeliers that flooded our salons. And we would shudder a little at the thought of these invisible presences peering at us greedily out of the dark.

Kasr el Nil, the other bridge, was the one our chauffeur took when driving me to school (my mother would not allow me to use public transportation for fear that *"des gens sales"* would pass their germs on to me by breathing into my face). The way to the bridge led past the Guezira Sporting Club, of which my father was honorary president. With its cricket and polo fields, this club had been built at the turn of the century for the British officers and administrators and remained for a long time out of bounds to "wogs." My father was one of the first members of the native aristocracy "honored" with admission to it. In time it turned into the pleasure haunt of illustrious members of the ancien régime and was later to become a favorite hangout of Nasser's New Class.

On my way to school, I would be driven by the pomegranate trees with their fierce red blossoms and the blue jacarandas that grew in lush abandon along the neatly trimmed lawns of the club. Of these trees, Lord Lloyd, the British high commissioner for Egypt in the 1920s, reportedly had said, "When I see the jacarandas in bloom, I know it is time to send for a battleship." Lord Lloyd believed that their scent had an unsettling effect on the minds of Egyptians and incited them to acts of political violence every spring.

Then we would wend our way past the horse stables and grounds that had once belonged to Khedive Ismail, who had ruled Egypt at the end of the nineteenth century, and where I took my riding lessons, until we reached the bridge. Flanking it was the high-rise building with the frilled facade that my parents found so grotesque—the Bourg Tower, topped by a rotating restaurant, which Nasser had erected as a symbol of modernity. Two majestic lions, relics of British imperialism, guarded the entrance to the other side of the bridge. They stood facing the luxury hotels of the Golden Strip, near the bank where the Pharoah's daughter supposedly discovered Moses in the bulrushes.

I got home on time for once that June day and headed for the veranda. Our servant entered with the handsome silverware and the Sèvres porcelain. Lowering his eyes with a reverence that always embarrassed me, he began to set the table, laying out the elaborately folded napkins before the wine glasses. A tall, striking Sudanese, he wore a flowing white silk caftan with crimson trimmings, sash, and turban. His cheeks were scarred with markings made with red-hot irons during puberty rites in his native village. He was soon joined by the other "boy," who glided silently over the parqueted floor as he passed around the heavy silver serving dishes.

Everything seemed perfect that day. The weather was warm but not too hot. My father's mood was excellent: I was not late, and the leg of lamb was pink and juicy the way he liked it. Then I made my announcement. Not daring to look my mother or father in the eye, I informed my sister of my plans—just loud enough so my parents would be sure to overhear. They should not count on my joining them on vacation in Europe this year; I was going to Israel instead. There was silence. My mother could not have looked more shocked if I had uttered an obscenity. "Listen, my dear," she said with that afflicted tone she frequently used. "Your father may not have a great fortune because he did not steal and accept bribes like so many of his colleagues in public office, but he is bequeathing you one thing that money cannot buy—a reputation of gold. His integrity has won him the respect of past and present regimes alike. You will not bring him dishonor in his old age!" And she added icily that if I went to Israel I would be completely disowned by my family and would not be permitted to set foot in the house ever again.

In the end her tears prevailed where her threats had failed. Her argument that my father would be imprisoned on my account also helped. But I clung to my resolve to visit Israel as soon as circumstances would permit it.

I arrived in the United States in September 1973 in time to register at Harvard, where I was to pursue courses for a Ph.D. in political science. A few weeks later, there was war between Egypt and Israel. With every day of war, the classroom theorizing on international relations seemed more irrelevant, as did the nightly television news broadcasts, which offered the spectacle of Arabs and Israelis killing each other for the entertainment of civilized Western viewers.

In the afternoons, other Arab students and I pored over the newspapers in the Middle East Center reading room, counting Israeli casualties—two thousand, no, two thousand six hundred, no, it's really three thousand, but the Israelis are concealing the truth. One day, an Israeli student came in and, overhearing our conversation, warned us not to be so pleased with ourselves. Israel, he contended, had knocked out Lebanon in '48 and Jordan in '67, and would knock out Egypt in this war. And next time around it would make mincemeat out of Syria. Bristling at his arrogance, I pointed at Israel's high casualty rate. He retorted that Arab casualties were even higher. That is when I heard myself saying that this was a price we were prepared to pay. My voice sounded foreign to me. I remembered the trip to Luxor I had taken the previous Christmas with a friend visiting from France. On the Pharaonic murals were portrayed a multitude of severed hands. The guide explained that these were trophies that generals had brought back to their Pharoah after each battle. That bit of historical lore had made me shudder, but wasn't my present joy at the enemy death-count only a more refined statistical version of my ancestors' grisly practice? Indeed, what right had I, sitting here at Harvard, to dispense with the lives of others so freely?

Shortly thereafter, I went to the Israeli consulate to apply for a visa.

I had hardly seen my husband since our honeymoon in Cannes in the summer of 1973, because I had had to leave shortly thereafter for Harvard, while he was to prepare for his departure for the Geneva peace talks as President Sadat's spokesman. He had turned up in the States a few months later, with Foreign Minister Ismail Fahmy, to explore ways to break through the Syrian-Israeli stalemate. But the week we spent together at the Shoreham Hotel in Washington, where a floor had been reserved for the Egyptian delegation, was hardly blissful.

His arrival in February of 1974 coincided with the publication of my first public appeal for peace, published in the *New York Times Magazine* under the title "An Egyptian's Vision of Peace," an article that was sharply criticized by the Arab press. Most characteristic was the reaction of the Lebanese magazine *Beyruth el Masa*:

> Every indication points to this article as a prelude to an upcoming Zionist plot aimed at exploiting certain Arabs who call for an understanding with Israel and making peace with her. . . . The importance of this article lies in the fact that it is the first open invitation coming from an Arab person, and published in a prestigious paper like the *New York Times*, for making up with Israel and having wide-scale cultural and economic relations with no limits and conditions—without even regaining all the occupied land.
>
> In her view, the right of Israelis to Palestine is unnegotiable, and if the Palestinians have suffered . . . because of the founding of Israel, the Israelis did not mean to cause them any harm. Besides, all the sufferings of the Palestinian people pale in comparison with the courage, perseverance, and creative imagination and other Jewish qualities which have transformed a dream into reality.
>
> This is an example of the thinking of a class of people whom Nasser stripped of its social influence and removed from power . . . the daughter of King Farouk's ambassador to Washington shares the philosophy of the former ruling class in regard to her country's dignity and the Egyptian, Arab, and Palestinian cause. It is a philosophy which does not make an Arab proud.

Beyruth el Masa followed this with a series of articles entitled "Words Never Before Uttered by an Arab Tongue," which were tantamount to an accusation of treason. The "Words" that so outraged them were to be found in the seemingly innocuous concluding paragraph of "An Egyptian's Vision of Peace":

> Neither of us has been absolutely right; both of us share the responsibility for the Middle East tragedy: Both the Arabs, who did not empathize sufficiently with the Jewish plight and failed to recognize that the Jewish claim was of equal moral validity with their own, and the Zionist settlers, who either ignored the Arabs out of moral myopia or were aware of their presence, but felt their interests could justifiably be sacrificed for the sake of creating the State of Israel.

Our foreign minister, who was much later to resign in protest against Anwar Sadat's trip to Jerusalem, was furious at what I had written.

Though we had previously been on excellent terms—he was our next-door neighbor in Cairo and related to us through marriage—he cold-shouldered me in Washington. And at his bidding, the Egyptian ambassador, Ashraf Gorbal, followed suit. When I tried to see him in order to clarify matters, I was subjected to the humiliation of being shown to the door of the very embassy my own father had had built.

Likewise, I had many cross words with my husband in Washington; he accused me of jeopardizing his career by antagonizing the foreign minister, scolding me as though I were a little girl. Filled with moral indignation, I protested that he should have the courage to stand up to the foreign minister, while he tried to explain that as a man in high public office, he was not as free as I to speak up publicly, no matter how much he might agree with my political views in private. But I insisted that it was precisely in a country like Egypt, where truckling to the ruler had become almost second nature to a people subject to arbitrary power for centuries, that the call for individual revolt was the most pressing. For too long high officials had allowed the president to set their tune, had changed their song at his bidding for fear of losing their posts, and had said one thing in private and another in public. And I could not help feeling it was degrading to bend with the wind.

Even though I exhausted myself trying to get him to see my point of view, Tahsin just walked up and down the hotel room with an irritated expression on his face, shook his head, sighed, and wrung his hands. When I had finished talking, he told me I had spoken the "most utter childish nonsense" and begged me to "think things over like a grown woman" and promise him that I would never again write articles calling for peace with Israel.

I could not agree to this. Undoubtedly, my anger that he would not, could not understand my sense of urgency accounted for the cold, harsh light in which I now saw him. The difference in our ages suddenly loomed large. At fifty, Tahsin was old enough to be my father. His small eyes had sunk deeper into his face; his hair was quite gray. To be sure, he still seemed an energetic, successful man. He was honest, intelligent, broad-minded, praised by the Western press for his charm and erudition. But the imaginative grasp, the brave idealism of youth, had left him, it was clear—they had been sapped long ago by the stifling immobility of Egyptian officialdom. I had always admired Tahsin, but now all I could see was the waning power of his vision, and most of all his inability to adapt life to his own ends. I saw, too, the weary dejection with which he contemplated his future as a glorified government clerk. Was he successful? To be sure, he was the presidential spokesman and would no doubt one day be appointed ambassador, but he had passed the highwater mark of his life. And what about us? What did love have to do with my dispassionate regard for this forthright, hardworking official? As I calmly studied him and his words, I felt a chill.

Tahsin and I parted without being able to come to an understanding. I did not tell him about my intention of going to Israel for fear he would make use of his governmental post to stop me. It was in his power to prevent my trip by seeing to it that my passport was revoked, which would make it impossible for me to leave the United States.

And here I was, barely a few months later, in July of 1974, aboard an El Al jet on my way to Israel. I was also ignoring the warnings from my family that had followed the publicaton of the now-notorious article, about the dire consequences of my actions. I had hurt Tahsin "in the worst possible way," my sister wrote. He would not be sent to the Geneva peace talks, even if Ismail Fahmy, the foreign minister, wanted him there. There were calls for his removal from office and for some action to be taken against me. The head of the U.N. desk at the Ministry of Foreign Affairs had even paid a special visit to our home to express his disapproval. My sister's letter continued:

You should have known that when your husband is in the middle of confidential and important negotiations *you* should not publish anything *at all*. In the second place, you should not publish anything against your government's official position when *they* are in the process of bargaining.

The reason everyone here is furious with the article is not so much because of the concession you wish us to make over Jerusalem and Sharm el Sheik (though, of course, they are angry about that, too), but more so because you have betrayed your sentiment as being entirely with the Jewish position. You speak of their "right" to Palestine. It is one thing to say we must make peace with Israel because we can't defeat her militarily, an argument some people here are even now prepared to accept, but quite another to argue, as you do, that these invaders have "equal moral rights with the Palestinians." And you praise Dayan's "courage" for opening the Jordan bridges to Palestinian workers, etc., etc. People who have just lost a close relative in the war are bound to be bitter against one of their own praising the enemy's courage.

Naturally, we have stood behind you and said you are ahead of your times and you're free to have your own opinions which are not Tahsin's. However, we are all very annoyed for his sake. As you know, Mother and Father have come to look on him as a son.

I don't want to depress you—you and Tahsin will both survive this, and put it behind you, if you have a little bit of sensitivity and awareness of what people feel and think in this part of the world.

A postcript from my mother read:

> We know that in America a husband can be a Republican and his wife a Democrat, but need we remind you that this is not the case in the Orient! Besides, I'll have you know that even an American Jewish journalist who accompanied Kissinger on his recent visit to Cairo told us you lean much more toward Israel's side than you do toward your own country. If, let us assume the impossible, you were ever to think again of going to Israel, this time at that country's invitation, it would be catastrophic. Not only will you be considered a traitor in your own country, but we ourselves will be considered no better, not to mention the fact that your life will be in danger because of some fanatic Arabs. So choose between your parents and your country or Israel!

Now I had chosen. I was, of course, under no illusion that my trip to Israel would make a major contribution to peace. In the face of Phantom jets and the interests of superpowers, individual action was pathetic. But I was determined not to give in to circumstances that seemed increasingly dangerous, to views that seemed increasingly myopic. Other nations, like the French and the Germans, had fought protracted wars, but at least their citizens had spoken to each other, traveled to each other's countries, read each other's literature. The hostility of Arabs and Israelis was historically unique: It was autistic. We had not even reached the most basic level of human communication, that of finding a means to explain to each other our rage. I believed that refusing to negotiate directly with Israel was a mistake, that all our differences could be resolved through dialogue.

"Let Us Begin: A Rigorous Dialogue Between an Egyptian and an Israeli," my second appeal in the *New York Times Magazine*, this time in the form of a joint article with the Israeli writer Amos Elon, had been my way of trying to find a means. And now, I thought, what could be a more natural way to make a dent in the wall of prejudice and ignorance that separated us from each other than the simple act of braving a taboo by going to Israel as a tourist to show that Arabs and Israelis could talk? This is how I began a voyage that was planned as a six-week summer vacation—I had reserved a plane ticket for July 21 to September 5— and turned out to last nearly three years.

A sudden jolt made my heart skip a beat. We had been sucked into a squall. The plane alternately shuddered and plummeted at a frightful speed. Silence had fallen over the cabin. The passengers sat upright, tense and drawn; only their eyes moved. For a brief moment I conjured up the image of a crash—the ironic end to my expedition, brought about by some hidden design.

The buffeting ceased just as suddenly as it had begun, and the plane resumed its smooth course through the sky. Only then did I realize how tired I was. My eyes felt dull and foggy, and there was a bitter taste in my mouth. I had not had a moment of rest since leaving Harvard well over a week ago. First there had been that eerie telephone call on the eve of my departure, an unidentified man with a strong Arab accent warning me that if I took this trip it would be my last one. The fact that I had kept my trip a secret from everyone, aside from a handful of close friends, made this threat all the more terrifying. Then there had been those strained days in Geneva.

Instead of flying directly to Tel Aviv, I had decided to stop over in Geneva, where my parents were on holiday, to break the news of my journey to them. On the way over from Boston I had rehearsed a hundred times what I would tell them. But my courage failed once I arrived. It had been a long time since I had seen them, and I could not bring myself to spoil the joy of the reunion. I decided to wait till the next day—and then the next, and then the next. Finally, I talked myself into believing that an explanatory letter sent from Tel Aviv would be preferable to a face-to-face confrontation. Was I afraid that their outrage would in the end break my resolve?

On the last day of my stay in Geneva, I sneaked out of the Hôtel du Rhône and made my way to the El Al Israel Airlines building. Through an unfortunate coincidence, it stood on the very same block as our hotel, which boasted a large clientele of rich Arabs, many of whom were friends of my parents.

The wait at the El Al ticket counter seemed interminable. I kept my eyes on the street, from which any passerby could get a good view of the people inside the plate-glassed office. My fear of being discovered was aggravated by the presence of the two not very friendly-looking German shepherds who guarded the office; they had been brought in to assist the security officer following a recent hand-grenade incident at the El Al office in Brussels.

I finally decided to go first to Rome and leave from there for Israel in order to conceal my destination from my family. It would not have been possible to fly out directly from Geneva to Tel Aviv, since my parents were bound to insist on seeing me off at the airport. Adding deception to deception, I therefore invented a friend in Italy whom I had to visit before returning to the States.

On the morning of July 21, 1974, I arrived at the Rome airport. There seemed to be an unusual commotion at the El Al baggage check-in point. Upon inquiry, I was told that all flights to Israel had been canceled because the outbreak of war in Cyprus was causing the obstruction of the air corridors. No one knew if the flight cancellations would last a few hours, days, or weeks. I could, if I wished, go into town and return to the airport that evening to find out whether El Al would be flying.

Not knowing a soul in Rome, I decided to wait it out and sank down, exhausted, on the floor near the El Al counter, with the first symptoms of the asthma that invariably attacks me in moments of stress. Opposite El Al was Libyan Airlines, and once more I began worrying about being recognized. The fact that I did not know a single Libyan hardly reassured me. I watched the Italian soldiers on the overhead ramp prowl up and down, machine guns in hand. Some months before, I had heard, thirty-six passengers headed for Israel had been gunned down by Palestinian commandos at the Rome airport.

I remembered how, in 1967, my mother had warned me that if I went to Israel the commandos would kill me. At the time I had dismissed these fears as the product of an old woman's overwrought imagination. Now I was no longer so sure.

I started. A smiling, plump face was bending over me. *"Scusi, non volevo farle paura,"* its owner apologized for scaring me. He just wanted to know why there was no one behind the El Al counter.

I began explaining, in hopelessly broken Italian, about the war.

"A war! Not again!"

"Yes. The Turks have sent their armies into Cyprus and . . ."

"Cyprus? Why didn't you tell me? Thank God! For once it's not our war!"

Only then did I notice he was wearing a skullcap.

I had been waiting since seven-thirty in the morning. At eight in the evening, the El Al steward reappeared and announced that a plane would be departing that night.

At the appointed time, a long line formed, with much shoving and pushing. People were tired, irritated, and quarrelsome. At last my turn came, and I presented my passport. There was a moment of surprised silence. The man's small, hairy hands leafed through the pages, and then he studied my picture intently, comparing it many times with the living specimen before him.

"What kind of passport is this?" he finally asked, in apparent disbelief of what his eyes told him.

"Egyptian."

"I am afraid you'll have to wait a few minutes. Please step aside."

I hated to lose my place in line after such a long wait and was tempted to make a scene, but the horror of attracting attention was enough to cow me into submission. An hour later I was still squatting on the floor.

At long last, the security officer, a tall, gaunt fellow, arrived and told me grimly to hand over my passport. When I did, he vanished. After another seemingly endless wait, he reappeared.

"It's okay, El Al has been notified about your departure," he said without looking at me. "I'm sorry, but it's not every day we get an Egyptian passenger, you understand." Then he handed me an embarkation card on which he had scribbled the roman numeral III with a Magic Marker. I wondered whether it was some kind of secret code designed to identify highly suspicious characters like myself for special attention.

Another checkpoint, near the gate. This time it was my hand luggage. The lean, long-necked woman with the harpy face who was in charge proceeded with deliberate slowness. Roughly, she dismantled my tape recorder down to the last screw while I tried to contain my panic that she might wreck it. At her side, a young El Al steward was studying me with a critical but not unfriendly look. He seemed moved by my wheezing and obvious exhaustion. "*Va bene, va bene*" ("It's okay, it's okay"), he told her. "*Fa i cazzi tuoi!*" ("Fuck off!"), she snapped back, confiscating the batteries of my tape recorder and shunting me into a booth for a body check.

There she proceeded to pull my hair with such ferocity that I could have sworn she was enjoying it, though she assured me it was a routine check for a wig. She pinched my breasts with an equal excess of zeal, once more insisting she was only doing her duty. And before I had time to protest, her long, slithering fingers had invaded my privates. Then she stepped aside and pulled back the curtain, smiling venomously at me. At three in the morning I was finally allowed to board the plane.

A tap on my arm pulled me out of my reverie. Someone had bent over me, a handsome, dark steward whose snub nose and square chin reminded me in a peculiar way of my cousin Rafik's. I asked him where he was from.

"Israel, of course!"

"But originally," I insisted.

"Morocco."

Was I imagining things, or was there a tinge of annoyance in his voice? He wanted to know if I was ready for dinner. I did not think I could get a meal down, but I told him I would very much like a cup of tea with milk.

"Sorry, we serve only kosher food on El Al."

I decided to have some dinner after all. Halfway through the meal I must have fallen asleep, for I was awakened by a hand on my shoulder. Too tired to rouse myself, I tried to ignore it, but the hand started shaking me. I opened my eyes. It was the dark-skinned steward who had brought me my dinner. Thinking he had come for the tray, I handed it to him; he waved it aside and ordered me to remove my shoes and place my leg up on the seat in front of me. I was too tired to resist.

"Not this one," he said brusquely, "that one." He pointed at my other leg. Once more, I complied. He drew a rod out of the overhead rack, and I realized that he was about to beat my right foot—no doubt he was aware that the ankle was feeble, having been broken and operated on the previous summer. "He's speaking Hebrew," I thought to myself. "He must be an Israeli who works for the intelligence service." But then I remembered reading in the *New York Times* that the Palestinian commandos who had broken into an Israeli school at Maalot a few months earlier had also spoken Hebrew. I wondered if he himself was a commando who suspected me of treason against the Arabs. No, it was not Hebrew he was talking, it was German! Of course! He must be a Nazi!

"Nazis, Israelis, Israelis, Nazis." The words kept running through my head. The German voice grew louder and louder, so loud that I finally woke up. It was an old woman, across the aisle, animatedly gossiping in Yiddish with someone two rows back.

I gazed out the window. Night was receding. The black sea glimmered in the twilight.

I began to take stock of the passengers next to me. In the next seat was a corpulent American matron with many double chins. From her massive coif, which peaked in all directions and was carefully tucked away behind a turquoise kerchief, I had at first assumed that she was wearing a wig. But presently she emerged from the bathroom, scarfless, her hair stiffly crimped, carrying a whole battery of rollers and bobby pins.

Seeing me stare at her, she turned toward me and asked, "Where are you from, honey?"

"Egypt."

"You mean they actually let you out of that awful place! And your family is with you?"

"My family is in Egypt."

"You poor thing! It must be terrible for Jews with that horrid man Nasser. He's just like Hitler, isn't he?"

"There's another president now, Sadat."

"Oh, yes, Sadat. Well, if you ask me, the Arabs are all the same. I don't trust any of them. And what's your name, honey?"

"Sana."

"Hannah?"

"No, Sana."

"Sarah?"

"No, no, Sana."

"Sama. Never heard that one before. Must be a name from over there. Oh well, now that you're going to Israel you'll get yourself a pretty Israeli name. Maybe Shoshana? You *are* going to live there?"

"No, I'm just visiting."

"Who knows, you might meet a nice Jewish boy to marry and settle down with. My daughter met her husband there."

"I wouldn't care to live there."

"Why not, Sama? The country needs young people, you know."

Up to that point, her conversation had mildly annoyed me, but now I was interested. Why not, I thought, why not pass myself off as a Jew in Israel whenever possible in the course of my casual encounters? If people know I am Egyptian they will be either hostile, and therefore unwilling to disclose what they genuinely think of their country in my presence, or else artificially kind, to show me how nice Israelis are to Arabs.

The idea of concealing my true identity tickled me, and I laughed up my sleeve as I mulled it over. All of a sudden, the words of the Israeli consul in Boston came back to me. After I had braved the massive iron gate, which gave his consulate the uncanny appearance of a medieval fort set in the middle of a modern high-rise building, and the security guard, who hulked impassively in the darkened embrasure of the doorway, I was reassured to find a beefy, languid, rather harmless-looking fellow seated behind the desk. The Israeli consul was all smiles as he proclaimed himself "deelighted" that I wished to visit Israel. All he needed was three days to clear the matter with Tel Aviv—a mere formality.

Since I had been led to believe that my departure for Israel was imminent, I returned my scholarship to Harvard and took a leave of absence. But as the weeks passed and my repeated phone calls failed to evoke any word from the consul, it occurred to me that I should drop in on him again in order not to lose the second semester as well. This time he informed me, somewhat curtly, that he could not assume the responsibility of issuing me a visa. What if I were a spy? When I protested, citing as evidence of my good faith the article I had just written calling for peace with Israel, he replied: "Aha! A very clever spy would resort to precisely such a diversionary tactic! And once I let you into the country, what is to prevent you from passing yourself off as some kind of tourist in order to get information out of people?"

I had just about given up any hope of dissuading the consul from the notion that I was a spy when I remembered my father telling me about a request for a meeting once put to him by Israeli Foreign Minister Abba Eban, through the intermediary of the *New York Times* Cairo correspondent. It was back in 1947, when Eban was the Jewish Agency's liaison officer with the U.N. Special Committee on Palestine and presented the Jewish case in the Palestine debates before the General Assembly. My father, as the first Egyptian ambassador to the United States, had been appointed Egypt's delegate to the Security Council in 1946 and was part of the Arab delegation that argued the case for an independent Palestine and against the Jewish state before the first special session of the General Assembly in 1947. Although my father had refused to meet with Eban then, I decided to write to him anyway to ask for his help. And it was thanks to his intervention that I finally obtained the visa in June, nine months after my initial application.

The Fasten Your Seat Belt sign had just been turned on, followed by the announcement that we would be landing in Tel Aviv in a few minutes.

The plane began its descent, rocked by the wind. Outside the window, a coastline loomed against the pale light of dawn. The Promised Land.

A Hebrew song, "Hevenu Shalom Aleichem" ("We Have Brought You Peace"), started to sound over the radio. Silence fell over the cabin; then, as if on signal, a glad roar swept through the plane: shouts of ecstasy, applause, even sobbing, as everyone joined in.

And I? Why did I feel so singularly drained of emotion, so indifferent? Hadn't I, too, arrived? Was this not the climactic moment after all those agonizing decisions, the anxious months spent waiting for a visa, the fear of being discovered, my guilt for having to lie to my parents and husband? Should I not feel greatly relieved to know that it was all finally over, that here I was at last? Why, then, did I feel so empty, so disappointed by this first view of the land?

I recalled how mortified I had felt at the age of eight when, after a long, hazardous climb up the Great Pryamid of Khufu, I reached the top and found no mystery or magic in the panorama. All elation had left me, and I gazed, disconcerted, at the view—desert as far as the eye could see, interrupted to the north by the vegetation that fringed the city.

Curious about what there was to be seen from above, I had taken advantage of a few moments of absentmindedness on the part of Fräulein Broch, my nanny, to sneak off in the direction of the pyramid. I had been warned that except for guides who knew their way about the pyramid blindfolded, only a few crazy tourists, intrepid northern alpinists, attempted its ascent. There were no steps to the top of the 137-meter pyramid. One had to cling by one's fingers to cracks and fissures in the stones, hoisting oneself up while groping around for footholds. But the erosion of the stones had made their surfaces so smooth and slippery that one's grip was tenuous at best.

Halfway up the pyramid, I remembered a story Mother had told me about the debauchery of King Farouk. To entertain himself one day, he had ordered two servants from his retinue to race to the top of the pyramid, promising one hundred pounds to whoever reached the peak first. One of the two men had slipped and fallen to his death.

It was not only the fear of vertigo that kept me from looking down, but also the even greater terror of the sight of my nanny's face below. She would have made the perfect prison guard. Her matronly figure had the dense solidity of those squat, robust women one sometimes sees in police uniform. She had short, powerful legs and muscular arms, and her perfectly symmetrical features made her face resemble a mask pierced by blue eyes colder than steel. The most remarkable thing about her was her golden, waist-length hair. Even that, thick and coarse as a horse's tail, had about it a metallic quality which made it not quite human.

Fräulein Broch took great pains with her hair. She would sit before her mirror for half an hour twice daily, upon rising and before going to bed, brushing her hair with swift, vigorous strokes that sent off electrical sparks. Then she would carefully braid it and coil it into a tight bun, which sat on her head like a crown declaring the sovereignty of her iron will.

She had a large collection of brushes—boar-bristle, nylon, metal—which she liked to apply liberally to my rear. The choice of the brush depended on the magnitude of the crime; the one I most feared was the metal, because it drew blood. The memory of Fräulein Broch's bulldozer voice calling out, *"Runter mit deinen Hosen!"* ("Down with your pants!") set my teeth on edge.

Back home, my mother had dragged me by the ear all the way down our long corridor to force me to apologize to Fräulein. My "deplorable conduct" had already led to the resignations of Miss Boden, Miss Duffy, Miss Geoffrey, and Miss Scanlon in rapid succession, causing Mother to switch from British to German nannies. She was understandably anxious not to lose Fräulein Broch as well. But my lips had remained stubbornly sealed.

Maybe some of the same defiance underlay my trip to Israel. I knew I would have to pay a price for this trip—at the very least, shame and ostracism for me and my family, and quite possibly prison or exile. And I will not pretend I was not afraid of that. But at that very moment when we were about to land, I was even more afraid of seeing Israel. The truth is that I wished I had not come at all. For if I liked Israel, would I not be a traitor? And if I disliked it, would I not feel I had paid a heavy price in vain?

Outside my window, right below the edge of the plane, Israel was now clearly visible. Burdened with life, the small land seemed abandoned in the open sea. The waves rushed in on her from all sides. A chain of buildings ringed the Tel Aviv shoreline, their embattled walls braving the turmoil of the waters. In the center, rising up above the city like a prison's guard tower, was a single skyscraper—the Shalom Tower.

2

A Vienna in the Middle East

DIASPORA JEWS often have overblown fantasies of the Holy Land, and in their own way, so do Arabs. Having expected something on the scale of Charles de Gaulle Airport, I was surprised, perhaps even disappointed, to find a small, provincial airstrip with a single building of middling proportions whose ugly front resembled a warehouse. Inside were a few cheap, glossy posters—depictions of Eilat, Tiberias, and Jerusalem—dog-eared and peeling off the concrete walls.

The jostling and pushing began once more, with the passengers pressing forward toward the passport checkpoint. I lingered behind, delaying the moment when I would have to cross into enemy territory.

But my turn came. Inside a small glass booth, a man with a beaked nose and jerky movements perched on a stool. I presented my passport. His keen eyes moved back and forth over my visa. "*Ya Allah!*" he cried involuntarily, and dashed out of his booth. These were the first "Hebrew" words spoken to me.

A moment or two later he reappeared, followed slowly by another clerk, who was staring at my passport with arched eyebrows and a supercilious grin. At last he let out a low whistle, raised his eyes, and without a word, motioned me to follow him.

Once we had reached what seemed to be the director's office, the clerk told me, in a lofty tone that became his sense of racial superiority, to wait outside. He entered and whispered something into the ear of a fat man who blurted, "*Ma? Mitzria!*" I recognized the Hebrew word for "Egyptian," because it was the same as the Arabic. Then the door was unceremoniously slammed shut in my face.

Shortly thereafter, the director threw the door open and called two officers. For a while all three stood on the threshold, locked in an agitated discussion. I listened, baffled by the shrill babble of the Hebrew tongue. I did not understand a word of what was going on, but instinct told me that the fat man was not to be trusted, and the suspicious glances the officers intermittently darted at me over their shoulders hardly reassured me. I could already picture the dark cell that awaited me.

Had I been tipped off about the notorious ineptitude of the Israeli bureaucracy, I would have been spared much of this unnecessary worry. But since I was still under the illusion that Israel was a superefficient, modern state, I never doubted that information about my arrival had been relayed to the airport and that I was now being trailed by a secret service agent. That, however, was hardly the case: Whoever had notified the El Al people in Rome had neglected to do the same with Tel Aviv. I had walked into a typical Middle Eastern mess. (Later I learned that the Israelis had a name for it: *balagan*.)

Three-quarters of an hour went by, during which not one of the men offered me either a chair or a word of explanation. Oddly enough, Frenchmen were another matter: A French passenger who had been standing alongside me, passport in hand, had received a courteous apology and a seat. The long wait was all the more intolerable in that I was suffering from acute stomach cramps. I stood outside the office as long as I could and then, overcome by urgent need, entered. Hardly had I opened my mouth when one of the officers swung around and, addressing me in Arabic, said, "Hey you! Get out!"

"*La!*" ("No!"), I retorted, looking him coldly in the eye. We were interrupted by the arrival of an officer escorting an Arab.

The Arab, whom they interrogated in my presence, explained that he was from Ramallah in the West Bank. There were some problems with his papers, and while his case was being looked into, he anxiously scanned the officers' faces. A brief exchange in Arabic followed. The director's tone was insolent, the Palestinian's plaintive and resigned. Those few moments brought home to me the whole meaning of the occupation.

When my turn finally came to be interrogated, the director addressed me in a friendly manner, though I sensed a touch of haughtiness in the forced simplicity of his tone. He asked me to state the purpose of my visit to Israel.

I told him it was tourism.

Subdued titters broke out at the end of the room. The director stared fixedly at me and asked again:

"Why did you come here?"

"I just wanted to see what Israel was like."

"How long do you plan to stay?"

"Six weeks." To prove it I showed him my return ticket, which was booked for September 5.

"Where will you be staying?"

"I'm not sure yet. Jaffa at first, then Jerusalem. But I expect I'll be traveling around the country most of the time."

This answer clearly did not satisfy him. Again my passport became the object of heated discussion among the men. The director went to telephone and made call after call. Was he talking to the Foreign Office? To the Central Intelligence Agency? His bland face brought to mind other Israelis I had hated. There was that insufferably arrogant student at Harvard who sat across the table from me in a seminar on nationalism. When I made the point that, like some other developing countries, Egypt suffered from an overabundance of engineers and a dearth of mid-level cadres and skilled technicians, he snickered, saying, "Egypt? Engineers? That's a good joke!" And then there was the Israeli officer at the Paris airport. On the bus into town I overheard him talking with a distinguished-looking French lady about the recent burning of the Aksa Mosque. He told her that he was sure the Arabs had done it themselves, just to create trouble for Israel. I turned around and said to him in French, "You must really hate Arabs!" Unaware that I was Egyptian, he replied, "No, I have no feeling for them one way or another. They are animals. They behave like animals, they live like animals, they think like animals."

Apparently finding no further grounds for detaining me, the director handed me my passport and, smiling sanctimoniously, motioned that I was free to go.

There was one thing I was absolutely sure of as I left the terminal: I was going to hate Israel.

As I set out in search of transportation to the house in Jaffa that I was borrowing from a French friend, I ran into my fellow passenger, the matchmaker. This time she advised me to open my suitcase before leaving the airport grounds to make sure that nothing was missing. According to her, the Georgians who unloaded the planes were thieves; recently, a friend of hers had found nothing but bricks in her trunk. Since she was so free with her advice, I asked about the cheapest way of getting to Jaffa. She recommended a *sherut*—a collective taxi.

Anxiety overwhelmed me again as I stepped into the taxi. I began to wonder if word of my arrival had gotten around and I was being followed. I scrutinized the other passengers in the taxi, trying to figure out which one of them had been planted there to spy on the Egyptian who said she was a tourist.

Up front, an El Al stewardess in a tight, short skirt was exhibiting her shapely legs for all to see. The three young American women behind me, who must have been roughly my age—somewhere in their mid-twenties—were absorbed by their own gossip. Like me, they had curly black hair, ruddy complexions, and a style of clothing that my mother would have disapprovingly labeled "hippie." It comforted me to think that I was not so conspicuous after all in my long Indian skirt and red poncho; I could easily have passed for one of them. To my right sat an Orthodox Jew dressed in a black coat, notwithstanding the heat. A black felt hat rode low over his forehead, and what little remained to be seen of his face was lost in an immense growth of beard.

I decided that the spy had to be this person beside me portentously bearded and hidden behind dark glasses. Wasn't Israeli intelligence reputed to be the best in the world? Wouldn't they try to outsmart me by choosing the person I would least suspect?

The man must have noticed I was studying him out of the corner of my eye, for suddenly he turned to me and asked whether I spoke English. (Given his unmistakable British accent, I reckoned he was probably not a secret service agent after all.) I nodded. He then asked where I was from.

"Italy," I said, without batting an eye.

Now he wanted to know if I was a new immigrant. No, I was here to look the country over and learn some Hebrew. I told him I would probably attend the summer *ulpan* (language institute) at Hebrew University. He shook his head disapprovingly. The academic reputation of Hebrew University was, in his opinion, undeserved. Its graduates might be competent technicians, but they were uncultured, utterly ignorant of their Jewish heritage. As a rabbi, he felt, a much better place for me would be Jerusalem's religious college for women, Neve Yerushalaim.

"Perhaps you have an Orthodox relative in Italy?"

I had to confess that I didn't.

"What about your parents, are they religious? Do they at least observe the Sabbath and Kashrut?" I was spared the embarrassment of having to give another negative answer by the driver's calling out, "*Sheket, bevakasha. Hahadashot!*" The rabbi translated for me: "Please keep quiet. The news!" The driver turned the radio up to full volume.

Despite my ignorance of Hebrew, I sensed from the outraged murmurs of the other passengers that an act of violence was being reported.

Forgetting that I had just passed myself off as Italian, I tucked myself in, trying to become invisible. A discussion followed in English, from which I learned that a parcel with detonators had been discovered in a bus and dismantled moments before it was due to go off.

"Well," the rabbi said to me, "it's no wonder these things happen with a government as weak and indecisive as ours is in its dealings with the Arabs. Letting the terrorists off without capital punishment—in fact, making things easier for them, with its policy of open bridges over the Jordan, so they can come and go as they please. They never had it so good! You see them traveling all through the country, making piles of money from the jobs we give them, living it up. It's a wonder they don't do these things even more often!"

"Luckily the Arabs are too stupid and primitive to take advantage of all the opportunities for mischief we offer them," the El Al stewardess added amiably.

Alarmed by the nasty turn the conversation was taking, I tried to change the subject. "From what I read in the paper, life isn't much safer in London because of the IRA," I said brightly.

But the rabbi dismissed my remark with a disdainful wave of the hand: "Who cares about that? It's only goyim killing goyim! They can all go to hell as far as I'm concerned. None of them ever lifted a finger for us."

Fortunately, just then the driver put an end to the conversation by screeching to a halt before a flock of sheep. A Bedouin child waved his stick to hurry the animals, but they gazed up at us with phlegmatic indifference. Without waiting for the last of them to cross, the driver stepped on the accelerator and we raced on.

I thought about the words of my fellow passengers, trying to come to terms with the painful discovery of this kind of casual and vicious prejudice against Arabs. I told myself that I should not be too hard on these people and reminded myself of the caricatures of Israelis I'd seen as a child in Egypt—images of demonic hunchbacks with crooked noses, thick lips, and evil, beady eyes that used to adorn newspapers during the Nasser era. And for the first time in my life and despite everything my parents had claimed, I began to realize how thin the dividing line between political hatred and racial prejudice really was.

By the time I started school in Cairo in the 1950s, the Egyptian revolution had taken place, but a residue remained of the cosmopolitan mosaic of languages and nationalities that had characterized Egypt during the ancien régime. (It was not until the "socialist decrees" of the early 1960s, which led to the nationalization of all major industries and businesses, that the foreigners and Egyptians of foreign extraction, who dominated the financial and commercial life of the nation, began to leave the country en masse.) In my family's milieu, Egyptians, Lebanese, Italians, Greeks, Armenians, British, French, Muslims, Christians, and Jews intermingled in a world that bore a remarkable resemblance to Lawrence Durrell's *Alexandria Quartet*. The very language we spoke reflected this cosmopolitanism. Like the Russian aristocracy of old, the Egyptian upper class was polyglot and particularly prone to lapsing into French or English, though French was generally considered more chic. It used to be said that the Egyptian nation had two languages: Arabic, the language of the masses, and Franglais, that of the elite. It was only toward the end of the nineteenth century that Arabic was made the official language of Egypt; throughout most of the century, all government business had been conducted in French, the international language of the day. For centuries before, Egypt's rulers—both the Mamluk slave princes imported from Georgia and the Caucasus to be trained as administrators and their successors, the Ottomans—had spoken Turkish.

My own lineage was a typical example of the kind of intermarriage that went on in the Egyptian upper class. My grandfather, Hasan Pasha Mahmoud, who had been the dean of the Faculty of Medicine at Cairo University and the king's private physician, had first married a Frenchwoman he had met during his student days in Paris and, after her death, a Turk—my grandmother. Grandmother's family came from Kaballah, a port on the Macedonian coast. Her great-grandfather's name, Topuzoglou (in Turkish, "Son of the Cannon"), is said to indicate his linear descent from a slave who had been kidnapped from his family at a time when it was still standard practice to abduct little boys from the European provinces of the Ottoman Empire, convert them to Islam, and bring them up as soldiers in the sultan's army. After he came to Egypt with Muhammad Ali at the beginning of the nineteenth century, he led the troops that repelled a British invasion from the coast of Rosetta in 1807 and was rewarded for his military exploits with the governorship of Alexandria. Grandmother's own brother, the former prime minister Roushdi Pasha, likewise married a Turk—the daughter of the Ottoman sultan's chief of staff, who was brought over from Istanbul for the wedding—and later a Frenchwoman.

My father had grown up at a time when the condition of Egyptian Jews had not yet been affected by the Palestinian conflict. In fact, Jews of the Suwares, Rolo, Harari, Cicurel, Moseri, and Quattawi families were still a large and thriving segment of the country's political, financial, professional, and cultural elite. The minister of finance and the

First Lady at the court were Jewish, as were several members of Parliament, the king's private lawyer, Mizrahi Pasha, and his physician. Many Jews wore the title *pasha,* the highest title of nobility in the land, and some had married into the best Muslim and Christian families. Of my father's three brothers, one was married to a Jew and another to the daughter of Prime Minister Riad Pasha, himself a convert from Judaism.

It was this experience that my father contrasted with what he saw in the United States when he was posted there as King Farouk's ambassador during World War II. He held this office for ten years and became very fond of the country, treating us to endless tales about the hospitality and generosity of Americans. As a child I had heard over and over again his story about how, when Rommel was at the gates of Alexandria and the fate of the Egyptian embassy in Washington seemed uncertain, American friends had flooded him with gifts of fruit, cheese, and liquor and offers of summer residences and blank checks. But for all that, my father liked to poke fun at American racism and anti-Semitism.

The anecdote Father most loved to tell was about the spring he spent in Florida with his friend, the millionaire Greek shipping magnate Embericos, at a time when Miami had not yet become a favorite resort of American Jews. Embericos happened to be dark-skinned, with a rather prominent nose. When they checked in at the Hotel Versailles, a worried receptionist cautiously approached him and whispered, "Excuse me, sir, are you Jewish?"

"No, why? Is this hotel only for Jews?" asked Embericos cagily.

"No, not at all, sir. Quite the contrary," the receptionist replied with obvious relief. Shortly thereafter, the hotel was bought by Jews.

On another occasion, at an exclusive country club in Pinehurst, North Carolina, my father was bending over a water fountain when he heard the senator who had been golfing with him call out, "Hold it, Mr. Ambassador, hold it!" Alarmed, he jumped back, thinking he was about to tread on one of the rattlesnakes that occasionally strayed onto the golf green. It turned out that there were two water fountains—one painted blue for the black caddies, one painted red for the white players. Father had been about to drink from the blue fountain.

A similar incident occurred at a White House dinner given by President Truman for diplomats and their wives. The Ethiopian ambassador was standing near the reception desk when a southern senator walked in. Thinking he was one of the help, the senator automatically handed him his coat. Silently, the ambassador took the coat and gave it to the desk clerk. Later in the evening the senator, who was seated next to my mother, noticed the Ethiopian ambassador at the other end of the table.

Recognizing him, he bent over to my mother and muttered in dismay, "Who on earth is this Negro?" Mother took pleasure in informing him.

Such anecdotes had often been the occasion of hearty laughs at the expense of the United States, but at the time they educated me against racial prejudice far more succinctly than any amount of parental moralizing could have done.

None of this liberal upbringing, however, had modified my hostility to Israel in the least, or my fervent conviction that we had to "root out the Zionist cancer." Growing up in Cairo during the Nasser era, I was imbued with the same animosity against Israel that every Egyptian child absorbed—a political animosity that only my uncommon upbringing kept from turning into racial prejudice.

We drove along the sea, past a deserted no-man's-land—the border between Tel Aviv and Jaffa. There was now a truce between the two cities that had once been such bitter enemies, though a long strip of abandoned Arab houses lingered on as a haunting memory of the '48 war.

On one side of the road there were only ruins—metal ribs sticking out of broken walls, crumbling white stones, and bits of blue painted on doors to ward off the evil eye. In the midst of all that wreckage stood the isolated and nearly intact tower of some ancient mosque.

In a few minutes, the cabbie called out, "Jaffa." I looked up and saw a small clock-tower with stained-glass windows. I could not help feeling somewhat bitter, for Jaffa had been ours until 1948, and I had expected at least a sign to indicate the beginning of the city. But there was none. Tel Aviv had erased all traces of a separate Arab identity here. Yet I was to learn that though most of its original inhabitants had fled during the '48 war, Jaffa's paving stones, alleys, and arches, every crack in its walls, its colors and smells, pulse and rhythm, were inalienably Arab.

On Boutros Street we drove past large, dark Arab houses with shuttered windows, and past shops whose signs, displaying names like Moshe Crankow or David Yiblansky, had flaked away to reveal the Arab names in the original script underneath them. There was something eerie and intangibly alien about this street; it gave Jaffa the feel of a colonized city.

The cabbie let me off near a piazza, telling me that to reach the house I was staying in, I should follow the road until I came to a church on the edge of a cliff overlooking the sea. When I got there, I saw that a large stone staircase ran alongside the church to a pathway below. In the back alleys, I knew, as all Arabs did, some of the hardest house-to-house combat between Jews and Arabs had taken place during the '48 war. Now the area had been restored: Israeli artists and writers inhabited the charming Arab houses, which architecturally were the finest in Israel. Exterior staircases led to the second-floor apartments, while the first floors had been rented to antique shops and art galleries. The traditional arched entrances had been filled in with glass to create windows. The shops displayed carved stone brooches from the port of Eilat, Yemenite silver work, Roman coins, and Turkish rifles alongside hand-embroidered dresses that were labeled MADE IN ISRAEL, but were in fact Palestinian. The luxurious Arab home that my friend had lent me flanked one of these antique shops and had a broad terrace overlooking the sea.

I stepped onto the terrace to get a breath of air. The Tel Aviv skyline loomed in the distance. The same skyscraper I had noticed when we were landing faced me once again. Alone, rising out of a confused jumble of clouds and roofs, the Shalom Tower seemed to stare back at me insistently.

As I stretched out on the elegant living room sofa upholstered in white leather, I thought I would rest only a short while before going for a stroll through the town. But I fell into a deep sleep, and when I opened my eyes it was already evening. Feeling hungry, I went out to search for a restaurant. On the dark staircase at the end of my alley, I stumbled into a garbage can and woke a half-dozen stray cats. A wall whose gaslights cast tremulous shadows over the lane led me to a mosque that Jews from Bombay had converted into a cafeteria. I could not face eating there, so I continued and once more came upon the clock-tower. I had no idea where to head from there, but I kept walking south until I found myself beside an Arab school by the name of Hassan Arafe. I was excited at the thought that I might have discovered an Arab neighborhood that housed some of the few remaining Palestinian residents of Jaffa.

A couple of stores were still open. The air was thick with the aroma of spices. As I walked past mounds of oily halvah and fibrous *konafa* cakes piled on copper trays, past two men sipping Turkish coffee and playing backgammon on the pavement, past a score of shrieking, barefoot children, I felt Egypt reawakening within me. For a moment the fear of not being allowed to reenter my country and the pain of exile almost overpowered me.

Chasing away sorrowful thoughts, I entered a small, dim shop with

34

half-empty shelves: dusty cans of apricots and peas, a few packages of cigarettes, glass jars with sour balls, toffees, and mint drops. A Milka chocolate bar that lay amid the humbler local species caught my eye. I hesitated; the blue sky on the paper wrapping had turned a sickly green and the venerable Swiss cow looked eons old. Regard for my own welfare told me I shouldn't buy it. But since I did not have the heart to disappoint the young man with the thin brilliantine-coated strands of hair, who was gesticulating excitedly in the direction of the Turkish delight, I asked for a baklava. He smiled gleefully, displaying a row of tiny black teeth notched like a saw, picked one cake out of the pile, and folded it artistically between two sheets of rustling paper. I took a cautious bite: Surprisingly, it was quite good. I paid and stepped out into the street, followed by a trail of baklava-loving flies.

I kept exploring, now down a side street called Margoa ("Relaxation") to a cluster of Arab mansions that overlooked the sea. They had belonged to the affluent Palestinians of Jaffa, who had either fled or been chased out during the '48 war. The plaque on one of the handsome villas read SADEH, the name of the Red Army officer who became the founder of Palmach, the celebrated Jewish shock battalion during the '48 war. I cut across a rocky path bordering his house to the shore. From a distant minaret came a call to prayer. Hundreds of tombstones clustered along a cliff with pale yellow chrysanthemums blooming in its dark cracks. Across from this old Muslim cemetery, the shadowy trees of Sadeh's garden fringed the black waters. The air tasted of seaweed and oranges—Jaffa oranges.

Irresistibly, I felt stealing over me the memory of those other oranges in Zurich. Whenever we were away on vacation, it was Mother's solemn duty to fix Father a glass of freshly squeezed orange juice every afternoon following his siesta. One afternoon, she noticed to her horror that we were out of oranges. She was seized by such panic that she violated one of her cardinal principles, which was not to let me go out by myself. I was whiling away my time as usual in the big swimming pool of the Grand Hotel Dolder when I saw Mother rushing toward me, panting and flustered. I was to hurry to the store and back before Father woke up. Proud at being entrusted with so august a mission at age ten and determined to show myself worthy, I headed straight for the cable car that wound its way down to the foot of the hill where the shopping area lay, not even pausing as usual at the little booth in the station that sold my favorite chocolate, Toblerone. But when I returned with my package, instead of the reward I expected for having acted so responsibly, I received a slap. I stared dumbfounded at Mother's flushed face, unable to make out the nature of my heinous crime. I had, it turned out, just made my first contribution to the Israeli economy: Stamped all over the orange rinds in violet was the label JAFFA ORANGES.

Now I headed back toward the piazza, still in search of a restaurant. On the way, I came upon a cobbled lane filled with the pungent odor of roasting meat. All the way down the street, I could see skewers stacked with chunks of lamb, tomatoes, and charred onions broiling over glowing red coals. Tired, I sat down beside the first grill I came to. Mounds of decomposing refuse and garbage littered the pavement, yet the customers, seated on the plastic chairs set out on the sidewalk, did not seem to mind. The neon light cast a lurid glow over the walls, lending them that vivid pink hue common throughout the Mediterranean. These colored walls resembled the ruins of Arab houses I had seen earlier that afternoon. Here and there one could see the joint of the floor or ceiling that had once been. To be sure, the colors of the walls had faded with time; the blues had turned violet, the greens yellow, the reds pink. But nonetheless, the walls had survived the demolition squads! They stood alongside the taller, newer houses of Jewish residents, clinging to them stubbornly. In surviving, I liked to think, they had preserved the lives of their Palestinian inhabitants, who had fled.

To my surprise, the young, dark-skinned waiter stared at me uncomprehendingly when I gave my order. The restaurant, it turned out, was Oriental Jewish, not Arab as I had supposed. So I switched to sign language. As I began to eat, a group of soldiers appeared at the end of the alley. The cobblestones rang under their heavy tread, and the loud jokes they exchanged echoed along the walls. They pushed their way into the crowded restaurant, ostentatiously trailing their Uzis behind them. Something about them changed the taste of the food in my mouth. I paid and left.

Back home, I sat outside on the terrace. Evening had cast its shadows upon the empty beach, and the neighboring houses were receding into the dark. Foaming black waves beat against the cliffs. Down below, in the old abandoned Palestinian port of Jaffa, warehouses hulked.

Shortly after I went to bed, I thought I heard the voice of the Egyptian singer Um Kalsum. I crept out onto the terrace that overlooked the neighbor's house. In the glare of the electric bulbs strung up on the trees of the garden, I could see a party gathering; a woman with platinum hair and rippling bronze flesh was singing and swaying in rhythm with the music. Her shiny green satin dress, with a tight, low-cut bodice, exposed her breasts: two large balls of jelly heaving up and down as she sang. One of the men, who had been writhing to the music's rhythm in his chair, suddenly jumped up, overcome by excitement, and, strapping a belt around his hips, began to belly dance.

Until that moment I had assumed it was an Arab party, but then I heard that she was dedicating the songs to the Mizrahi and Cohen families.

I returned to bed and looked at my watch. It was no longer on my wrist, but hanging on the wall. There was something odd about it; it resembled the Jaffa clock-tower. Its hands did not move, and though I could see them clearly, I was unable to interpret them. I wondered what time it was as I puttered about the house, trying to tidy up. It was an abandoned Arab fisherman's shack, with only a rusted fisherman's lamp hanging by a long chain from the ceiling and a dead plant. I really should get rid of the plant, I thought to myself; it wasn't nice to have junk lying about. But somehow I could not bring myself to throw it out.

A narrow spiral staircase led to a bull's-eye window in the roof. I climbed up and was surprised to find the beach jammed with Israelis. They were all seated on a single small towel; I took my own and spread it at some distance from theirs. As I was about to lie down, I noticed a huge, oddly shaped wave; it rushed toward us, roaring wildly, ringing the shore like a high wall. I ran up to the Israelis, yelling that they should evacuate the beach. But they would not move. So I left them and tried to get to the cliff before we were flooded. As I reached the peak, I saw the water rise up and tower above me like a mountain. I closed my eyes in terror. Moments later, I reopened them. The waves had begun to recede and the shore had reappeared. The Israelis were nowhere to be seen.

I tossed and turned. The dark seemed oppressive now that the party next door was over. Creaking boards and the sound of the wind whistling against the rooftop made me jittery. For a long time I lay on my back, unable to sleep, alert for distant sounds. Even the occasional lights of passing cars flashing against the windowpanes and walls made me jump. Finally, unable to resist the urge, I got up to inspect the house. I walked briskly up and down the rooms to give myself courage, checked out dark corners, opened all the closets, even looked under the bed. Then I double-locked the front door and lay down once more, reassured. But soon the old disquietude returned.

Remembering how I had detested Fräulein Broch, my nanny, for shutting off the light my mother had left on for me in the corridor, I went to turn on the light in the hallway. From that day, I never slept in Israel without a light. During the day I was strong, courageous, full of bluff. When Israelis asked me if I wasn't afraid an Arab would kill me for treason, I would laugh at them. But at night, I was alone with my nightmares.

In the morning my eyes, blinded by the strong light, scanned the unfamiliar blue walls. My body stiffened under the sheets. Then I remembered I was in Israel.

The telephone was ringing. It was a television producer. How had he gotten my phone number? I wondered. It was a question I would ask many times. I have yet to fathom how it happened, but virtually the entire Israeli press had been alerted about my arrival.

Just as I was congratulating myself for having turned down his request —he had brazenly scolded me for refusing to give my impressions on the evening news—there was a knock on the door. A good-looking young man with curly black hair and manners at once courteous and diffident had been sent over to persuade me to change my mind. I continued to refuse, knowing full well that in a country as small as Israel no one was likely to forget a face seen on TV and that the safe anonymity I treasured would be lost. And indeed, I held my ground throughout my stay: Though I later agreed to speak with newspaper reporters, I never gave a television interview.

But I did offer the reporter a cup of coffee that morning, so he would not feel his trip was a total waste of time. He expressed genuine pleasure about my coming to Israel, and his friendliness and warmth won me over. Soon we were chatting away like old friends. He asked me what my first impressions were, and upon hearing that I had mixed feelings about Jaffa, he graciously offered me a key to his Tel Aviv apartment. It was really no more than an attic, he said half-apologetically, a relic from his bachelor days that he had kept for occasional overnight stays after moving to Jerusalem. I was grateful for the offer; I wanted to be in the atmosphere of a Jewish city, which Jaffa simply did not afford. I took a *sherut* to Tel Aviv the next day.

Israel is a nation of early risers, and though it was only seven in the morning, the traffic was already heavy on the outskirts of the city. Amid the maddening din of horns, the throughway to Tel Aviv looked like the bumper-car arena of an amusement park. I was watching the Volkswagen ahead of us struggle to overtake an enormous bus when suddenly I was jolted out of my seat. Our taxi had come to an abrupt stop. The accident was our cabbie's fault; he had switched lanes without signaling and had consequently been rammed in the rear by another car. This did not prevent him, however, from sticking his head out the window and heaping abuse on the other driver. I understood only the first of his invectives, because the Hebrew term *chamor* ("donkey") was the same as the Arabic.

An American passenger offered a translation: "You donkey, I see you don't want to spend next Sabbath with your family!" To which the driver replied in kind. Arabic curses like *"ibn el kalb"* and *"kus omak"* ("son of a bitch," "cunt of your mother") punctuated the stream of vituperation that followed; apparently biblical Hebrew was deficient in good four-letter words.

A horrendous whistle brought the traffic to a standstill, and a policeman on a motorcycle entered the scene. From the vehement exchange and gesticulations, I gathered that our cabbie was now engaged in a life-and-death struggle over the amount of fine to be paid. Israelis seemed to have the same healthy, if somewhat exaggerated, skepticism of authority as Egyptians and, like them, to believe that laws apply to everyone except themselves. Without a knowledge of Hebrew, I unfortunately could not tell what compelling excuse the culprit had come up with, but the policeman ended up by tearing up the ticket, which I took to mean he had been outsmarted or, more likely, outshouted.

We drove past some hitchhikers. I was startled by the sight of a young soldier who stood in their midst, lost in an embrace with his girlfriend. Photos from the Western press flashed before me: heavy armored columns moving through the West Bank; soldiers with faces distorted by fury pulling Arab women demonstrators by the hair and bashing the skulls and backs of men; other soldiers indifferently blowing up Arab houses in Gaza. I remembered one picture in particular, that of a soldier kicking a suspect against a wall. It was disconcerting to see this odious uniform on an amorous eighteen-year-old. I could not tear my eyes away from their passionate kiss.

More cars, more noise. The traffic inched through the thick air. Little workshops, garages, printing houses blackened by the smog.

We had reached the city.

Tel Aviv was a surprise. I had always thought of Israel as a marvel of Western technology, not just because of its military might, but also because Amos Perlmutter, an Israeli professor who had visited Harvard, had told me it was "definitely part of Europe." In his view, at the root of the Middle Eastern conflict lay a clash between Western and Arab cultures. This only confirmed what I had been taught as a child: The Zionists of Palestine were an alien, *European* element, "a thorn in the heart of the Arab nation." Given all this, I had expected a grand metropolis, the gleaming jewel of Israeli dominion and efficiency. Instead, Tel Aviv resembled a Middle Eastern bazaar.

Central Station, where the *sherut* dropped me off, had regulations of its own: Pedestrians, buses, horse carriages laden with fruits, bicycles, trucks, cabs—all had right of way. Masses of people zigzagged between cars. Buses suddenly zeroed in from side alleys. Taxis pulled up in the middle of the street without warning to let off their passengers.

Vendors crowded the sidewalks. A huckster selling ice cream ran among a throng of soldiers in a queue—older soldiers, perhaps reserve officers, red-eyed, unshaven, pot-bellied under sloppy shirts, and youngsters who seemed to be returning from furlough, with short haircuts, freshly polished shoes, and pressed uniforms. Another peddler, seated at the edge of a bathtub planted in the middle of the sidewalk, was hawking toilets, sinks, gravestones, tiles from Italy, and a needlepoint portrait of Moshe Dayan. Next to a butcher's stall with the fanciful name "Le Coq d'Or—Kosher" was a stand with all kinds of bagels. The grocer, wearing a sweaty red T-shirt and flashing a gold canine tooth when he smiled, held out a steaming ear of corn and asked me if I was an American tourist and would I go dancing with him that night.

Architecturally, Tel Aviv was a nightmare. In lieu of the streamlined terminals, gleaming skyscrapers, stately mansions, and elegant parks with statues and lush fountains I had imagined, it was a town of four-story cubes. The drab brick buildings, with their unwashed slate-colored windows and walls corroded by pollution and the salty sea breeze, lent it the atmosphere of a shabby provincial town. Everything about it was oppressively square: no curved windows, no rounded ornamental portals, no arches or columns. It was a town of identical balconies running along all the floors, all with the same metal railings, the same protruding drainpipes, and the same plastic shades: striped gray and black alternating with a weather-beaten green and blue.

Before each building stood a bleak little plot, presumably a garden. The scraggly lawns looked as if their only source of moisture came from the runoff of the balconies. A few blades of grass fought for their lives under mounds of discarded yogurt containers and ice cream wrappers, while the balding hedges seemed to have surrendered to the impact of children's soccer balls and mailmen's bicycles. Trees apparently had a better chance of survival; each building had at least one.

I found Rheines Street and went by a series of peeling housefronts with uniformly narrow entrances and dingy staircases. I stopped before number 32, entering by way of an unhinged fence gate. A small old woman with a polka-dot handkerchief tied around her head like the ribbon of an Easter egg was beating her carpets on the first-floor balcony. Noticing my suitcase, she asked: "Vere have you come from, young lady?"

"America," I said. Feigning a reciprocal interest for the sake of politeness, I asked her in turn if she was originally from Germany.

"Ja, ja, zat is vere I come from. How clever of you to tell zat right avay!"

But alas! The conversation did not end there. Mrs. Dorfman proceeded to cross-examine me: Which apartment was I headed for? Was I married? Had I any children?

Her face puckered sympathetically when she learned that I hadn't.

"Oh! Vat a pity. Vell, never mind, you are still young."

Meanwhile I had been fumbling for the light switch above the staircase, but she advised me not to bother. The landlord had long ago stopped replacing the light bulbs because they were always being stolen. "People here are no goot!" she added, shaking her head.

I couldn't tell her how much I agreed.

"My" apartment, situated near the rooftop, consisted of a single room with a bed that took up nearly all the space, a tiny fridge, and a hotplate. The bathroom was so small one had to stoop when entering. Oddly enough, a pair of long, narrow Pharaonic eyes, heavily fringed with black, had been painted on the hot-water boiler.

I dropped off my suitcase and headed straight for Dizengoff Circle— the city's major tourist attraction, or so at least I supposed, having read a book by the famous Israeli "dove" politician Lova Eliav, who wrote that the day Israeli tourists would be allowed to see the Pyramids and Egyptian tourists could visit Dizengoff there would be a real peace.

I had imagined the Israeli equivalent of the Pyramids to resemble the Champs Elysées. To my surprise, it turned out to be much like any other street in Tel Aviv, except that its entire length was devoted to the junk-food business. I walked past pizzerias displaying stale, triangular slices and synthetic juices bubbling in transparent plastic tubs—the choice was between a greenish mauve and a greenish yellow. Farther on, a seedy little restaurant spilled out into the street, its window featuring stacks of greasy chicken and cold, soggy french fries. Beside it, on the sidewalk, gray slabs of meat were being cooked beyond redemption.

My eyes traveled exultantly the length of Dizengoff Street and I thought to myself, "Wait till I tell my friends back home about this. They'll never believe me. Here we've been saying all along that Israel must integrate itself into the Middle East if it wants to be accepted, but

Israel *is* the Middle East!" For facing me was a scene right out of a crowded Cairo quarter. On both sides of the street were two enormous posters: To the right, Bruce Lee in karate posture was taking on the Dragon; to the left, a half-naked woman with a grotesquely large bosom lay sprawling on the floor while two men were literally fighting over her. Crowded underneath the posters, tiny shops displayed sesame-paste salad and balls of falafel behind dirty glass stands. Everything seemed to get stuffed into pitas so that it could be eaten on the run. Couples strolled by arm-in-arm, their chins jutting forward to keep the chick-pea paste off their shirts. Olive-skinned men in mod clothes (clumsy plat-form heels, flashy bell-bottoms, flowery pink and garish purple shirts unbuttoned over their hairy chests) accompanied girls who looked at once overdressed and naked, with vermilion toenails, high cork heels, flimsy blouses, and minimal shorts. Farther down, Arab music wailed forth from under a peddler's pile of combs, Israeli colognes, and Amer-ican chewing-gum. Squatting on the sidewalk beside him was a dark-skinned beggar in a skullcap. He held out a bony hand to passersby, who tossed their coins into it. An isolated Wimpy stand jarred with this otherwise Oriental setting.

The sight of so much food parading down Dizengoff had made me hungry. I went in search of the only restaurant in my guidebook recom-mended for its Jewish food, Kiton. On the way, I passed a little bank and decided to stop and convert some traveler's checks into liras. For this simple transaction, which in America would have taken five or ten minutes, I was referred to three separate departments, and the amount of paperwork involved was phenomenal.

The bank clerk, a bald man with a tiny red nose stuck like a button in the middle of his fleshy face, asked to see my passport, because Israelis were subject to foreign-currency restrictions. Staring at it dumbfounded, he inquired in Arabic if I was a Cairene.

"Yes."

"But so am I!" He beamed.

He asked me what district I was from. I told him. "Zamalek," he breathed, why, he knew it very well. He added with a wistful smile that when he was a boy, his mother used to send him there every Passover to purchase *batarech* (salted mullet roe, commonly known as Egyptian caviar) from the Greek grocery Vassilakes, which had the finest in town. His voice trailed off nostalgically. He was no longer with me; he was in the little juice shop where he stopped on the way back from the grocery for his favorite drink—freshly squeezed guava juice. He stopped short, as though troubled by an afterthought: "You *are* Jewish, of course?"

42

"No."

"Then you're working for us?" he asked, dropping his voice.

I could not help laughing. No. I was not nearly as exotic as Mata Hari, I was merely an Egyptian tourist.

He looked skeptical.

Meanwhile, the line behind me was getting longer, so I tried to steer him back to business by asking him why bank transactions took forever in Israel.

He sighed. "Yes, it's like Egypt. We even have a word for it here—*bureaucratia*. Do you know how many hours an Israeli bureaucrat puts in each day?" he asked me. I shook my head. "Eight-oh-four," he declared. "He comes at eight, does zero, and leaves at four." I laughed, but the crowd behind me sounded far from amused. The bank clerk, however, was not going to let any disgruntled customer spoil his fun. Before I could stop him, he had already embarked on a new joke.

At the opposite counter, another interminable wait. The Englishman just ahead of me lost his temper because the young teller was flirting with the cashier at the adjoining window. He protested.

"Mister, you can see I'm busy! If you don't like the way we do business here, go to another bank!" the teller snapped at him, and went on chatting with the girl.

Having spent over an hour in the bank, I was ravenous when I finally reached the restaurant. By this time I should perhaps have anticipated that reality would be quite different from my expectations, but I was not prepared for the dish that arrived when I asked the Polish couple who ran the small establishment for a "typical Jewish meal." The *kishke* they recommended turned out to be a revolting darkish intestine oozing a gooey white substance. I did not know what it was, but I was determined not to let it enter my mouth. I ate the accompanying potato pancakes (*latkes*), which were strangely sweet but tasty, and then left to wander about in the sweltering heat.

By the end of the afternoon every move had become an effort. My heels cleaved to the pavement, and I had to gasp for air. Israel in July was even worse than Egypt. When I unexpectedly came upon the sea, I thought at last I would be able to cool off. I removed my shoes, hobbled over scorching sand to the shore, rolled up my skirt, and stood soothing my feet in the water. A few minutes later, I stared in bewilderment at limbs I could barely recognize as my own. They were black. Luckily, there was a large tin of benzine in the middle of the lifeguard's platform, for the purpose of removing the ubiquitous tar.

It seemed the entire city was at the beach. Here in the crowd the

Israelis were more impolite and irritable than ever. The place festered with quarrels because it was impossible to set down one's foot anywhere without stepping on someone's towel, thereby infringing on jealously guarded terrain. I began to feel I was the target of everyone's malevolent attention. A row of fat pink matrons seated on rented folding chairs stared at me with hostility from behind their violet plastic sunglasses. A group of teenage girls in tiny bikinis whispered and giggled behind my back as I passed them, and a boy on the beach yelled at me when I inadvertantly stepped within range of his racketball game. Something told me the hard rubber ball that hit me from behind was no accident. I tried to walk along the shore instead, but now I sighted a giant, placid turd wafting toward me.

As I was hurrying away from the mobbed beach, I noticed a large crowd in front of a theater. I did not know if the film was any good, but I knew it was a chance for a few quiet moments in a cool, air-conditioned place. When I got closer I saw they were lining up to see *The Towering Inferno*. I bought a ticket and walked in. Since no usher was in sight, I picked out a seat at random. No sooner had the feature begun than Russian curses rent the air, followed by a crash of broken glass and furious screams. I jumped out of my seat, ready to rush to the door, but the woman next to me caught my sleeve, forcing me to sit down. "Don't worry," she said in English. "I see you are a foreigner. It's nothing. This happens all the time in Israel. Someone must have sat in someone else's seat, and there's a fight. That's all."

But soon even she grew alarmed, as the irate man, who had been hit by a Coke bottle, swore he would not leave the theater without killing his attacker. Some of the viewers got up and tried to persuade the pitcher of the bottle to leave. Meanwhile, the Russian pulled out a knife. Finally the manager was able to settle the row by a compromise. The two parties were placed at opposite ends of the theater, and things settled down to a relative quiet.

I say "relative" for, as I soon realized, in Israel it was a time-honored custom to talk uninterruptedly through movies. In this case, since most of the audience did not understand English, it hardly paid to listen anyway. My own command of English yielded me no advantage, for the hubbub totally drowned out the voices of the actors. Fortunately, someone had had the foresight to insert French subtitles in addition to the Hebrew ones. To the murmur of voices was added the continuous crackling of sunflower seeds, which Israelis seemed to consume in enormous quantities, and the wailing of a baby.

The rest of the movie unfolded uneventfully to the accompaniment of the audience's running commentary. As the movie fire spread in a newly built skyscraper during its inauguration ceremony, the audience shouted advice to the hero, Steve McQueen, who was in charge of the rescue operation. "*Lo, lo mikan, idiot!*" ("No, not here, idiot!"), someone would call out to him as he tried to elude the flames. Catcalls and hisses would follow. "*Ta'azov oto, hu mistader tov me'od*" ("Get off his back, he's doing fine"), another viewer would respond. "*Eze chor batachat! Tishbor et hachalon!*" ("What an asshole! Smash the window!"), a third person would yell. The heckling gave way to smacks and sharp whistles whenever a romantic love scene alternated with the action. I giggled as I remembered how my father had refused to set foot in movie theaters ever since the revolution had allowed the populace to invade the balconies, bringing their sunflower seeds and lewd jokes with them. And I thought of how Theodor Herzl, the founder of the Jewish state, would turn in his grave if only he could see how his dream of building a Viennese polity in the Middle East had fared. Had he not rallied the Jews to form "a wall of defense for Europe in Asia, an outpost of civilization against barbarism"?

It occured to me then that perhaps Israel's desire to perceive herself as part of Europe was a way of gaining the acceptance historically denied to the Jews. Building a second Vienna in Israel would certainly prove to the West, which had humiliated and rejected them, that the Jews were every bit as civilized as any people in Europe.

I, too, had expected that Tel Aviv would be like Vienna, but there in the dark theater, tired, sunburned, exhilarated, I realized that I felt disturbingly at home in this city, because, with its shabby four-story houses, its balconies, its teeming beaches, and its people's endearing vulgarity, it could have been Alexandria.

3

The Politicians

THE NEWS about an Egyptian visitor to Israel spread quickly when *Le Monde* published an article about my arrival, which was followed by a piece in the *New York Times*. The Egyptian press responded to this as could be expected. The well-known journalist Anis Mansour, writing in *Al Achbar,* a paper generally considered to reflect government views, assailed me, calling me *sazga* (an Arabic term for naive and stupid) for allowing myself to fall into the Zionist trap, while the highly regarded left-wing journal *Al Talia* carried an article a few weeks later that stated:

> Since the middle of July 1974, Zionist newspapers, radio and television in Israel, the United States and Western Europe have been describing a young lady from Egypt who is preparing for her doctoral degree in political science at Harvard University. . . . According to the news reports, the passport officials could hardly believe their eyes when she arrived at Ben-Gurion Airport and they found themselves holding a real Egyptian passport with an Israeli entrance visa. . . .
>
> This was all part of an Israeli plan to mislead international public opinion into thinking that educated Arabs supported coexistence with Israel and opposed the Arab liberation movement in general and the Palestinian liberation movement in particular.

Not surprisingly, the Israeli media were somewhat kinder to me. Though a few of the local newspapers, like the *Jerusalem Post,* had earlier displayed their skepticism by reprinting "An Egyptian's Vision of Peace" under a caricature of a vulture flying over the Pyramids with an olive branch in its beak, others seemed prepared to make the hazardous leap of faith. Their yearning for peace was perhaps best expressed by a newspaper editorial welcoming me to Israel, published shortly after

46

my arrival under the heading "The First Swallow." Thus overnight I had become a symbol, of foolishness or treachery to some, of peace and hope to others—but in either case a target for manipulation by politicians and propagandists.

One of the great advantages of being an Egyptian in Tel Aviv, as I quickly discovered, was that one could hobnob with the high and mighty.

Among the welcoming notes I received at my Rheines Street apartment in the days following my arrival in Israel was one from Menachem Begin, head of the parliamentary opposition to the Labor government, inviting me to lunch with him at the Knesset. It was accompanied by a gift parcel, which included a book of his memoirs, *The Revolt,* and another by the founder of the Jewish right-wing movement, Zeev Jabotinsky, entitled *Prelude to Delilah: The Story of Samson,* as well as a record of Jabotinsky's songs.

I played it:

> Two banks to the Jordan,
> One is ours, the other too.

> There will be plenty and happiness,
> For the Arab, the son of Nazareth, and my son,
> Because my flag, a flag of purity and rectitude,
> Will purify the two banks of the Jordan. . . .

I could not bring myself to listen to the rest.

I dreaded that the news of our lunch would travel back home; I was terribly uneasy about being seen with such a notorious right-wing figure. But I was too curious to resist.

In all my time in Israel, I can hardly remember feeling more trepidation than on making my entrance into the Knesset building. I stood on the threshold of the cafeteria reserved for cabinet ministers and parliamentary members, my heart beating. The distance I had to cross to get to Begin, who sat in the back of the room, seemed enormous, as great as the one that had greeted me on arrival at the huge ballroom in Cannes where I made my debut at the age of fifteen. I felt the same bashfulness —only this time I was not imagining it, everyone *was* staring at me. As I headed for Begin's table, the rumpus so characteristic of Israelis at mealtime subsided abruptly, and there was such a stillness that one could have heard a paper napkin flutter to the floor. Here, in person, were all the ministers and former ministers who had been known to me only from the grotesque caricatures in the Egyptian newspapers. I stared at them as if they were animated cartoon figures. Abruptly, the silence was shattered by chairs and tables being pushed back. Within seconds, dozens of welcoming hands stretched out toward me, and I was trying to clasp them all simultaneously. As the eager faces pressed toward me, I felt a lump in my throat, for these were not naive, idealistic young people, but hard-boiled politicians and cynics.

Suddenly, it seemed the whole Israeli army was closing in on me. There was General Sharon, who had led the incursion into the western bank of the Suez Canal during the 1973 war, his enormous pot belly pushing before him the diminutive General Yariv. And hugging me effusively was General Bar-Lev, whose formidable fortifications along the Suez Canal we had successfully stormed a few months earlier. Squeezed in among them was the former chief of staff and now the prime minister of Israel, Yitzhak Rabin, accompanied by a thin gentleman with a funereal air who turned out to be his press secretary, Miron Medzini. My husband and Medzini had been students of Henry Kissinger's at Harvard and had met again in December 1973, in the lobby of the Intercontinental Hotel, during the Geneva peace talks.

Now Begin, the devil incarnate in Arab mythology, was edging toward me. He lowered his head with a jerk, as though he had horns and were going to butt. Instead, he kissed my hand with exaggerated gallantry. And before I knew it, Begin was steering me, with a repertoire of polite amiabilities, toward a table where an elegant, heavily bearded man sat. I recognized him at once as Ben Elissar, Begin's right-hand man. Next to him was Begin's personal secretary, an unremarkable-looking gentleman by the name of Yechiel Kadishai. Once we had joined his men, Begin said to Kadishai, "Have you met our Egyptian guest? She's a doctoral candidate at Harvard, you know."

"No, I have not had this honor," replied the latter, fixing me with a stare at once mistrustful and supercilious, as though I were some kind of shoddy merchandise with a pretentious name that Begin was trying to pawn off on him. I could not help blushing.

We ordered lunch, and while we were waiting to be served I chatted with Ben Elissar, who was soon to become Israel's ambassador to Egypt. He spoke to me in perfect French and was what might be called a *beau parleur*. But there was something too suave about him; he seemed engaged more by verbal gymnastics than by real conversation, and he kept fingering his beard and stealing glances at his slender, graceful fingers.

The food arrived. I tackled a steak stiff with age and some flotsam that went by the name of vegetable stew. Eager not to offend, I ate every scrap. The food put Begin in a buoyant mood, and he began telling anecdotes halfway through lunch. His two cronies hung on his every word, greeting even his drabbest sallies with squeals of laughter.

And then the hilarity abruptly stopped as Begin directed his attention to me. Addressing me unctuously, he praised the Egyptians, who were a more civilized, gentler people than other Arabs, he said. With them, he intimated, peace was possible. "Only if you're ready to give up the West Bank," I immediately retorted, to show him I would not be manipulated by flattery. Even if it meant being rude, I would not let Begin think that my trip to Israel and acceptance of his invitation meant I had turned my back on my people and my beliefs. My statement clearly disturbed him: his jaw stiffened and his mouth twisted into a jeer, while Ben Elissar's hand trembled with rage, spilling soup on his beard.

"You must get one thing straight at the outset," Ben Elissar said imperiously. "Judea and Samaria are the heartland of the Jewish people, and we have exclusive sovereignty there."

"Yes, exclusive sovereignty," reiterated Begin.

"And what about the Palestinians?" I asked.

Ben Elissar gave a little laugh.

And Begin echoed, rhetorically, "What of them? Their standard of living has gone up by four hundred percent, thanks to the jobs we have offered them. We have brought full employment to the West Bank. If they don't like it here, they can go to Jordan."

After a moment of smoldering silence, Begin asked me if I had been to St. Jean d'Acre, a Palestinian town and celebrated Crusader fort, incorporated into Israel after the '48 war. I told him I hadn't.

"A pity. You would have been able to see for yourself how well *our* Arabs are doing," he said, with a superior smile.

I answered that I doubted I would find the condition of Israel's Palestinians enviable.

He looked up at me in pained surprise. Suddenly, he raised his arm and gestured to someone at a neighboring table. The man leapt up and rushed over eagerly. He was one of the so-called friendly Arabs in Begin's party. His paunch and the rings on his puffy fingers, which were constricted at the joints like link sausages, told eloquently how well *he* was doing.

Begin greeted him affably, and the "Arab-Israeli" dissolved into a profusion of bows. Having ordered a cup of Turkish coffee for him, Begin spoke to him in a condescending tone. He explained who I was and said that he was trying to enlighten me on Arabs in Israel but that I refused to believe him, so he wished me to hear it from the lips of one of my own kinfolk.

The coffee arrived. The Palestinian drank it. After licking the foam off his mustache and running his fingers twice through his hair, he obligingly echoed Begin's views on the "Arab-Israelis" and on the many gains that benevolent Jewish rule had brought the Palestinians in the occupied territories.

I ignored him and, addressing myself to Begin, pressed on him the urgency of putting a stop to Jewish settlement in the West Bank. "There are Jewish settlements all over the world, including the United States," Begin remarked with a dry and haughty air, "and there are already hundreds of Arab settlements in Israel [he was referring to the Palestinian towns and villages within the 1967 borders]. I see no reason why there should be no Jewish settlements in the West Bank. We expect in the future to receive millions of Jews from Russia and South America, and we have every intention of settling them there."

I argued that if there was to be peace between Israel and the Palestinians, those Jews who felt a religious attachment to areas within the West Bank could go and live there, provided they had a visa issued by a sovereign Palestine—just as an American Catholic who wished to reside permanently in the Vatican would have to get the permission of the Italian authorities to do so.

He laughed at this and said: "If a stranger comes to your land, on the first day you will invite him over and give him dinner. Then, if he stays overnight, you may still offer him breakfast the next morning. But by the third day he will have begun to get on everyone's nerves, including the children's, and you will throw him out. You don't seem to understand that we have no intention of being guests in our own land."

I was in a cold rage.

Begin realized this, but nonetheless went on: "I want you to tell your president, when you go back, that we have no designs on Sinai whatsoever, but that Judea and Samaria are our homeland, and we intend to keep them."

"Judea and Samaria, as you call the West Bank, are no concern of Sadat's, but I'll be happy to tell the PLO, who will be interested to hear it," I replied sarcastically. (In actuality, the closest I had gotten to the PLO was watching Arafat on television.)

At the mention of the PLO, Ben Elissar began to tug angrily at his beard, and Begin's eyes narrowed in irritation. Recovering a thin smile, he informed me that the PLO in no way represented the Palestinian people and that the majority of the Arabs did not approve of their acts. "Ask him," Begin said, pointing at the Palestinian, who nodded like the utterly spiritless creature he was. I was ashamed for him. "You see!" Begin said to me triumphantly.

The craven Palestinian angered me even more than the pompous Begin, and I couldn't keep myself from launching into an impassioned defense of the PLO. I praised their actions as deeds of heroism—savage, but legitimate guerrilla tactics. And I defended the PLO as idealists who sacrificed their lives for a cause, knowing as they did that almost certain death awaited them the moment they crossed the border into Israel.

As I was saying this, I was sure that I noticed an understanding gleam in the Palestinian's eyes—as if he were signaling me that he shared my views, even though he did not dare articulate them. This unspoken complicity revolted me even more; in my contempt for him, I did not want us to have anything in common. But now, suddenly, he spoke up:

"Arafat—" he began.

"Arafat is a murderer!" Begin exploded.

He had a lot of nerve calling Arafat a murderer, I returned, when he himself was responsible for the massacre of an entire Arab village in 1948, old people, women, and children included.

Smiling with forbearance, Begin accused me of being a victim of the propaganda of the Israeli Labor party, which had "fabricated" the Deir Yassin massacre in order to discredit the right—thereby providing the Arabs with excellent ammunition against Israel.

It was obviously futile to push the argument further. Exasperated by Begin's dogmatism and contemptuous affability, I was anxious to leave. But just as I was preparing to flee, he pressed another helping of dessert upon me.

As I sat glumly munching my cake, I saw Moshe Dayan enter the cafeteria. Every eye followed him as he swept past the parliamentarians, his body perfectly erect, his head held high, and seated himself in the remotest corner of the room. Like a mighty god presiding from afar, he scanned the assembled crowd. A smile of complete indifference played about his lips.

I gazed at him with undisguised curiosity, thinking back to the time I had encountered him many years ago aboard a TWA jet. I was just a schoolgirl on my way back home from New York, where I had gone as the Egyptian delegate to a political forum for teenagers after winning a contest organized by the *International Herald Tribune*. TWA had offered a free ticket in the first-class compartment, and I ended up sitting behind Dayan. As he pushed his seat back I caught a glimpse of his profile.

At first I did not recognize him, for I had not seen him board the plane, and I felt pity for him, thinking, "Poor man, he must have lost his eye in an accident." As the outline of his features became sharper, it began to dawn on me that I had seen his face somewhere before. Then I realized with a start that this was none other than our perennial foe, General Moshe Dayan, the leader of Israel's imperialist incursion into Egypt in 1956—the man whose eye patch had confronted me daily from the front pages of our Egyptian newspapers as the very emblem of Israel's malevolent designs.

A thrill of revulsion ran through me. I was literally within arm's reach of the enemy. Would I dare go up to him and look him straight in the eye? I leaned forward. "Sir," I whispered in his ear, but so timidly that he did not even hear. Then I tapped him on the shoulder.

He turned around and looked at me with a puzzled air. Having exhausted my entire stock of courage in this one act of heroism, I could not force a single word from my lips and merely let out a nervous giggle. He beckoned me to come sit next to him. I hesitated, looking about me furtively to see whether anyone was watching. My heart pounding with terror and delight, I sat down.

Smiling at me, he asked how old I was. I blushed. He noticed my shyness and took my hand encouragingly in his. It only made matters worse: The thought of the terrible retribution that would await me on arrival if anyone saw me fraternizing with the enemy struck me dumb. Dayan burst out laughing and said I should not be so frightened by him, he was very fond of girls.

By then he must have gathered who I was from the identity tag I still wore on my blazer (all delegates had been asked to wear tags so they could be recognized at the airport by the people assigned to meet them). He began to talk about the conflict between the Arab world and Israel, all the while keeping my hand in his. I let it stay there limply out of embarrassment. But my conscience compelled me to disown it: Sweaty and cold, my hand began to feel eerily dissociated from the rest of my body.

Apparently oblivious of my qualms, Dayan went on to deplore the hatred of the Arabs for Israel, telling me how in the old days he had been on the best terms with many of them. He had often been the guest of King Abdallah of Jordan, where he had feasted on charcoal-broiled lamb wrapped in mint leaves. After dinner, he and the king would drink syrupy tea out of gold-rimmed blue glasses and play backgammon. He had managed to endear himself to His Majesty by always letting him win, he said. One day, after Abdallah had won his third game in a row, he told Dayan in a burst of enthusiasm that he was very fond of him; it was that woman Golda he could not stand.

Since I had never heard of the secret negotiations between Israel and Jordan in 1948, I did not believe a word he said, and congratulated myself for being immune to Israeli propaganda. I wouldn't let him talk me into believing that an Arab monarch would agree to meeting one of the enemy. I felt like a great statesman negotiating her country's affairs, and my only regret was that I was wearing my school uniform in honor of the reception party awaiting me at the Cairo airport. I felt silly in my gray blazer, tie, and pleated skirt, and kept tugging nervously at my long woolen socks, wishing I were dressed in something more grown-up.

The announcement that we were about to land at Orly jolted me out of my secret fantasies. Dayan had not stopped talking since I had sat down next to him, and the hours had flown past. He was getting off in Paris to catch an El Al connection to Tel Aviv, while I was continuing on the same flight to Cairo. I realized with a pang of regret that my adventure would soon be over. Suddenly it occurred to me that none of my school friends would believe me when I boasted of our meeting, so I decided to ask him to sign my autograph book. He wrote pointedly: "I wish you all the best, Sana. —Moshe Dayan, commander of the Israeli army in the 1956 campaign." He then told me I could be his guest in Israel anytime I wished, kissed me on the cheek, and disappeared.

On the way home from the Cairo airport, I wanted both to show off my autograph and to hide it for fear of chastisement. But since vanity had always been stronger in me than fear, the former triumphed. Mother was irate. How could I have disgraced my country this way? And what if the customs official had spotted it? It would have meant no end of trouble, not just for me but for my family. Not to speak of the shame of it all, when the neighbors and friends found out. . . . She made me promise I would never mention the incident to anyone, not even to Father.

Though I kept the secret, I never forgot the meeting. Later, in those tense weeks before the '67 war, when Dayan was made Israel's minister of defense by popular demand, I would creep up to the roof (for fear that our house was bugged) and tune in to the Voice of Israel, broadcast in English. On clear days, when the station was not jammed, I would follow the news about him. Sometimes there would be excerpts from interviews he had given to foreign reporters, and the sound of his voice would send the blood rushing through my veins. It was a risky thing to do, because anyone caught listening to the enemy broadcast could be accused of spying.

Now here I was, a grown woman, and he an aging man. I looked at his head—a perfect, balding oval. The face had hollowed, and the cheekbones stood out a little more prominently than before. But he had the same fierce eye—so intense that it seemed to burn right through his skull.

The thrill of Dayan's distant presence turned me suddenly garrulous; I wanted to shine. Raising my voice enough to be overheard, I began to regale Begin and his cronies with Egyptian jokes about Goha, one of our comic folk heroes. They shook with laughter. I waited for Dayan to notice me, but he continued to sit impassively at his table.

Just as my spirits had begun to sink again, a portly gentleman with a broad, placid forehead and shaggy gray eyebrows entered the cafeteria. He had a look of genial astonishment at the world. Shooting a few bewildered glances around him, he advanced with a timid step. When he caught sight of me, he seemed overcome with joy. His handshake was not the cold, stiff gesture of a politician; it was full of genuine warmth. He asked me, almost humbly, if I would do him the honor of having coffee with him. I accepted and, after thanking Begin for his hospitality, let this friendly stranger lead me to another table.

We sat down together, and I discovered that he was Lova Eliav, a member of the Knesset (and the future founder of a small, liberal party called Peace for Israel).

On hearing what had transpired between Begin and me, he knitted his brow and said: "Begin's claim that the West Bank Arabs never had it so good has a terrible ring to it; it's an echo of our own exiled past when the anti-Semites used to say, 'Those Jews have it good, just look at all the money they make.' Unfortunately, it's not just Begin who thinks this way. I must confide to you that I am terribly afraid these years of occupation have eroded the values of many people in this country. Some of them have become kulaks—worse still, petty slave-drivers. Every morning they go down to the cheap labor market in Ashkelon, where all kinds of Arabs from the surrounding refugee camps congregate—old men, young men, women, children. And I have observed with my own eyes how my countrymen look them over, feeling the arms of children to make sure they are strong, the way the white plantation-owners once examined the teeth of black slaves. They prefer to hire children because they can pay them a pittance, and sometimes they cheat them, paying them less than they promised or nothing at all.

Because what can a twelve-year-old boy do against a Jewish land-lord who has given him a kick in the pants and chased him off his fields?"

When I asked Lova why he did not raise this issue in the Knesset, he lifted his hand to his forehead in a weary, discouraged manner. "I have done so time and again, but no one listens, no one cares! Years ago I brought this to Golda's attention. I told her we are creating here, in Israel, the equivalent of an Uncle Tom's Cabin—a Cousin Muhammad's Cabin—and related to her how I had seen whole Arab families herded into chicken coops and stables on the *moshavim* [cooperative farms] which I had helped build in the Lachish desert. The same thing is happening in our cities today. Since the West Bank Arabs are not al-lowed to reside in Israel—supposedly for security reasons—and they find it too exhausting and expensive to commute back and forth to their villages every day, they are locked into the workshops at night by their Jewish employers and sleep on the floor. The government knows that there are tens of thousands of Arabs who live and work in subhuman conditions, year in and year out; but it has chosen to ignore them, because if it recognizes their presence it will have to provide them with decent housing and all kinds of services, which are expensive. Only when there is a fire in a carpentry shop and the next morning they discover the charred bodies of three Arab refugees—who were unable to escape because they were locked in—do the press and the public show some concern, but this lasts half a day and then they forget all about it."

Lova sat silently for a few moments with a disillusioned look in his eyes. Then he got up, saying, "That's why our house is falling apart. It does not mean the state will wither away as the PLO may wish it to, it means we will turn into a 'normal' state, a small state of two and a half million Jews ruling over a million and a half Arabs, a state of terrible inbred social injustices like Guatemala, El Salvador, Ruanda, and so many others. And I don't think that's what my father came from Russia to build." Pressing my hand in his, he nodded and walked out, his silvery head bowed.

Shortly after this Knesset luncheon, Ben Elissar extended an invitation to me in Begin's name to attend the convention of their party, Herut. That year the convention was held in the West Bank town of Hebron, in a building that looked like a bunker. It was a relatively small place filled to the gills with more than 2,500 guests, including television crews and journalists from all over the world. People were everywhere, hanging out of doorways, sitting on ledges, huddled on the steps that led to the podium. The air was stale in the windowless room. Along the ceiling, a wooden railing shaped like a cross let down a maze of twisted ropes that cast snakelike shadows on the walls.

I had been placed in the front row, which was reserved for former ministers and top state dignitaries. On one side of me sat former finance minister Pinchas Sapir, and on the other former president Ben Zvi's widow, Rachel Yanait. Our chairs had been set a little apart from each other, but in all the rows behind us the seats were crammed closely together, with some people sharing chairs. To save space, no allowance had been made for aisles, and often as many as fifty persons would have to get up in order to open a passage for a latecomer. But it was not so much the cramped physical quarters that made this hall too intimate for my comfort as it was my knowledge that almost all of the other guests shared memories of the years they had spent together in the right-wing youth movement Betar, and later as hounded renegades in Irgun, the underground movement under Begin's command. In their fierce devotion to the leader, those gathered here tonight were not so much a political party as a cult.

The walls quivered with suppressed excitement as, one by one, the dignitaries filed in: the heads of each of the five factions that made up the right-wing Likud bloc; the Ashkenazi and Sephardi chief rabbis; the three ministers for the religious parties; Moshe Levinger, the head of the religious settlement in Hebron; General Ariel Sharon; and, finally, the leader of the Labor party, Shimon Peres.

It had not been so long ago that a Labor party luminary, David Ben-Gurion, had called Begin a Hitler who would have no qualms about decimating the Arabs in order to ensure Jewish sovereignty over the whole of Palestine. Behind the animosity of the two leaders lay years of ferocious infighting between Jewish "terrorist" organizations and socialists. The latter, appalled by the "terrorists'" indiscriminate killing of women and children, had arrested many of them and turned them over to the British authorities for imprisonment. This had earned them the sobriquet of "traitors," while they, in turn, dubbed Begin and his followers "fascists." The socialists looked askance at the right-wing motto "In blood and fire hath Judea fallen, in blood and fire shall it rise again," and at its emblem, a hand aiming a gun across the map of Palestine with the inscription "Only by the Gun."

The mutual suspicions and recriminations were exacerbated by the assassination in 1933 of a venerable member of the Labor establishment,

Chaim Arlosoroff. Though the mysterious circumstances surrounding his death—he was shot one evening on his way home, along the seashore of Tel Aviv—made it impossible to establish the guilt of the right, there was no doubt in the minds of the socialists as to who was responsible. Thereafter, Ben-Gurion's abhorrence for Begin was such that he would never agree—no matter how pressed he was in his search for a coalition partner—to sit with Begin in the same government. He coined the slogan "Without Herut and without the Communists" and remained true to it; his boycott extended not only to the living, but often to the dead. The Irgun dead were not recognized as having died in the service of the country, and their widows were denied state pensions. Ben-Gurion even went so far as to refuse permission for the remains of Jabotinsky, the revered right-wing leader, to be brought home for burial.

But now Ben-Gurion was dead, and the country as a whole had gravitated steadily toward the right. Ben-Gurion's successors had long since made their peace with Begin, as the presence of Shimon Peres—one of Ben-Gurion's most fervent disciples—on the podium that night testified. In fact, later in the evening, Begin was to call upon "the pupils of Ben-Gurion and Jabotinsky to join hands in defending the country," adding that "all differences are irrelevant now." Begin's choice of Kiryat Arba, the Jewish settlement in the Arab city of Hebron, as the site of his convention was not accidental. It was his way of thumbing his nose at the Labor party, which initially had been opposed to this settlement, and at the world at large. He was signaling that there would be no withdrawal from the West Bank, or, as he preferred to call it, Judea and Samaria.

When Begin himself finally mounted the podium, the hall seemed to go into seismic convulsions. He smiled coquettishly, like a prima donna relishing bravos. From the wall behind him, the portrait of Jabotinsky stared down on the scene. Abruptly the applause ceased, and the crowd fervently sang the anthem Jabotinsky had composed:

> With blood and sweat,
> Will rise a nation,
> Proud, generous, and fierce.
>
> Sacrifice blood and soul,
> For the sake of the hidden glory.

With the words "We have come back to Hebron and we are here to stay," Begin launched into his speech, and the audience thundered its approval. The man was a splendid orator. Shaking his finger, he warned the Arabs not to try to destroy the Jewish national homeland again. They would have to contend with a new Jew, he admonished, a fighting Jew, a *lion*—the word reverberated through the air like a roar. Continuing to address himself to the invisible foe, he said: "Ten times in the course of the last fifty-five years, you have tried to drown our aspirations for a Jewish national renaissance in blood. The result is that we have gotten stronger and bigger, and it will be the same in the future if you continue in your senseless ways."

Then, suddenly, singling me out of the audience, he addressd me in a voice oozing sweetness: "Return to your country and tell your people that Jewish soldiers have mothers who hate war just as much as Arab mothers do, and the Jewish people love peace and respect their neighbors. But also tell your people that if they try again to destroy us, the Jewish fighter will defend his homeland with all his might!"

Resuming his exhortation to his audience, he announced—and at this point his pitch became positively fierce—that the state was today in possession of military technology capable of bringing about the *devastation* of the Arab countries. This veiled allusion to Israel's nuclear might was greeted with an explosion of joy.

When Begin wound up his speech, a file of children dressed in blue and white, who had stood in back of the hall holding placards in the form of lotuses that bore the names of the Jewish settlements in the occupied territories, looped around to the podium. Raising their lotuses like halos above the heads of Begin and the ministers, they surrounded them like a celestial chorus, their rosy faces smiling beatifically. There were forty-four boys and girls in all, one from each settlement. The audience saluted them by snapping to attention and remained standing in silence for a full minute.

The meeting came to an end, and everyone staggered out in a paroxysm of excitement, reeling about with their arms around each other's shoulders, yelling, stomping the ground with their feet, and clapping their hands. Columns of people began chanting:

> From Dan to Beersheba,
> From Gilead to the sea,
> There is not an inch of land,
> Which was not redeemed with blood.
> Soaked in Hebrew blood,
> The fields, the mountains, the valleys.

I watched them march out arm in arm. I was quite alone.

As I was on my way out of my Rheines Street apartment one day shortly after the Herut convention, I found a letter from my father in my mailbox. I opened it with trepidation. First it described how shocked he had been to discover that I was in Israel from the French television news broadcast, which he and Mother watched every night in Geneva. Then he went on:

A friend of mind, an officer who was director general of passports and exit visas, informed me that you have been placed on the blacklist for having gone to Israel, a country with which we are still officially in a state of war. They have instructions to arrest you at the airport upon reentry, following which you are to be tried by a military tribunal. I do not have to spell out for you what that means—no less than fifteen years in prison, probably torture, since you are suspected of being a Zionist agent, and they will want to know if you have passed information to the enemy. Your marriage to a high official and your extensive contacts with cabinet ministers make you all the more suspect in this regard.

I have the intention of meeting with the minister of the interior to discuss this matter. I know that the Ministry has a complete file on you. The Egyptian intelligence service has kept an eye on every one of your moves. So before I talk to the minister and act as your lawyer, I want to know *every detail* very frankly. Is it true, as some Egyptians are saying, that you are in Israel's employ and receive money from them? Have you ever received funds from any Jewish institution? How much? The fact that you travel on El Al for half price is already an indication that you receive favors or bribes from the Jewish side. So tell me everything and send the letter with a person you trust, for I don't want to be confronted with your "file" when I go to see the minister. I am both a lawyer and your father. As your lawyer I have to know everything; as your father I am ready to forgive.

For a while after I read the letter, everything around me blurred. Only one thing pressed upon my consciousness—an agonizing homesickness which was for me something new and disconcerting. The dread I now felt of not being allowed to return to Egypt made my previous attitude seem flippant by comparison. I had paid little heed to my mother's warnings, following the outrage from Arabs that greeted the publication of the first *New York Times* article, that if I continued in this vein I might be barred from reentry to my country. Now I was worried: Had a report on my visit to the Herut convention already made its way into the Ministry of the Interior's files? It must have, since Begin's address to me had been widely quoted in the Israeli press. And would that visit not be interpreted, back home, as lending legitimacy to Israel's presence in the occupied territories?

Lost in my thoughts, I had not noticed the enclosure that had slipped out of the envelope onto the floor. I picked it up. It was an article from *Le Monde*, which my mother had forwarded to me after marking it with a huge red exclamation point. It read as follows:

Cairo—The arrival in Tel Aviv of an Egyptian, Mrs. Sana Hasan, about whom we wrote in our July 23rd edition, continues to be a subject of discussion among the press and among political and society circles.

Mrs. Hasan, who is not, strictly speaking, a journalist, but a student at Harvard University in the United States, is especially well known in Egypt as the wife of Mr. Tahsin Basheer, the official spokesman of the Ministry of Foreign Affairs, a high official who is amiable and cultured, and who was regarded until now as a candidate for a ministerial position.

Although he divorced his wife shortly after the announcement of her arrival in Israel, Mr. Tahsin Basheer is now in disgrace. In the press and in the Cairo salons, one hears that Mrs. Sana Hasan has "gone over to the enemy," and has been stripped of her Egyptian nationality. . . . A young Cairo journalist, however, has declared: "Mrs. Tahsin Basheer can only be faulted for being ahead of the politicians."

Thus I learned of my divorce. In an attached note, my mother added that I should understand that "poor" Tahsin had no choice because the foreign minister, Ismail Fahmy, had called him into his office and told him that he had to decide between me and his job. (This was to be confirmed later in Fahmy's memoirs, in which he stated he had received this order directly from Sadat.)

When I read this, my sorrow turned to sullen anger. I could not help feeling that Tahsin should have stood by me. I put the letters in my pocket, reminding myself that I had gone to Israel fully cognizant of the price I might have to pay. And if the talk in the Cairo salons had me betraying my own country, so be it. I would pursue my course.

The Begin visit was just the beginning. That summer I took advantage of my easy access to Israel's rulers by calling on and accepting invitations from leaders representing the whole political spectrum, including Golda Meir and Shimon Peres. The day I went to visit Golda Meir, the sun shone so implacably on the somber, rectangular villa with the forbidding front that I felt disinctly unwelcome. I rang the bell at the garden fence. The front door opened. From high up on the porch, two eyes glittered mistrustfully. It was Golda Meir.

She took in my casual clothing. "Come in," she said stiffly, without a smile.

There was something intimidating about Mrs. Meir's appearance. Perhaps it was the way her frizzy gray hair was severely pulled back into a bun. Maybe it was that her squat build, heavy legs, and laced shoes with thick square heels reminded me of a strict headmistress. At any rate, I felt tongue-tied.

"I am delighted by your visit, my dear," she said coolly, "but I would have been happier if President Sadat had come in your place." And she went on to tell me that she had invited him to Israel during her tenure as prime minister in order to negotiate with him directly. But he had refused, which only showed that he was not interested in peace, she said. While thus remonstrating, Mrs. Meir escorted me into an austere living room. Three lugubrious Israeli paintings adorned the wall opposite the sofa, where I was asked to sit, while next to it, on a small table, stood an ebony sculpure of a bearded violinist in traditional Orthodox garb. To my left, an antique menorah hung over a bookshelf, which featured several volumes on Zionism and socialism.

"And what if Sadat had come?" I asked. "Would you have been prepared to return to the '67 border?"

"Never!" she snapped, and proceeded to rattle off her list of what could and could not be given back: "Jerusalem must remain united and under our control. We can't give up the Golan Heights and have the Syrians shoot down at our kibbutzim again. Sinai we don't need, though we must keep Sharm el Sheik with a corridor to Israel because it is vital to our security. And Gaza we must keep, of course. But enough of this . . . will you have juice or tea with your *apfel strudel*?"

The Golda Meir who emerged from the kitchen a few minutes later, *apfel strudel* in hand, seemed to be a different person. Her tone was jovial and relaxed now, and the expression on her face had softened. With her gray silk dress, pearl necklace, and amethyst brooch, she might have been an aunt receiving her niece for tea.

She bent over and cut a parsimonious piece of strudel, which she placed on my dish.

"I hope you like this cake. I baked it myself, you know."

Her graciousness brought about an immediate resurgence of my table manners. Sitting stiffly upright, my knees tightly locked together, I delicately lifted the cup up to my mouth (instead of diving into it as usual) and was careful to take only small mouthfuls of cake at a time. I watched Meir's movements out of the corner of my eye, for Mother had taught me it was not polite to go on eating once the hostess has finished, no matter how hungry I might be.

The cake's crust was tough and stale, but I praised it, a gesture that seemed to win her over. But not for long. The Palestinian question brought the curtness back to her tone, as she stated that Israel was *not responsible* for them.

"Look, my dear, whenever there is a war there are refugees. What did the million Sudeten Germans do when they were driven out of Czechoslovakia at the end of the Second World War? Where did the hundreds of thousands of homeless people go after the war between India and Pakistan? They solved their problem without putting the onus on others. So let the Palestinians solve their problem within Jordan."

"Mrs. Meir, you sound like Leonid Brezhnev, who once scolded the Jews for raising such a fuss about their six million dead. He said that twenty-five million Russians and Poles had died in those same camps. Besides, the Palestinians have a national identity which is separate from Jordan's and—"

"And what about me?" she exclaimed. "Do you think *I* have anything in common with a Moroccan Jew? They have more in common with the Jordanians than I have with the Moroccans. When the Oriental Jews came here, they were ignorant, dirty, and disease-ridden, but we gave them homes and medical care, and we built them schools. We did the same for *our* Arabs. And what have the Arab countries done for the Palestinians? Nothing!"

Upset and angry, I had nothing better to say than to ask her if I might use her bathroom.

The tiny bathroom she led me to was immaculately clean. Just as I was about to reach out for the starched towel, I spied a hair in the sink. Dismayed, I picked it up and looked around me to make sure I hadn't shed any more. The sink seemed to have lost some of its former luster. I decided that I had better clean it out with the towel; it wouldn't do for her to think Arabs were dirty. As I was rinsing the sink, I spotted a splotch on the small glass shelf above. I didn't know if it had been there all along or if I'd inadvertently dirtied it by splashing water over it, but I decided that I'd better polish that, too, so she wouldn't suspect me of having done it. But now the towel, which had been sparkling white and neatly pressed just a moment earlier, looked drab and limp. I tried to iron it out by stretching it over my knee, and then hung it carefully over its bar.

When I returned to the living room, I sought to assuage my paranoia by immediately taking the offensive. Israel *owed* it to the Palestinians, as an act of restitution for all they had suffered, I said, to negotiate with their representatives—the Palestine Liberation Organization. "Why are you so afraid of the PLO, Mrs. Meir?" I asked her. "They have already moderated their position, and if you negotiate with them they will eventually be brought to recognize the Jewish state—"

She cut me off: "Listen, the other day my grandson told me he had a nightmare about dying. I tried to explain to him that little boys don't die. I told him first he'd go through the stage of being a boy, then through that of being a young man, then an old man, and only then would he die. But he said he did not want to die—not even in stages."

"Mrs. Meir," I said, pleadingly, "we all have to be willing to take risks for the sake of peace. Don't you ever let yourself go and dream about peace?"

She leaned back in her armchair, brushing me with a glance at once proud and grieved.

"Sure, I dream," she said. "I have nightmares; I see cossacks charging down our streets massacring Jews. I don't want my grandchildren to have to live through pogroms the way I did as a child."

Her pained expression affected me more than her anger had. But my sympathy cooled with the stinging sarcasm of her next remarks: "I know the kind of state your Palestinian friends have in mind—a secular democracy in which Jews will be welcome. Thanks a lot. If I'm going to live in a pluralistic state, I'd rather go back to America."

She added, laughing, that President Qaddafi of Libya had also said he would be willing to take in some Jews, but she did not think Libya would be a very nice place to live. Nor would she like to live in Saudi Arabia. Its king believed that all the evil in the world came from two sources, the Jews and the Communists, and he had attacked her for being both. "Isn't it funny that he should have attacked me for being a Bolshevik, while the Bolsheviks have branded me an agent of American imperialism?" She went on to say that she would "not like to live in Iraq either, they have not been very nice to the Kurds." As for Syria, they had shown the world what Arab democracy and socialism were all about by their barbaric treatment of Israeli prisoners of war. "Frankly, all this leads me to the conclusion that it is not possible for Israel to make peace with the Arabs before they develop democratic regimes. And that, as you know, will take at least another century."

I sat silent for a few moments before this short, stout woman sheathed in her ironclad virtue, and then I asked her, ironically, "And how about Egypt, Mrs. Meir? How do you rate it on your list?"

"Well, you know, my ancestors were there four thousand years ago. . . ."

After this coup de grâce, I felt there was nothing left me for to do but to leave. I got up, saying, "Mrs. Meir, maybe I should go now and come back in a hundred years' time, when you think we will be ready for peace."

I had underestimated the vast stock of indifference she seemed to have at her disposal. She told me in a peremptory tone to sit down again and proceeded to treat me, for another twenty minutes, to her views on the cause of the Palestinian "problem." The whole problem, as she saw it, was the result of the struggle between the forces of light, the Israelis, and the forces of darkness, the Arabs, who were hordes of barbarians surrounding the small, valiant state of Israel and its heroic citizens.

As soon as I could, I rose again to leave. As she accompanied me to the door, she emphasized her desire to live at peace with the Palestinian people. When I stared at her doubtfully, she said, "Don't you think I want peace?"

Not wanting to hurt her feelings, I uttered some platitude, but added that it was not just a question of wanting peace; everyone wanted peace. The issue was what one was prepared to do for it.

On hearing this, she went to her bookshelves and pulled out three heavy volumes. She told me that they contained pictures of every Israeli soldier who had fallen in war; a small biography accompanied each photograph.

"To my sorrow there is now a fourth volume in the process of being edited. Do you think that a nation that cares so much for its war dead does not want peace?" She added that she deeply regretted that no such volumes existed in Egypt. It seemed the Egyptians did not put much stock in human lives, she said. This time I lost my temper outright: "You think Israel is the only perfect nation on earth, don't you, Mrs. Meir?"

"No, I don't think Israel is perfect. For one thing, it is not as socialist as I would have liked it to be. . . ."

I left her house baffled by the kiss she planted on my cheek by way of good-bye: It was so sudden, so inexplicable, so imperious.

Like the Israelis who flocked en masse to their balconies during the summer months to escape their stifling little apartments, I sat every night on mine, pen in hand—for I kept a diary throughout my stay in Israel. Ensconced in my wicker chair, I recorded what Mrs. Meir had told me, ruminating over my disappointment that I had found no greater receptivity or enlightenment in a Labor leader like her than I had in the official right as represented by Menachem Begin. I wondered whether this intransigence was a generational matter: I knew Menachem Begin's family had been decimated in the Holocaust, even though he himself had not mentioned it to me, and possibly it was this that made him reduce Palestinian enmity to the age-old phenomenon of anti-Semitism. And Golda Meir, as her dream had revealed, was pursued by childhood memories of pogroms. I decided that I had to meet leaders from the generation of the sons, those born or raised in Israel and therefore freer of the traumas and prejudices of the past. For my visit to Israel coincided with the stepping-aside of the "old guard" to make room for "young blood," as the press referred to the fifty-year-old men like Yitzhak Rabin and Shimon Peres by contrast to the septuagenarians and octogenarians who had come to Palestine from Russia and Eastern Europe in the 1920s and 1930s and had dominated the cabinets up till now. In this sense Golda Meir represented the last of a line.

I was therefore happy when I received an invitation for dinner from Shimon Peres, the Labor party leader, who was then minister of defense and who would become prime minister in 1984. He lived in the northern suburb of Ramat Aviv.

I reached his residence and walked past the dreary clump of trees that flanked it. The buildings, somewhat taller here than in the center of the city, were daubed with that same grayish wash that lent a lackluster quality to Tel Aviv.

On stepping out of the elevator, I was stopped by the soldier who guarded his door. Having cross-examined me, he signaled for me to wait and rang the bell. Shimon Peres came to the door, and the soldier told him that I claimed to have been invited for dinner. The minister of defense listened to him without evincing the slightest glint of recognition in his eyes. He allowed me to writhe helplessly before his motionless gaze for what seemed to me an interminable moment. Just as I was overcome with embarrassment at the thought that perhaps I had mistaken the day and he had not been expecting me, he half-extended his hand in my direction.

I was even more unnerved when Peres declined to address so much as a single word to me throughout the meal, at which were present his wife, his father, a secret-service man, and some friends. They were all agitatedly discussing the problem posed by a group of Israeli religious settlers who, that very day, had taken possession of some land in the West Bank and were squatting there in defiance of a government eviction order. It was Peres's responsibility, as minister of defense, to send the army to remove them forcibly.

During this conversation, I cast a sidelong glance at Peres, who sat next to me. His large face was impassive, and in his eyes lay a cold, pitiless energy. He was a master of the clever epigram, like "Democracy is a bird which needs two wings; if you cut one of them off, it won't be able to fly." Thus did he rationalize his acceptance of the right wing's support of the settlements. I listened to him without saying a word.

After dinner, we moved to the living room. On the walls were a number of fine modern paintings. But the drab coloring of the upholstery and the mechanical arrangement of the pictures and furniture lent the room an indifferent, impersonal quality.

It was then that someone saw fit to address me for the first time. The secret-service man asked me my opinion of the Palestinian problem. When I told him I thought Israel should get out of the West Bank, he treated my remarks with disdain. As I went on to argue the right of the Palestinians to a state, Peres pretended not to listen, but I could see his eyes flicker as his interest in hearing my opinions alternated with the contempt they inspired in him.

When I had made the arguments in favor of the Palestinians, he told me: "We are prepared to give up part of the West Bank, but not all of it, because the moment we do, a PLO government will install itself there, which means we'll have the Russians at our gate. You cannot blame us for feeling that the farther off the Russians are, the better off we are. The rest of the West Bank Arabs will have to adjust to living with us, just as the Basques had to adjust to the French, and the Catalonians had to learn to live with the Spaniards. Since we cannot redivide the country, the only alternative is to find a way of dividing the government—in other words, working out some kind of autonomy for the Palestinians. If you don't like the word 'autonomy,' you can call it a federation, confederation, whatever—the name is not important; what counts is that we maintain military control over the West Bank."

Then he began to question me about Egypt and responded scornfully to my suggestion that Sadat wanted peace. He obviously believed that all of Egypt's peace initiatives since Nasser's death were of no consequence, and he treated my accounts of them as amusing little stories to be consumed as entertainment by his Israelis guests, superior Western-ers. The misinformation about my country on which he based his opin-ions was shocking to me; he delivered it with an ignorant self-assurance that was even more troubling. But I could see here too that there was no hope of wrenching him away from his fossilized point of view, so I fell silent.

Sensing my annoyance, Peres changed the subject and asked me where I had learned to speak English and what other languages I knew, after which he began to interpolate French expressions into his conver-sation.

When I got up to leave, he said good-bye to me without the slightest glimmer of warmth in his eyes. I was therefore greatly surprised by his offer to provide a ministerial car and a guide to show me the reclaimed lands in the Negev Desert. I accepted and arrangements were made for me to take the tour the following week.

The guide who came to pick me up was a Labor party veteran and a longtime Peres supporter. Rivka Guber had arrived in Israel on the same boat as Ben-Gurion, and she had just been awarded the country's most prestigious prize—the Israel Prize—for her exemplary patriotic devo-tion. She had been a pioneer who had helped thousands of Oriental immigrants settle in Lachish, a desert strip near the place where her firstborn had fallen in battle with the Egyptians. Her other son, too, had died in the '48 war, at the age of seventeen.

No sooner had the Mother of the Sons, as she was known to Israel, caught sight of me than she threw her arms around me, calling me her Egyptian daughter. I submitted to her effusions with patient resignation, even though I was unable to summon up much filial affection for her. Soon I found myself in the back seat of the car, sandwiched between Rivka and her husband, Mordechai, and forced to endure an endless barrage of "flattering" remarks on the order of "Isn't it amazing! Sanale [she used the affectionate Yiddish diminutive of my name] does not look at all like an Arab, she's not in the least dark!"

"Yes, dear," said the old man meekly.

Shortly thereafter she was again amazed, this time by the fact that I spoke English so well. Never, she confessed, would she have dreamed that she would one day meet a young woman from "Arabia" who was as highly educated as herself.

As it turned out, Rivka had only two subjects of conversation: herself and Israel. She drew on a store of countless tales about "the quiet heroism of our poor men" and kept repeating, with a breathless catch in her voice, that every inch of the "liberated" territory (the Negev) had been redeemed with Jewish blood. Then she told me of all the Oriental Jews in Moshav Noga whom she had introduced to soap and water and shown how to use a toilet. Her husband, who no doubt had heard this litany of her accomplishments before, kept dozing off until such time as she chose to put him back in the picture by jabbing him fiercely in the ribs.

And so, lulled by her virtues and Israel's, I rode for two or three hours past the flower fields of the reclaimed areas, all cultivated by Oriental Jews and Indian immigrants; occasionally we stopped at her imperious order to inspect the gladioli Rivka herself had charmed out of the barren soil.

From then on, I resisted all the gracious offers of government officials to "show" me the country, always insisting, politely but firmly, that I preferred to see it on my own.

4

A Summer Affair

BETWEEN MY visits with Israel's political leaders, I continued to lead the life of a tourist. Upon getting up in the morning, I would stroll by myself through Tel Aviv, taking stock of the shops, visiting museums, exploring different neighborhoods. My own was a respectable middle-class one, featuring a large concentration of *Yekes* (German Jews). In the afternoon, when it was time to walk the dogs, a whole procession of my neighbors would suddenly surge out of doorways and portals, poo-dles in hand, burbling away in German. *"Guck mal! Was für eine Schweinerei!"* ("Look! What a pigsty!"), they would exclaim on notic-ing the litter-strewn streets of Tel Aviv. There was a quaint, old-fash-ioned charm to these couples: the men with their bowler hats and bow ties, the women with their colorful parasols and white lace gloves. They were well-to-do Jews who had left Germany in the twenties and thirties, when it was still possible to get out with one's money, and had settled in this district, which was then considered the center of Tel Aviv. Now their children had left them behind and moved to the elegant new suburbs north of the city—suburbs that, with their well-tended flower beds and handsome villas, formed little Western enclaves in the midst of an Oriental setting as Meadi did in Cairo. For in Tel Aviv, as else-where in the world, the line from rich to poor ran from north to south. In the south lay the slum of Shechunat Hatikva, with its poverty and crime. As the southern periphery expanded and the center of town was progressively inhabited by Oriental Jews, the privileged classes fled northward, spilling over the sand dunes. So it happened that the loca-tion of the fashionable streets had switched from Herzog to Allenby, and later to Dizengoff. Now it was the turn of Dizengoff's cafés to be forsaken by the younger set.

To these cafés I repaired daily, after I had lunched and napped. They lay within a few minutes' walk from my apartment. On the way over, I would pass the tiny laundromat where Herr Professor Kranzendorf, a bachelor, brought his shirts for washing every Friday morning at eleven-thirty on the dot, and the grocery store owned by Moshe, a Czech immigrant, who sold me the chopped chicken liver his wife prepared. He did not get along with my fruit vendor, a Moroccan Jew with a stall opposite his, and had advised me not to buy from "that Arab," who he said cheated everyone by slipping rotten peaches into the bottom of the brown paper bags.

Having reached Dizengoff, I would install myself at Café Kassit, which in the forties had been a central meeting place for Israel's luminaries. But famous poets like Avraham Shlonsky and Natan Alterman had long ceased to grace its aluminum chairs; now Kassit belonged not so much to artists as to would-be artists, aging hippies, pimps, prostitutes, and tourists.

Next door, the clientele of the Café Roval had never varied. It was made up of pasty-faced old widows from Eastern Europe, who came in groups of three and four for their afternoon tea, and of nouveaux riches: foppish men and overdressed women painted, penciled, and dyed.

When, at the end of the day, I returned to Rheines Street, I would be greeted by its maze of balconies, homey to me because they were so Mediterranean. But no sooner had night set in than I would begin to hate them. I would have to relinquish all hopes of getting to sleep early. Miry, on the third floor, would be flirting with her boyfriend, who was sitting on a motorcycle down below. From the balcony next to mine, Zipka would admonish her eight-year-old son to come home now or she would break his neck, while Mrs. Dorfman, on the first-floor balcony, would be telling Rocha, on the balcony across the street, all about her friend's husband, who had taken a young mistress.

These balconies had no secrets from each other. By tying dwellings and whole neighborhoods together, they turned Tel Aviv into a little village. How long would it be, I wondered, before I heard my own secrets passed down the balconies by my solicitous neighbors?

For I now had more to hide from gossips than the news that an Egyptian was living in their midst. A chance encounter had irrevocably altered my life as a tourist, binding me to this city in a way I had not anticipated.

One morning Yoav, the young reporter who so generously had lent me his apartment in Tel Aviv, came to see if I was comfortably settled, and since he was planning to head back to his house in Jerusalem after visiting me, I asked him if he could give me a ride. I had not yet had a chance to see the sights there; I was eager to visit the Old City. Yoav said he would be delighted, as long as I did not mind making a small detour with him; he had to pay a brief business call on a women he wished to interview for television. When we arrived, he proposed that I come in with him and meet her rather than wait in the car.

As soon as we opened the little garden fence of the cottage, a German shepherd came tearing out of the backyard, barking viciously, followed by a ratlike, whining mongrel. I had already started to back away from the dogs in fear when a woman with limp, dun-colored hair and thin lips appeared at the doorway. Yoav introduced me. She greeted me somewhat gruffly and apologized about the dog, explaining that she had recently purchased him because of the alarming number of burglaries she said were perpetrated by Oriental Jews in the neighborhood.

After ushering me into the living room and inviting me to make myself comfortable, she drew Yoav off to the kitchen, leaving me alone with the two beasts. Figuring I had better try to win them over, I stretched out my hand to pat the German shepherd, but his snarl was none too reassuring; I beat a hasty retreat and sat tensely in the armchair in the remotest corner of the room until a middle-aged blond man came to my rescue. "Children, children," he called out in a gently reproving voice. The dogs promptly turned around and ran toward him, tails wagging.

The man looked up. His eyes were a melancholy blue. Glancing with a puzzled air at my red cotton poncho and the sombrero that lay on the table, he asked, "Are you a new immigrant from Mexico?"

I told him my nationality. It took a few moments to register, after which, afraid I might have noticed how startled he looked, he blushed and, stretching out his hand, said with a kind look, "Welcome, welcome here. My name is Danny." Then, pulling up a chair, he picked up the mongrel, placed him on his knees, and caressing the creature's ears, asked me what had brought me to Israel.

I answered mechanically, for I was taking in, slowly, every detail of his appearance. His face was pale and delicate beneath the dark gold of his curls. His slender body was at once hard and supple, more like a boy's than a middle-aged man's.

But it was not so much his looks that had attracted me from the first instant he stepped into the room, though he was without doubt a handsome man; it was something about the weary expression on his face, the lassitude of his gestures, his slightly stooped posture—all of which suggested the burden of some secret sorrow. I felt his melancholy as a bond between us.

My monosyllabic replies must have told him that I was not exactly involved in the conversation, for he suddenly stopped talking and looked at me with curiosity.

At that moment, Yoav entered and told me that Gila, Danny's wife, was insisting that we stay for lunch; he wanted to know if it was agreeable to me. It was. We went into the kitchen, where Tammy, their sullen fifteen-year-old daughter, was already eating. Gila continued to ignore me, addressing herself almost exclusively to Yoav, whom she had seated beside her, while I was banished to the other end of the table, next to Danny. As Gila and Yoav chatted about this and that, we two ate in silence. From time to time he would smile at me, and I would reciprocate, trying not to blush too visibly.

When Danny finally did speak to me, it was about his dogs. He was concerned because the German shepherd had recently bitten a friend of theirs. He had thought of enrolling the dog in training school, but he had not been able to stand the brutal way in which they tried to break him and so had withdrawn him from the program at the end of the very first session. Oddly enough, although the German shepherd was rough with people, he was very gentle with the small dog, who had been thrown yelping into the backyard one day shortly after he was born. Danny had felt pity for him; he had taken him in. I was pleased by this almost feminine sensitivity—what a relief from the typically Mediterranean machismo that was so much a part of Israeli culture.

After lunch I went out of my way to be nice to Gila, but she was insistently proper, dour, and chauvinistic. Her conversation with me was full of stock expressions such as, "There are forty Arab countries and only one small Israel; why can't the Arabs absorb the Palestinian refugees?" Then she began to gossip somewhat maliciously with Yoav, and I found myself wondering how an exquisite being like Danny could have married so self-righteous and petty a woman.

When Yoav suggested that it was time for us to leave, Gila insisted he accompany her first to her room so she could show him the clock-radio a friend had just brought her from the States.

While we waited for their return, Danny drifted into his study in search of his pipe. I followed him there and was surprised to find the room covered from wall to wall with poetry books, the sight of which immediately elevated him even further above the rank of other men.

Danny took out a book of Israeli poems and translated for me one called "My Country" by Rachel Blaustein, a pioneer:

> I haven't sung your praises,
> Nor glorified your name,

In great deeds
And in wars.
Only a tree I plant,
On the banks of the Jordan river . . .

Only a path my feet have traced,
Across the fields.

All too soon, Yoav and Gila came in search of me. Gila gave me a
chilly good-bye, which made me despair of ever seeing Danny again; our
slight acquaintance was hardly sufficient to justify future visits. But as
we were walking away, I heard him call out what I had longed to hear:
"Come and see us again soon, will you?"

For a long time I sat in the car next to Yoav without speaking, hardly
conscious of my surroundings. Buildings, bits of blue sky, and sea flew
past me. I was vaguely aware of the rumble of cars and murmur of
pedestrian voices. Then a few words spoken by Yoav jolted me back to
earth. He asked what I thought of the couple I had just met, and when
I said that the man seemed much nicer than his wife, he told me not to
judge her too severely: Her twenty-three-year-old son had just been
killed in the 1973 war. Danny had not said a word about that to me, and
I dared not ask Yoav what front he'd fallen on. I hoped it had not been
ours.

If I was shocked to hear of their loss, I was also secretly thrilled at the
thought that my intuition had been correct, that Danny was laboring
under some sort of private grief. I began to fire questions about Danny
at Yoav. But his replies stopped me in my tracks: Danny, he said, was
an officer in the army!

It seemed impossible. His love for poetry, his gentleness with animals,
his timidity—all to my mind reserved him for a more ethereal sphere, a
career in literature or the arts perhaps. But never soldiering. Soldiering,
in my view, was a step short of fascism. Career army officers were
professional killers or, at best, mindless autocrats who reveled in hierarchy and discipline, absurd pomposity and posturing, infantile marches
and parades. Undoubtedly class prejudices further enhanced my hostility to the army. For my parents' generation, the army had been a profession unworthy of a gentlemen; only the dull and debauched sons of the
aristocracy were enlisted there in the hope that they would be kept out
of mischief by riding horses and playing polo. Then, when the Military
Academy was finally opened up to the lower classes in the 1930s, it was
flooded with petit-bourgeois applicants, who saw it as an avenue for
social mobility; from this class came Nasser and his junta. I remembered

my grandmother's outrage when Hussein el Shafii, who was to become Egypt's vice president, asked for the hand of one of her granddaughters. "How dare this low-down officer think he can marry into our family? These people act as though everything is permitted since the revolution!" she had exclaimed.

But all these thoughts, which were racing madly through my mind as Yoav's car headed for Jerusalem, could not by themselves account for the intensity of my reaction. No, the shock I felt had little to do with my antipathy for the military. The dreadful fact was that Danny was an officer in the *Israeli* army: He was the enemy incarnate. Age-old feelings I had about the Israeli army welled up unbidden. Over and over again I tried to tell myself that Danny was clearly different from other Israeli army men like Rabin and Sharon, who with their brutal waxen faces and voices heavy with righteous solemnity seemed cut out of the same pattern. But all these fine arguments in Danny's favor were to no effect once the full impact of Yoav's words pierced through my defenses and I was left with no choice but to face up to who Danny was. It made no sense, but I could not help feeling betrayed, manipulated by his dovish poem and his sweet talk about dogs. He had toyed with my emotions— to serve what sinister design? I resolved never to see him again.

A few days later, Danny got in touch with me. He told me that his father, to whom he had described my visit, was very anxious to meet an Egyptian. And he proposed that he take me over to his house for tea. I excused myself on the grounds that I was too busy in Israel for social calls, and hung up. He must have sensed from the coldness of my tone that something was wrong, because the next morning, as I was leaving my apartment, I saw him coming up the stairs. According to my resolution, I should have stepped back inside and slammed the door, but I had not counted on finding myself face-to-face with Danny, and alone. He cast a "Shalom" in my direction and strolled nonchalantly past me, walking into my apartment as though he were in the habit of doing so. I followed him meekly to the couch, my heart racing.

He asked me if anything was wrong, and when I gave no answer, he pressed me for one. So I told him. He interrupted me with a laugh and, seizing me in his arms, said I was a silly girl. I pushed him away, but not with as much conviction as I ought to have done, I thought.

Assuming a grave demeanor, he began to talk about the Israeli army, how different it was from other armies because it was a civilian organization. He spoke about the "purity of its arms," claimed that it never shed innocent blood, and so forth. His recital irritated me, and I had to restrain myself from being rude to him. He clearly felt that he was foundering in unknown territory, because he went on and on as people do when they lack self-assurance and try to give their arguments more force by repetition.

Suddenly he stopped and looked at me, as though he were seeking my help.

So he wasn't just smugly inflicting this propaganda line on me, I thought with satisfaction, he was desperately trying to win my good will —albeit clumsily. I was moved by his vulnerability, and I searched for some amiable remark. He smiled weakly, either out of wounded vanity or with gratitude, and fell silent for a few moments. Then he began to talk about himself. For the men of his generation, he said, there was no choice but to join the army. He was only eighteen when the '48 war broke out, and Israel was in peril for her very existence. There simply was no question about the honorable thing to do in these circumstances; he had enrolled in the Palmach unit (the elite commando force). His voice was transformed by genuine emotion now, and I could not help believing him. Besides, I wanted to believe him. Rather than think he was trying to manipulate me, I chose to attribute his words to his age and circumstances, his sense of honor, and the like.

I was so delighted to have found a way to let myself see him again that when he got up to leave, I offered to walk him a few blocks. This must have emboldened him, because as we reached the little garden fence, he turned around and took me in his arms once more. This time I let him kiss me. It was understood that I would, of course, go with him to visit his father.

I roved about the streets for a long time after we parted, my emotions awhirl. The thrill of my forbidden attraction to him, my guilt at enjoying his kiss, my fear that someone might have seen us—almost every conceivable emotion battled within me. I told myself that I was just asking for trouble and decided never to set foot in his house again. But in the end I was irresistibly attracted even by the enormous obstacles that promised to turn this relationship into a grand passion. I had already decided to give the tumultuous feelings that agitated me the name of love.

On the appointed day, I arrived and found Gila alone in the living room—Danny was apparently not yet back from work. She offered me a seat and positioned herself opposite me on the couch, taking up something she was embroidering. Suddenly, she laid down her needlework on the table and, leaning over in my direction, remarked, "You never pluck your eyebrows, do you?" For a few moments she examined me in silence, with the horror-stricken air of one who has just run into a Neanderthal woman. Then she volunteered the name of her Moroccan beautician, who she said could work wonders on me. Taking my hands in hers, she added that I had better let her take care of my nails as well; the cuticles needed to be pushed back. I could not quite control a gesture of impatience. Fortunately, Danny arrived before the conversation went much further, and the smile he shot at me was ample compensation for the uncomfortable half-hour I had just spent. We left together for his father's suburb.

Ramoth Hashavim was in many ways unique. Populated almost exclusively by German Jewish immigrants, with a sprinkling of Czechs, it resembled a corner of Europe. When we arrived, it was evening. The twilight sky added another measure of dignity to the handsome old facades of the houses. The gardens were in bloom, and shadowy figures could be seen moving across torchlit verandas.

It was a sad irony that it had taken old age and German reparations money to finally bring a degree of gentility and leisure to the lives of these people whom I was to come to love. In the morning they read *Der Spiegel*, went to Hansi, the local grocer, for their precious half-pound of *Schinken* ("ham"), and then tried to learn Hebrew from *Elef Milim* ("A Thousand Words"), a popular beginner's manual. For though they had lived in Israel for some fifty years and were multilingual, they had never been able to accustom their ears to that harsh, guttural tongue. After dinner, they would sit out on their verandas with a glass of Unterberg and gossip. Outside of the wars, hardly anything troubled the luxurious indolence of these lives, except perhaps the occasional rattlesnake, indigenous to the neighborhood, that strayed onto their lawns and provoked them to cry, *"Furchtbar war es! Ganz unheimisch!"* ("Dreadful! Sinister!"). They moved in a closed circle of other German-speaking Jews, whose world was made up of the weekly chamber concerts, bridge parties at which *Kaffee mit Schlagsahne und Kuchen* were served, and the Goethe lecture series. Of Israel, the real Israel, they knew nothing, suspected nothing, and desired to know even less.

The man who came to the door with two poodles—one black, the other white—was still sprightly and sleek, though he must have been in his mid-eighties. He was dressed nattily in a navy blazer and gray corduroy trousers, and his voice rang with a vaguely German accent.

Like many German Jews I had met in Israel, Danny's father was exceedingly polite. I appreciated his somewhat old-fashioned gallantry, but I could not help feeling that he was all too aware of the great honor he was bestowing on me by inviting me to his house. While another Israeli might have displayed his sense of racial superiority to me by adopting a haughty tone, Danny's father affected a simplicity of manner which, I could see, covered a good deal of pride.

After he had offered me his arm and shown me around the house, which was simply but tastefully furnished, he led me to a room whose glass-paneled shelves held an entire collection of Mozart symphonies and concertos. As we sat down beside a delicate blue ceramic bowl filled with geraniums, he turned to me and kindly inquired, "Vell, vould you rather ve spoke in English or Hebrew? It's all ze same to me."

His accent was so amusing that I could not resist replying in my best German. At this, he very nearly choked with surprise. Clearly, the notion of an Arab who could speak idiomatic German was for him uncanny. He could probably picture Arabs only as poor fellahin who led a crapulous, abject existence, or as rich, fat effendis in *kaffiyehs* who built lavish villas in which to house their harems.

He sat in stunned silence for a few moments, running his manicured fingernails along the edge of the little napkin with embroidered edelweiss and forget-me-nots that had been stiffly folded into a cone and set up on the tea plate.

Then he began to tell me about the Palestinians he had known when he first arrived from Germany back in the 1930s. One day he found, squatting on a field he was supposed to plow, two Arab peasants who had been expelled from their farms by their Arab landlord because they had defaulted on their debts. They refused to budge, claiming it was their land. When he went to inform the landlord of this, the latter answered him, "Go back there and drive your tractor over them." Another time, he had hired two Arab farmhands to help him, and the same landlord, hearing the price he had offered them, shook his fist at him, saying, "Are you crazy to give them so much money? You are going to spoil our workers." This, the old man proclaimed in a tone that left little room for argument, and not the "so-called" Palestinian nationalist sentiment, was at the root of all the trouble between Arabs and Jews. "When the Arab landlords saw we were offering their workers such high wages, they grew afraid and incited them against us."

I pointed out that the ruthless exploitation of Palestinian workers, which undoubtedly had existed at the time, could not by itself account for the Palestinian revolt of the thirties. There must have been a national consciousness to sustain the months of boycotts, strikes, and riots. But the old man, who was at once hard of hearing and highly opinionated, cut me off: "Don't you tell *me* about the Arab disturbances," he shouted. "You weren't even born then, and I was nearly killed by a hand grenade that was tossed into my car as I drove through an Arab village on my way back home. I tell you, it was nothing but a handful of gangsters who were hired to make trouble for the Jews."

He had gotten so agitated by his argument that his face was flushed, and he was sputtering with anger. I looked at Danny in alarm, but he sat contemplating his father with a smile that combined wearied resignation with indulgence. Having decided it was best not to contradict him, I said nothing further. Once he regained his composure, he seemed a trifle ashamed at having let himself fly into a rage. To make up for it, he began to tell me stories that showed Palestinians in a more positive light.

Now he seemed so anxious to be kind to me that when the time came to say good-bye, I marveled that he did not put out his hand and pat me on the head, as he had been doing with his black poodle. This cultivated man would no doubt have been shocked to think that he was treating me the way enlightened aristocrats treat their servants.

While Danny was driving me back to my little apartment on Rheines Street, he began to tell me about his mother.

He had been much closer to her than to his father. She was a German Catholic, a quiet, unassuming, kindhearted woman who liked flowers and music and who had converted to Judaism in order to marry the man she loved. Raised in an upper-class Junker family in turn-of-the-century Germany, she reserved her highest admiration for displays of martial valor and *deutsche Kultur*. Her ambitions had been entirely fulfilled, for her son had become both a career officer and an accomplished pianist. Ironically, while Danny was fighting the Axis on the Italian front, as part of the Jewish Brigade in the British army, his uncle was a high-ranking officer in Hitler's Wehrmacht. When Danny's mother died, she left two stacks of letters, neatly tied with blue and pink ribbons, at the bottom of her linen trunk. They contained her brother's letters, with Wehrmacht insignia, as well as Danny's—along with the pressed dried poppies and edelweiss that Danny had picked in the Italian Alps, where the Jewish Brigade was stationed during World War II.

Danny's background did not come as a surprise to me. From the outset, he had struck me as having a certain exquisite delicacy—especially evident in a country where such qualities were patently absent. The notorious brassiness and vulgarity of the Israelis undoubtedly had something to do with the fact that Israel had never had a bourgeoisie to set standards of refinement; just as it had never had a genuine proletariat. Its founders were the children of the small merchants and artisans of Eastern Europe; the Western Jews, more assimilated than those from the East, had not come to Palestine. Outside of the trickle of German Jews, including Danny's family, that had arrived in the thirties, most of the German and Austrian Jewish bourgeoisie lucky enough to escape the Holocaust had gone to Britain and the United States. Jews from other parts of Western Europe had often chosen to remain in their own countries at the end of the war. And the more recent immigration from North America had been too small to alter Israel's fundamentally petit-bourgeois character. The Oriental Jewish immigration to Israel had been drawn mostly from the lower classes; those North African Jews with education and money went to Paris.

Class: Though I might rebel against it, it still exerted a hold on me, and I admired Danny's manners, his cultured mind, the tact he seemed to exhibit in all things. Even his style of courtship was very different from that of other Israelis, who, like many Mediterraneans I had met, were obsessed with their virility. It was impossible to go sightseeing anywhere in Israel without being accosted by some man who vaunted the quality and size of his member. When I mentioned this to Danny one day, he laughed and told me a joke: Do you know why Israeli men come so fast? Because they have to run and tell their friends about it!

After Danny took me to visit his father, he let a few weeks pass without getting in touch with me. I was filled with impatience to see him again, and tormented by growing fears that this had been just a passing flirtation for him after all and that he had forgotten all about me once the exotic attraction of my being an Egyptian had worn off. I dreaded being rejected if I called and asked to see him, so I opted for the tactic I always used when I was afraid of something: a head-on assault. I plucked up my courage and turned up at his house.

It was evening. Gila came to the door. She looked me up and down with her tiny, alert eyes.

"I just chanced to be passing by, so I thought I'd drop in for a visit" was my perfunctory answer to her unspoken question.

She informed me that Danny wasn't home and remained firmly planted in the doorway, as though determined to bar my passage.

I told her I did not mind waiting, if she did not mind letting me in. She was so astonished by my nerve that she moved aside. I entered and installed myself in Danny's study.

While I sat alone waiting for him, I fixed my eyes on the objects in his study, trying to imprint their exact lines, colors, and textures on my mind, so that when I was back in my apartment I would be able to call up their images.

From time to time, my eyes wandered toward the window that over-looked the street. I could feel the thrill of his imminent appearance. Suddenly, a figure stood out, sharp and black in the lamplit space outside the garden fence. I immediately recognized Danny: He always walked with a slight stoop, his head bowed as if weighed down by some invisible yoke.

He greeted me with eyes full of warmth, but the words I thought they promised were stifled by Gila's entrance.

We sat around the living room table, and Danny assumed that easy, tactful, assured manner he generally used to welcome guests.

After a while, he began to talk to me about his son, with modest paternal pride, telling me he was a boy of such deep feeling that once, when he was twelve and an army friend had taken them hunting, he had cried his heart out at the sight of the wounded birds.

As he was saying this, I stared at Gila's face. Grief had ennobled it, given it a simple grace, a quiet dignity. I was moved, in spite of myself, and began to feel sorry for her. But my generous sentiments did not last long. With his usual sensitivity, Danny had felt her distress and, pulling his chair closer to hers, had slid a consoling arm around her shoulders. My jealousy was almost more than I could endure; I couldn't help feeling resentful that his tenderness and concern were intended only for her.

By the end of the evening I was so persuaded of my insignificance in Danny's life that his offer to drive me home came as a complete surprise. Seated beside him, I was unable to say a word. He must have sensed my shyness, for he turned toward me and, with a smile, asked, "Do you know why I feel so drawn to you?"

"Why?" I asked, blushing in the dark.

"Because you are so full of contradictions. You are the only person I know who is at once cheeky and shy. Do you get my meaning?"

For a long time after that there was no sound other than the rumble of the motor. Once or twice he took a deep breath, as though he were about to say something, but he kept on gazing straight ahead, silently.

Then, as he was pulling up by my door on Rheines Street, he began again to talk about his son. He had died because he had gone to the rescue of a soldier trapped in a burning tank, and it had exploded. The morgue had not wanted to let Danny see the corpse, but he had insisted. When they pulled off the sheet, he saw that the head had been severed from the trunk. "There is something uncanny," he sighed, "about the way, in this country, it is so often the fathers who have to follow their sons' coffins to the graveside." Then he was overcome by grief.

I took his hand in mind and squeezed it, trying to put into my grip all the tenderness and sympathy in my heart. But I did it hesitantly, ashamed that part of me might relish the luxury of weeping with him over his son's death because it offered me the opportunity to comfort him with my affection.

Then I asked him, in a voice I endeavored to make sound casual, if he would like to come up for coffee. We went upstairs and talked for a long time, or rather Danny talked and I listened. He spoke about his son, but most of all he talked about Tammy, his teenage daughter—how threatened she felt by her brother's death and the empty space they reserved for him in the house, a space she knew she could never fill. He felt guilty at the knowledge that he was neglecting her, yet he could not stem the grief he nourished for his son.

We ended that evening in bed.

In the weeks that followed, Danny visited me regularly at my apartment. He began to talk about his wife. She had been a secretary at the army headquarters, and he had married her on the rebound, he said, after his first wife had left him for another man. He had been drawn to Gila because he felt safe with her; he was relieved that there was no great passion between them. But the apparent tranquillity of his life with her masked a secret sorrow, a sense of boredom, and a growing conviction of incompatibility. He had stayed on with Gila for the sake of their children. Later, when the death of their son plunged her into a profound depression, she needed him more than ever. Danny wanted to believe that he had remained with her all these years because he was honorable and upright, but there were times when, as he lay awake long after she had fallen asleep, he could not help wondering if it was not out of a kind of spinelessness.

Whenever he spoke this way, I felt less sad than usual to part with him. The thought that he was unhappy somehow comforted me. And I would pray for his misery to increase past endurance, so that at long last he would come knocking at my door, lonely and homeless, and I would offer him the comfort and shelter of my arms. As for my own husband, I had by then largely forgotten that he existed.

PART TWO

5

On the Kibbutz

I T MUST have been at the end of August that I was first seized by panic at the thought that I would soon be leaving, and without having learned much about Israel. I had spent most of my time with politicians, and I understood only after the fact that one learns very little from politicians. What could these great figures, so concerned with cultivating their public images and Israel's, possibly reveal to an Egyptian? Was not all sincerity imprudence in their eyes? Once the thrill of meeting our archfoes had dissipated, I was left only with a sense of frustration and annoyance at the thought that I had wasted a precious opportunity.

I realized that my voyage, which was drawing to an end, was in fact just beginning, that the mere crossing of a geographic boundary had not in itself constituted an arrival, that I would have to cross many more boundaries, both external and internal, before I finally reached my destination.

It was then I decided to start my trip all over again, this time determined to meet and get to know ordinary Israelis. The Ministry of the Interior was only too happy to extend my visa. I was obviously a public relations asset. I notified Harvard that I would not be returning for the following year and settled in for a long visit.

There was still another motive for prolonging my stay: Danny. When I announced to him my intention of going to live in the country because I had spent too much time with celebrities, he teasingly said that what I needed most of all was to get away from myself as a celebrity, and to that end he recommended Kibbutz Vatik, where, he assured me, I would be quietly ignored. The members of Kibbutz Vatik, which was one of the oldest kibbutzim in Israel, had the reputation of being *af le mala* ("with their noses up in the air"). They could still remember the days when their kibbutz had been visited by every politician of note from Ben-Gurion to Levi Eshkol, and by famous artists from Chagall to Leonard Bernstein. The presence of an Egyptian was hardly likely to make heads turn.

And so I decided to leave Tel Aviv—albeit sadly. As my bus pulled out of Central Station on its way toward Kibbutz Vatik, I contemplated the bustling, purposeless agitation of the crowds. I could already feel a pang of tenderness for this nervous, ramshackle little town—now reduced to human proportions. I was going to miss Tel Aviv. And truth to tell, although Danny had assured me that the company of so many illustrious pioneers would more than make up for the loss of his own, I did not share his enthusiasm for the kibbutz. Since I thought of myself as a socialist, I was forced to concede the superior merit of the kibbutz, but I was well aware that socialist Zionism had inflicted as much suffering on the Palestinians as had any other movement within Zionism.

As the presence of so many kibbutzim in Arab Galilee testified, the Israeli left, which saw itself as the champion of Jewish-Arab understanding, had not stuck to its principles when the '48 war offered it an opportunity to seize the farms of the Palestinians. Mapam, the Marxist-Zionist party, may have held out for a binational state until the bitter end and insisted on Jewish manual labor as a way of avoiding friction between Arab workers and Jewish landlords; but when it came to Arab land, its greed was indistinguishable from that of the right wing it hated.

The bus ran along the shore, past the suburb where Golda Meir lived. There was a cold sheen to the sea, and the stark white of the houses was harsh on the eyes. We passed sand dunes studded with vivid green stalks. Kibbutz peanut fields lined both sides of the road. We had reached the heart of the Sharon Valley, which had given Israelis their legendary reputation for converting swamps into green pastures. Great centers of civilizations lay buried beneath its sands. A succession of wars and conquerors from the Philistines to the Crusaders had devastated the land, reducing it for centuries to an economic backwater; water beds had dried up, degenerating into malarial swamps, and the soil, once fertile and abundant, had become arid.

Soon we pulled into the local station at Hadera, one of the first colonies to be set up in the Sharon Valley, where we picked up a dozen provincial Rumanian women and their husbands, all dressed in their best Sabbath clothing for a wedding in Afula. At the last minute, an old Yemenite Jew in a hooded robe pushed his way into the jammed bus, gripping his wife's wrist with his right hand and a live hen with his left. Once on the bus, he handed the hen to his wife, and she held it upside down by the legs, pressing against me to steady herself. Its wings flapping wildly against my face, the bird squawked till I thought my eardrums would burst. On our way out of the city, we passed a little memorial garden with a tablet listing the names of the pioneers who had died of malaria during the swamp reclamation, alongside the sons of Hadera who had fallen in Israel's wars.

The road ran down the middle of a gradually narrowing valley, Wadi Ara, made up largely of Palestinian villages. Clusters of lovely little cottages, fashioned from sunbaked bricks, graced the hillside. Rows of onions, their tubelike stalks erect and luminous in the sunlight, rose like tall candles against a dark green carpet of watermelon leaves. Farther on, the air was thick with the pungent smell of cabbage. Then the road wound upward along terraced hills planted with tobacco whose blossoms, now chaste and delicate like garden flowers, would turn a loud cherry-violet in the spring. The tobacco was being harvested, and farmers, naked to the waist, were stacking the leaves into brown jute bags. Their dwellings lay scattered throughout the hilltops. On the flat white roofs, above the blue windows and doors decorated with painted hands to ward off the evil eye, chains of tobacco leaves were drying in the sun. The rugged charm of the area was marred here and there only by a two-story cement shoebox that some rich Palestinian farmer had built in perfect Israeli style. It would seem that these farmers considered this appalling imitation of the characterless modern house, with the bleak concrete exterior that was so popular in Israel, superior to their own modest stone cottages, whose natural tones were so full of delicacy, brightness, and warmth.

The bus struggled to the top of the hill. From this vantage point the Jezrael Valley, encompassing Kibbutz Vatik, was visible.

Somewhere in the vicinity was the Palestinian village of Um el Fahm, whose history should shatter Mrs. Meir's complacency. It had been conquered by Israel during the '48 war. Although the Rhodes armistice agreement stipulated that the rights of "residence, property, and freedom" of these new Arab citizens of Israel were to be respected, the Israeli government had promptly confiscated their lands.

I recalled my visit with David Ehrenfeld shortly before leaving Tel Aviv. David was one of a handful of new millionaires whose appearance on the national scene had been greeted with barely concealed jubilation by those anxious to break away from Israel's "stifling egalitarianism." He had joined a socialist youth movement against the the wishes of his father, a diamond magnate, and later had become a member of a kibbutz. But at a relatively young age, he developed a heart condition that disqualified him from physical labor. Believing himself to be a parasite on the kibbutz, he left and decided to turn to the only trade about which he knew something—diamond cutting. He donated most of his profits to political causes supporting Oriental Jewish and Palestinian communities in Israel. He himself lived frugally in a tiny two-room apartment; he had no servants and owned no car.

I remembered David telling me: "I believed in the kibbutz. Oh, how I believed in the kibbutz! Socialist Zionism was my whole life. And then I saw what happened during the '48 war. There were a few Arab villages around us; we threw out their inhabitants at gunpoint, and our bulldozers destroyed every stone in those villages.

"After the war, the inhabitants came back to claim their lands, and they found out that the government had confiscated them on grounds of 'absenteeism.' The peasants were left with no choice but to work for us as hired labor on the land they had once owned."

The bus now angled down the slope, along a thoroughfare called the Ruler's Road, toward Afula, the capital of the Jezrael Valley. Founded on the site of a Palestinian village, this town, like most Israeli development towns with their ubiquitous jerry-built construction, offended the eye. Here, we pulled to a sputtering halt to let out the Rumanian passengers and pick up a bunch of rowdy volunteer farmhands, most from the United States, who were returning to their kibbutzim after an evening spent in the "big city." They filled the bus with a rancid odor of sweat, tobacco, and liquor, as well as the shrill notes of "Hava Nagilla" sung in a strong American accent.

Beyond Afula the sun was setting. Oranges glowed in dark green orchards, while at a distance, silver specks glistened against black iron nets. These were the turkeys that clustered in the poultry houses of the kibbutzim. Mount Gilboa loomed stark and gaunt in the gathering dusk. Here King Saul had fought the Philistines, and his three sons had died in battle. When news of his defeat reached him, he had committed suicide by falling on his sword. King David, in his eulogy to Saul, cursed the mountains, vowing they would never again see dew or rain and would forever remain barren.

The bus stopped. The mountains were within walking distance of Kibbutz Vatik.

Lugging my heavy suitcase, I made my way toward the kibbutz, discernible now by its flickering lights. I hoped I'd be picking potatoes in the morning. My eyes scanned the landscape, trying in vain to spot the fields that lay beyond.

My sister later wrote me that when my parents learned I had gone to work on a kibbutz, Mother had cried, while Father had merely shrugged his shoulders, saying it would do me some good—I'd lose a few pounds. It seemed to Mother the ultimate ignominy that her daughter should engage in fieldwork—and for the enemy, no less. After all, from her perspective, what could be more degrading than the toil of a peasant? In Egypt, the very word *fellah* ("peasant") had become an insult in common usage, connoting someone boorish, uncouth, stupid.

This contempt for the peasant was an attitude the children of the Egyptian privileged classes assimilated at a very young age. One day when I was only six years old, away at boarding school in Heliopolis, where the dry air was supposed to be good for asthmatics, my mother came to see me after paying a visit of condolence in the vicinity. She was wearing a long black dress, and her face was fashionably shrouded for the occasion in a black tulle veil. A little classmate of mine, who had caught a fleeting glimpse of her from a distance and had mistaken her mourning attire for the traditional black garb of the lower-class woman, ran to tell our friends that my mother was a peasant. That afternoon, on entering the refectory of the Sacré Coeur, where the children were assembled for tea, I was greeted by taunting looks and titters. Scarlet with shame and rage, I learned of the disgrace that had befallen me. But I held back my hot tears, for to cry would have been an admission of guilt. I had before me only two ways of assuaging my wounded pride: either to deny that my mother wore a black dress—which few were likely to believe—or to claim that the woman in black had not been my mother. I chose the latter course, explaining that she was a maid whom my family had sent with a message from home. That night I lay for a long time unable to sleep, my whole body shaking with sobs, for though I had settled the question of honor to my satisfaction, it had cost me a greater betrayal.

Mother's wealth, of course, like that of the rest of the Egyptian landed aristocracy into which she was born, derived from the sweat of those very peasants whom she scorned. The wealthy class had first risen to prominence at the end of the nineteenth century and, by the second decade of the twentieth, had become thoroughly assimilated into the Turkish ruling elite. But their roots lay deep in the villages. Most of them were families of humble origins who, by a combination of luck and cunning, had managed to profit from the introduction of lucrative cash crops like cotton into Egypt during the reign of the Ottoman viceroy, Muhammad Ali.

Although Mother's family, which settled in Egypt in the seventeenth century, shortly after the Arab conquest, traced its lineage all the way back to Arabia and the Prophet, it had been only moderately well off until the last quarter of the nineteenth century. Her grandfather was a village mayor and her father a wealthy landowner who was chosen because of his reputation for honesty to be caretaker of the khedive's estates in the Delta—a position that served to extend the family fortune further.

Ahmad Menshawi Pasha, Mother's great-uncle, had become a millionaire by introducing mango plantations into Egypt. He thought of it when his friend Orabi Pasha—the leader of Egypt's first nationalist uprising against Western domination and the privileges of the Turkish ruling elite—brought him a gift of mangoes from Ceylon, where he had been exiled by the British. To this day, one can hear Egyptian street vendors call out, "Menshawi mangoes, Menshawi mangoes." They remain the finest in the land.

I myself had never seen my great-great-uncle's estates, for by the time I was born the landed aristocracy had moved to Cairo, and their only links to the villages were the middlemen who commuted back and forth once a month to collect rents from the tenant farmers. Even my mother's generation, which had lived closer to the farms, had had no more than a perfunctory relationship with the peasants. Generally, the landowners isolated themselves in the provincial towns bordering on their estates. So it was that my own family had lived in Tanta—next to the village of Ishnawai, where they owned lands—on a street that was named after them and was lined with mansions belonging to members of the Menshawi clan. No one else would have dared build a house on Menshawi Street; it would have been considered an unforgivable affront.

What little I knew of Menshawi Pasha's life came to me from family stories and published accounts. It was the stuff of fable. In *Veiled Mysteries of Egypt,* an English book written in 1912, the author describes his visit to my great-uncle's estates and to his garden, "a place of Elysian delights. . . . I knew that the extent of the garden was eighty feddans [acres], that it produced flowers of all sorts and fruits in abundance and of marvelous rarity, but I was not prepared for such a vision of cultivated beauty as burst upon us as soon as we passed through the gate in the high wall. . . . Wealth alone could not have done it. Although wealth could bring treasures of fruit and flowers from the earth, it could not make them grow as they grow here."

Beyond this paradise, however, the peasants lived in the direst poverty, their relationship with their masters like that between serf and feudal lord in the European Middle Ages. Destitute peasants were utterly at the mercy of their landlords, who made the laws and virtually possessed the power of life and death over them.

When I reached the gate of the kibbutz, it was already bolted shut for the night. After the guard checked me over, a young man who said he was in charge of volunteers arrived to show me to my sleeping quarters.

Tall, muscular, and suntanned, and with a touch of arrogance and derisiveness in his manner that I had learned was uniquely Sabra, he walked on ahead of me, tight-lipped, without offering to help carry my suitcase.

I plodded on behind him in silence. After a fifteen-minute trek, we reached a handful of cottages. My guide came to a halt before one of them, and vanished with a curt "Good night."

"Wait a minute!" I called out. "You haven't given me a key."

"You don't need one."

"What about work tomorrow?"

"Breakfast at five. The truck will pick you up at six in front of the entrance to the dining room."

I trudged up the stairs, groped for the light, and looked around with dismay. I was in a cold, rectangular room with bare walls and a gray tile floor. Two narrow bunks were its only furniture. On one of them lay a neatly folded pile of sheets and pillowcases. At the end of the small corridor, which led from the room to a built-in closet, stood a rickety chair and a wooden table with an electric teakettle.

The starkness of this unfamiliar setting reinforced my inveterate fear of sleeping in strange places—a fear that years of being shunted from foreign country to foreign country, embassy to embassy, hotel to hotel, boarding school to boarding school, had hardly dissipated, and that the alienness of this land seemed to heighten. Was it here, then, that my nerve would fail? For a while, I shifted disconsolately back and forth from the hard iron bed to the wooden chair; neither, it was clear, was prepared to offer me any comfort. And my eyes kept returning to the unlocked door. How could I sleep in enemy territory without a key?

As I lay gazing up at the ceiling, I discovered that I was not alone: From the overheard lampshade an enormous gray lizard stared at me. Like a shot, I was out of bed and out of the cottage. But as far as my eyes could see, there was no help to be had—only the whisper of the trees huddled in the dark. Too embarrassed to wake up my neighbors, I tried to deal with the lizard alone. The broom I aimed at its head missed its mark, however, because my hands were trembling uncontrollably. At last I resigned myself to spending the night with this roommate.

I must have lain awake for a long time. The lizard's overhead movements, the stifling heat, the uninterrupted racket of crickets, and the buzzing of the flies and mosquitoes all kept me from sleeping. So did my fear that if I allowed myself to fall asleep I would not be able to get up in time for work, given my present state of fatigue.

I woke up feeling more tired than ever. But the sun was out, the flower box on the window ledge was overflowing with geraniums and irises, and outside tall cypresses lolled in the jasmine-scented breeze. Heartened, I dressed and headed toward the dining room.

Knowing no one but my Sabra guide of the night before, I felt too shy to enter and decided to skip breakfast. I sat outside by the entrance, where the truck was expected to pull up, waiting for the other volunteers to finish their breakfast.

The first to arrive was a slender, dark girl wearing a long lilac skirt, a flowery scarf, golden bangles, and hoop earrings. She could have been an Egyptian peasant dressed up for the Mulid (the celebration of the Prophet's birthday), but she turned out to be from Tashkent. Next came an English redhead in a sequin-studded blouse with a low-cut, frilly neckline. She was full of coquettish affectations, and she had a strong cockney accent. Having tried her luck with the girl from Tashkent to no avail (the latter spoke no English), she began to talk to me. Fortunately, however, a young man from Brazil made his appearance, and I was abandoned in favor of this more attractive target. Soon our working team of twenty-four people was complete, and we waited for the pickup truck.

We drove across a terrain bordered by mauve mountain slopes. Their barrenness contrasted with the richness of the fields. Our truck cut a swath through the dark, moist layers of earth, which crumbled on contact with the wheels like the frosting of a chocolate cake. A strong odor of freshly tilled soil filled the air. No wonder the pioneers fell in love with this land; no wonder the Palestinians refused to leave it.

The truck dropped us off at the edge of the potato plots; behind them towered a whole field of sunflowers, bowing under the weight of their crowns. After a while, our overseers arrived—all of them strongly built men, and all of them bare-chested. Nowhere was the difference between the generation of Eastern European pioneers and their offspring more apparent than on the kibbutz. The young people, a whole head taller than their parents, looked like another species.

How we volunteers admired those powerful sunburned torsos that glistened like liquid gold! But these handsome, proud sons of Israel had nothing but disdain for us. To them, we were only a pack of spoiled visitors who regarded their work on the kibbutz as an exotic way to spend a summer vacation before returning once more to their pampered, bourgeois lives.

We were divided into separate work teams, each with its own overseer. Some of us were to work in the fields, others on potato combines. Those aboard had to catch the potatoes, which the combines dug out of the soil at tremendous speed, wipe the mud and pebbles from them, and throw them into a huge bin. The other job—far more tiresome because of the bending involved—consisted of walking behind the potato combine and gathering the potatoes it had missed.

Our overseer assigned the combines to the females and the stoop work to the males. Because I disliked his patronizing assumption that women were suited only for lighter work, I traded places with one of the men, who was only too happy to oblige.

Hardly had the work begun, however, than I regretted my choice. My back ached, and my hands, raw from clawing into the rough soil, felt as if they were on fire. As the sun beat down upon me, I remembered a stout, red-faced Englishman I had seen in Upper Egypt who was felled by sunstroke. He lay stretched out on a bench in the garden of the Aswan Palace Hotel, alternately shrieking with pain and moaning in a mechanical, impersonal way. A black page boy in a flaming turban and ballooning pantaloons had run to fetch him ice, and he said as he attentively administered it, "You no worry, Meester Reechard, you be okay. Beoble no die from thees." But there wasn't a sliver of ice to be had here, not even a drop of cold water. Then I wondered what it was like to die of dehydration, and thought with pity of our poor soldiers who had been so thirsty in the Sinai desert during the '67 war that they had had to drink their urine.

After an hour's work, all sorts of mysterious objects began floating before my eyes, but I kept myself from fainting by conjuring up the embarrassing image of my body being carried off the field on a stretcher.

A jeep arrived with a water tank, and we drank at last. The overseer came by to ask me if I'd like to trade places with someone on the potato combine, now that it was halftime. Too proud to admit I was tired, I declined.

Those last hours were the worst. I had the feeling that this sweltering morning would never end; the rows of potatoes seemed interminable. I focused my envious eyes on the strong biceps of our handsome overseer; he seemed not in the least tired. How I hated the Israelis for their disgusting good health, and for all those yogurt-and-cucumber-salad breakfasts they had been fed since childhood!

Finally, the day was over. As I was dragging myself toward the big collection bin to throw in my last basket of potatoes, the overseer snatched it from me, yelling, "Not these, can't you see the ones on top are rotten?" He culled out some potatoes and, dropping them onto the ground, added, "Leave them, the Arabs will come for them. They always come around after we've finished a day's work to get what we've left behind. They'll eat anything."

Too tired to object, I let this remark pass. A minute later he came up to me and, patting me on the back, said that I should become a member of the kibbutz—implying that I had worked well. Swelling with pride, I looked patronizingly at the other women, who had done the easy job. Miriam Baratz, the first woman pioneer to earn the right to work in the fields alongside the men, back in 1910, could not have relished her hard-won recognition more than I did. I felt like dancing down the potato rows.

When, on the following morning, I bragged about my achievement to the young Sabra who was frying *gribenes* (a Jewish delicacy made from chicken fat) for our breakfast, she was not impressed. "Big deal!" she said, shrugging. To her, even the crassest house chore was preferable to picking potatoes under a blistering sun or driving a tractor. Being in no position to promote the virtues and values of potato picking, I merely noted that I'd rather drive a tractor any day than cook.

"But what if it broke down in the middle of the field?" she asked. The idea that a woman's inability to repair a tractor might have something to do with the school curriculum in this kibbutz, which offered the boys mechanics and the girls needlework, obviously did not upset her. She dismissed it with a scornful wave of her spatula, saying that, in any case, women shouldn't drive tractors because it made them infertile. Before such a compelling argument I remained speechless.

At Kibbutz Vatik, this line of thinking had dictated that women could work in the henhouses but not at the carp pond, pick apples in the orchards but not potatoes in the fields, while men could teach high school but not primary school. And clearly only men could fill the positions of kibbutz secretary, finance manager, and treasurer.

The idea of "proper" occupations for women was certainly familiar to me, though in a rather different form. My mother never tired of trying to teach me these "proper" interests, in spite of very little encouragement from me. Her efforts to cultivate my musical talents had been a total failure. I loved music, but my singing lessons always ended up with me in tears, even though my mother never ceased to assure me that if I only practiced singing "Do-re-mi-fa-sol" for ten minutes in the bathtub every morning, I would strengthen my vocal cords and develop a good voice. When I was eight years old, my piano teacher advised Mother to stop throwing her money out the window. But Mother held out, even insisting on giving me ballet lessons as well, until one day, at the school performance, she overheard another parent say, *"Cette petite a la grâce d'un bébé éléphant"* ("This little girl has the grace of a baby elephant"). That was the end of my dance career.

And then there was the question of the husband! What Mother had in mind for me was an early marriage and the life of leisure my cousins led—fittings at the dressmaker's, gossip circles at the Guezira Sporting Club, tea at Groppi's, and summer trips to Europe to stock up on the latest fashions. Since childhood she had always impressed upon me that *el sit ma tiswash ta'rifa mincheir gosha* ("a woman isn't worth a cent without a husband"), which might well have been the reason why she had spent her whole life in a servitude that alternated between agony and bliss. All of her mental and emotional faculties were given over to such worthy causes as making sure, day in and day out, that the soup was piping hot, that the butter balls to be served with the warm rolls had been taken out of the fridge half an hour before the meal so they would not be too hard, that the roast beef was not overdone, and that the strawberry tart was not mushy, lest the thing she feared most in her life should come to pass: Father would refuse to eat. She never uttered a word of complaint, though she had had to give up her friends, her habits, her very tastes—down to her daughter's name, which she had wanted to be Sonia in honor of a favorite Russian ballerina but had had to tame into its nearest Egyptian equivalent to avoid offending her husband's patriotic sensibility. Nor would she form an opinion on any subject until he had formed his, and if we chanced to ask her what she thought of this or that, she would first look up at him as though trying to fathom the mystery of his superior mind before venturing an answer.

But surely times had changed since Mother used to scribble on the door of her school locker: *"Mon Dieu, envoyez-moi un bon mari pour me délivrer de la tyrannie de mon père"* ("My God, send me a good husband to free me from the tyranny of my father"). And surely things were different in Israel, I had thought. It took me a while to realize that the glamorous image of women pioneers plowing fields and carting manure, which came to us through Israeli songs, folktales, and old photos of women striding off to work in their tough hiking shoes with pickax and spade slung over their shoulders, was largely mythical. Whatever illusions I still clung to were further dispelled by Chava, the oldest cook on the kibbutz. When I brought up the question of female occupations with her, she gave a short, ironic laugh and then told me: "The attitude of our male comrades toward us has always been, *kvod bat hamelech penima*—'true honor for the king's daughter lies in her own home.' When I first started out, in Degania, we had to wage a long, hard battle to even be allowed to work in the fields. We had come to make a revolution, only to find ourselves pushed back to the occupations of our mothers in the *shtetl*. And it was all the more hard on us because there were only three of us to twenty men, and we had to do all the housework. We complained about this at every kibbutz meeting—particularly about the laundry, which had to be done by hand. But the men—they were led by Moshe Dayan's father—said it was out of the question that they help out with the laundry. It was a woman's job. When I moved to this kibbutz, I found the problem was even worse here because we had to carry the heavy baskets of wash all the way up three flights of stairs to hang it up to dry on the roof. The men were very selfish. They refused to invest in machinery that would lighten our burden, claiming the kibbutz could not afford it, but they somehow always seemed to find the money for their own field equipment!"

When I told Chava what the younger cook had told me, she said in a tone of sorrowful resignation: "Today's women don't want what we wanted. They have all kinds of social pressures on them to be good wives, beautiful, and so on. The media tell them, 'Buy this and you'll be Marilyn Monroe.' The ads that ran during the war were scandalous! Instead of appealing to the women to help with the war effort, if not by fighting then at least by driving trucks and ambulances to the front lines, they said, 'Be beautiful for him, he deserves it.' No wonder women in the kibbutzim started to ask for beauty parlors! At first they rationalized it by saying, 'We polish our shoes, so why not our faces?' Then they just went ahead and did it. Now everybody does it, and when you've fixed your hair and done your nails, you certainly don't feel like picking potatoes!"

To be perfectly honest, I didn't feel very much like it either. But having made it a point of honor to stick it out, I could only pray for the end of the potato harvest. In the meantime, I scanned the bulletin board every morning in the hope that I had been transferred to another job, since volunteers were often shifted around to fill in for regulars who were sick. No luck: My name remained as resolutely on the list of potato-pickers as if written in indelible ink.

One day, long after I had ceased to believe in the possibility of a transfer, a small miracle occurred: I was to work in the cow shed, in place of a young man who had been given a leave of absence to attend a seminar at Kibbutz Givat Brenner.

That evening, I set out in search of the manager of the cow shed, whom everyone addressed, curiously, as Nikolai—an abbreviated form of his Russian family name, Nikolayev—rather than by his new name, Onn. Nikolai, like most settlers, had Hebraized his name on arrival in Palestine. While many of them had changed family names like Gelb into Gilboa, after the mountains of their beloved new homeland, many more had preferred to take on names connoting strength. Onn ("Vigor"), Kabiri ("Powerful"), Oz ("Strong"), Eshet ("Steel"), Tzur ("Rock"), and Arie ("Lion") were among the most common at Kibbutz Vatik. To my surprise, Nikolai turned out to be a spare old man whose frail body seemed, on first view, hardly able to support his absurdly large head. I remember thinking, "The work must be easy if *he* can do it!" I should have known better. When I asked him at what time he expected me to show up the next morning, he replied, "Oh, not too early. I myself start at four, but you can come half an hour or so later."

After that strong hint, I felt compelled to show up at the crack of dawn. Nikolai took one skeptical look at me and muttered something under his breath. I could not understand his words, since they were in Hebrew, but his tone convinced me they had not been wholly complimentary. I wondered if he was lamenting his bad luck at being sent a female helper, but soon found out that his displeasure was directed more at my clothing than at my gender. Nikolai had tucked his trousers into a pair of knee-length rubber boots and wore a black plastic apron; I had turned up in a long skirt and sandals. The first job to be done was the cleaning of the stalls; before long I was wading up to my knees in mud and cow dung, trying not to slip. Raking this slush would not have been so hard if it weren't for the nauseating stench of excrement, intensified by the terrible heat. The swarms of flies were so thick I kept my mouth closed to avoid swallowing one.

After cleaning out the stalls, we were to feed the cows. The hay had to be carried from an overhead loft and pitched into troughs—by no means an easy task, since each bale weighed some fifty pounds. Moments after we had started, I was so drenched in sweat that my underwear was glued to my body, and I could have sworn I heard my spine crack each time I speared a load of hay with my pitchfork.

I was sorely tempted to sit down, but the sight of this spunky old man bustling about tirelessly compelled me to go on working. I later found out that the song he was humming to himself ran as follows:

> Work is our life's elation,
> For all our troubles, the salvation.
> Ya halili, oh! labor mine.

Nikolai went out to fetch the cows in from milking, and presently returned, fussing and fretting as he cracked his whip behind them. But these willful creatures continued to dawdle along, taking their own sweet time.

When they had finally been prodded back into their stalls, he ordered me to fetch them water, another onerous chore, which involved carrying what seemed like hundreds of heavy pails to the troughs. As I stood watching two cows who had gotten their heads stuck in the railing, Nikolai sidled up to me and whispered despondently into my ear that Rachele (little Rachel) was sick. I had no idea who little Rachel was, but thinking it must be one of his granddaughters, I sought to find some appropriate expression of sympathy. When he told me I should try to make her eat, I began to suspect he was referring to a cow. I followed him into one of the stalls, where, sure enough, a cow was sitting diffidently in back while all the others were up front ruminating. Nikolai went up to the trough, picked up some hay, and brought it to her, cooing enticingly, "Rachele, Rachele," but she turned her head away. Looking heartbroken, he left and returned a few minutes later with a huge thermometer. I was to take her temperature while he went next door to give the calves their milk.

After Nikolai left, I realized he had forgotten to tell me how many minutes were needed to measure a cow's temperature. Figuring that he would be back any moment, I did not let that worry me and advanced smiling benevolently at the patient, who was still seated on her derriere. No sooner did she see me, however, than she sprang up and lurched toward the railing, sending the other cows scurrying about in a panic. I lost her in the fray and began wandering from cow to cow in a state of fearful agitation, calling out, "Rachele, Rachele," in vain. The beast would not answer. What on earth was I going to tell Nikolai when he came back? That all the cows looked alike to me? Just as I was about to leave the stall in despair, one of the cows suddenly slumped to the ground. Delighted at having found Rachele, I ran up to her and hugged her warmly. But getting her to open her mouth so I could put the thermometer in was quite another matter. Every time I managed to shove it in, she would stick her tongue out at me, grimacing horribly, and out it came.

While we were engaged in this contest of wills, a piercing howl rent the air. I swung around and found myself looking directly into Nikolai's ferocious blue eyes. "What are you doing?" he shouted. I started to explain about the cow. "You idiot, this is Yossele, can't you even tell a male from a female? *Ya Allah!* The kind of volunteers they send us nowadays!" He shook his fist at the powers beyond. "And whoever heard of putting a thermometer in a cow's mouth! It's up her rump you have to stick it, you . . ." He punctuated his remark with an unprintable Russian word.

As his vociferations continued, I began to wonder whether honor did not call upon me to make a dignified protest. After all, how was I supposed to know? I had never set foot on a farm, and the only cows I had seen had been from train windows—the charming creatures whose little bells tinkled throughout the Swiss Alps.

But I remembered that my job was more important to me than my pride. I started apologizing to Herr Nikolai, and since my Hebrew was as rudimentary as his English, I spoke to him in German and he answered me in Yiddish. Repressing my disgust, I stuck the thermometer up Rachele's posterior. Nikolai, far from mollified, ordered me about with a vengeance. For my punishment, I had to scrub all the pails with soap, even though I failed to see why rinsing them out with water was not good enough.

The next morning I was late for work. I braced myself for Nikolai's recriminations and, not feeling nearly as humble as the day before, resolved to tell him, in the event he got too abusive, that I cared not a whit for this job as cow-dung queen. But when I reached the gate and spotted the old man's stooped, brittle frame, I was moved by his frailty and began instead to rehearse a genteel little speech of abdication. To my surprise, he turned around and, without uttering a single word of reproach, smiled at me whimsically. Then he went on with his job, singing:

> Strike, hammer! Rise and fall!
> We shall stretch our concrete roads in the sand!
> Wake up, desert! We have come to conquer you.
> The asphalt is hot,
> Our hands are bleeding,
> But we have, we have the strength!

After translating this rousing ballad from his pioneering days, he overwhelmed me with little attentions. I musn't exert myself too much—he even offered to help me carry the pails—and of course it was all right if I took a little break!

At midmorning, therefore, I went to sit down for a few minutes. He followed me, asking me if I found the chores he had assigned me too taxing. It wasn't the chores I minded, it was the heat and the flies. "Ah!"

he said, with a touch of merriment in his blue eyes. "I have just the thing for you: *kartivs*." When I asked him what they were, he winked at me and hurried over to the giant refrigerated milk tank, which stood at the entrance to the cow shed, where he broke off a couple of icicles that had formed underneath it. Handling them as though they were the most precious things on earth, he brought them over to me.

As I licked the icicles, he told me that his biggest problem when he came over from Russia had been his inability to get used to the heat. Sometimes when he was out working in the fields of Degania under a broiling sun, he would faint. His friends would throw a bucket of water over him and carry him back to the tent, and he'd lie there crying at the thought that he was too skinny and weak ever to make a good manual laborer. "Just to give you an idea of how bad the heat was, we used to carry a big barrel of water from the Kineret [the Sea of Galilee] and place it in the middle of the fields. It stood there all day, and the sun was so ferocious that by the time we came to drink it, it was literally boiling. What with this foul water and a poor diet, we were constantly suffering from diarrhea. Our toilets then consisted of four holes at the edge of the settlement, with no partition between them. The comrades always went there in pairs so that while one of them crouched, the other stood guard. It was dangerous to be in an isolated area all by oneself, because of the sniping. One day Ben-Gurion visited us. Now, he was the kind of man who could not even take his shirt off in front of another man, let alone bare his bottom. When he had to do his business, he was beside himself with anger. Only animals, as he saw it, could relieve themselves in front of each other like that. After returning to Tel Aviv, he went straight to the Histadrut [labor union] headquarters and threatened the workers' committee that if they did not build us proper toilets he would resign. Nothing came of it, but the next time, when Weizmann [the future president of Israel] came to visit, we dug him his very own hole!"

When we finished work that day, Nikolai shook my hand warmly.

Not finding any cogent explanation as to why this irascible old man had turned overnight into the kindest of bosses, I concluded that my pleasant nature had finally won him over, and to show myself worthy of Nikolai's good opinion I redoubled my zeal. But soon afterward, I was to discover the reason for the compliments he rained on me. Nikolai had been unaware on the first day that I was an Egyptian. The work manager in charge of job assignments, having had to run an errand in Tel Aviv that morning, had neglected to inform him. When Nikolai went out to complain that to "bring over these specimens who don't know how to work is a waste of good Jewish money," the manager explained how embarrassing it would be for him to ask me to quit the job. Despite Danny's opinion that I would be ignored, I was still treated as someone special. The idea of having an Egyptian in his cow shed greatly tickled Nikolai, and from that day on we became fast friends.

Our work together provided me with handy pretexts for visiting him at home, though in truth I hardly needed them. Like other kibbutzniks his age, he was hungry for company. As one of the first kibbutzim established in Palestine, Kibbutz Vatik had a sizable elderly population. I saw them everywhere, stooped figures dragging their heat-weary bodies down the tree-lined lanes, or sitting by themselves in the dining room—forsaken by children and grandchildren alike. It was a bitter fact that in this community, which had been founded on the ideal of brotherly solidarity, the absence of an old person from the dining room, whether due to sickness or depression, could go unnoticed for three or four days.

One day, on returning from work, I saw an obituary on the bulletin board. The young kibbutznik who had been in charge of our potato-picking team was standing beside me, so I asked him who had died. He shrugged his shoulders and raised his eyebrows to indicate that he hadn't any idea. Later, I found out that the deceased was one of the founders of the kibbutz.

By devaluing intellectual and commercial occupations and by glorifying manual labor, the pioneers had contributed to the precarious status of the elderly. The kibbutz placed the highest premium on work that required physical stamina. As a result, young men acquired higher status than their middle-aged fathers, and in kibbutz meetings the suggestions of twenty-year-olds were often listened to more respectfully than those of the pioneers who were in their seventies and eighties. They were aware of this attitude toward them, and they felt ashamed about being parasitic in a community that had made a religion of work, which led them to push themselves to keep on working until their dying day.

Young kibbutzniks often teased me about my partiality for octogenarians, but I felt happy and proud to be in Nikolai's company. Now that I had come to admire Israel's pioneers, I could not understand how this man, who for me was a repository of Israel's vanished greatness, could leave them so incurious. I would often skip dinner in order to have more time with him, because he was in the habit of turning in early. But I never had to go hungry; Nikolai would collect old bread slices and grill them on a square wire net set over a kerosene flame, and then show me how to peel garlic with my teeth and rub it hard against the buttered toast. This had been his dinner every night as a boy in his little village, and for dessert we would have tea, Russian style: a sip of the hot liquid followed by a spoonful of marmalade. He had been too poor to afford sugar.

Nikolai described his miserable childhood in Russia, where his mother died in childbirth when he was only four years old, leaving six children. He talked of his father's struggle to feed the ever-hungry family; of his apprenticeship at thirteen with a cruel master carpenter; and of his first encounter with Zionism, at the house of a rich man who had offered him a meal after seeing him being beaten in the street by his master. The man turned out to be a local Zionist notable and chanced to be entertaining several Jewish writers, including Chaim Nachman Bialik, for dinner. As Nikolai sat eating in the pantry, he overheard their passionate debates about Zionism. That evening sufficed to convert him. He resolved to run away from home and to go to Palestine.

He planned his escape with a handful of friends from his village. It was 1918, and the Bolsheviks had made it illegal to leave the country. Nikolai and his friends did not have the money to pay the Russian guides who smuggled people in boats across the river to Rumania, so they had to wait for the winter, when the river froze and they could traverse it on foot.

"One night we decided the time had come to undertake the journey. We could not see a thing; it was pitch-dark. We only felt the ice beneath our feet. None of us could afford boots. Our feet froze, which made walking very painful. The river was about a kilometer in width, and we had been warned that the moment a spotlight went on, we should lie down so the guard couldn't see us. We all wore white sheets in order to be indistinguishable from the snow. One member of our group went ahead of the others with a long metal stick to test the ice. If it felt strong he proceeded forward, and we followed him. We walked in single file at two-meter intervals from each other, so that if one person fell through the soft ice, at least those behind would be safe. In this way we hoped some of us, if not all, would make it to Eretz-Israel."

Among the group of adolescents who made the daring escape across the river of ice was Nikolai's fiancée. Though they were engaged in Russia, they abstained from sex altogether to avoid "accidents"; they were determined not to give birth to a child outside Palestine. And indeed their child was "the first child born in the swamp." Mosquitoes were the bane of their lives then, and the kibbutz was so poor it could not afford mosquito nets; members had been allotted only half a yard to cover their faces when they slept. At the age of three months, Nikolai's child contracted malaria. The doctor confirmed their worst fears: The baby would have no chance of survival unless they left the kibbutz. Nikolai thought his prognosis so much nonsense; after all, the Arabs had lived in the valley for generations and had plenty of children. He rode off to the neighboring village and asked the first peasant who came his way how many children he had. The Palestinian told him he had four children, but four others had died of malaria; of the surviving four, one was sick.

Nikolai returned home to his wife and began to cry as he recounted what he had seen. But they were pioneers: They decided that they had to stay.

"We felt it was a historic test, like the one God had set for Abraham. Weeks went by; our baby seemed to shrink like a lemon from which the juice was being slowly squeezed. We would sit by her bedside at night, and she lay there without crying or sleeping, as though she had no strength to do either. She would just stare at us with those huge blue eyes of hers. Sometimes I had the feeling the little one knew we were sacrificing her on the altar of Zionism and accepted her fate. I felt I was murdering my own child. But a miracle happened. The rains started in November, and the mosquitoes fled. Her fever gradually fell. She lived. I had been vindicated! Our faith in the absolute rightness of our cause had triumphed. I knew now there would come a time when all the obstacles before our people in Palestine would vanish."

When Nikolai did not reminisce about his past, he sang me old songs. He would haul forth a *garmushka*—a Russian accordion that he had carried, strapped on his back, the night of his flight across the ice—and would sing me patriotic Russian songs:

> On the Dnieper banks horses are storming,
> With rage and wrath they are mauling the enemy,
> Cossack riders from the Boudyonin Brigades.
> They are crushing the fascists.

Though he had lived in Palestine more than sixty years, Nikolai still pined for the landscapes of Russia. As he described them to me, I could sense in him a sweet intoxication that resembled the feelings of early love and longing. He used to tell me that there was something unreal about Israel: It had no dense forests, no great rivers and lakes, no high mountains, and not a single cathedral!

One evening, he told me he wanted to show me something. He pulled a picture out of his tattered wallet and handed it to me with a wistful look. I expected to see a photograph of his youngest brother—the only member of his family still alive in Russia, of whom he had often spoken. But it turned out to be a yellowed, poorly focused shot of the forest near the Russian village where he used to play as a boy. When I said it was nice, he smiled gratefully at my words. Most of all, Nikolai liked to sing this sentimental little ditty:

> Far away the Volga is storming,
> And in one's heart, one feels a little pain.
> We knew then what was a homeland,
> We knew then what was an enemy too.

The words "homeland" and "enemy" reverberated within me, tugging at some invisible cord in my heart. Many a night, when we sat together in the moonlight on the little hillock where his shack was and I heard him sing this song in a doleful, quavering voice, I was so moved that I would begin to weep out of yearning for that Volga I had never seen—and perhaps, though I was blind to it then, yearning for the Egypt from which I might be barred forever.

One day when I turned up at the cow shed, Nikolai announced to me glumly that his assistant had dropped out of the seminar at Givat Brenner and returned to the kibbutz; I would have to look for another job. I was bitterly disappointed, but I could see that the old man was just as upset, so there was no point in making a fuss.

When I reported to the work manager, he told me that there was no opening anywhere on the kibbutz just then. If I wished, I could lend a hand at the cemetery, and he'd transfer me out as soon as something else came up. I did not jump at the offer because I had always been afraid of cemeteries. But neither did I relish the prospect of idle mornings spent waiting for the others to return from work. Faced with the choice between boredom and gloom, I opted for the latter.

I set out at dawn the next morning in search of the cemetery. The moon drooped sadly over the horizon as an uncertain light announced the rising sun.

The kibbutz graveyard lay hidden deep in the mountain crest; above it, the sky formed a black arch. Everywhere, flowers had been planted by friends and relatives. Pink roses lit up the black basalt, and yellow lupines twined around the mossy tombstones. Outside of the warble of birds, no sound could be heard. The cemetery seemed deserted.

Suddenly, a figure stepped out of the shadows. A reedy wisp of a woman, she came softly forward and stood motionless beneath the spreading margosa tree whose blossoms rained on the graves. Bending over, she started to dust the petals off five huge basalt tombstones that seemed to mark a particular burial site. Then she paused, and from a slight stiffening of her back I guessed that she had begun to cry. At first she wept silently, with a subdued grief, but a moment later she was shaking with sobs.

I started down the stairs in her direction. She turned around, looking up at me with swollen eyes full of tears. I recognized her. I had seen her many times in the dining room, accompanied by the woman they told me was her sister-in-law. She had a delicate face framed by a golden braid, and the simplicity of her dress enhanced her gentle grace. Slender, tall, and pale, she resembled a calla lily.

Both she and her sister-in-law, who was black-haired, plump, and sensual, had a certain aura about them. Their entry into the dining room was always greeted by compassionate sidelong glances and whispers, and they always sat alone. People seemed to shun their company out of a mixture of awe and reverence, an attitude that aroused my curiosity from the outset. When I asked Nikolai about them, he told me that the blond woman was the daughter of a friend of his, David Belahofsky, a tall, shy, red-haired man from Russia. In the 1920s, the tension between the Jewish settlers and the Palestinian villagers was at an all-time high. The settlers, having purchased the land from absentee Arab owners, evicted the tenants and deprived the peasants of their age-old grazing rights. The Palestinians retaliated against these foreclosures by raiding Jewish settlements—stealing cows, uprooting newly planted trees, and defiantly bringing their flocks to graze on the fields. David Belahofsky had the job of guarding the fields of Kibbutz Vatik on horseback.

Belahofsky had unlimited confidence in his ability to settle the conflicts peacefully by talking to the Palestinian raiders. Once, a settler came looking for him and told him that an Arab shepherd was squatting on the fields, threatening to shoot anyone who tried to remove him by force. Belahofsky rode up to him, dismounted, and walked calmly toward him. He spoke to him quietly for a few minutes, without threatening him, and the Palestinian left. On another occasion, during the Palestinian uprising of 1936 against the British occupation and the Jewish settlements, an English commanding officer ordered his men to open fire on an Arab village whose residents had attacked a British convoy. But Belahofsky stood defiantly before the cannons and told them they would shoot over his dead body.

Two years later, during that same uprising, he was killed riding down a track in the Gilboa Mountains when his horse stepped on a mine. On his tomb, the British colonial administrator for Palestine had inscribed: "Here lies an honorable Jew, a friend of the Arabs, who was killed by the Arabs."

This dramatic story intrigued me, and I asked Nikolai if he could introduce me to his friend's daughter, Shoshana. He hinted that it would be more discreet if I left her alone, which made me suspect that she hated me because I was an Arab. From then on I trembled in her presence like a guilty person, and if by chance I passed her on the lawn, I would look away awkwardly, not knowing whether our vague acquaintance was a sufficient excuse to say "Shalom."

Now, when I asked Shoshana if she knew whether I should start my work in the cemetery or wait for the others, she said that there were no others. She was the "regular" on the job, and a volunteer pitched in for whatever weeding or watering needed to be done. Then she gave me my instructions. I was to rake the leaves that cluttered the narrow passages between the rows of gravestones.

I worked by her side till noon without daring to speak to her, and afterward I could not shake off the poignant impression that quiet, sorrowful woman made on me. It was the same in the days that followed. A trivial conversation seemed unwarranted, even indecent in this kind of setting, and a sort of delicacy kept me from asking the one question I was burning to have answered: Why had she chosen for herself such a morbid occupation? I could not help thinking at times that she liked the sadness of the cemetery. There seemed to be something soothing for her in the company of these silent, invisible presences.

One morning, after I had exhausted the stock of polite remarks I habitually addressed to her on arrival and the silence weighed more heavily than usual on me, I summoned my nerve and asked her why she worked in the graveyard. She brushed the question away with a shrug of the shoulders. "Everyone who has loved ones here wants the place to look nice, but no one else wants to do this. So here I am to do it."

Here I am to do it. This, I came to see, was her family's motto. I wanted to question Shoshana about her feelings, to probe more, but for the time being I did not push on with a conversation she was obviously reluctant to pursue. Yet her refusal to talk only enhanced that undefinable melancholy charm with which my imagination had endowed her.

On a particularly hot day, when we had both worked ourselves to exhaustion plucking weeds, I noticed that she had a rash. Alarming sores, rather like blisters, spread across her hands and arms. When I pointed this out to her, she made light of it, claiming it was only from tension, a kind of eczema. She had been afflicted with this malady periodically since her son had died, she said, and it usually lasted no more than a couple of days. There was no cure for it, though the ointment her doctor had given her relieved some of the itch. This was the first allusion she had ever made to her son. I expressed much concern, suggesting she go home early and allow me to finish the job. Washing the tombstones was all that was left to do, and I told her it might be best not to expose her hands to the water. She seemed moved by my gesture, but declined the suggestion that she go home, saying she would sit in the shade and wait for me.

So I went to work, first soaping and scrubbing the nineteen marble tombstones that had been set up for nineteen sons of the kibbutz who had fallen in the 1973 war. Then I turned to the other gravestones, which were of flint, basalt, and granite, and began spraying them with the hose. When I was done, she thanked me, suggesting I come and cool off with some ice cream she had in her freezer.

Her first overture had come, at last! As we walked back, I was already imagining that she had an instinctive feeling for me and that we would become friends.

Shortly after we had settled down with our vanilla ice cream, we were joined by her sister-in-law, Leah, and by Shoshana's husband. A tall, good-looking blond man with a charming, genial manner, he exchanged a few pleasantries with me, talked a bit about soccer, and then withdrew, leaving us three women to our own resources.

We sat quietly. All lightness seemed to have left the room with Shoshana's husband. Hesitantly, I began to ask Shoshana about her father. And I finally learned why this venerated family seemed enveloped in a mystique of tragedy.

Shoshana described how, on the day of her father's death, her mother had tracked up the mountain path to where he lay, removed the sheet from his face, and looked at him one last time. "She had him carried home, cleaned him, and dressed him for the coffin, and then she sent for me. 'Shoshana,' she said, 'your father was killed, but you mustn't cry.' Later, they carried the coffin out to the fields, and a lot of people crowded about us. She still didn't cry. She just put her arms around the coffin. But I couldn't hold back my tears."

Up to this point, Shoshana had spoken in a stark, flat tone, as if she were narrating the tale not of her father but of some legendary epic hero. But now, as she recalled how her mother had grabbed hold of her shoulder and said, "Shoshana, control yourself, in our family we don't cry," her voice cracked.

To give her a chance to regain her composure, Leah took up the thread. She talked about Shoshana's brother, Joseph, who had been her childhood sweetheart and later became her husband. She was with Joseph when he heard his father had died: "It was the only time I saw Joseph cry. He was only seventeen, but he picked up the gun and field glasses that lay next to his father's body and took his place as guard. From that day on, the idea of treading in his father's footsteps became an obsession for him. He always said to me, 'We'll have a son and I will call him David. He will grow up to be just like his grandfather!' And I would laugh and say, 'What if you have a daughter?'

"Relations with the Arabs were not as bad as they had been in the twenties and thirties, but there would often be fights—with long sticks, called *nabuts*—when the Arabs brought their sheep to graze on our land. Joseph suffered many injuries, but he liked his post because it made him feel close to his father.

"You know, the things that happened to this family are so strange, it's hard not to become superstitious. Joseph's father was killed on the anniversary of the founding of Kibbutz Vatik—we were decorating the dining room for the celebration when we heard the news—and Joseph used to tell me our son would be born on the same date. I knew that was impossible; I wasn't due to give birth until a month later. But my son was born prematurely, on the exact day of the twenty-fifth anniversary of Kibbutz Vatik. Since it was also the memorial day of his grandfather's death, the whole family was gathered at the cemetery when they rushed me to the hospital. Well, you can say it's only a coincidence. . . ."

After a pause, Leah began to talk about the '48 war. Jospeh had been one of the first men to volunteer for the Palmach commando unit. She knew that he was in combat because every night as she tried to fall asleep she could hear the echo of cannon fire in the mountains. But she wasn't afraid; Joseph was so self-confident, so convinced that nothing could happen to him.

Then, one night when the cannons sounded from the Gilboa Mountains, they came and announced to Leah that Joseph had been killed not far from the spot where his father had died. By a cruel irony, he had fallen on the last day of the war, the very day the armistice had been signed with the Arab countries. He was twenty-seven, and Leah twenty-four.

Leah's color had drained from her face, as though the effort of telling her story had quite exhausted her. She suddenly looked older. It was time for me to go. I quietly thanked Shoshana and Leah and left them to their private thoughts.

After this day, it was as though Shoshana and Leah both regretted having offered me too much and were trying to take it back. I became convinced that Shoshana was avoiding me; though she did nothing directly to offend me, she had a way of quickly finishing her meal just as I entered the dining room, or remembering some urgent business she had to attend to whenever our paths crossed accidentally.

She wore her usual expression at work, but her affability seemed to disguise a considerable reserve toward me. Once or twice I caught sight of her eyes surreptitiously taking stock of me, so coldly that it made me shudder.

With great trepidation, I started to call on her uninvited. But her exaggerated courtesy whenever I visited hurt me more than unkindness would have. Nothing would have been simpler, at this point, than for me to withdraw, yet it was precisely this that I could not do. Something drew me to Shoshana. What it was, I didn't know.

I felt somewhat more comfortable with Leah, who sensed my affection and reciprocated it. She had a warm, expansive nature, but there were days on end when it was impossible even to speak to her. She would sit on the lawn of her cottage, hiding behind her dark glasses, and stare straight out in front of her as though waiting for someone's return. Posting myself at her side, hour after hour, I would say nothing. I could think of no way to communicate to her the sympathy that welled up inside me. My attachment to her and Shoshana seemed eerie, even to me.

One evening there was a dance in the kibbutz dining room, and I wanted to go. Too shy to arrive alone, I searched out Leah and begged her to come along. She demurred, and her continuing refusal annoyed me. I began to nag her.

"Leave me alone," she cried.

Offended, I lost my temper and shouted back at her: "I *am* leaving. It's awful to be around a person who does nothing but feel sorry for herself all day long."

The careless words that escape us sometimes do more harm than our cruelest deeds.

She bowed her head meekly, saying in a sad tone of voice, "You are right. I am sorry; I will go with you if you like."

Her words put me to shame. I retorted somewhat gruffly, in order to cover my discomfiture, that she needn't bother, I was not that keen on going after all. Then I sat in silence, gazing sheepishly down at my shoes.

"Please don't be mad at me," she pleaded. "It's hard for me to go there, I see my son everywhere . . . the spots where he used to dance and sing, the girls he flirted with. . . ." She gave a little laugh that sounded more like a sob.

I went and sat by her side on the sofa and, not knowing what to say or do, took her hand in mine and held it. It was then that she spoke to me about her son for the first time.

David was only two years old when his father was killed, but he was very much affected by it. A nervous, sensitive child, he would come to Leah and say, "Where is my father? I don't want a father in a picture, I want a real father!" Communal living offered scant help: "People think it's easier here because the members of a kibbutz form a community. But it's not true. The children see that everybody else has a father; they watch other fathers putting their children to bed in the children's home. And when they quarrel among themselves, they are very cruel. More than once I overheard one of them telling David scornfully, 'You don't have a father, your father was killed.' "

David grew up to be like his father, handsome, strong, and fun-loving. But there was also a more sensitive side to his nature. During the '67 war, he got into trouble for defying the orders of his commander: He untied the hands of the Syrian prisoners of war, unable to bear seeing their faces so tormented with flies.

In Israel, parents must give their agreement in writing before an only son can be accepted into a combat unit. Leah had signed; she did not feel that she had the right to prevent him from doing his duty. David volunteered for one of the most perilous marine units—the Frogmen. In 1969, during the War of Attrition with Egypt, his unit was ordered to attack Green Island, an action that was to open the way for the Israeli offensive along the Suez Canal the following day. At the end of the battle, which lasted fifty-five minutes, five Egyptians and nine Israelis lay dead. David was one of them. He was twenty-three.

Leah had been on her way to Europe when she learned of her son's death. The kibbutz offered each member a paid vacation overseas, a benefit that could be claimed only once in a lifetime. It had been Leah's turn to go. Aboard the ship, she heard a sailor mention the attack on Green Island, and an hour later she received a telex. She returned home immediately.

When she got to the kibbutz, she found that someone had already broken the news to her mother-in-law, who had just turned eighty and had to bear the loss of her husband, her son, and now her grandson. A strongly built, square-jawed Slav of sturdy pioneering stock, Sara Bela-hofsky was a very dignified woman and, as usual, displayed nothing of her grief. She continued to rise punctually at seven every morning, but the work that had always been such a joy she now went about mechanically. Even the garden in which she had taken such pride no longer meant anything to her. Something had broken. Her one consolation was her other grandson, Shoshana's son, Roni. Shoshana told me, "After David was killed, Mother used to say to me, 'You will see, by the time Roni gets to the Sinai there will be peace, I am sure of it.'"

A few years later, it was Shoshana's turn to take the trip abroad. Before leaving, she made Leah promise her that if anything should happen to the family, she would let her know. She was in London when the telephone rang at midnight. Roni had been killed. He had fallen along the Suez Canal on the first day of the 1973 war, when the Egyptian troops stormed the Bar-Lev line. He was nineteen. Shoshana flew back immediately.

Shoshana had no time to cry for her son because she had to pull herself together and take care of her mother. She had dreaded breaking the news of Roni's death to his grandmother, and indeed Roni's loss was more than Sara Belahofsky could endure. Little by little, everything became confused for her. She would suddenly get up and say to Sho-shana, "We have to go to Roni's . . . to David's . . . to Joseph's funeral." "You know, David has come back, he's not dead."

"It's a horrible thing to say," Shoshana said, "but I suffered so much seeing her that way that I used to wish her dead. But when she died, it was terrible. Everything came together—her death, the death of Father, of Joseph, of David and Roni. I couldn't take it anymore, I collapsed. Then I looked around me; I saw others in the kibbutz who had also just lost sons in the war, and I realized that I had to shake myself out of my depression and help them. I remembered Mother's dying words. She was in the hospital and suddenly she got up. A friend asked her, 'Where are you going, Sara?' and she answered, 'I'm going on duty, I have to guard.' And the friend said to her, 'Sleep, Sara. Don't worry. Shoshana will take over from you.'"

On hearing this, I grasped for the first time the significance of the five huge basalt tombstones in the kibbutz cemetery: They symbolized the strength of the Belahofsky clan, their fortitude in the face of overpowering sacrifice. Who could help admiring them? There was something majestic about their pain.

And yet those tombstones also symbolized a fortress the Belahofskys had passed on to their children to enable them to fight war after war without question. It was this aspect of their impossible heroism I found difficult to accept. How could all they had gone through not have altered their trust in their leaders, their unwearied devotion to their country? While I was moved by their pain, sometimes, in noting the admiring glances cast upon them in the dining room, I struggled in vain to banish from my mind the suspicion that they savored their martyrdom. There seemed to be a secret obstinacy in that sorrow, something I could not understand—as if their grief were a form of strength that packed the force of a weapon. Could their sorrow be hostile? Before its incomprehensibility I became conscious of anger, my old anger against Israel reawakened. Were they not exploiting their grief the way Israel sometimes did the Holocaust victims and its own war dead—for political ends? And if so, was it not incumbent on me to resist being manipulated? My heart constantly vacillated between deep sympathy and mistrust. I felt I could not pity them without a risk.

I became haunted by the price this family had paid for the state of Israel, and wondered whether they ever felt that it was too high. One day when I was in Shoshana's house, I inquired, "Did you ever ask yourself if the demand for Isaac's sacrifice was justified?"

She looked at me uncomprehendingly. It was clear she was reluctant to answer. But at that moment I was driven by such savage curiosity that I would have scratched her heart out to get at the truth. I asked her bluntly, "Did you ever think that if your leaders had been more flexible, your son might still be alive today?"

She began to tremble, and finally she answered: "I could wonder whether my son would still be alive if our government had been more conciliatory, and I could wonder about many other sophisticated things. There are so many questions you can raise. . . ."

She was very agitated, but I went on with heartless obstinacy to spell out all the opportunities for peace that had been lost because of Israel's intransigence. I subjected her to a scathing account of all the wars, leading up to the 1973 war, that could have been avoided had it not been for Golda Meir's policy of creeping annexation—her bad faith in claiming that everything was negotiable if only the Arabs would come to the bargaining table without conditions, even as new Jewish settlements kept being established in the occupied territories.

She listened to me with a look of complete bewilderment on her face and then stammered: "I—I—I don't know. . . . Maybe you're right, but it's best not to think too much about . . . You see, when there is a war, you have no choice. You have to say, 'My country needs soldiers, so *here I am to do it.*'"

A flood of tears ended her words.

Terrified by the spectacle of this sorrow I was beginning to comprehend, and ashamed of having provoked it, I wanted to flee. Instead, I tried to console her. I apologized and begged her not to cry, but all to no avail.

As I stood helpless and numb before the frenzy of her grief, Shoshana looked up at me kindly and said, "Don't worry, it does me good, I haven't cried since Mother died."

When I left her that evening, I tried to quiet my guilty conscience by telling myself that what I had done was justified by the need to make people less ready in the future to serve up their children as cannon fodder for the wars brought on by the ambitious designs of their leaders. But I realized, of course, that like the generation of the founders before her, Shoshana was strong in her innocent patriotism and courageous in her single-minded devotion, and I had no right to rob her of this. By tormenting her, I had been trying to escape my own uneasiness. Every time she mourned her son, I would travel back to those gatherings in Harvard's Middle East Center reading room, when my Arab friends and I would gleefully pore over the newspapers, counting casualty figures and drawing up inventories of all the tanks "we" were blowing up during the 1973 war on the Bar-Lev line. It was almost impossible to believe that all this had happened only a few months before, impossible to contemplate that one of the casualties "they" suffered had been Shoshana's son. Here, among the people who paid for the politicians' wars, it was impossible to remove myself from their agony.

6

In the Melting Pot

WHEN THE day of my departure arrived, I went to bid Nikolai farewell. We looked at each other for a few seconds, unable to speak. Then he held out his wrinkled hand to me, saying, "I will have to get used to being alone again, now that you are leaving." I was deeply moved and promised to visit him before I left Israel. All at once, we were both struck by the same thought, and he uttered the very words I dreaded: "Who knows if I'll still be here when you come back?"

I pretended not to understand and said in a tone that I tried to make cheerful, "Don't be silly, of course you'll be here, you know you haven't left Kibbutz Vatik in years!" As I spoke these words, all the hollows and lines of his face suddenly came into harsh focus for me. I felt compelled to lower my eyes, as though it were an act of impiety to notice how worn and diminished he seemed. Or perhaps I simply wanted to preserve in my memory the image of Nikolai as I had known him in the cow shed, bubbling over with playful vitality.

I bent forward and placed a soft kiss on Nikolai's forehead. He did not say a word; he merely clasped me tightly in his frail arms. Trying to harden myself, I said, as dryly as possible, "I've got to go, the kibbutz car is waiting." Then I bolted from the room and ran downhill, letting the tears come.

Though I had grown very attached to Nikolai and to the Belahofskys, I had planned to leave Kibbutz Vatik and go to live for a while at Ulpan Etzion, a home in Jerusalem for new immigrants, in order to participate in the intensive language-training programs offered in these "absorption centers." The Hebrew I had picked up on the kibbutz did not suffice for anything beyond the simplest conversation.

And then there was Danny, from whom I was virtually cut off during my entire stay on the kibbutz on account of the distance, a four-hour drive, and lack of time; volunteers had only one Sabbath free every three weeks.

I had lain awake night after night, reliving our meetings and conversations, recalling the sound of his voice, his bashful smiles, the way he had of shunting a lock of hair from his brow or brushing his mustache with the back of his hand—and I yearned for that hand, for the soft brush of his hair on my skin, the prickle of his mustache on my cheek, my neck. It comforted me to think that Jerusalem was only forty minutes from Tel Aviv and that I could commute back and forth to the little apartment on Rheines Street whenever I wished.

In a sense, my joining Ulpan Etzion was the fulfillment of a long-standing dream. As a teenager I had thought that if only I knew Hebrew I would not be confined to Israel's English radio station, which was often jammed, but could tune in to its other stations as well. Our government did not concern itself with Hebrew broadcasts because, outside of a handful of people especially trained for the army and espionage, hardly anyone in Egypt understood the language. Since there were no schools or foreign language institutes that taught Hebrew, I decided to turn to the local synagogue, where for a certain fee the rabbi agreed to give me lessons even though I was a Muslim. But when I informed my mother that she would have to increase my weekly allowance because I would be taking Hebrew lessons, she was beside herself with anger. "Are you out of your mind? Do you realize what trouble we would be in if someone saw you going into a synagogue? What if people find out you are taking Hebrew lessons? Do you want everyone to think that you are a spy?"

That evening, when Father returned home, I heard her telling him, *"Taala elha'! Bintak hat wadina fi dahya!"* ("Come to the rescue! Your daughter is going to bring down a calamity on us all!").

Needless to say, my mother refused to dole out the money. But I was at least as stubborn as she, and that summer, in Geneva, I walked into the Naville bookstore and bought a set of Hebrew vocabulary cards— the kind that have the Hebrew words written out in Roman alphabet on one side with their French translation on the other. As I sauntered down the street, turning over in my mind the problem of how to get this subversive material past customs, a charming little panda at the toystore across the street caught my eye. It gave me an idea.

I locked myself in the bathroom that night and performed a feat of surgery, carefully cutting open the panda's belly, removing part of the cotton lining, and replacing it with the cards. Two days later, a roly-poly official with prominent nostrils and a coarse mustache heaved my overstuffed suitcase onto the counter in the customs zone of the Cairo airport.

As he pried it open, he asked routinely, "Anything to declare?" I told him the same story I had told Mother, that I had only a teddy bear I had bought for my little cousin. *"Zarif, zarif awi"* ("Cute, very cute"), he said, picking it up and fondling it. Then he confided to me how fond his little boy was of stuffed animals, and I quaked with fear lest he should decide to confiscate my panda for his son under the pretext that it exceeded in value the hundred-pound limit that had been set for gifts (I had heard that this was common practice among customs officials) or worse still, notice the imperfect stitching. But he replaced it carefully where he'd found it and obligingly placed his massive derriere over the lid of the suitcase to help me press it shut.

Now, when I arrived at Ulpan Etzion, my enthusiasm for learning Hebrew came up against Israeli officialdom. On pushing open the gate, I was greeted by a sour-faced woman who peered at me suspiciously from behind her spectacles. The idea of an Egyptian installing herself in a center for new immigrants was clearly not to her liking, and the fact that I had been accepted as an Ulpan resident by the Jewish Agency in New York made no impression on her whatsoever. She proclaimed that if I wished, I could study Hebrew as a day student—the classes were open to people of all nationalities and creeds—but she could not allow me to board. The Ulpan, she asserted, was funded by money donated by world Jewry to encourage immigration to Israel, and it simply did not make sense for me to live there.

I asked to see the director. When she said he was too busy to receive me, I made for his door anyway, but she jumped up and barred my passage. I raised my voice at her, and the ruckus we were making instantly produced the director. Couldn't he try to clear up this matter by placing a call to the Jewish Agency in Jerusalem? I asked. No, impossible. He must have it in writing, he said curtly. He showed me the door, growling all sorts of disagreeable things.

I took the bus to King George Street, where the Jewish Agency was located, fully expecting to spend the whole afternoon enmeshed in the usual red tape. I was therefore quite surprised when, after only half an hour's wait, the person who was taking care of me presented me with a brief, to-the-point note. Delighted, I rushed back to the Ulpan, burst into the director's office, and triumphantly waved my letter at him. He did not seem nearly as pleased, but I was too happy at having won the right to live there to care. At the time, I thought of it as a rare privilege.

That evening, when I entered my new room and turned on the light,

I saw hordes of giant roaches scurrying away across the floor and along the walls to disappear in the cracks around the moldings and pipelines. I lay down in that dismal penitential bedroom, whose cracked windowpanes let in a thin stream of freezing winter air that pinched my cheeks. For a long time before I fell asleep, I was sure I could hear the roaches crunching away in the sugar pot that had been left out on the table. I tossed and turned. I would have borne the torments of the hard, narrow bed with the convex mattress graciously enough had it not been for the convulsive plumbing that made my walls groan each time the toilet was flushed. The worst blight, however, was the stench that emanated from the bathroom, next to which, by misfortune, my room was situated. The flush boxes were old and did not work well, so there were notices warning us against blocking the toilets by throwing the lavatory paper into them. We were expected to put the used toilet paper into a bin. The problem, I would learn, was that the bins were emptied only in the morning, when the maids came to do the cleaning. Until then, they overflowed with tissue paper smeared with feces and attracted throngs of ravenous flies. By evening the soiled paper littered the floor, and whenever the tank had one of its periodic fits of hiccups and flooded, we had to slither in the slime to reach the toilet.

Notwithstanding my troubled sleep, the next morning I entered the classroom bright-eyed and eager. Since I could neither write nor read, I had been placed in the beginners' class, the only one that taught the alphabet. After our first grammar class I was so eager to try out my syntax on someone that I dashed down the street and flung into the face of the first passerby the sentence we had been practicing all morning: *"Slicha, adoni, effo autobus mispar shesh?"* ("Excuse me, sir, where is the number six bus?"). "I'm sorry, I don't speak Hebrew" was the reply I received, delivered in a clipped, upper-class British accent.

Soon the pride and joy I had experienced in tackling the complicated repertoire of the Hebrew vocabulary were offset by the annoyance I felt at the uses to which the words were put. Every new lesson was turned into an indoctrination session. We would learn the adjective *yaffa* ("beautiful"), and the teacher would make us repeat over and over again: "Israel is *beautiful.*" Next would come the noun *lev* ("heart"), and the sentence would run: "The Wailing Wall is the *heart* of Jerusalem, Jerusalem is the *heart* of Israel, Israel is the *heart* of the world." It was no better with the pronouns. On the third day we were taught the word *shelanu* ("ours"). And so, all hour long, I had to repeat: "The land of Israel is *ours,* not theirs," until I myself was confused.

Another pedagogical device used to bolster our patriotic feelings was the *tiyul* ("excursion"). We would be taken on a bus either to visit battle sites like Kastel, where we would be treated to glorified accounts of Israeli armed feats, or to tour the occupied territories.

One day, when I could finally find my way through the alphabet, I saw the following notice on the bulletin board of Ulpan Etzion: "Ulpan Etzion is organizing a two-day trip to Southern Israel during the Passover holiday. Listed below are the places we will be visiting: Eilat, Abou Rhodeis, Nuweba, Dahab, Sharm el Sheik. Please sign up now." Furious, I crossed out "Southern Israel" and wrote "Egypt" in its place. All week long, I debated whether or not to go. It was humiliating to visit one's own country while it was under occupation, especially in the company of the occupiers. But curiosity overcame my qualms.

As luck would have it, our guide was a rabid nationalist who supported Begin. He lost no time in appropriating all of our Egyptian beaches for Israel, and just to make sure there was no misunderstanding, he renamed them in Hebrew. Overnight, Nuweba became Neviot; Dahab, Di Zahav; Sharm el Sheik, Ofira; and the Gulf of Aqaba, the Gulf of Eilat. He even took offense when I complained about the heat, and defended "our" weather with such a miffed expression on his face that one would have thought it was his very own personal property.

Barely had we crossed over into Egyptian territory when the bus broke down. Everyone got out, and the men were told to push while the driver stepped on the accelerator.

As I sat on top of an asphalt bank by the roadside, gorging myself on matzos and chocolate spread, I could not help enjoying the spectacle of our guide's red face and lurching bottom as he heaved and shoved in vain. A wicked thought crossed my mind, and I began chanting, in my best Hebrew, *"Avadim hayinou le Paro bemizraim"* ("Slaves we were to Pharaoh in Egypt"). Everyone burst out laughing and joined in singing this traditional Passover song, except for the guide.

Eventually the bus was repaired and we continued toward Nuweba, where we would spend the night. Along the way we made a stop in Dahab to cast a quick glance at the coral beach. An Israeli tourist bus was unloading a full cargo of Scandinavians, and I felt resentful at the thought of our beaches being exploited commercially by the Israeli travel industry when such profits would have been invaluable to Egypt's development. An old Bedouin peddler who boarded our bus helped me place things in their proper perspective. He was selling oranges, and one of the French girls was thirsty, so she bought a dozen. I heard someone behind me saying in French, "How can you buy from him after all the Arabs have done to us? When I go to the Old City, I never buy anything from them—not even a postcard."

I, on the other hand, was thrilled at seeing the Bedouin. In this isolated setting it was like meeting a brother. I told him how happy I was to see him and said that he was the first Egyptian I'd talked to since my arrival in Israel. He shrugged his shoulders indifferently. "Egypt, Israel, it's all the same."

"What do you mean?" I exclaimed, barely suppressing my indignation.

"You see that?" he said, pointing toward an old fortress in ruins. "This is all that remains today of the Ottoman rule. I am an old man, so I still remember the Turks. After them came the British, then the Egyptians, and now the Israelis. One day, they too will be blown away like the desert sands." He shrugged his shoulders again and clambered out of the bus.

By evening we reached Nuweba. There was an ethereal loveliness to the deep turquoise of the sea. Puffs of white mist swathed the rugged cliffs of the Saudi coastline across the water.

As we were busying ourselves getting a campfire started and preparing dinner, someone asked the guide if there was a restroom within walking distance. "What do you need one for?" he quipped. "Just go over there. All of Saudi Arabia is a toilet." The others guffawed.

There was much singing and carousing that evening, as everyone joined hands and danced a hora around the campfire—everyone, that is, except me. I went down to the surf to watch the sunset. The soothing sound of the water must have lulled me to sleep, because when I opened my eyes it was morning. There was a light breeze, and the sand felt wondrously soft and warm underneath me. Everyone else was still asleep, so I let myself sink luxuriously into the limpid blue-green water, inhaling the piquant fragrance of seaweed.

But this tranquillity was soon broken by the arrival of hordes of sightseers. Going on excursions amounts to a craze in Israel, perhaps because of the claustrophobia from years of sealed borders. First, some picnickers from the neighboring Moshav Neviot—yes, there was already a Jewish settlement here—then busload after busload of city folk. By midday Nuweba was seething with people, and the lovely landscape had been transformed into a vast mound of garbage. Scattered everywhere on the sand were piles of sardine cans, watermelon and grapefruit rinds, onion peels, and rotten tomatoes on which throngs of flies and other insects feasted.

When we boarded the bus for Jerusalem the following evening, I had had my fill of the scenic seashore of "Southern Israel." I did not hide my disgust. At one point I said to our guide that, as far as public civility went, Israeli standards were no higher than those of the most underdeveloped countries. He vehemently denied my accusations, and I asked him how else he could explain why, under cover of night, Israelis defecated on the beach right next to their tents when it would cost them nothing to move behind a bush, or why in public restrooms they seemed so often to mistake the floor for the toilet. Why did it never dawn on them, I asked, that their blaring stereos might be hard on their neighbors' sanity, or that it was inconsiderate to blast a car horn in the middle of the night? What made them vandalize the public telephones? Metal wires, wooden sticks, old combs, buttons—anything was okay to rip off the telephone company. Why did they fail to reprimand their children for throwing garbage out their apartment windows? Not only the guide, but everyone on the bus resented these remarks. All the way back to Ulpan Etzion, the discussion raged; I couldn't stop myself, and neither could they.

When I got to class the next morning, two words greeted me from the blackboard: *"Aravim masrichim"* ("Stinking Arabs"). During the class break that followed, my red poncho was burned; I had left it behind on the chair, and it had mysteriously made its way over to the paraffin heater. From then on, I was snubbed by many Ulpan residents.

But I was not the only target of my classmates' ill will. There was another non-Jew in our class, a German by the name of Ulrika. She was a strapping country girl with coarse yellow hair, freckles, and red cheeks. A person of remarkable moral conviction, she belonged to a German youth organization whose aim was to imbue the nation with a sense of responsibility for what had been done to the Jews during World War II. Her partiality for Israel occasionally blinded her judgment, at least to my mind, and yet the rest of the class mistrusted her. Since she was kindhearted and a bit naive, she became the butt of everyone's malicious jokes.

One day Ulrika arrived with a basketful of *Brötchen* (the buns Germans eat for breakfast), which she had baked for the class, and started passing them around. The teacher, who was in the midst of illustrating the various declensions of the word *tov* ("good") on the blackboard, wrote: *"Ulrika tova"* ("Ulrika is good"). Suddenly, an American girl who was seated in back said in a loud, clear voice: "The only good Germans are dead Germans."

It was as though a shell had exploded in the class. Everyone was silent, hardly daring to look at Ulrika. At first, I blushed as though I were myself the injured party, and then I turned angrily toward the American girl and asked her how she could say such a revolting thing. The class immediately rushed to her defense, arguing that her feelings were perfectly understandable in view of what the Jews had suffered at the hands of Germany, while I insisted that someone like Ulrika, who had not even been born at the time of Hitler, could not be held responsible for his crimes. In the midst of all this, Ulrika, who had not said a word, burst out crying and rushed from the room. We never saw her again.

My classmates tended to look upon newcomers with great suspicion, and though they pretended to take no notice of them, their curiosity was enormous. Ulrika's departure left me as the only outcast until a batch of fresh arrivals—Russians—momentarily deflected the hostility away from me. Great excitement had greeted the director's announcement that some new immigrants from the Soviet Union would be joining us soon. Days in advance, the corridors of Ulpan Etzion were buzzing with the news.

But the two young men who graced our classroom door one morning —a spindly, balding engineering student and a squat artist of sorts— immediately fell short of all expectations. They greeted us gruffly, and from then until the day they left, they maintained an insolently overbearing manner. Their barely concealed contempt for us was a reflection of their own ambivalence toward Russia. On the one hand, they depicted everything related to the Soviet Union in demonic terms, while on the other, they expressed a nostalgia for a country that had given them, no matter how oppressed they might have been there, the pride of feeling part of "the greatest nation on earth." They never tired of boasting—particularly in front of the Americans—about their astronauts, athletes, musicians, dancers, and scientists. In their eyes, Israel was a village by comparison. If they felt a loss of status in being uprooted from a great civilization, they suffered too from their ignorance of all languages but Russian. Immigrants from countries with less grandiose self-images were not as crippled by the language problem.

The Russians constantly criticized Israel for being "too socialist" and were ardent supporters of Begin's right-wing policies. At the same time, they had inherited the Soviet scorn for Western democracies: Capitalism was inherently degenerate, and the Western way of life was frivolous and chaotic. In their view, Western democracies, particularly the United States, were in decline, because their people had lost all sense of self-restraint, all notion that there are limits to freedom. At the Ulpan, the object of their opprobrium was an American who also happened to be a leftist. In the middle of the night, they marched down to his room, swinging their belts over their heads and hollering, "We smell a Commie here! Give him to us and we'll hang him!"

Shortly after the Russians arrived at the Ulpan, they wrote a petition on behalf of the free immigration of Soviet Jewry to Israel, which they planned to hand in person to Henry Kissinger, who was then in the country. It demanded that the American secretary of state put pressure on the Soviet leaders. They decided to organize a small demonstration of Ulpan students outside the building where Kissinger was scheduled to meet with Israeli cabinet members, and they asked us all to join. When the Soviet artist, still unaware that I was an Egyptian, approached me in the dining room, I did not quite know how to answer him. I favored action on behalf of Soviet Jewry on humanitarian grounds, but I could also envision my picture in the Arab press with the caption: "Instead of demonstrating for the return of Palestinian refugees, Sana Hasan marches on behalf of Jewish immigration to Israel!" And so I told him somewhat sheepishly that I needed time to think the matter over. His veiny cheeks flushed with anger. "What is there to think over?" he snapped. I told him the issue was a little delicate, since I was an Egyptian. He gasped, for the notion of an Egyptian allowed to travel freely—let alone in Israel—was unfathomable to him.

For days I repeatedly explained to him that despite the absence of parliamentary democracy, the people of Egypt did not live in terror at home and enjoyed the freedom to study and live abroad if they wished; nor were torture and executions frequent in modern Egyptian history. But he jeered; he simply could not imagine a centralized government on any model outside of a Stalinist one, and therefore conceived of Sadat as some kind of bloodthirsty tyrant. One day, when I had to run errands after lunch, I asked the Ulpan students who were sitting with me at the table if they wanted me to pick up anything for them. Since the artist was also present, I thought I should ask him out of politeness. "Yes," he said, "there is one thing you can bring back for me: Sadat's head!" And so it went.

For all the conflicts I had with the Russians, and with the other students, I did not regret living at the Ulpan. For one thing, I had never had a chance to see so many people with such different backgrounds from mine. As a child I had been barred from the company of working-class people. But here there was the American girl, Sarah, whose father was a butcher; a Moroccan, Arlette, whose uncle, a bricklayer, lived around the corner; a Polish boy, Betzalel, whose family were dockers in the port of Ashdod; a French boy, Gaby, who was an electrician.

One of the consequences of my privileged situation was that I was virtually the only one in the class who did not have a part-time job; almost all my fellow students worked in the afternoon. I decided to do it, too. Since my purpose in looking for a job was not to make money, which I still had plenty of at this point in my trip, I decided to try for a job as a menial worker, a position that to me seemed very exotic. Having learned from our janitor that the man who owned the grocery down the street from us was looking for a temporary replacement for his wife, who was in her last month of pregnancy, I presented myself there one day. At first the grocer, a stout little man of fifty with a kindly face, seemed pleased enough with me. He told me I'd have to sit under the awning by the huge barrels of olives and pickles that were set out on the sidewalk and keep a sharp lookout for the flies that had a tendency to fall in and drown. If I happened to notice one, I should spoon it out discreetly when the customer was not looking. Then he broached the subject of my pay, and finally, almost as an afterthought, asked me if I was Jewish. His face fell when I said I wasn't, and I sensed that it might not be prudent to add that I was Egyptian. For a few seconds he fingered his closely shaven chin, mulling over what he had just heard. Then he told me to check back with him the next day. I did and found that he had given the job to someone else. When I told this story to a group from the Ulpan, a Finnish boy said I had been a fool to let on that I was not Jewish. He himself had made the same mistake, with exactly the same results.

Having been tipped off by the Finnish boy, I made sure, when I presented myself some weeks later for a job in the kitchen of the King David Hotel, to wear a huge Star of David. I assumed the identity of Suzy Leibowitch—a name I had agreed upon with an American friend of mine who was a manager at Bank Leumi and who opened an account for me there—and was hired on the spot.

It was with considerable trepidation that I turned up at the hotel the first afternoon. The King David, which dated back to the heyday of British imperialism, had once been a favorite haunt of the Egyptian Queen Mother Nazli, and it had been built by the same group of British entrepreneurs responsible for Egypt's most illustrious hotel, Shepheard's. Like Shepheard's—where, according to Kipling, sooner or later one was bound to run into every person of importance—the King David had in its time seen some of the most eminent political figures of Britain: Viscount Allenby, Lord Mountbatten, Sir Winston Churchill. As symbols of the hated British occupation, both hotels had been the targets of violent action. Shepheard's was put to the torch by rioting mobs on the eve of the 1952 revolution, and the King David was blown up by the Irgun—an action that killed innocent Arabs and Jews along with the British officers who were its target.

My thoughts, however, did not linger on such tragic events that sunny afternoon, but rather on the kitchen of the King David. In the past, before it was bound by kosher laws, it had served caviar, champagne, and oysters shipped in specially from Marseilles and featured French cuisine and elegantly clad Sudanese in flowing white caftans who catered to reigning princes and peers.

But its famous clientele and world-renowned menus were only part of the reason I was so thrilled about the prospect of working at the King David Hotel. Kitchens have always held a great attraction for me, perhaps because I had been forbidden to enter ours as a child, for fear I would pick up "bad language" from the cook. The prohibition, however, only made the life of the "help" appear more glamorous to me. Whenever we visited one of my aunts, I would slip away to the servants' quarters while the grown-ups chatted together. My aunt had a whole retinue of maids of all ages, hired from the village where her husband owned lands. I would squat beside them on the floor and eagerly take in all their stories, some of which made my hair stand on end—stories about *afrits* ("devils") and ghouls; about the camel caravans that used to come to the landlords' estates bearing little black slave boys, whose testicles were then cut off and who were half buried in the sand until their wounds dried; about village girls whose clitorises were cut off at birth so they would be spared the temptation of sexual pleasure; and about young brides who were deflowered by their husbands in the presence of their mothers-in-law. The husband would accomplish this feat with a handkerchief wrapped around his finger, and the bloodstained cloth would be exhibited to the assembled relatives and friends, who waited at the threshold and greeted it with ululations of joy.

These terrifying tales were told to me while the maids sat combing out their long braids with lice combs. One day, when I was suffering from a stomachache, one of the maids plucked a louse from her hair, stuffed it into a raisin, and told me to swallow it. When I made a face, she swore in the name of Allah and His Prophet that this "pill" was an infallible cure.

And then there was the food. As in our house, the servants had quite a different menu from the masters'. We were entitled to the best cuisine of the West—lamb chops, filet mignon, and shrimp, creamed carrots, scalloped potatoes, and sautéed peas—while they ate peasant stews. We had the iced chestnuts and fondant, they the candied sesame and chickpeas. But I far preferred to eat their food, and I loved the freedom of being able to do so without a fork and knife. With them I did not have to sit rigidly upright and risk having my elbows knocked if I leaned on the table or my hand slapped whenever I let it wander into the serving dish. Here, I was not frowned upon for soiling the tablecloth, for there was no tablecloth—nor were there any tables or chairs or serving dishes, for that matter, but only the cheap crockery out of which the servants ate. They sat cross-legged on straw mats and scooped out the stew from a common dish with pieces of pita bread. How I loved dipping mine into that sauce and watching it trickle all the way down my arm onto the floor!

Then there were the goodies I never got at home: sugar cane, which we peeled with our teeth, chewed, and spat out onto newspapers; *halawa,* a gooey caramel prepared by boiling sugar with lemon juice, which the maids also used for depilation; *mish,* a wormy old village cheese that made ripe Camembert smell like a rose by comparison; and *leban daker,* a rocklike, unrefined, and sugarless chewing gum, which made my jaws throb.

The combination of gory stories and too much food invariably made me sick at night, and my unsuspecting mother would be completely mystified by my sudden attack of asthma. One of these nights, as I lay wheezing and gasping for breath, unable to sleep, I overhead her in the bedroom next door, telling my father that she didn't understand why *la petite* became overexcited every time I visited my aunt.

These adventures lasted until the day I picked up lice from one of my aunt's maids. Horror-stricken, my mother forced me to confess to her the company I'd been keeping, and from then on my aunt's servants' quarters were decreed off-limits.

It was not until many years later, when I was already in my teens, that I had another chance to make friends with people *"pas de ma classe,"* as my mother would say. I befriended Helga, the fifteen-year-old maid who made up my hotel room every morning in Bad Gastein. Through her, I got to know many of the hotel's waiters and kitchen staff, and as a result I had a brief romance with one of the scullery boys, a fourteen-year-old Austrian named Ewald. We would slip out every night, after my parents had retired to their room, and go to taverns and movies. Ewald would give Helga little billets-doux to put under my pillow. One that I recall went as follows:

Felsen können brechen,
Bergen niedergehen,
Aber dich vergessen,
Das wird nie geschehen.

(Rocks can break,
Mountains crumble,
But to forget you,
Will never happen.)

Our relationship lasted until the day my father went to my room in search of aspirin and found an empty bed. He waited for me at the hotel entrance and gave me such a thrashing that it almost cured me of the desire to see Ewald again.

The King David Hotel had hired me as an apprentice kitchen hand with the proviso that I'd be on trial for the first week and, if the chef found my zeal lacking, I would be discharged. By dint of sycophancy and slavishness, I managed to weather the probationary period.

The first test was getting the chef's blessing for my appointment. After I had been fitted out in appropriate work clothes, I was led to the kitchen by the manager, to whom I had said that I was a new immigrant from Portugal. The four long rows of ovens gave off so much heat that the place was suffocating. A motley crew of cooks, faces dripping under their white caps, clothes sodden with grease and sweat, were scurrying about clanging pots and yelling curses at each other in every conceivable language from Russian to Cambodian.

Sitting imperturbably in the midst of this rumpus, encased within a glass cubicle, was none other than the great chef himself—an Austrian with a broad face and sleepy eyes. The work manager entered the cubicle and whispered at length to the chef, who peered at me dubiously from behind the glass pane. I waited outside, nervously fingering the lapel of my white coat and trying to look as if I had been stricken with reverence at the very sight of him.

After a few minutes the chef roused himself and, stepping outside of his booth, grabbed me by the coat sleeve and shoved me past a horde of gesticulating cooks into a clammy hole. This was the pantry of the splendid King David, and it was here, under the dominion of a nasty Iraqi boy and a buxom matron from Libya, that I was to be employed from then on. The boy, a pimply, sallow-faced teenager with filthy nails, asked me in Hebrew where I was from. When I said Portugal, he snorted with all the superiority of someone who had never heard of the place and felt none the poorer for it. Then the woman, who had the kind of haughty insolence that left no doubt as to who the boss was, pointed at a mound of thick, whitish roots that lay on the counter and ordered me to peel them. I was to make horseradish. The task would have been simple enough if there hadn't been several hundred of them and if their skins had been less resilient. Still, I pulled away at them until, after wrestling with one particularly stubborn root, I let the knife slip and cut myself. To my dismay, the blood gushed all over my sleeve. Embarrassed by my own clumsiness, I went over to my boss and asked if I might be excused for few minutes. "Already!" she exclaimed. "What for?" Then, noticing my soiled sleeve, she interrupted herself in mid-sentence to take a swing at me. *"Tembelit!"* ("Fool!"), she blustered in bad Hebrew. "Look what you've done to your uniform! Do you think you'll get a fresh one every five minutes? Go wash this off and get your hand bandaged." Seeing my stupefied expression, she yelled: "Go on! Move!"

I looked up at the boy for some sign of commiseration, but he sat at the edge of the sink, gazing stolidly before him and swinging his legs back and forth in a gesture of supreme indifference. So I slunk out of the room, thinking that I had better not make a fuss on the first day if I wanted to hold on to the job. It had not taken me long to find out that scullions ranked low in this hierarchy, and I was the lowliest among them.

In an order where everyone lorded it over everyone else—the waiters over the cooks, the cooks over the scullions, and so on—we were kept in our proper place by curses and name-calling. *Tembelit* was the term my boss reserved for me, *espèce de conne* ("cunt") the address preferred by the Moroccan assistant cook (which would have ruffled my feelings had I not heard them refer to my boss as *cette pute,* "that whore"); the first cook liked to call people *'alf-wit* in his broad cockney accent, and the chef's favorite term was *Schwein* ("pig"). I believe the only person the chef addressed by name other than the first cook was me, and that was because Suzy rhymed with the word *zuzi* ("move," in Hebrew); he liked to stick his head out of his booth and bellow, *"Zuzi!* Suzy! *Zuzi!"*

We worked in a reeking little den whose floor had by lunchtime become so clotted with mayonnaise, eggshells, and sardine oil, not to mention salad and vegetable peels, that I had to move about gingerly in order not to slip in the mush. The heat from the ovens made the stench of decomposing food unbearable; the rancid odor of sweaty armpits did not improve matters.

My Iraqi co-worker looked as though he had never been near a bath in his life. When it was time to mix the coleslaw, he would stand over a gigantic bowl of shredded cabbage and, doing away with the wooden spoons, plunge his arms into it—grease-encrusted sleeves, filthy hands, blackened fingernails, and all. Then he would draw his arms out slowly, a pinkish liquid running off his sleeves and all over the floor. I could not help wondering what the refined clients of this five-star hotel would say if they knew that the same hands that had tossed their coleslaw had been used moments earlier to scratch an oily scalp, wipe sweat off a forehead, pick a nose, and engage in other activities best left unmentioned.

By three o'clock we had put away the leftovers from the buffet lunch —hard-boiled eggs, gefilte fish, herring, Russian salads—and could take a break at last. The late-afternoon activity was less hectic. But at eight o'clock on the dot, a good two dozen harried, panting waiters would come thundering down the stairs, clamoring for the food. Precisely at eight, all the cooks would start running amok, struggling to push through the narrow passages between the ovens, with the hundreds of pounds of roast beef they held up in the air headed for inevitable collision. Punctually at eight, a crimson-faced chef would charge out of his glass cubicle straight into this seething mass, armed with a battery of four-letter words. (I was assured that the chef's repertoire had grown immensely in recent times because of the added pressures brought on by the visits of President Nixon and Henry Kissinger. What happened to his vocabulary later, when President Sadat was a guest of the hotel, I can hardly guess.)

I would stand in the middle of this pandemonium, trying to hear above the clamor of their oaths what the waiters wanted, all the while skidding out of the way of the British first cook, who was threatening to stuff the veal roast up my "arse," and the Moroccan assistant cook, who promised to scorch it with the baking pan if I didn't "shake it." In the meantime one of the waiters would be bellowing for his potatoes, while another would be ranting away because the roast beef I had served him was overdone and the guest had sent it back. Their tempers were hardly improved by their having to run up and down two flights of stairs with heavy trays several times in the course of the evening, since the kitchen was not on the same level as the dining room.

In the midst of this customary chaos, one night the Moroccan assistant cook rushed at my boss with a knife, swearing he would teach *cette pute* a lesson. I stepped between them and calmed down the cook, thereby earning the gratitude of my boss—and the advice that came with it. She took me under her wing, offering to procure me a husband and tipping me off on how to seduce a man: by putting a drop of menstrual blood into his coffee. But before my new ally could advise me on the more pressing issue of how to negotiate the confusion of the kitchen, my stay at the King David Hotel ended, in as abrupt and disorienting a way as it had begun.

Cats were the bane of our existence in the kitchen. It was because of them that we were obliged to work in the awful heat with closed windows. The chef hated them and was devoted to keeping them out at any cost, but this did not prevent them from slipping in through the basement doors when supplies were delivered. I had never seen his face turn as livid as it was the morning he discovered a frozen cat in the cooling room. He turned around, sizzling with rage, and asked who was responsible for this. No one dared answer him. "Who," he shouted, "put away the grapefruits last night?" Someone pointed at me, and I was instantly fired.

But I wasn't ready to give up working yet. Having noticed that the number 4 bus drove past a big dairy factory called Tnuva, I decided to try seeking employment there. They had nothing available but told me to try the chicken-packing firm Off Meshek, nearby.

Off Meshek was run by a Czech who spoke not a word of English. I introduced myself again as Suzy Leibowitch but this time concocted a story about being a new immigrant from the United States who had gone with her husband as a volunteer to Kibbutz Vatik and, after falling out with him, had come to Jerusalem in search of work.

The owner led me to the punch-in room, where I was immediately surrounded by women who fired questions at me in Georgian. I looked at them in bewilderment, wondering why they mistook me for one of them. To be sure, there was some physical resemblance—all the women had Mediterranean looks, and most were on the stocky side, no doubt because of their Soviet diet of bread and potatoes. Before I had a chance to answer, the owner pushed them roughly aside, yelling that I was no *Gruzinit* but an American.

Instantly the women fell away. I could hear the gasps as the magical word "America" was whispered down the line. Some leaned forward, studying me intently as though I were a rare and wondrous species that had accidentally fallen into the midst of common mortals. Others smiled at me with delight. There was no doubt at all in my mind as to which, for these women, was the Promised Land.

But they did not keep their reverential distance for very long. No sooner had the owner left the room than they thrust themselves upon me with violent enthusiasm. One tossed up my skirt, giggling wildly as she exhibited my "American" nylon petticoat to the others, who craned their necks to get a better view. In the meantime another was solemnly trying to pry my mouth open to see how many gold teeth I had. From the glittering smiles all around me, I at first surmised that neglect had brought the women tooth decay at a relatively young age and that their poverty had kept them from having the gold coated with enamel. Later I discovered that the gold caps on their front teeth were purely ornamental.

An elderly woman with no fewer than seven gold teeth tottered up to me and squeezed my bosom to see if my bra was padded. Then she unceremoniously unbuttoned her blouse, displaying a baggy green satin bra decorated with rosebuds, a model clearly designed for buxom country girls. "Russian bras no good, no support!" said the woman, clutching at her withered breasts and lifting them up to illustrate her point. Why, then, didn't she buy American bras now that she was in Israel, where they were widely available? She rubbed her fingers together to indicate to me that they were beyond her means. How about Israeli bras? I asked. But she puckered up her nose in disgust at my suggestion, after which I felt compelled to offer to send her some bras when I returned to the States. What kind would she like? I inquired. "Maidenform!" she replied without hesitation. I dutifully noted down her size, and was rewarded with a resounding kiss on the lips.

The supervisor, an impressively tall woman with thick black braids pinned about her ears, stalked into the room. She clapped her hands, calling the women to order. It was, as I found out, time to dress me for work. The women continued to frolic about, gabbling away and gawking at me. Meanwhile, the supervisor brought forth a large roll of plastic, which she kept locked in the closet, and swaddled me from head to foot in it, saying I should be careful not to rip it because plastic was expensive and the owner's policy was that workers should have no more than one piece a day. Then she proceeded to pin up my hair, explaining that, in accordance with factory regulations, all female employees had to wear their hair above their ears, tucked under a plastic cap.

She led me to a murky subterranean work hall. A nauseating reek of decomposing chickens filled the airless space, along with the endless creaking of the revolving conveyor belts. As the supervisor ushered me to my place, she began to explain the various stages of chicken gutting.

At one end of the circular assembly line stood the *shochtim,* or religious butchers, who were set off from the other workers by their blue coats. Every twenty minutes or so a van would drive up to the factory and drop hundreds of squawking chickens down a chute. The *shochtim* would then grab them and slit their throats with razor-sharp knives.

Such was the power of these holy men that they were able, by holding several chickens together by the legs, to do them in simultaneously with a single slash. By the end of the day, each one of them had butchered no fewer than a thousand chickens.

I used to watch the dangling severed heads with fascinated horror as they continued to emit their blood-curdling cries. But the *shochtim* were unimpressed. Kicking the twitching bodies to one side, they would turn impassively to their next batch of victims. The chickens were then picked off the floor and strung up on the iron spikes of an apparatus designed to pluck their feathers. From within the machine came the smothered squawks of those unfortunate enough to have survived the throat slitting. All were quite dead by the time they emerged at the other end.

Then our job would begin. As the chickens were propelled forward, the workers stood by, scissors in hand, ready to chop off their heads. For some reason this task was reserved for the men, who were paid a higher hourly wage—no doubt because they handled a more respectable part of the chickens' bodies than the rest of us. The next batch of workers was made up of women whose job it was to plunge their hands into the chicken's cavity and flip out the entrails so that they dangled on the outside of the carcass. Then came our turn. We had to seize hold of the intestines, pluck them out, and cleanse the cavity of any remaining feces or bile, while the women after us grabbed hold of the "good" parts, the hearts, livers, and gizzards. Finally, the last group of women cut off the birds' feet.

The work was extremely fatiguing because there was no proper foot support. Whoever had designed the factory must have had in mind a race of giant Jews, for the conveyor belts were above the reach of anyone under six feet tall. In order to reach the chickens, we had to stand on crates, a most uncomfortable position that gave us all backaches and sore shoulders by the end of the day. In addition, we had not a moment of respite: If anyone so much as stopped for a second to wipe the slime off her brow, she might miss the entrails of the next chicken as it sped by. Unsavory sights assaulted us no matter where we looked. If we glanced up, chicken bile would drip on our faces; if we looked down at the bloody gutter below, we would be treated to the spectacle of distended intestines and heads and feet floating in a stream of slime.

When I was a child, the dangling head of a turkey with a severed jugular vein had made me cry. My mother had grabbed hold of my hand and, as she pulled me away from the butcher's stall, told me that the Muslims and Jews killed their fowl in a far more "humane" way than did the Christians, who strangled them. But when she turned to Father for a corroboration of her reassuring words, he registered his skepticism by reciting a verse:

La tahsibu arkus beinakum taraban;
F'al teir yarkus madbuhan min al alam.

(Don't think I dance in your midst out of joy;
The birds dance too when they feel the butcher's knife.)

A howl greeted the lunch bell. The women jostled past me, stampeding through the open door and down the staircase; in a flash the room had emptied. For myself, as for the others who rushed toward the dining room, the chairs were a far greater attraction than the food.

I tried to keep tabs on the vanishing trail of plastic aprons, but in vain. The last one shot through the revolving door, and I found myself on the second floor, abandoned by all. I opened one or two doors but found no trace of a dining room. Just then, a man with a giant torso and a small, egg-shaped head came out of the bathroom. I asked him where the dining room was.

Flashing his gold tooth in an insinuating smile, he led me with many gallant flourishes of his hand toward a door, which he held open for me. I stepped inside an immense work hall, and before I had time to focus my somewhat dazed eyes on the mountains of chicken carcasses that lay about, I found myself lying atop a bed of crushed ice, smothered by an avalanche of hot, sticky kisses that descended down my neck and throat. How I would ever have extracted myself from under this load I cannot say, for it is certain that no matter how much I hollered, no one would have heard me. But as chance would have it, Shaul, the Moroccan rabbi who was in charge of the salination of the chickens in accordance with Jewish religious law, happened to walk by. Hard as it was to believe, my three-hundred-pound assailant turned white at the sight of this mere gnome of a man. I did not linger long enough to see what ensued.

Halfway down the corridor, I met a woman who pointed me in the direction of the dining room. I went down one more flight of stairs, pushed open a door, and almost fell into the arms of my supervisor. I told her indignantly what had happened. "That must have been Krysztof," she said, and burst out laughing. Then, pointing out a slender, middle-aged woman with wispy gray hair at a table across the room, she whispered to me that he was her husband.

"What?" I exclaimed, shocked. "You mean his wife works here, and he behaves like that?"

"Oh, don't take it so seriously! He just likes to have some fun once in a while. All men are animals when it comes to sex. They can't help themselves. Why, I bet your husband would do the same thing if he had the chance," she said, winking at me.

"He most certainly wouldn't!" I asserted.

"Really?" she said, her eyes wide with astonishment. "Then he can't be much of a man!" Later, I discovered that the Georgians were the Latin lovers of the Soviet bloc; the male workers at the factory constantly boasted of their prowess, bragging that all Russian women vied for their favors and preferred them to their own husbands because of their passionate foreplay.

As the days passed, my life took on a certain stable rhythm. I worked at the factory from 12:30 to 10:30 P.M. and went to classes from 8:00 A.M. to noon.

One or two evenings a week, I traveled down to Tel Aviv to meet Danny on Rheines Street. Often he could stay only a short time, but it was enough to renew our passion and our connection. I regaled him with stories of my adventures, each time managing to tell a bit more in Hebrew. He praised me, he teased me, and after each visit I returned to Jerusalem tired but anchored, refreshed, happy to see my colleagues in the Ulpan and especially my fellow workers at Off Meshek.

Indeed, I seemed to be getting along famously with my Georgian comrades. I was accustomed to hearing Israelis speak of the Georgians as a boorish, violent, rather seedy lot. These prejudices were shared by the Russians at Ulpan Etzion, who referred to the Georgians as *khuligani* ("hooligans"). Nevertheless, I liked the quick-tempered Georgians, whom I found warm, hospitable, and extraordinarily generous.

The Georgians and the Bukharan Jews figured among the poorest ethnic groups in Israel, but they had a truly striking dignity of bearing. The interiors of the Georgian homes I entered were always immaculate, always ready to welcome visitors; a kettle was kept simmering on the stove, and guests were served a strong tea in the cheerful porcelain set that had been brought along from home. The children were well-groomed and unusually polite. Though Georgians were every bit as disgruntled with life in Israel as the deprived Oriental Jews, their disillusionment did not seem to have demoralized and brutalized them as much. Their families had not disintegrated under the new pressures, as so many Oriental Jewish families had done. Instead, they had managed to provide support and shelter. The father of the house, despite his low earnings, retained his patriarchal authority, and the mother, who in most cases had never worked before, was successfully absorbed into the labor market.

One of the first Georgians I came to know was Sonia, a woman who plucked out chicken intestines next to me on the assembly line. She stood out from among the other Georgians by virtue of her bright yellow hair. With her pudgy red cheeks and pug nose, she resembled a Raggedy Ann doll. Although she worked overtime because she could barely feed and clothe her six children on the salaries she and her husband earned, she was never too tired to cook a special meal for me in the evening. Meat appeared on her table no more than three times a week, and even then only chicken, which the workers were allowed to buy every Thursday from our plant at a discount. But she had such an inventive way with parsnips, beets, and cabbage that although I was always offered the same thing for dinner—chicken gizzards and wings—each dish seemed to me exotically new. And when she donned her exquisite scarlet folk dress, lit the candles, and warmed our blood with a home-brewed potato liquor, the meal seemed regal.

Sonia was a vivacious, temperamental woman, quick to fly into a rage, but she never bore a grudge except against Israel, about which I never heard her say a kind word. For the most part the Georgians had been small artisans and merchants back home and, unlike the Russians, had not been drawn to emigrate by material aspirations. Nor did they attribute their departures to anti-Semitism, as the Russians sometimes did. Sonia was rather typical in this regard, she claimed. "My daughter was the only Jew in class, and no one ever hurt her. We lived side by side with Arabs [presumably she meant Muslims], with no problems, and believe me, the goyim were kinder to us there than Israeli Jews are here. When I go to Machane Yehudah [a food market in Jerusalem], the children throw stones at me and call me *Gruzinit* ("Georgian"). So what if I am a Georgian, am I not a Jew? You wouldn't think so from the way we are treated. People tell us we are dirty. Even at school, the children say these things to my daughter. It's not nice. People here have no manners, no respect."

The Georgians were devout Jews who had come to Israel at the bidding of their rabbi, believing it was their duty as Jews to go and live in the Holy Land. Instead of the spiritual Jerusalem depicted to them in the Bible, they were confronted with the reality of Israel, and in their disappointment they segregated themselves into their own Georgian community, living in a kind of ghetto and being extremely unwilling to do anything for the state that had so let them down. They viewed taxes as just another attempt to cheat them out of the little they earned, and they strongly opposed the drafting of their children into the Israeli army. Sonia, availing herself of a law that exempted married women from army service, had already found a match for her seventeen-year-old daughter and planned to marry her off in time for her to avoid the draft. And she constantly griped about the fact that her son, the owner of a small laundry, had been drafted, asserting that the state had no right to disrupt his business and take him away from his family.

One night, Sonia's husband, who was generally absent in the evening because he supplemented his income by working as a janitor in the neighboring Tnuva dairy factory, joined us for dinner. Alexander had the standard Georgian physique—a short, stocky body, gnarled limbs, and a round face. He sat silently throughout the meal, hunched over his plate, chewing away at the chicken wings, sucking the sauce off his fingers, and stuffing huge chunks of bread into his mouth. But when Sonia took out the family album to show me their house in Georgia, saying, "Judge for yourself where we lived better, here or there," he sputtered: "Life under communism was a hundred percent better than here. The problems only started when Jews applied to emigrate to Israel. The government said, 'You were born here, you were given a nice job, a nice apartment—why do you want to leave?' The troubles are only for people who want to leave. They say you are selling out the Russian government, and they are right. Everything there was good, why did I have to leave?"

"Why *did* you leave?" I ventured. He looked at me indignantly, wiped the gravy off his tiny, comblike mustache with the back of his hand, and yelled, "How was I to know that they are like this here? When I was in Georgia, I was a Zionist. I didn't know that in Israel people don't have any manners and they are all liars and thieves. As soon as we got here, the people at the Jewish Agency—who are all horrible people—started to create problems. They wanted to give us an apartment in a horrid place [Afula, the developmental town in the Jezrael Valley], and I didn't know anything about Israel, so I was going to be had. But my brother-in-law put me on guard against their offer. So we lived with him in Haifa for a year and a half, until we could get an apartment in Jerusalem. The first time I took a look at this apartment it was worth seventy-five thousand liras. I went to Amidar [the government building company] and said I wanted it. They said sure, just wait a bit. Two months later they finally said we could have the apartment. The price had gone up, in the meantime, to a hundred and twenty thousand liras. Of course they knew all along that the price was going up—that's why they didn't want us to occupy it right away, so they could increase their profit. That's how it goes here. It's not just the government people who lie, it's everyone. The other day in the store, a man shortchanged me. I didn't notice at first because I am not so familiar with the currency, but when I pointed it out to him he denied it. Stealing is a profession in Israel. So, now, when the family writes to us from Georgia to ask if they should join us, I write back and say, 'No, here is no good.' "

When Alexander had finished eating, he confided to me that he had a brother who worked in an auto plant in Detroit. "He writes to me that it is excellent for the Jews in America. They earn a lot. Here you work like a mule and you earn nothing." He added that he wanted to join his brother in Detroit, but it was not possible because his brother was not a citizen yet. Then he wanted to know if I would be able to help him get to America, and was disappointed to learn that I could not pull any strings for him with the immigration authorities either.

It was in the house of Alexander and Sonia that I first got a taste of impulsive Georgian generosity. I rarely left them without being laden with gifts. Once, after Sonia had led me on an inspection tour of the closets in her bedroom in order to show me the trousseau she had brought along from Georgia for her daughter's wedding (she had had it ready since the girl was four years old), she begged me to take along an embroidered pillowcase, saying it would bring me luck on my wedding night. All my arguments to the effect that I was not likely to try my hand at marriage a second time were to no avail. Another time, Sonia's mother —a gaunt, gloomy old woman who was always dressed in black but sported a magnificent array of colorful peasant shawls and golden hoop earrings—insisted on giving me her earrings, which I had been so ill advised as to admire. Only when she saw my terror at the prospect of her freezing my earlobes with a chunk of ice and piercing them was she dissuaded.

I thought the Russians at my Ulpan were effusive in their Slavic emotionality, but compared to the Georgians they were arctic. Whenever I left Alexander and Sonia's house after a visit, I would be trailed all the way to the bus station by a whole contingent of well-wishers from the neighborhood. While they stood waiting to see me off, they would inundate me with kisses—strong, noisy, wet kisses on the forehead, on both cheeks, even on the lips. Any stranger who chanced to pass by and witness the emotional outpouring with which they greeted the arrival of my bus—the anguished lingering over the departure, the warm hugs and embraces following their good-byes, the affectionate mutterings that lasted until the driver wrenched them away from me by pushing them down the steps—would have been puzzled to learn that the journey I was about to take was to carry me no more than a few blocks away, and that we would all meet again at work first thing in the morning.

7

A Prostitute

ONE DAY as I left the Ulpan, I caught sight of some Oriental Jewish girls jeering at a Palestinian woman who was dressed in colorfully embroidered peasant garb. She came toward me with short halting steps, balancing a basket of grapes on her head and carrying a bare-bottomed infant in her arms. The hecklers tagged behind her, chanting the following ditty in Hebrew:

> An old Arab man, wretched and lame,
> Married an old Arab woman, wretched and lame.
> They had a son,
> Wretched and lame,
> Who married an old Arab woman, wretched and lame . . .

The woman kept on walking as though she were oblivious to their presence. Suddenly one of the girls lurched forward and pushed her from behind. The woman's face flushed with panic as she struggled momentarily to maintain her balance, but the grapes fell. Frightened by the commotion, the baby burst out crying. The pedestrians continued to pass by without even casting a glance in their direction.

Excited by her cruel deed, the assailant, a strikingly beautiful young woman, began to trample the grapes, yelling, *"Aravia meluchlechet, Aravia meluchlechet!"* ("Dirty Arab!"). I ran up to her, jerked her away, and salvaged what grapes I could. Then I did my best to console the woman, who did not stop her lamentations until I offered to pay for all the damaged fruit. Her tears dried up, and she smiled and told me, in surprisingly flawless Hebrew, that I was a *Yehudiya im lev tov* ("Jewish woman with a good heart"). It was not the first time I was struck by the rapidity and expertise with which Palestinians from the occupied territories had caught on to the language.

When I turned to the girl and asked her what had prompted her to do such a thing, she replied that these were Arabs from "the territories" who came to sell their fruit, and that she and her friends did not want them in their neighborhood.

The girl's name was Leila, and that is how my acquaintance with her began. Her callousness infuriated me, but it did not surprise me, for I knew that she and her friends were from a nearby home for juvenile delinquents. I had seen them hanging around the gate of our yard at the Ulpan in the company of some boys from the school just across the street. As soon as we ventured outside, their harassment started. Any one of us was fair game, but the kids had their favorite scapegoats and their own rules: Girls would tackle boys, and boys girls. Leila and her friends always picked on Richard and Tim. Tim, a Britisher, was singled out because he was tall and scrawny, with abnormally long legs and a stiff walk that made him look as if he were on stilts. The American, Richard, was teased about his ponytail and his earring. The girls would wiggle past him, smoothing their hair, jingling their bracelets, and calling out, "Hello, beautiful, you boy or girl?" The females among us were left to the tender mercy of the boys, who followed hot on our heels, rocking their hips to and fro and rhythmically hissing, "Fuck, fuck, fuck, fuck."

Not long after I witnessed the assault on the Palestinian woman, I decided to do some volunteer work in the home. Many of the Ulpan residents did social work; notices that urged us to volunteer were plastered all over our bulletin boards. As "new immigrants," we were expected to participate in the building of the nation, and since we were located in a poor Oriental Jewish neighborhood, this meant working with deprived segments of the population. Some people gave free English lessons and others "adopted" kids from the nearby Hadassah orphanage, taking them out twice a week for walks, picnics, or movies. Still others worked in the rehabilitation center for the mentally disturbed that was located down the street.

The idea of working in a home for delinquent girls was particularly appealing to me; I felt a natural sympathy for girls who wouldn't stay in line. The lives of these young thieves, drug addicts, and especially prostitutes represented the height of rebellion to me, carefully raised as I was in the puritanical climate of Egypt.

The first time I had gone out alone with a boy in defiance of parental orders, Mother had shouted hysterically after me that the only thing left for me to do now was to "go down to the street and open your thighs," and Father, who had waited up for me, greeted my return with an angry tirade. When I persisted in this course of action despite the threats and thrashings I received, Mother's lamentations became somewhat more subdued. After repeating to me for the nth time that she could never live down the shame of knowing that the doorman, who saw me returning home after midnight, considered me a prostitute, she would shake her head dolefully and mumble in French, "It's sad, my poor girl, how sorry I feel for you! You are really not cut out for life in the Orient." Or she would wring her hands in despair and remonstrate, "Poor imbecile! You are your own worst enemy! When will you finally understand that without her reputation a woman is lost?" By that time, however, she had given up, saying, *"J'espère que tu vas te marier en blanc!"* ("I hope you will be married in white!").

During her own childhood, Mother had been kept in absolute seclusion, guarded over jealously by *Dada* ("Nanny," in Arabic) Safran and *Dada* Morgan—the first a black eunuch, the other a Circassian slave girl. All the girls in her family wore veils, and whenever they were driven anywhere outside their estate, the car blinds were drawn shut and the peasants had to turn their backs to the vehicle so that they would not risk soiling the girls with their eyes. When her father scolded her for gazing out her bedroom window one day, she protested, "But I was just looking at the garden—no one was there." "No one indeed!" he answered. "And the gardeners—aren't they men?"

Patriarchal power reigned absolute at home. Mother had to kiss her father's hand every morning on waking up and every night before going to bed. Each day after lunch she had to stand by his bedside, a fan of ostrich feathers in hand, and shoo way the flies while he napped. Her father had given instructions to the Mère de Dieu, her boarding school, that his daughters were not to be let out on Sundays. Their sole entertainment was to go up to the school roof and observe the passersby in the street. As for vacations, they were always spent at home with my grandmother. Although my grandfather traveled to Europe every summer, taking an interpreter because he spoke no foreign languages, he never once agreed to replace him with one of his daughters—or, for that matter, with his wife. Even so, Grandfather was thought to be terribly progressive for his time because he had only one wife and because he consulted his daughters instead of imposing a husband on them. Still, the suitor was not allowed to see any of the girls before the wedding contract had been signed, and only after the engagement was announced could the couple exchange pictures.

Grandfather considered Father debauched for taking Mother dancing in St. Moritz during their honeymoon. During a visit one day, Father asked him, "Do you know that your daughters deceive you?"

"What do you mean?" my grandfather exclaimed, outraged.

"They only wear the veil when they come to visit you," Father replied. "Wouldn't it be less hypocritical if you told them of your own accord not to wear it?"

Having resolved to work in the home for delinquents, I went to see the director, who turned out to be an exceptionally dedicated young woman. Though she had never used volunteers before, she told me that she had nothing in principle against the idea, provided that my taking the girls out did not interfere with their schedules. They all received practical training in sewing and home economics in the morning, as well as courses in the Bible and instruction in reading and writing, since many of them were functional illiterates. Daily sessions with the social worker and the psychiatrist were also mandatory.

As she led me to the door, she warned me: "The most important thing for you to learn, if you are serious about working with us, is not to give in to despair yourself—to the feeling that nothing can be done for them. That was the attitude the government had toward their parents —whom they used to call the 'generation of the desert,' because they believed that, like the Jews Moses led out of Egypt, they had to die out for a generation of healthy Sabras to emerge. Well, here you have the result of this policy. The children have inherited their parents' sense of impotence, and this can be very frustrating for those who are trying to teach them to help themselves. I can tell you from my own experience, it's difficult not to get discouraged, because what you'll be up against is their apathy, their indifference, and their hostility."

I would have liked to work with several of the girls, but the director suggested it might be better if I limited myself to one in order to be able to develop a closer personal relationship with her. So I chose Leila. Why I did remains to this day a mystery to me. Perhaps it was because she had been the instigator in the act of outrage carried out against the Palestinian woman and was therefore the most challenging. Or perhaps it was something about her eyes—those narrow slits of piercing jade that had met mine the first day at such close range and with such boldness. I felt drawn to her in a way that reason could not account for.

Leila had been born in Tunisia, though like many Oriental Jewish youngsters who were ashamed to admit they were born in an Arab country, she lied and said she was a Sabra. Her father, a Jewish shop-keeper, had been very prolific; of his thirteen children—all girls—Leila was the youngest.

When Leila's mother died in childbirth, her father had brought his children to Israel, where many of his relatives had been recruited by *shlichim* (Zionist recruiters) to settle during the 1950s. He had entrusted the care of their Nazareth household and of the younger siblings to his oldest daughter until she got married, after which he ruled over his household with an iron grip. He watched over the girls constantly and lived in fear that they would lose their virginity. If they were a few minutes late after school, he would slap them and call them *zonot* ("whores"), and if they wanted to go out with a boy, they had to lie. Eventually his fear became a self-fulfilling prophecy. Late one night, when Leila returned home from a date (she had told him she was staying at a friend's to study), he flogged her, shaved her head, and threw her out of the house.

Leila sought refuge at the house of some Arab neighbors. Shortly thereafter she met and fell in love with Ali, a pimp who had just been released from jail. At fourteen, she gave birth to their child, and he convinced her that she would make more money whoring in Tel Aviv, where prostitutes were in great demand. It was there that the social worker had found her. When she had tried to convince Leila's father to take her back home, he refused, saying that as far as he was concerned his daughter was dead. It was decided that Leila would be brought to the home and that her child, whom she did not want to put up for adoption, would be raised by one of her older sisters.

At twenty-one, Leila was now the oldest of the girls in the institution. Whenever I came to see her she would greet me in a disdainful manner that reminded me of the way I had dodged my mother's caresses at boarding school—even though I had secretly warmed to her tenderness, I had been ashamed because I knew my friends were watching me. So I did not react to Leila's standoffishness with the kind of hurt my Mother had exhibited; on the contrary, it pleased me. I liked her bored look, the pouty droop of her mouth, the indifference with which she treated me and my gifts. Pointedly disregarding my arrival, she would go on sitting and gossiping with her friends. And I would listen to their fever-ish voices, which sounded to me like the clucking of excited hens, marveling at the pettiness of their conversation and the extent of their spite. Most had been prostitutes, and typically, they lavished torrents of abuse on men even though they lived exclusively for them.

Having always been plagued by a strong drive toward self-improve-ment, I could not help envying Leila's utter satisfaction with herself. I remember remarking to her once that the night guard at the home bore an eerie resemblance to a dwarf in a painting by Velázquez. She had responded by asking me if he were a friend of mine, and when I explained to her who he was, she shrugged her shoulders and told me that the social worker had once taken them to look at paintings in the Jerusalem Museum, and that she had found them a deadly bore. She made no attempt to conceal her reactions, and often, on the street or in a bus, when it would have been seemly to appear not to notice someone's odd clothing or strange features, she would gawk, point, or shriek with laughter. Having grown up in a class where social refinement was often mistaken for delicacy of feeling, I could not help reveling in her lack of restraint, however much it embarrassed me.

The lures of another class did not stop here, for in my hunger for revelation even the silly conversations of Leila's friends appealed to me, and I longed to make their acquaintance. It was a pleasure her possessiveness could not grant me, and whenever I asked her any questions about them, she would groan with impatience. Since I never did manage to get to know any of her friends, it was only through her portraits of them that I had access to her peers—and her portraits were invariably colored by her passionate affections and hatreds of the moment.

More than once I witnessed her rolling over on the ground with her "soul buddy," screaming, biting, pulling at her hair, and refusing— despite my intervention—to let go until she had torn out a fistful. At such moments Leila's voice would become fierce and lewd.

Leila always hung out with the same gang of girls I had spotted on the day I had seen them assault the Palestinian woman. They all shared a background of poverty and shame and came either from broken homes or from families whose fathers had been unable to adjust to the terrible loss of their status when they gave up being small merchants and traders in the Arab countries to become unskilled laborers in Israel. Another thing the girls shared was the inability and unwillingness to help one another; it was as if their suffering had completely exhausted their capacity for sympathy, either for one another or for those even less fortunate than themselves.

One day, on our way to a café in Ben-Yehuda Street, Leila and I passed a blind beggar wearing a greasy beret and a filthy old blazer. I handed Leila a lira and told her to toss it into the pea can he had put out on the sidewalk. When she did, the beggar let out a squawk, to which she responded with an ugly curse. I asked her what had happened, and she laughed, telling me that she had tried to filch a few liras from his can, but the "wretch"—who, it seems, was not as blind as he had pretended to be—had caught her at it. Shocked, I asked her how she could stoop so low as to rob a beggar. She replied that she saw no reason for supporting beggars; it just encouraged them to be lazy. If she were in the government, she would abolish welfare altogether, and then people would be forced to go out and look for work, she said. Her reply annoyed me all the more because of its hypocrisy. After all, she herself, like most of the other girls in the home, was supported by welfare. I admonished her severely, but her features, which remained impassive throughout my little sermon, told me I was wasting my breath. There was no room in her heart for compassion. She had received too little of it herself to have any to spare.

The plight of the Palestinians awakened equally little sympathy in her. Ever since the day I had seen her tormenting the old woman, I had striven in vain to change her attitude toward the Arabs. To that end I had even revealed to her my own true identity, hoping it might modify her prejudice. But I was deluding myself. Leila could handle quite well the fact that I was an Egyptian without its making the slightest dent in her contempt for Arabs. She said, "You are different," and simply put me into a separate compartment. In the course of time, she became so accustomed to me that she seemed to forget what I had told her altogether. For her, I was just "Sana" and the Arabs were still "them." More than once she made pejorative remarks about Arabs in my presence without even realizing that she might hurt my feelings.

Leila's prejudices did not stem merely from national chauvinism, and even less from her own personal experience with Arabs. On the contrary, her father had always told her that his life in Tunisia had been a good one and that he had had cordial relations with the Muslims. At home, her older sisters spoke Arabic with their father, and she herself had been rescued by Palestinians from Nazareth when her father had thrown her out of the house. No, things were much simpler, and much more complex. As was often the case with Oriental Jews who felt scorned by the Ashkenazim (the European Jews), it enhanced her self-esteem to be able to look down on someone.

Once, when I invited her to a picnic, I left her off on the highway to buy some soda and sandwiches. Having had to wait a few minutes to be served, she returned to the car fuming: "Did you see that? Did you notice that *Araboosh* [a pejorative term for Arab, the equivalent of "Yid"] who pushed himself ahead of me? What nerve they have, these people! You give them your hand and pretty soon they want to take your whole arm. Because we are so good to them, they think everything is allowed!"

"What do you mean?" I exclaimed indignantly. "That fellow was ahead of you in line! Why shouldn't he be served first? He's a human being just like you—your equal."

"Are you crazy?" she burst out. "These people are not my equal! They're nobodies, flies compared to us Jews! We could crush them just like that if we wanted to," and she snapped her fingers contemptuously in my face to emphasize just how easily this could be accomplished.

Her gesture made me so furious that for the first time I lost control of myself and slapped her. My anger must have frightened her, for she began to cry—those bright tears that she often shed out of wounded vanity rather than real grief, all the while dabbing the corners of her eyes with her little handkerchief to keep her mascara from smearing.

But there were times when I saw Leila shed genuine tears. I had taken her to a Turkish movie she had been badgering me about for weeks. It was a mawkishly sentimental film about a self-sacrificing mother who was married to a poor farmhand. The couple was ruthlessly exploited by their landlord till the day the husband was crushed by a huge boulder he had tried to haul off the field with the aid of his water buffalo. Though his life was saved, his arms had to be amputated. This episode marked the beginning of an endless epic about the woman's heroic struggle to save her family against all odds. She toiled alone from dawn to dusk, frequently going without food so that her husband and children could eat. One night, her husband, feeling himself a burden, slipped away and was never heard of again. Then a drought ruined her crops and her youngest boy died of starvation. When she went to seek the help of her landlord at his estate, begging him to lend her some flour for her children, he would not give her any unless she sold herself to him. . . . And the movie continued to unfold in this vein.

Leila cried her heart out, and as we left the cinema she said, "Wasn't that a great film? And wasn't the mother wonderful? My mother would have been just like her if she had lived."

The only other genuine tears I recall seeing Leila shed had to do with her dog, a small gray poodle that her pimp had stolen for her.

For Lucky, nothing was too good. Leila shared her choicest food with her, rubbed her with her best perfume, and spent all the money she had on ribbons, fancy raincoats, and an endless array of rubber balls and dolls. She bathed Lucky every day, even though the poor dog obviously hated water. When I spoke up on the creature's behalf, Leila, who would brook no interference when it came to her dog and became insanely jealous if she saw someone else caressing her, retorted curtly, "It's good for her; cleanliness is very important."

Lucky was a sickly-looking animal with a doleful expression brought about, no doubt, by being tied up all day. When I told Leila it was not fair to the animal to imprison her in this manner, she gave me her "it's good for her" line, claiming that if she let the dog run loose, someone might poison her just for the fun of it.

The only time Leila let her dog off the leash was during the twenty-minute walk she took with her every evening. On a day that I accompanied her, the dog had run on ahead and was at a good distance from us when a mutt jumped over a fence and mounted her. Leila ran after them, beside herself with rage, calling the mutt all kinds of names yet afraid to get close enough to try to dislodge him. When he finally dismounted, she fell on Lucky, crying piteously. She was in an absolute frenzy and could not be consoled, even when I offered to drive Lucky to a veterinarian if she was worried about her becoming pregnant. No, that was not the cause of her distress: She was upset, she said, because female dogs hated sex; it hurt them. I could not help laughing, and replied that Lucky did not seem the worse for it. My tactless remark stirred Leila's vague moral sense. "How could you say such a cruel thing?" she exclaimed. "Didn't you see how she wrenched and whined while the brute laid her?" And she began to howl even more loudly.

She cried well into the night, and when I returned to see her the next day, the director told me she had had to call in a nurse to give her a tranquilizer.

The only being in the world Leila loved as much was her pimp, Ali. (Like many Oriental Jews, he had a Muslim Arab name.)

One day she prevailed upon me to take her to Tel Aviv, where Ali lived. Though I was well aware that the social worker had warned Leila several times to stay away from him, I gave in, partly because it was common knowledge that the girls continued to meet their pimps in secret and partly because I was curious to find out what he was like.

We reached a seedy little café in Shechunat Hatikva, a dilapidated southern suburb of Tel Aviv. Almost completely inhabited by Oriental Jews, it was one of the worst slum areas in Israel and had the highest rate of crime and juvenile delinquency. Inside, Leila hailed a burly man whose long, furry arms hung limply on either side of his foreshortened torso, making him resemble an ape. He turned, and sizing up her breasts with the gaze of a connoisseur, he bent down to kiss her on the cheek.

"How have you been?" she asked him.

"With a stiff prick, because I haven't had you in so long," he answered, roaring with laughter and giving her a friendly whack on the bottom.

He greeted me warmly, but his excessive familiarity made me take an instant dislike to him. "Well," he said, "how do you like this dump? Nice place, isn't it? I bet you none of your fancy Ashkenazi friends ever brought you here. Fine people, those Ashkenazim. Too bad Hitler didn't get rid of all of them for us. I tell you, it's no wonder there was anti-Semitism in the West. When you see how awful these people are, you understand how they caused it. Nothing like that ever happened in the Arab countries, because Oriental Jews just aren't like that!" He accompanied these words with a sneer that crumpled his face.

"I know them, these Ashkenazim, well," he went on, after escorting us to a table in the corner. "I used to work for one of them. What a shmuck he was! He had a little workshop right under his house, and for twelve hours a day I would have to stand there beside that infernal machine grinding gravel till I was ready to scream. Even when I was asleep at night I would hear the noise of that machine, as if someone was grinding inside my head. Well, the boss liked to pose as the great *sahback* [Arabic for "buddy," a word that has become part of Israeli slang]. Like he really understood his workers. *Kus omo!* ["Cunt of his mother!"] What could *he* know about how it felt to stand on your feet twelve hours in a row?

"And his wife, you should have seen her—thin like this [he raised his manicured little finger with the fat emerald ring] and tits like this [he cupped the palm of his hand to the size of a plum]. Their tits, that's everything to these Ashkenazi women, more important than love, honor, family—anything in the world, except maybe their poodle! They'll never have more than two children because they're scared their tits will sag. And then they come to us with all their fine speeches about how we should cut down the size of our families for the good of the children. I'll tell you their true motive—they're afraid of us because we are already a majority in this country!"

I examined Ali as he spoke. His hair was naturally curly, but it had been slicked back by brilliantine. The greasy reddish bangs that fell over his forehead set off his cruel green eyes, lending his face a predatory look—an impression to which his large, flat nostrils further contributed. He wore a shirt of the brightest orange imaginable, so loud that even Leila, for all her garish taste, felt compelled to comment on it. But it was his hands, with prominent, fiery tufts on the knuckles, that arrested my attention. Something about them sent a thrill of disgust coursing through me. Suddenly, in the presence of this beastly male, I felt lust.

"*Habibti* ["my love," in Arabic], are you still with us?" He was addressing me, and I blushed as if he had actually been able to read my thoughts.

Having assured himself of my attention, he went on: "Anyhow, I would go up once a day to help the wife with the heavy work—mopping the floors, the bathroom, the balcony. The boss even let me keep the key to his apartment to show me that he trusted me. Well, one day I seduced his wife. It wasn't hard. These Ashkenazim are all whores. You should have seen how my prick made her squirm and pant. She couldn't have enough of it. Another time when I came up to clean, I found their fifteen-year-old daughter home all by herself. Well, you know me, I'm not one to resist a fuck for long. So I had her too. Each one of her thighs was as plump as this [he held out his hands as if around a watermelon], and her . . ."

I listened for a few more minutes, concealing my disgust and trying to maneuver him to another subject by asking him what he was up to at present.

No one, least of all the police, knew exactly what Ali was up to. He was a notorious figure in Israel's criminal underground, and pimping was only a marginal activity for him now, he said, though he had indeed started out as a member of a ring of pimps linked to the organized crime syndicate in Tel Aviv. Each of them had been placed in a key job—as bartender, porter, waiter, or taxi driver. Ali had first worked at a bar, then in a discotheque, and later at a hotel—a highly coveted center of operations because it gave one direct access to the tourists on whom a good part of the trade depended.

Ali described how he performed his job as the night porter: When a guest arrived during the night shift, Ali would carry his luggage up to the room. If the man was traveling without his wife, Ali would ask him whether the journey had tired him and whether he would care to have a drink before he went to sleep. Once Ali returned from the bar, they would chat a little and Ali would gradually shift the subject to women; as soon as his prey seemed duly warmed up, he would ask him how he would like to meet a nice Israeli girl. If the tourist showed interest, he would bring him one of the prostitutes the next night. The money would be paid directly to Ali; he would then pay the woman as well as the night concierge, who had to be bribed to allow the women on the premises. Ali would keep a certain percentage for himself and hand the rest over to the organized crime syndicate. The syndicate was involved in other activities as well, ranging all the way from scalping to illicit gambling, theft, loan-sharking, and extorting protection compensation from small businesses—most notably in Tel Aviv's HaCarmel market, where the vendors, all Oriental Jews, were beaten up if they refused to pay for the service. The profit from these activities would then be channeled into the syndicate's legitimate businesses, which were used to launder dirty cash and functioned as a front for income tax purposes.

Ali had ended up making big money and invested part of it in Israeli-owned brothels in Frankfurt and Hamburg. His front in Israel was a chain of *steakias,* fast-food joints that sold cheap steaks stuffed into Arab bread and smothered with all sorts of Arab condiments. He had been in and out of prison all his life and had just recently served time for setting fire to a meat-packing plant operated by one of his rivals from the syndicate.

Ali spoke to me at great length about the bestiality of Israeli wardens, who, he alleged, beat up and sexually assaulted the prisoners. On the other hand, he was enthusiastic about American prisons, for he had been imprisoned even in America, having emigrated there in the hope of starting a new life. But he had soon gotten drawn into the drug business in New Orleans and was eventually picked up by the police for peddling cocaine; after serving time, he was deported to Israel. "On my life," he said, "American prisons are like fancy clubs. They treat you like a human being, you get plenty of recreation—Ping-Pong, basketball, football, you name it. And the food—what can I tell you, I had never eaten so well in Israel! Such quantities! Believe me, I was sorry to leave. The only education I ever got in my life was in that prison. I learned English and I read a lot. You should have seen their library! There isn't a school in Israel with a library like theirs! I tell you, that's some country, America! Even a crook like me would come out of a place like that straight!" He chuckled.

I asked him if he had ever considered going straight since then. He made a face. "Me, straight? I was only joking." Then his expression turned deadly earnest, almost sinister: "Listen to me," he said. "I grew up right around the corner from this café—in the garbage. We lived eleven kids to one room after we came from Iraq. In our house there were only mattresses, three kids to a mattress. When all these nice Ashkenazi children were being tucked into their warm little beds, I was sandwiched between an older brother who kicked me in the balls and a younger brother who farted in my face. For ten years I slept like this. During all that time I was fed on the unfulfilled promises and the lies of this government. When I was old enough to read, I opened the newspapers and saw that nothing was ever written about our problems. Oriental Jews were just spots on the wall, people walked right past us without even seeing us. But about the Ashkenazim there was always plenty in the papers, about the thefts and the corruption of the government—there were enough pages of scandal to cover entire walls. So I understood one thing. This is a country where only those who steal thrive. And I said to myself, If the socialists can do it, why not me? That's when I started to steal, and, believe me, I've never regretted it. It's true, I've been in and out of prison ever since. But so what? Would it have been better for me to go on in the workshop? No thanks, I'm sick of slaving for Ashkenazi bosses. Just look at how the Oriental Jews around you live: They work, they fuck, and they sleep. Is this a life? At least me, when I'm out of prison, I live like a king."

As the days went by, I discovered new facets of Leila's personality that captivated me. She had become a woman without ever being a child, and in many ways she seemed older than I because she was so much tougher and, I suppose, more cynical. Yet it was perhaps the very fact that she had had to grow up so fast that made her so infantile. She really knew how to play in ways that adults have long forgotten. Her charming games needed no more than a few pebbles or bits of paper, for they arose from the powerful, uninhibited imagination of childhood. It was enchanting to watch her. While she played she captured for a few precious moments the pure bliss of childhood, when guilt and remorse had not yet laid their claim on her—nor had the world yet dared to criticize, judge, or torment her. She took delight in buses and would ride for hours around the city, going from terminal to terminal without getting off and studying everyone and everything with ravenous intensity. Often she would tell me that only on the bus did she have the sense of being free at last, of really going places. "I let my fantasy go and travel with it: I am in Venice, in Paris, in Rome, I am surrounded by all these slick, well-dressed men and women. The handsome man who has just climbed aboard is rich and famous, he has eyes for me only, soon he will propose, and I will send postcards to my friends in the home telling them about it. They will be green with envy."

Though she had never been inside an airplane, Leila was crazy about flying. Whenever we heard the sound of a jet rumbling overhead, her face would light up with exhilaration. I bought her a toy propeller plane that could fly around the room, and she kept it with her constantly. One day I learned that the Jerusalem Museum was going to be holding a kite-flying contest the following week and told her I would take her. She, who was in the habit of regarding whatever we were going to do with contemptuous indifference, could not control her joy. Though she was perennially late without reason or excuse, she arrived early that day and could hardly restrain her impatience as she waited for me to buy the colored paper, wood, and string we needed to build the kite. Later, I watched her tearing back and forth with it in front of the museum pavilion, screaming ecstatically; I had never seen her so happy.

After the contest was over, she kissed me and told me this had been the most wonderful day of her life. I believed her. She added that when she had been a small girl, she would stand on top of her bed, close her eyes, and jump, flapping her arms in the process. For a few moments, she said, she had felt like a bird soaring in the air.

The only other time I saw Leila as carefree and joyous was while she was playing *chamesh avanim* ("five stones," a game that worked on the same principle as jacks) with her son. She was not very tender with him, and I was often shocked to hear her yell such things at him as *"Halevai shetikaver chayim!"* ("I wish you'd be buried alive!"). But she loved to play with him when he came to visit her. They were like two kids wrangling about how many points each had scored and whose turn it was to toss the stones.

Her son, to whom she had given the Arabic name Sami, lived with her sister in the district of Nachlaot, a predominantly Oriental quarter laid out along twisting alleys.

Over the course of several visits to see Sami and Leila's sister, I came to know Nachlaot well. It was an intimate place. Everyone there knew the alleys, but no one knew their names. If one asked where to find a certain street, the answer was likely to be "Who exactly are you looking for?" Old people sat silently on minuscule straw stools out in the street by their houses. Having lived in such close proximity for decades, they already knew everything about each other, so there was little left to gossip about. But occasionally one of them would pipe out a precious morsel of news in a thin, tremulous voice, and it would be passed along from stool to stool until it reached the end of the street.

The narrow, cobbled lanes and balconies overflowing with red castor beans and pink coriander blossoms lent an exotic air to the poverty of Nachlaot. As in the cramped, poor districts of Cairo, everything took place on the staircase: People did their wash out on the stairs, ate on the stairs, quarreled on the stairs. Going to visit someone in Nachlaot was like peeling back the layers of an onion. By the time one had climbed to the fourth floor, one could report on the private lives of everyone on the three below: The woman on the third floor is always in bed because she is dying of syphilis; Mazal has taken up with an ambiguous-looking youth; Maklouf, on the second floor, beats his wife; old Mr. Nissim is too lazy to use the toilet in the courtyard.

All kinds of people lived in Nachlaot: hawkers who sold fish, fowl, eggs, vegetables, and fruit at the neighboring Machane Yehudah market; street peddlers of sunflower seeds, falafel, chick-pea salad, razors, combs, ballpoint pens, needles, thread, penknives, condoms, laxatives, and *mezuzahs* (the tiny scrolls that contain the Sh'ma Prayer); street cleaners, laborers, barbers, carpenters, handymen, one or two clerks, tradesmen, welfare families, pimps, prostitutes, magicians, fortune-tellers, street performers, beggars, and boys who sold their services to men with "peculiar tastes" for a hundred liras.

On my first visit to Leila's sister, when I had yet to meet Sami, I passed two old women dressed in black, squatting on top of a staircase. One, with a mauve kerchief tied low over her forehead, was picking stones out of her rice. Her belly flabbed over her knees, and the jutting veins on her hands told of endless hours of washing and cooking for the many children who had since grown up and left Nachlaot. Her friend, a stringy woman with a long, thin gray pigtail, was sucking at a dark cigarillo that she had rolled herself. She held it between thumb and index finger, and her brown, bony joints looked like an extension of the cigarillo. As I walked on, a voice behind me rasped in Hebrew, "Child, child, where are you going?" I looked around for a child, but it was I who was being addressed.

The woman with the mauve kerchief, whose brown face was as wizened as a raisin, smiled at me; she had no teeth. When I told her I was looking for Aziza Cohen (Leila's sister), someone reading a newspaper on the first-floor balcony overheard me. He stood up and cackled at me in Hebrew, "The blacks are no good! The blacks are no good!" The gentleman was trying to warn me against speaking to the dark-skinned old woman at the foot of the staircase. "Poor soul," one of them sighed, twirling her finger against her temple. "He is a little crazy." (She used the word *meshugah*.)

Later I found out that this Mr. Blumenthal was the only Ashkenazi resident in the building, a relic of the days nearly fifty years ago when German Jews still inhabited the quarter before it was "overrun" by Oriental Jews. Soon, all traces of the "white" man had disappeared save for a handful of impoverished students from Hebrew University, who came and went. One morning, Mr. Blumenthal awoke to the news that the man who was to be his neighbor on the same landing was an Iraqi, and that two Moroccan families were moving in upstairs. From then on, he hated the "blacks." Mr. Blumenthal's attitude toward Oriental Jews had acquired a mystical, quasi-religious dimension. For him, the "blacks" were devils fashioned out of darkest night.

Like many of the old people in this neighborhood, Mr. Blumenthal had a passion for collecting and hiding things. Every morning one could observe him wandering through Nachlaot, rummaging through the odds and ends that lay strewn across the lanes. He would bend over, examining each item carefully as he talked to himself. If he had too many things to carry, he would hide some so no one else could take them until he came back to haul them off the next day. His bedroom was packed to the rafters with corks, papers, bits of glass, bottles, old newspapers, cardboard boxes, pieces of rope and metal. No one was allowed to touch anything; the hill of broken tidbits by his bedside was his own kingdom, over which he was the sole ruler.

One day Mr. Blumenthal became very sick. He would not consult a doctor, but the neighbors found out about his illness by hearing his groans through the paper-thin walls. They called the police, who came and took him away by force. He stayed in the hospital for six months, and when he was finally allowed to go home, he found an empty room. The "blacks" had played a practical joke on him and stolen everything.

Mr. Blumenthal was heartbroken. He no longer ventured outside; his passion for digging up odds and ends seemed to have left him. He just sat out on his balcony all day long, silent except for those few times when he stood up and shouted, *"Hashchorim lo beseder!"* ("The blacks are no good!").

Mr. Blumenthal's warnings notwithstanding, I got directions to Aziza Cohen's and entered one of the low-roofed hovels that ran along a sunken, cobbled path some five feet wide, interrupted here and there by a seedy little shop. A foul smell of sewage permeated the street, and several of the outside staircases were plastered over with the blood and feathers of the unfortunate birds that had been chosen for that day's meal.

The dark hallway led to a steep, fetid flight of stairs. I was about to descend to the basement apartment when a little girl in yellow rubber boots came tearing up, followed by a screeching little boy in a grimy T-shirt. As they whooshed past me, my eyes widened with horror at the object that dangled from the boy's hand—a huge black rat with long yellow fangs and a crushed skull. In a matter of seconds, I had scuttled down the stairs, almost knocking over an old woman, who tittered and asked, "What are you so afraid of rats for? Over here, they are our good neighbors."

There were no nameplates over the basement doors, so I knocked on the first one. I was lucky: The disheveled creature who came to open it was Aziza, Leila's sister, though I found it hard to believe. Instead of

Leila's beauty, which caused men's heads to turn toward her as if by a kind of tropism whenever we went out together, I was startled to see a woman with eyes set so wide apart in her square, pockmarked face that she looked like the battered front of a bus. Her lanky arms and legs were awkward and ill matched.

Aziza admitted me to a one-room apartment whose wallpaper hung in tatters, revealing open chinks in the walls. At one end of the room stood a disemboweled armchair and a double bed with a flaking metal frame, while at the opposite end was a huge old refrigerator—a gift of the welfare organization—which served as a closet. Like all the appliances donated to the poor in Israel, it could not be used once it had broken down, for there were no funds available for repairs.

Hardly had I introduced myself when a man with a dyed mustache and an ill-fitting blond toupee came clattering down the stairs, dragging behind him the same little boy I had seen with the rat a few minutes earlier. The man hurled the child into the room, screaming, "This piece of garbage will end up a no-good pimp like his father!"

The handsome, dark-skinned boy with striking eyes was Sami, Leila's son. He knew now, at seven, that his mother was a prostitute and that his aunt was ugly and "black." He knew too that he was poor, and he was ashamed of it. Sami attended school in the neighboring upper-middle-class suburb of Rechavia, because the Jerusalem municipality had started a busing system that channeled underprivileged Oriental Jewish kids into the better schools of the wealthier neighborhoods. There he had met and become deeply attached to a little girl whose parents were German Jews, and she had taken him to play at her house. He was always telling me about her beautiful blond curls and about her mother's hands, long and white with pointed pink nails. And then there was their toilet! It was not just a hole in the courtyard, like his, but a real toilet with a shiny white seat. They did not use old newspapers and wrappings to wipe themselves, as his family did, but had rolls upon rolls of soft, pastel toilet paper.

I was curious about the little girl and asked him once if I could meet her, but he retorted scornfully, "What! You want her to see this filthy hole and my ugly aunt? I would die of shame!"

Sami was a bright boy, full of fantasies. He read the Bible at school, and it triggered his imagination. Casting himself in the role of the hero of each story, he would tell me that he flew in the air, that he spoke to God, that he sailed in Noah's ark. He was also very observant, and because he saw so much and wanted even more, he could be vicious, full of jealousies and bitter hatreds.

His aunt was afraid of him. He spoke of her only rarely and always referred to her as "ugly." Sami never spoke of Leila, but he talked constantly about his father, whom he had never met. He said he admired his father because he was a very strong man, a pilot who had killed a lot of Arabs. Thanks to him, Jerusalem had been captured in the '67 war, he explained. (As far as I could tell, Ali had indeed been drafted when he had come of age, but he had never made it to the front lines. He had been assigned to kitchen duty, the menial jobs in the Israeli army being relegated almost exclusively to Oriental Jews. Soon after that, he was discharged on account of his criminal record.)

On the other hand, Sami was not very fond of the man with the dyed mustache—his aunt's husband, Busseino. When he was at home, Busseino made few demands on his family except that they leave him in peace. He would lie in bed with the sheet over his head and snore until Sami's din could no longer be ignored. Then he would thunder from beneath the sheet, *"Nishbar li hazain!"* (literally, "My prick is broken!") —a Hebrew expression for "I am fed up!"). If that produced no result, he would spring out of bed and either cuff the boy and vow to crack his head open or offer him five liras so he would take a trip to the candy store. The bribe never worked for long; five minutes later Sami was back, clamoring for more money to buy a Coke, sunflower seeds, ice cream, marbles, or whatever else he happened to fancy at the moment.

This daily ritual could be repeated five or six times until Busseino lost his temper altogether and throttled Sami. Then the boy would huddle in a corner of the room whimpering, and Busseino, unable to sleep, would storm out of the house in disgust.

Once I was so bold as to ask him why he did not try to find a job so as to set the little boy a better example. "Listen, I'm a realist," he answered me. "I know I can bust my ass working, but I still won't get anywhere. There is no future for me in this country. Maybe up there," he said, pointing at the heavens, "things will be different. And you can be sure of one thing: It will be the same for the boy, he knows it and I know it. When he is eighteen, they'll take him to the army. Perhaps he'll get killed, perhaps he won't. If he survives, this is the future that is waiting for him." He patted the bed.

"That's absurd! Why?" I exclaimed.

He laughed. "Why? Because my name isn't Goldberg or Moscowitz, that's why. It happens to be Naggar [an Oriental Jewish name]."

Busseino's life was pretty routine. He got up every day at about noon and carried a barrel of white beans that Aziza had cooked to sell to the nearby bean restaurant. Then he disappeared until dawn. Every night Aziza went to work for him; like Leila, she was a prostitute, and brought clients to their home. But though Busseino pimped, he was not connected with organized crime as Ali was. For that, he had neither the talent nor the ambition; he was interested only in making enough money to get by. Besides, he had always been a loner, he said. The son of Moroccan immigrants, he had run away from home at thirteen and drifted about, living off petty thefts and camping out in abandoned Arab houses. He had returned to his home only twice: for his father's funeral and for his sister's wedding.

I asked Busseino why Aziza did not seek some less disreputable employment outside the house in order not to embarrass Sami. Though the little boy had never said a word about his aunt's activities, he slept in the alcove immediately adjacent to her room. He told me only that at night there were always many *dodim* ("uncles") who came to visit.

Busseino answered with a shrug of the shoulders: "My wife is no professor, what could she do?" I mentioned work in a shop or restaurant, but he said, "No, she can't do that. She hasn't the patience, and besides, she can't read, she can't write, she can't count.... What do you want her to do, wash floors? Do the dishes? We have one and a half million Arabs in this country who can do that, so why should she go and do menial work for other people?"

Two months after I had gotten to know Leila, she was released from the home. The director was happy with her progress and thought she was ready to start a new life. I had doubts on the subject, for I feared that Leila would soon tire of her new job as salesgirl in a downtown shoe store. Since it was hardly remunerative, and since the municipality had made no provision for a halfway house in which the girls could lodge once they left the home, I knew she would have to depend on her pimp for a place to live, thereby once more falling under his influence.

I had reason to believe that she had been reverting to her old ways from time to time in order to pick up a few extra liras even before she was released. The social worker who saw her each day had told me that during their brief outings, the girls often plied their trade in the dark alleys and courtyards that abounded in Jerusalem.

One day I received a confirmation of this. I had taken Leila to a movie, and after dropping her off in a taxi at the home, I continued to the Hilton, where I had been invited for a drink. When we reached the hotel, I handed the cabbie a hundred-lira note, asking him to break it for me. He began fumbling in his pocket, mumbling a vulgar little Israeli ditty to himself:

Pocket Ping-Pong,
Pocket Ping-Pong.
Everyone can put his hand inside his pocket
And play Pocket Ping-Pong.

I pretended not to hear. After a few moments, the cabbie asked: "Do you mind helping me find the change?"

When I told him that I did mind, he raised his chin derisively and exclaimed: "Oh, come off your high horse! I know you girls. I've been with your friend before. When I was on reserve duty in the army, I would go to that home with some friends; we'd whistle, and the girls would come out to the fence. They were always game for a fuck."

When I reported to Leila what he had said, she laughed. I pressed her for an answer, and she confessed that she had occasionally picked up a client here and there, but mostly by the wall of the Old City (in Arab Jerusalem). I was curious about it, so she explained that Jewish and Arab prostitutes worked side by side there: The terrain had been divided up between them by a kind of tacit agreement. The Old City was an ideal place for someone who was pressed for time, and she had to be back at the home by midnight. She could always count on picking up a yeshiva boy on his way to pray at the Wailing Wall, she said, and turning a quick trick with him in one of the dark niches. Jerusalem was a paradise for prostitutes; it was blessed not only with an abundance of tourists but also with the largest single concentration of ultra-Orthodox Jews. Since Orthodox women were immured in chastity before marriage, and Orthodox wives were off-limits for at least twelve days out of every month because of the religious strictures concerning menstruation, it was Orthodox men who formed the prostitutes' most avid clientele, Leila said. There were also the Arabs.

The only time I ever heard Leila say something nice about Arabs was in this context: "They're not like the Israelis, who just shoot their stuff into you. They're real gentlemen, they whisper nice things in your ears, and caress your tits—I like that—and afterward they always take the time out to invite you for a coffee or a glass of *arak*."

My own attitude toward Leila vacillated constantly between amusement and exasperation. I did not feel comfortable with my official role as reformer; on the other hand, the authorities at the home—the director, social worker, and psychiatrist—expected me to exercise a salutary influence over her, and perhaps I was not totally immune to the gratifying self-image of the liberal who is impelled to save wrongdoers from themselves. Still, I hardly related to Leila from on high. I had the fondness and regard for her that one has for a friend. Her conversations were far more entertaining to me than the endless political talks I had with most Israelis. And her boisterous gaiety was in no way displeasing: The touch of coarseness in her voice, her shrill, tumultuous laughter, and the unselfconscious vanity with which she flaunted her flamboyant wardrobe distracted me and cheered me when I was most tired and disheartened. Upon spotting me at the entrance to the yard she would come up to me and, taking me coaxingly by the arm, whisper in my ear the latest rumor about some teacher of hers in the home. We would spend hours like this, strolling about arm in arm, idly gossiping and giggling like two schoolgirls. Later, when she left the home, I would sometimes stay overnight at her place. She would sit at the edge of my bed and breathlessly read romantic stories to me from some cheap Israeli magazine. Then, when I was too tired to concentrate anymore and had begun to doze off, she would turn off the light and sing me smutty or sentimental lullabies in that voice of hers, which was at once husky and childish. On those happy notes I would fall asleep.

Given my feelings for Leila, it was not surprising that soon after she left the home my relationship with Ali reached an all-time low. He was jealous of my influence on her, and for my part, I resented the hold he had over her. I knew that she would do anything for him, while if I asked her for the least thing she would not lift a finger.

Leila had an unthinking affection for Ali. He had been her first man and was still her only love. "He's quite a stud," she told me one day in a tone at once boastful and plaintive. "I got pregnant the very first time. I was only thirteen when my father threw me out of the house. I had never had a man before Ali. I had been kissed and once or twice I had let a boy from school touch my breasts—you know how it is—but that was all. Then Ali came along and he said if I loved him I had to let him do it to me. When he took me to the hotel room, I was too embarrassed to remove my clothes, so I only took off my panties. But he said, 'Yala, yala' ["Come on, come on," in Arabic], so I had to take off the rest too. I was frightened to death when I saw how big his thing was. It was the first time I had seen a man naked, and I began to cry and begged him not to do it to me. But he pushed me down on the bed. It hurt me terribly; I screamed loud enough to bring down the walls.

"After I had Sami he put me to work for him. He wouldn't touch me up front anymore. I had to let him have my ass. He said he was afraid one of my clients might have given me the clap. But I think he just enjoyed it better that way. I hated it. One day he ripped me up so bad I had to go to the hospital. Well, that scared him good. Now, whenever

I'm on the job, he only has me suck him. It's pretty disgusting; still, I'd rather have him squirting in my mouth than ramming his telephone pole up my rear!''

A few weeks after Leila left the home, she had a very bad row with Ali, in the course of which he smashed the toy plane I had given her. She told me that when she responded by threatening to stop working for him, he took a penknife out of his pocket and vowed to cut her face if she ever quit. "Just a little souvenir," he had said with a leer, "before we say good-bye, so you won't forget me."

On hearing this, I left a message in the café on Ben-Yehuda Street where Ali hung out whenever he was in town "on business," saying that he should call me the next time he put in an appearance. When he called two weeks later, I told him that if he ever threatened Leila again, I would report him to the police. "Oh yeah," he jeered, "I would just love to see you prove your accusation. Leila is the biggest liar!" Then he went on to tell me in a voice trembling with anger that I was a *chor batachat* ("asshole") and that I had better get one thing into my head: His quarrels with Leila were none of my business. "Just lay off her. She's a toy for you. You come here as a tourist and you stuff her head with all kinds of crazy ideas. But one day you'll leave, and then what? She'll have to go back to the same old life and the same old shit. Don't kid yourself about that."

Much as I hated to admit it to myself, there was a lot of truth in what Ali said. But I was not yet ready to give up my role as Leila's savior, nor for that matter to concede the victory to Ali. After speaking to him, I immediately rushed over to Leila's place and, without the slightest hesitation, told her she must choose between us. She sat on the bed gnawing her nails but would say nothing. I lost my temper and yelled that if she had such a low sense of self-worth as to put up with this kind of treatment, I did not want to see her ever again. Then I left.

Three days later a door slammed downstairs to announce her presence—Leila could never resist slamming every door she passed through. By then I was firmly resolved not to talk to her, but when I saw her standing there in her red muslin dress and gold bangles, her gold-flecked Byzantine eyes looking at me penitently, I weakened. In a disdainful, petulant voice, she offered never to see Ali again. I knew, of course, that she would not be able to live up to her resolution; still, it flattered me to think I had wrenched this concession from her. For that moment, the satisfaction of scoring against Ali was probably more important to me than the benefits Leila would reap by leaving him.

Our friendship took up again where it had left off. I was aware that she was capable of any meanness or betrayal, and I would have liked her to believe that my indulgence came purely from my goodness of heart. Unfortunately, I knew she was far too intelligent not to realize her power over me.

Why was I so attached to Leila? She exasperated me and made me love her at the same time. I hated that she would abandon herself to someone like Ali and resented that I couldn't give her the self-worth that had been so long denied her. Yet I also understood: The hunger in her for intimacy, excitement, and attention, even at great cost, was a quality I recognized in myself. Leila was no stranger to me, no charity case. Even as I fought against what she revealed to me, I could not deny my identification and affinity with her. I fought, but not only on her behalf.

8

The Soul-Snatchers

ON THE SABBATH, in the part of Jerusalem called Mea Shearim, the men stow away their black costumes, and the bleak old quarter is buoyant with color.

There are old men whose long beards spread out majestically over Ottoman robes of crimson satin or priceless golden caftans, tokens of their descent from old Jerusalemite families; there are Sephardic Jews with black conical hats and striped Arab gowns, and Chasidim from Eastern Europe who, with their black trousers tucked into knee-length white stockings and their frock coats fastened around the waist with silk cords, look as though they have just stepped out of a Rembrandt painting.

Young men wearing plump fur hats, the height of fashion in seventeenth-century Europe, strut about holding their heads high like falcons. Behind them—always at a respectful distance—come their wives, dainty young women in long, puffed-sleeved frocks, their newly shaved heads covered with black silk scarves or with wigs freshly crimped for the Sabbath.

On the Sabbath, Mea Shearim isolates itself even more completely from the twentieth century. No cars are allowed in the quarter. No movies. No television. No radios. All the shop grilles are lowered and bolted.

The quarter's gnarled alleys teem with people, but they are filled with another time, another rhythm. They reverberate with the soft tones of Yiddish and the rippling laughter of children: pale-faced little girls like antique dolls from Poland in their pink organzas and lilac tulles, little boys in blue sailor suits with wide linen collars. The streets swell with the cantor's low wail from the synagogue and with the thick warm odors of *cholent* stews. On Sabbath, Mea Shearim takes a deep breath of the crisp Jerusalem air and rests under a peaceful blue sky.

The name Mea Shearim ("Hundred Portions") comes from a sentence in the Bible that begins with those words and was read in the synagogue the day the quarter's foundations were laid in 1874. It was built to accommodate the numerous new arrivals from Eastern Europe—the Chasidim ("Pious Ones")—for whom there was not enough space inside the walls of the Old City. Their spokesman, an ultra-Orthodox Dutch lawyer and journalist by the name of Dr. Jacob de Haan, was a charismatic man of many talents and a known homosexual who composed moving poetry about being torn between his love for God and his desire for the Arab boy. He wrote of waiting for his lover by the synagogue wall at night and the next day contemplating the hands that clasped the holy book, lamenting, "What have these same hands touched last night, in the dark!"

De Haan, bitterly opposed to the Zionist settlers, led the fight against them. In his hatred of them he went to lengths that some considered treacherous, establishing contacts with Arab leaders and British politicians opposed to Jewish statehood and trying to organize a joint front with them to combat Zionism. This aroused such bitter hostility that he was assassinated by the Haganah, the Jewish military organization in Palestine, which denied the act, claiming he had been killed by one of his Arab lovers.

The residents of Mea Shearim still withhold the payment of taxes to a state they refuse to recognize, and therefore do not receive the same amenities as other Israeli citizens. Until recently, they baked in the communal oven, fetched water from the local well, and lit their homes with oil lamps. And while Mea Shearim today has electricity and running water, it remains a poor neighborhood that depends heavily on charity from religious Jews overseas. The men in Mea Shearim have no time to earn a living; their lives are consecrated to God.

I first became interested in the neighborhood when I was promoted to an advanced course at Ulpan Etzion. I had caught on to Hebrew quickly because of its similarity to Arabic, and after I had been at the Ulpan for four months, my teacher thought I was ready for a more challenging program. My new classmates, who read the highly literary biblical Hebrew with the greatest ease even though they could not speak the language, were for the most part young men in skullcaps. They were either currently enrolled part-time in a yeshiva or headed for one. This pleased me, for I was eager to meet Orthodox Jews. I had had no contact with them until then; religious Jews were none too popular in the ferociously secular Kibbutz Vatik. During those occasional forays we had taken into the city, whenever my kibbutz friends chanced to encounter someone in black frock and earlocks, they would make a face behind his back or mimic him so derisively that they would have been considered anti-Semitic if they had been Gentiles.

The most interesting of my classmates at the Ulpan was Saul, a black Jew from Ethiopia, whom I befriended. He told me his people, the Falashas ("Wanderers"), were a Jewish aristocracy that dated back to the reign of King Solomon. According to him, after a visit with King Solomon, the Queen of Sheba, an Ethiopian, returned home pregnant and eventually gave birth to a son, who was sent to his father to be reared as a Jew. When the son reached manhood, King Solomon asked him to return to Ethiopia and establish a royal line, the Solomonic dynasty.

But the rabbinate in Israel did not recognize the Jewishness of the Falashas, because as a community that split off from the mainstream of Judaism very early on, they had only the Bible to rely on—not the rabbinical interpretations of it (Mishnah and Gemara), which were compiled later—and as a result they did not follow the Jewish rituals prescribed in the Talmud. Though they adhered, for example, to the biblical commandment to circumcise baby boys on the eighth day following birth, they did not follow other regulations of rabbinic Judaism. Saul would have to be symbolically circumcised as part of his "conversion" to Judaism—a drop of blood drawn by a pinprick—failing which he would not be allowed to marry a Jew; in fact, he could not marry anyone in Israel, since no civil marriage existed.

Saul attributed all this to racism, and the fact that he had difficulty finding an Israeli girl who would go out with him on a date no doubt contributed to his feeling. "Just look how different Israeli attitudes are toward the Russian Jewish immigrants here," he told me, his indignation all too plainly visible in his lean face. "They have been intermarrying with Christians for generations, so there is no way of knowing which ones of them qualify according to the *Halacha* [religious laws] as Jews. Many of them don't follow religious practices and have never been circumcised—yet no one says they have to be! Everybody recognizes them as Jews, and the authorities moved heaven and earth to get them here, while for years and years no one would lift a finger to help us emigrate to Israel. Quite the contrary, we were discouraged by the Israeli consulate officials in Ethiopia, even though they knew our people lived in extreme poverty often bordering on starvation. It's only recently that they've begun to admit us."

It was Saul who first showed me around Mea Shearim. He was attending a yeshiva there part-time, since he wanted to become a rabbi. After that day, I returned to Mea Shearim again and again. Through Saul and my other religious classmates, all matters relating to Jewish tradition had acquired a great fascination for me. I would stand for hours on end at the entrance to the quarter, watching the animated crowd, intoxicated by their rhythms. Secretly I nurtured the hope that someone would stop and talk to me, but no one ever did. Occasionally some child might point a finger at me and giggle, reminding me that I was as exotic to him as he to me. If I crossed the paths of men, they never looked at me; only their cringing as they backed away hinted that they were at all conscious of my presence. Once, catching sight of a black-frocked youth scuttling down the alley with downcast eyes, I barred his way, hoping to get him to speak to me. But he merely shot a side-glance at me and, before I had a chance to open my mouth, spat in my direction. The spittle landed on my shoe.

For a long time after that, I kept my distance from men in black garb, effacing myself like an abject shadow at their passage to spare them the defilement of my womanhood. But one evening I went back to Mea Shearim and boldly ventured into the large internal courtyard of its main compound. It was empty. It seemed as if the inhabitants of these somber dwellings, acting on a premonition of my visit, had fled to their shadowy walls and remained invisible. I wandered about aimlessly for a few minutes and then came upon a notice posted on a wooden shopfront. It was a quotation from a Talmudic authority: "A man shall not walk between two women, two dogs, or two pigs, and two men shall not allow a woman, a dog, or a pig to walk between them."

Engrossed by these words, I had not noticed the person who was threading his way down the narrow spiral staircase behind me. When I heard steps, I whirled around and grabbed the dark figure by the sleeve. Surprisingly, the man did not seem in the least unnerved, nor did he pull away. Instead, he smiled and asked in American-accented Hebrew what I wanted. Encouraged by this, I introduced myself and found out his name was Rabbi Hirsh. Then I begged him to let me come visit one day. "Why?" he asked, somewhat taken aback, and since I could not think of anything terribly persuasive to say, I told him the truth: that I wanted to see how the residents of this neighborhood lived, that there was nothing I desired more ardently than to be admitted into one of their houses. He replied that it was out of the question; he could not have a woman visitor. When I continued to implore him, he was finally moved by my eagerness to agree at least to come to the Ulpan and tell me about life in Mea Shearim.

It was terribly inconvenient for me to receive him at Ulpan Etzion, since the common room was noisy and I clearly could not talk to him in my bedroom. But rather than lose this chance, I decided to beg the director to allow me to use the staff room after classes were out. I gave Rabbi Hirsh the address; he showed no trace of recognition. He explained that in order to minimize their contact with Zionists, the members of Neturei Karta, his sect, rarely left their own quarters. As their secretary and spokesman, he got around more than the others. He had to meet with foreign visitors and sometimes undertook purchases or banking transactions for the community. But he added: "I would not touch that filthy Zionist lucre with a ten-foot pole. I always refuse the hundred-lira notes because they have the picture of Theodor Herzl, nor will I accept those with President Weizmann on them. I take only coins or small bills with pictures of non-Zionists, like Einstein and Montefiori [the English-Jewish philanthropist]."

Since he had never had cause to set foot in my neighborhood and hadn't the foggiest notion of how to get there (although it was a mere ten-minute drive from Mea Shearim), I gave him detailed directions: He should walk up to Rechov Strauss, which intersected Mea Shearim, and catch the number 6 bus . . . Here he interrupted to inform me, somewhat caustically, that he never took a Zionist bus because they did not observe the Sabbath; he traveled only in taxis driven by religious Jews or Arabs.

Notwithstanding all these reservations, Rabbi Hirsh did arrive at the Ulpan. And there he was, in a closed room, all alone with a young Arab woman. He refused to take off his black coat and hat and sat stiffly upright on the edge of the couch, his legs virginally clamped together, his pale hands resting rigidly on his knees. For him to have ventured so far out of Mea Shearim into the jungle of secular society must have been like undertaking a dangerous safari. But Rabbi Hirsh was a brave man. His face was composed, and he even managed to smile.

I, on the other hand, was very nervous. Feeling too intimidated to talk at first, I retreated into the kitchenette, where the faculty prepared their morning coffee. As I stood there, mentally wrestling with the enigma of what to offer him, I heard him call out: "Please, I can't have anything. Your Ulpan is not kosher." I returned to the staff room, and we sat for a few moments, staring at each other in silence. Then he apologized for not having received me in his house, but assured me that he had made a special concession by coming to meet me. He would not have done it were I not an Arab, he said. I expressed some surprise at this, to which he replied: "Why are you surprised? For centuries, the Jewish people lived more peacefully with their Arab neighbors than with any other goyim. There have also been Jews in the Holy Land ever since the destruction of the Temple, and they never had any trouble with Arabs until the Zionists came. As a result of the Zionist movement we have had nearly twenty thousand Jews killed in Palestine, and another six million killed in Europe. The Holocaust was God's punishment, because the Talmud teaches us that we are bound by oath not to take the Holy Land back by force—that we are to endure our exile. The Zionists have in effect said, 'Look here, God! Exile is not very pleasant, and if you won't return our land to us, we'll just roll up our sleeves and take it ourselves.' "

I stared at him incredulously. The specter of divine retribution had brought color to his long, pale face. The tip of his bulbous nose was flushed, his blue eyes were smoldering, and even the wisps of reddish hair that sprouted limply on his chin bristled with animation.

I wondered why he should fear God's wrath, since he was not a Zionist.

"As Jews," he explained, "we don't believe in individual responsibility; we are responsible for one another and subject to collective punishment. The Bible says that during our term of exile, we are to be scattered among different nations of the world so that no tyrant will be able to annihilate all of the Jewish people at once. This is precisely what we fear will happen here at the hands of the Arabs as a result of the premature ingathering of the Jews. We don't want to suffer the same fate as the Zionists."

At this point he interrupted himself and asked me what I thought of the Palestine Liberation Organization. I replied that in my view it was the only legitimate representative of the Palestinian nation. He smiled approvingly, saying he could not agree more: He himself had written a letter of congratulations to Arafat following his recognition as leader of the Palestinian people by the U.N. In it he told Arafat that if he were to form a Palestinian government in exile, members of Neturei Karta would be happy to serve as consultants on Jewish affairs. As Rabbi Hirsh saw it, there was a striking accord between the views of Palestinians and those of Neturei Karta, as well as between their circumstances. Both of them wanted a distinction to be made between Judaism and Zionism, and both favored a secular, nonsectarian government in Palestine. Furthermore, Rabbi Hirsh informed me, for years Neturei Karta had been agitating to get the United Nations to recognize them as refugees. There was no difference, in his view, between a people that was "pushed out of its land and one like ourselves whose land is being wrenched from under it by the Zionists."

A Palestinian government in the Holy Land was preferable to Zionist rule: "God first gave the land to Isaac," he continued, "then exiled us and gave this land in trust to the sons of Ishmael until such time as the Messiah comes and our Temple is rebuilt and a Jewish king enthroned. Until then, we are obligated not to rebel against any government by the sons of Ishmael in the Holy Land."

By that time, nothing Rabbi Hirsh said would have surprised me. But I couldn't help playing devil's advocate, and I asked him how he could justify taking up with people the Israelis considered to be the killers of their women and children.

To which he replied without batting an eye: "Would you meet with Prime Minister Rabin?"

I said that I *had* met with him.

"Well! Mr. Rabin orders the bombing of refugee camps in Lebanon every day—he does not shy away from the spilling of civilian blood. And when the Americans threw their atom bomb on Hiroshima, was that not an act of terrorism at its most potent? Nobody looked at America and said, 'Those terrorists, they are spilling the blood of innocent people!' "

We had been talking for nearly two hours, and he now seemed remarkably at ease in his new setting. I decided to venture a second attempt at offering him a beverage. I was aware that he couldn't eat anything at my place, I told him, but surely he would have something to drink.

"No, no," he said, holding up his palms in front of his face as though to shield himself from invisible germs. "I really don't want anything, thank you very much."

"I'll just make you a cup of tea, that must be okay!"

He raised his eyebrows as though he had some doubts on the subject and then said with a tone of resignation, "*Nu, meile* ["Never mind," in Yiddish], let it be tea."

Pleased with my victory, I retired to the kitchenette and took pains to prepare a cup of Earl Grey. I placed it before him and slumped into the armchair, but the expression on his face made me straighten up anxiously.

"That's milk!" he exclaimed.

"Don't you like milk in your tea?" I asked, already regretting my excess of zeal.

"Yes, I do. But I can't have it here, your milk is not kosher."

This time I was totally bewildered. It was my understanding that all food products in Israel were kosher, processed under strict rabbinical supervision.

I expressed my puzzlement. He explained that Neturei Karta members could never be certain of milk produced outside their own premises. "What's to assure me that this is not the product of some kibbutz that disregards the commands and milks its cows on the Sabbath? These Zionists have no morality, I tell you, no fear of God." He made as if to spit.

There was clearly no room for argument, so I hastened back to the kitchenette and sorrowfully poured out the expensive imported English tea. Lest he should suspect that I had merely rinsed out the cup, thus allowing a few invisible drops of milk to remain behind, I discarded it in favor of a mug with an engraving of the Wailing Wall, which I thought appropriate. I had barely reentered the room when his dismayed voice brought me to a halt: "Earthenware cup? I am sorry, I can't drink out of that. It is porous and may have absorbed some milk from previous usage. I only drink from a glass when I'm on a visit."

Back to the kitchen. I put fresh water on the fire. By now, I felt like Louis Pasteur working feverishly in his lab to overcome a pernicious epidemic. At last, looking as congenial as humanly possible, I presented him with the glass. He thanked me and put it on the table. Just as I began to relax, I heard a crack: The heat of the tea had shattered the glass. We both burst out laughing.

When he got over his mirth, Rabbi Hirsh seemed to remember my mug with the Wailing Wall: "We, the people of Neturei Karta, never go to the Wailing Wall, although we have more feeling for it than any secular Zionist, nor have we ever set foot in the Tomb of the Patriarchs in Hebron. We'd rather live in peace with our Arab neighbors than have access to our shrines. We despise the way the Zionists manipulate the Wall for nationalist purposes! We would prefer to see Jerusalem internationalized."

In Rabbi Hirsh's view, the only way to foil the Zionist plan of using religion as an instrument for their nationalist goals was to insist on a strict separation of church and state.

I was nonplussed. It was the first time I had heard a rabbi pronounce himself in favor of this. I asked him if he realized that by favoring such a separation he was opting for a secular state. "Absolutely! We want the Jewish religion to remain completely separate from the political and secular activities of these perfidious Zionists. Without the church, without Mafdal [the largest religious party] and the chief rabbi legitimizing all their parades and their affairs, the state would be out of business in no time—the Jewish people would not be tempted to terminate their exile and come here without waiting for the Messiah."

We had gotten on famously, Rabbi Hirsh and I, so as he began to leave I pressed upon him once more my plea for an invitation to his house. Finally he agreed to let me visit him, and I felt as though I had received a pass to the gates of heaven. Time after time I had been led to believe that to visit the residents of Mea Shearim was an extraordinary privilege that I would never attain.

When the day came, I put on a blouse and a long skirt. The blouse seemed filmy; I removed it and tried on a jersey instead. It molded my breasts too much, so I decided to wear the blouse underneath it in order to flatten out my chest. Finally, I slipped on a blazer over the lot—the more wrapping the better, I thought.

Swaddled so from head to foot, I set out for Rabbi Hirsh's house. Once I reached Mea Shearim, I passed under the arcade with the warning, in English, "Kosher daughter of Israel, do not go about in whorish clothes: Wearing short sleeves is defilement," and entered the internal courtyard. Still other posters inveighed against the drafting of girls into the "brothel-like" Israeli army and warned women not to go to the "lewd" public swimming pools, where men and women swam together. On the doorway facing the arcade was a sign reading A HOUSE OF LEARNING. I peered through the window of that building and saw the lolling heads of little boys with cherubic faces and golden earlocks listening to a dour-faced, black-frocked teacher who read sternly from the Torah. Then I came to a wall covered with scrawled messages: "Jews: Remember to hoist a black flag on Independence Day: Mourn 37 years of rebellion against God" and "It is forbidden to take part in government elections." Rabbi Hirsh's apartment lay within arm's reach.

I made my way up to the overhead landing and saw, underneath the gilded nameplate on the door, a notice in English, Hebrew, and Arabic that read: "I am a Jew, not a Zionist."

Rabbi Hirsh's wife greeted me coldly, with the haughty air of an irreproachably devout woman, and then plunged into the kitchen, where she spent the remainder of my visit furiously scouring the pans. It was clear, to say the least, that she disapproved of my presence. I caught a fleeting glimpse of two kids scurrying off into the bedroom. Then I was left alone with Rabbi Hirsh.

To judge from the little I could see, the Hirsh apartment was modest but dignified. The living room, where we sat, was actually a study and served as the family's dining room as well. Aside from the table, the furniture consisted of a few old wooden chairs and a glass bookcase whose left side had been smashed. A beautiful white lace curtain adorned the tall window, and the brass oil lamp and candlestick on the ledge had been so well polished that they sparkled like mirrors.

My eyes lingered rapturously on every object, for the magic with which I had imbued the lives of these religious people was not dispelled now that I had at last succeeded in making my way into one of their homes.

Rabbi Hirsh told me that his family had emigrated from Poland to New York City. They had been part of an ultra-Orthodox community in Williamsburg whose residents still refused to recognize the state of Israel.

"What about your wife?" I asked. "Is she Israeli?"

He chuckled. "Now you are talking like a Zionist! No, she is Palestinian, a Jerusalemite whose lineage in the Holy Land goes back many generations." When I asked how he had met her, he told me it had been through a *shadchan* ("matchmaker"). He described the initial meeting, arranged by the *shadchan* for the purpose of matrimony, and the few visits that followed, always in the presence of a chaperon.

Just then, we heared a faint creak. The door at the other end of the corridor was slowly opening, and presently a sprightly little girl with long red braids burst into the room. She looked very much like her father, except that the same features in her were harmonious. She had sparkling blue eyes, an ivory complexion, and a small round nose. Her chin was dimpled, and her full lips drooped slightly at the edges, cutting an enigmatic smile across her otherwise angelic countenance.

I tried to engage her in conversation by asking if she was going to school, but I extracted no more than a smothered giggle before she hastily ducked out of sight. Her father told me that she attended a religious school where the language of instruction was Yiddish rather than Hebrew, because the use of Hebrew would imply an acceptance of the Zionist goal of a Jewish national renaissance. The members of Neturei Karta believed the sacred language should be used only in prayer. I asked him if all she studied at school was the Bible, to which he replied that they got one hour a day of "so-called" secular education—arithmetic, reading, and writing.

"We find the Talmud rich enough to satisfy their secular needs. Our daughters aren't going to go on to become whores in college—if you'll excuse the expression. We don't even want our sons to go to college."

"And how does the education of the girls differ from that of the boys?" I asked.

"It says in the Talmud that it is forbidden for the girls to study the Torah—any woman who does so is a demon. The girls go to separate schools where they study only the laws that apply to women and they have cooking and sewing lessons. In a word, they learn how to bring up families, Jewish families, who will follow all the commandments."

"Can't a woman have a profession at all?"

"She can teach other girls, be a seamstress or a salesperson in order to provide some economic assistance to her husband so he will be able to devote more time to his Torah studies. But her main role is to have many good Jewish children. We take very seriously the biblical injunction against wasting the seed. To refrain from having children because you want to study a few years in peace, or because you are poor, are not good reasons. You have to believe in God—He will find a way."

"But what about these huge Oriental families, Jews whose children finish up in the street as dope pushers and prostitutes?"

"I'll tell you, those children should be sent to religious orphanages; we have many of them in Palestine. They will grow up much better there than at home—not only materially, but spiritually. Besides, who says that the large families of the poor have more problems than the rich? Go to Savion [a rich suburb of Tel Aviv] and you'll see the children. They are sick in the head, they become homosexuals, Zen Buddhists, all kinds of things, and end up spending half their lives on the psychiatric couch."

I could see that when it came to girls, Rabbi Hirsh's mind was quite made up, so I switched to the subject of the opposite sex, asking him how he expected to get the doctors and the engineers his community needed if the boys were taught only the Torah. "Listen to me, Sana, the world needs two types of tradesmen—the perfumer and the tanner. Both are necessary to civilization, but every parent would prefer his child to deal with good odors than with bad odors. Each Jewish parent chooses for his child what is most nutritious for his soul, which is everlasting, while its material counterpart is cast aside. The highest aspiration of every Jewish father is for his boy to become the greatest Talmudic scholar, the greatest sage, and to study the divine law twenty-four hours a day for a hundred and twenty years!"

"And what if your body is sick?"

"Doctors are in the world whether I or my children provide them or not. God will provide them. There will always be plenty of goyim. My wife and I go to Arab doctors and to Arab hospitals—never to Jewish ones. In fact, when our leader, Rabbi Blau, God bless his memory, was dying, he refused to go to Hadassah Hospital because they perform autopsies and all kinds of experiments on the sick. Many times we've demonstrated against the postmortem autopsies carried out in Jewish hospitals.

"We have had many battles against the state," he continued. "Sometimes we won, sometimes not. In the fifties, we demonstrated against public transportation to the beach on the Sabbath. It was a very violent demonstration and one of our men was killed—a policeman clubbed him over the head. We also demonstrated against the traffic through our streets on the Sabbath. We won those battles. Then we demonstrated against sexually mixed swimming in the first public swimming pool in Katamon, but we were defeated. Recently we demonstrated against a pornography shop in Jerusalem, and an incendiary bomb was thrown through its window. The case went to court, and we won. You must have noticed the scandalous clothing of women in Jerusalem, which is supposed to be the holiest city in the world. Even Arab women, whose attire would be to the credit of the Jewish people, are being led astray by Zionist immodesty. And have you seen the billboards with movie advertisements in this city, which is sacred to a billion and a half Jews, Christians, and Muslims? You don't have to be a Jew to be offended by them; an animal would be insulted!"

I asked him whether he himself had ever taken part in any demonstration.

"Have *I*?" he exclaimed, puffing himself up till I thought his coat buttons would burst. "I was in prison on account of one of them not too long ago. And it wasn't my first time, either. This last time there were eighty of us jailed, and I was thrown into solitary confinement with a Fatah man [a Palestinian guerrilla]. I arrived there in the middle of the night during Passover, and the Fatah man was overjoyed to see me. He offered me bananas and apples, and he gave me his address and a message for his mother that he was alive, which I conveyed to her after my release. He understood that I was a Jew, not a Zionist—he saw that the two of us were in jail, and the Zionists were outside."

Rabbi Hirsh beckoned me over to his bookshelf and pulled out a copy of a print with the silhouette of an armed guerrilla, under which was written *"Palestine en lutte"* ("Palestine in struggle"). His Fatah friend had given it to him during their stay in prison, he said with a puckish smile. Then he leaned over and whispered, "Some of our group are in Cairo distributing pamphlets this very moment."

"Really! What kind of pamphlets?"

"Anti-Zionist pamphlets. Would you like to see one?"

"Of course!"

He puttered around gathering up a few pamphlets and flyers and handed them to me. One of them read: "Zionists—it is not enough that the blood of thousands of Israelis is spilt on the altar of your unbelieving state. Give back at least the territories you captured with the blood of thousands in the Six-Day War, for their blood will be sought from you."

The address at the bottom read pointedly: "Neturei Karta of the Orthodox Jewry, P.O. Box 5053, Jerusalem, Palestine."

"Would you like to take some of these home to Egypt?" he asked.

"Sure," I replied, unwilling to offend him.

"The Zionist customs officials at Ben-Gurion Airport might be awfully interested in them!" He chortled, halfway between exhilaration and defiance.

I did not see Rabbi Hirsh again, but my religious indoctrination did not stop with him.

One day Ulpan Etzion organized an excursion to Masada, the fortress where a group of Jewish Zealots, who refused to accept Roman rule, had lived for six years before committing mass suicide. I was quite exhausted by the time we had climbed to the top of the mountain, and decided that instead of going on to the nearby springs of Ein-Gedi with the rest of the group, I would hitch a ride back to Jerusalem.

For some time I walked along the dusty shoreline road without seeing a single car. Beneath the bare cliffs, the sea lay torpid and motionless, ringed by a crust of brine as thick as glass. Nothing violated the awesome tranquillity of these waters except for a few blackened tree stumps and the pillars of salt left behind to commemorate the fate of Lot's wife.

When I saw an old jalopy coming toward me with a young couple in the front seat, I flagged it down. The driver said they were headed for Jerusalem, and I sank exhausted into the back seat. As soon as we were off, the woman asked me where I was from. I did not feel like unraveling the whole of my life history just then, so I said, "The States," and closed my eyes, hoping she would get the hint. Instead, she said joyfully, "So are we! My husband and I!" Then I noticed her wig, and she immediately acquired fresh interest in my eyes. She was fair, and she squinted a little behind her glasses, which added a touch of innocence to her wide blue eyes. He was slender, with blond locks tucked behind his ears and a sparse tuft of hair at the tip of his round chin, which, because he had no growth on his cheeks, made him look like a prepubescent trying to grow a beard.

Afraid they might notice that I had no American accent, I proceeded to cook up a story about being born in Egypt and having left with the Jews who emigrated to the States after the '67 war. And what was I doing in Israel? the woman asked. When I told her I was a tourist, she whispered something to her husband. Then she asked my name. I had to lie again: I said it was Sarah. She told me that hers was Judith and her husband's David; they both came from Milwaukee.

I asked Judith why they had come to Israel, and she seemed surprised by my question. Then she said fervently: "Like the eel that swims thousands of miles to reach the ocean, like the salmon that returns to spawn where it was born, like the birds that fly to faraway countries, the Jews —all of them—have to come here. It's the spiritual center that brings them closer to God."

I sat silently for the rest of the trip, gazing across the sea at the Jordanian mountains, which were reddening like bricks in the fire of the late-afternoon sun. At the entrance to Jerusalem, Judith asked me if I'd like to come home with them for a cup of coffee. I hesitated, because I was very tired. Yet visits to religious people's homes were still a rarity for me, and I hated to pass up this opportunity.

It was dark by the time we reached their neighborhood, so I was unable to get a good view of it, but it seemed to me on first sight to have none of the quaint charm of Mea Shearim. With its modern concrete apartment buildings, it would have been indistinguishable from any Jerusalem quarter were it not for the black-frocked men who hurried back and forth.

Judith led me up to a plainly furnished two-and-a-half-room apartment. We sat at the dining table in a corner of the living room, and she offered me some cake with the coffee. I accepted gratefully, for I was hungry. I drank the coffee hastily and was going to work on the cake when I noticed David's reproachful look. Apologizing for wolfing down the food, I started explaining that I had had no dinner, but he interrupted by saying that I should have proffered the blessing first. Blushing, I confessed that I did not know the blessing and began to panic at the thought of being exposed. But Judith told me comfortingly not to be embarrassed: She sympathized with my problem, having herself come from a Reform background, with parents who neither observed the Sabbath nor kept kashrut. As it turned out, two separate prayers had to be offered, one for the coffee and the other for the cake. But since I had already disposed of the former, Judith told me, "Now take a piece of cake on your fork and say, '*Baruch Ata Adonai Elocheinu Melech Haolam, Bore Pri Hamezonot. Amen*' ["Blessed are Thou, O Lord our God, King of the Universe and Creator of Nourishment"]."

The incident left me uneasy, and I resolved to eat quickly and flee before they discovered I was an impostor. What followed, however, made me change my mind.

When I had finished eating, Judith said that there was something she felt compelled to tell me. She and her husband had consecrated their lives to missionary work. Masada was their base of operation; they visited it often because it was always teeming with tourists, and when they saw young Jews who, like myself, were aimlessly drifting about, they tried to bring them back to the true path. They would invite them home for coffee and seek to revive their interest in Judaism. More often than not they succeeded, and would then offer to have them spend the night or, if there was already a houseguest, find another home for them in the neighborhood. Such hosts were not hard to find, because it was considered a divine duty (*mitzvah*) in this Orthodox neighborhood to make a secular youth repent and embrace Orthodoxy. Guests were then asked to prolong their stay for a few days, and religious instruction would begin almost at once. A pair of scissors applied to a young man's long hair made for beautiful earlocks, and a girl would exchange her jeans for black stockings and a "decent" hemline. Then they would be channeled into Mount Zion Yeshiva (the only one in Israel to accept girls). Sometimes the girls would be kept on as household members to help out with chores and with the host family's often numerous children until suitable marriages with Orthodox youths could be worked out for them by a *shadchan*.

Judith proposed that I stay on in their house for a few days to discover the beauties of the religious life, for, while most of the missionary work in their neighborhood centered around the saving of young men, she herself believed in the importance of reeducating young women because of the vital role they played in raising the future generation.

Moments before she had revealed her motive to me, I had been about to tell her my real identity, but now I thought to myself, why not? Here at last was a chance to live the religious life, which I had so far witnessed only as an outsider. I stifled my scruples and accepted her offer. Judith and David were obviously elated and went out of their way to make me feel welcome. David drove me back to the Ulpan that evening and waited in the car while I got a few things and left word in the office that I would be absent for several days.

My initiation into Orthodox Judaism began the next morning. Judith and I sat at the dining room table while David was in the next room, immersed in his holy books. "The first thing you should know is that the Torah was created one thousand years before the world," said Judith. "And the second thing you should know is that the Torah is the blueprint for the world. The world was created to fit the Torah, and not the other way around. Take, for example, the palm tree. The reason it was created is that during the feast of Sukkot, which celebrates the last harvest of the year, the Torah commands that a bouquet be made of a branch of the palm tree together with a citron, a bough of a leafy tree, and a branch of the willow."

Then Judith wanted to know if I understood why God had left His creation unfinished. "Why, for example, when a man could have been circumcised, was he left uncircumcised?" When I confessed I was at a loss for an answer, she hugged me with delight and, pulling out a book called *The Jew and His Home,* told me the answer: "The author of this work starts out by saying that in his kindness to us, God left His world incomplete. At first, this might seem paradoxical. The incompleteness of the world looks more like an inconvenience, a cruelty on God's part. The idea behind it, however, is that God wants us to be partners in His creation—just like a mother who will call on her small child to give a last stir to the cake batter in order to let him feel he's helping her."

In addition to my Bible lessons, there was practical instruction. The first thing I had to be taught was how to keep a Jewish home. Judith taught me the many special duties that were incumbent on a woman, such as the baking of the Sabbath bread and the lighting of the candles. This had to be undertaken no sooner than an hour and a quarter and no later than eighteen minutes before sunset every Friday night. After I had covered my hair with a kerchief, I would draw my hands around the candles and toward my face three times and say the blessing to thank the Lord for separating light from darkness, the Sabbath from the workdays, holiness from profanity, and the Jews from all other nations.

Judith had a splendid silver menorah, a family heirloom, taller than any I had seen. It dominated the small living room, as it must have done the altar of some temple of old. Four animals were encrusted on it: a lion, a gazelle, a tiger, and an eagle—the ones that, according to the prophet Yechezkel, sat on the throne of God. Every Jew, Judith taught me, had to combine the strength of the lion, the dexterity of the tiger, the sharpness of the eagle, and the fleetness of the gazelle in carrying out God's laws. I could well see why so many talents would be needed when I learned how many of those laws there were: six hundred and thirteen.

First came the kosher laws. On my second day in the house, we all had to go to bed hungry because I had inadvertently used the cheese knife to slice the cold turkey, thereby making it nonkosher. Then there were the laws of purity *(tahara).* Judith explained that once I was married, I could neither have intercourse during my menstrual cycle—the minimum period of abstinence was five days, plus another seven after the bleeding stopped—nor let my husband come into contact with any part of my body, even my little finger. After the first child was born, the period of abstinence would be increased to seven days, plus another seven blood-free days. In addition, after each delivery I had to do without sex for three weeks if it was a boy and double that if I was "not so blessed" and had a girl. She warned me that if I violated these rules, my fetus would, according to the Talmud, never see the light of day, and any child I already had would be stricken dead. Before my husband could touch me again, I would have to "purify" my body through immersion in the ritual bath at the local *mikvah*. Judith showed me how to undergo this bath, which, not surprisingly, turned out to be a complicated affair. First I had to wash myself thoroughly in order to make sure that no dried blood was left on me, that my hair, toes, and nails were perfectly clean, and that all traces of any facial cream had been removed. As an extra precaution, I then had to roll a piece of white linen into the shape and size of a tampon and insert it into me, examining it afterward to make sure it was not stained. When I asked her why I need go to such great lengths, she answered that it was absolutely crucial that I do so because, according to the Talmud, at the time of the woman's "impurity" her blood contains poisons dangerous to the man. Only after I had tested myself in this fashion could I take my ritual bath. I would stand, feet apart, arms stretched forward with fingers outspread, and, closing my eyes and lips, kneel in the pool of water, immersing myself till my head was covered. After this, I would say, "Blessed art Thou, O Lord our God, King of the Universe, Who has made us holy with Thy commandment."

On the morning after my arrival, Judith slipped out of the house while I was still asleep to buy me what she called modest clothing. When I woke up, she presented me with a long-sleeved, ankle-length white dress. I was touched by her kindness, even though the small gilded ribbons, the frills, and the lace around the cuffs and waistline made me look rather like a garish statue of the Madonna decked out for a religious procession in a Spanish village. As I was slipping on the dress, Judith asked me shyly whether I was a virgin. My bold-faced lie seemed to reassure her—at least temporarily. But two days later she returned to the subject with a preoccupied look on her face that told me she might have been having second thoughts about my chastity. Did I think it was right for a girl to have sex before her marriage? she asked. When I equivocated, she stated firmly that prior to marriage, the relationship between a man and a woman was not holy (*kadosh*). Making love was permissible only with the idea of the divine duty (*mitzvah*) in mind—that is, in order to bear a child.

To counteract my obvious skepticism about submitting to such restrictions, Judith often gravely read me little parables, plucked for the occasion from an endless library of all-purpose religious instructional booklets. In this instance, she read me the following parable: "A blind man and a cripple went into an orchard to eat fruit. The blind man said, 'How can I eat the fruit, I can't even see it,' and the cripple said, 'How can I eat the fruit, I can't even walk over to it.' Then the cripple had an idea: He got on top of the blind man and directed him, and they were thus both able to eat the fruit. Shortly thereafter, the king came and caught them. The cripple said, 'It's not my fault, I could not have walked without the blind man's help,' and the blind man said, 'It's not my fault, I could not have seen without the cripple's help.' So the king said, 'You are both at fault, so you will both be punished.' "

Judith left me in no doubt about the interpretation. "On the Day of Judgment," she explained, "when we are brought to trial before the King of Kings, the soul will plead not guilty and will say, 'I was dragged into this by my sex-crazed body,' and the body will claim, 'I'm not guilty, I was only the slave of the desires of the soul.' But they will both be judged guilty because they are inseparable, they work together."

When Judith talked to me about marriage, she told me earnestly that the Hebrew word for marriage was *kiddushin,* which came from the word *kodesh* ("sanctity"). But in marriage, only the woman is sanctified, not the man, so it is incumbent on her to stay pure, while even if her husband sleeps with a different woman every night he will not impair the sanctity of the marriage. That is why, although only the man in Judaism has the right to divorce, there is one way a woman can force her husband into it: by committing adultery. Jewish law commands that an adulteress be cast out.

By the end of the week, I had become a well-integrated member of the household. Judith clearly enjoyed having me, for I was company for her during the long hours when David was away in the yeshiva. She liked to reminisce with me in English about how things had been back home in the States.

To enable her husband to devote all his time to the study of the Torah, Judith supported them by selling wigs she made to other Orthodox women. Occasionally, she would ask me to deliver a wig to one of her clients. The first time she sent me, I trembled lest someone in the street should recognize me, but I soon became so engrossed in the life of the neighborhood that I forgot my fears. I passed a tiny shop with a window as dirty as the thick spectacles of the lonely octogenarian owner who sat hunched over a Torah, squinting at letters his tired eyes could barely decipher. The shelves were crowded with odds and ends: bulky religious tomes in musty crimson bindings, books on Jewish law, phylacteries, and white prayer shawls with black stripes. I watched a customer enter and saw the old man move reluctantly up to the shop window and tug at the enormous book of psalms that was on display, reeling under its weight. One hefty thrust upward with his belly and he had hauled it onto the counter, where it landed heavily, raising a mighty puff of dust straight into the client's face. The customer beat a hasty retreat; clearly, these venerable old books did not like to be disturbed.

Just across the way, another store defiantly flaunted its gaudy vermilions, its windows cluttered with a bewildering assortment of cheap china: purple salt and pepper shakers fashioned into oversized tulips, fruit bowls looped with orange ribbons and blue apples, enameled candy boxes smothered in gold leaves, vases laden with strawberries and Stars of David, heavily embroidered linen coverlets for challah bread.

Next door was a barber shop. Everything in it was an institutional green, and on one of its two revolving chairs sat a customer. With a flurry of theatrical gestures, the barber was shaping the most popular neighborhood hairstyle—a completely shaven head, with the sole exception of ornately curled earlocks. The earlocks had been secured on either side of the client's ears with black tape. When he was finished, the barber dexterously removed the tape and raised a hand mirror in back of the client's head, beaming with pride at the reflection of a smooth, pink, shiny billiard ball. The client nodded approvingly and, taking a black velvet skullcap out of his pocket, carefully placed it over his bald skull, paid, and left.

By the end of three weeks I had begun to feel as though I had grown up in Judith and David's neighborhood. Paradoxically, it was the only place in Israel where I was able to forget that I was not Jewish. I had also become quite attached to Judith and David and was finding it more and more difficult every day to maintain the double deception of my Jewishness and my authenticity as a potential convert to Orthodoxy.

At first David had been more reserved than Judith, but I could see that he too had grown quite fond of me. He demonstrated this one evening in a dramatic way. Calling me to his study after dinner, he told me that he was pleased with my progress and convinced of the sincerity of my repentance. Then, to explain why this was a matter of such concern to him, he confessed to something that was a source of great shame to him. He had been born a Christian. He enjoined me to keep this a secret; no one other than his wife, the rabbi who had converted him, and the head of his yeshiva knew that he was not of Jewish blood. "In other religions, when people convert, there is no spiritual change, nothing happens. They just go from one belief to another belief; but when a person converts to Judaism, he becomes a new person. So I can only speak of my past self as I would speak of a person now dead, whom I once knew. That person was named Walter and is now named David. They have similar-looking bodies, but a new spirit inhabits the body."

"But why did you convert?" I asked.

"Why? Suppose you had a choice between being a very simple cleaning lady who does the floors or being the personal secretary of the king. Which would you choose? Well, the Jews are the secretaries of the king, and the others are just common help. It's because the Jews are closer to God that they are asked to observe so many commandments, six hundred and thirteen in all, while the goyim need to obey only ten. But my own conversion was truly and completely an act of God, I can't really explain it."

Nonetheless, he told me about it.

His parents were German Catholics who had emigrated to America during the thirties. David was born in Milwaukee and had lived in a lower-middle-class Catholic neighborhood not far from the factory where his father worked as a foreman. A bright boy, he had won a college scholarship, and it was there that he met and fell in love with Judith, an upper-middle-class Jewish girl. At first he decided to convert to Judaism in order to enhance himself in her eyes and went to see the rabbi of the university's Orthodox congregation. "When I went to speak to him, he threw me out of his office, because it says in the Talmud that if a non-Jew wants to convert, you should do everything in your power to discourage him. Two, three months passed, and still he refused to see me. But I was persistent, I kept calling him, even though he hung up on me every time. And meanwhile, I read about the Jewish religion, so that if he ever agreed to see me I would know enough about it to convince him.

"Finally, he condescended to speak to me. I was scared to death when I went to see him. He told me that he was prepared to let me study with him, but he would not promise to convert me. Then he proceeded to give me my first lesson. He explained who Moses was and what the Torah was; I realized that even though I had been a devout Catholic and had attended a parochial school, the Old Testament was never properly taught to us. And the New Testament, as you know, is a joke!" Seeing his contempt for his own background, the price he had paid for acceptance, filled me with unease.

"I tried to start living in accordance with the Torah. This meant keeping the *mitzvot*. Of course, a goy isn't allowed to keep all the *mitzvot,* but I tried to keep kosher and observe the Sabbath. I let my beard and my earlocks grow, and I always wore a skullcap and *tzitzis* [a fringed ritual undergarment worn by Orthodox men]. I even moved out of my home in order to be closer to the synagogue—of course, by then I would have had to leave anyway, because I was a source of great shame to my family; everyone in the neighborhood thought I had gone insane. After that I behaved in every way as a Jew should behave, except that on the Sabbath, when a Jew is not allowed to carry anything, I would carry a handkerchief to remind myself that, not being a Jew yet, I was not privileged enough to carry out the commandments in full."

Finally, before David's unflinching commitment, the rabbi relented. He would convert him, he said, if he passed one final test. He had to agree to give up the woman he loved so that it would not appear that he was converting merely because he wanted to marry her. David agreed, and the rabbi asked him to send Judith to see him the next morning.

For Judith, the tearful meeting with the rabbi was only the climax of a painful ordeal that had begun two years earlier: "It all started with my teaching David the alphabet in Hebrew. Soon he was reading Hebrew more easily than I could. We had met at the beginning of the academic year, in September, and in February he came and told me, 'You know, I'm studying to become a Jew!' I thought he was crazy, and I told him so.

"I'd never been religious, but he was very enthusiastic about his Torah studies, so devoted that finally I became intrigued myself. I started going to the library just to read up on Judaism because I was curious to know what was so compelling to David about what he was learning. Soon I was spending more and more time there; that's when my academic courses began going down the drain.

"After a while the shoe was on the other foot. Now I was the one who wasn't Jewish enough for David, and he would tell me that we couldn't see each other without a chaperon because it was forbidden by the Torah, and he couldn't marry me unless I observed the *mitzvot.* Doing this was very hard for me, because it meant endless fights with my family. My father is prosperous, very assimilated, and utterly nonobservant, and we had a non-Jewish cook, which created complications because Jews can't eat something cooked by a non-Jew unless a Jew helps in its preparation. Well, anyway, it was a big hullabaloo. I finally insisted that they make me a separate kitchen with separate sinks and refrigerators for dairy and nondairy products. I also asked for my own set of plates and cutlery.

"I started going to the services at Rabbi Israel's *shul.* It was my first exposure to Orthodoxy, and I was shocked to find out that these rabbis were real people who talked, joked, and laughed like everyone else. I couldn't take a cab because it was the Sabbath, and it was a good two-hour walk, so I'd get up at six in the morning and take along a chocolate bar to eat on the way, not realizing that I was breaking one Sabbath law by carrying it and another one by eating it, since it wasn't kosher. Then I would come home again, eat a cold meal, and go to bed for the rest of the day in order to avoid any contact with the television and to stay out of fights with my family.

"And now, after all of this, Rabbi Israel called me to his office to tell me that if I really loved David, I had to stop seeing him. He was to be sent for two years to Israel for religious studies, at the end of which he would be converted. Provided our love survived those two years of separation, he would be free to marry me, the rabbi said, but only if in the meantime I myself became an Orthodox Jew. Ironically, Rabbi Israel had stopped doubting David's motives; somehow now it was I who was suspect. According to him, all my efforts to keep the *mitzvot* were worthless, because I had done it for David, not out of true conviction. If I really wanted to prepare myself to embrace Judaism, I had to give up college—I was a premed student—and he would send me to a religious school for girls in New York.

"I was weeping hysterically, but I accepted for David's sake. Those two years of separation were very hard, because we both knew that our love was subservient to the will of God and that either of us might have to give up the other for the sake of the Torah."

I asked Judith if she had ever regretted giving up a career as a doctor to lead this life. She denied it but admitted that there were times when she wished David were less observant. At this point David interjected: "For me, there's no question that I should do all the *mitzvot.* I have no choice. A Jew who sins is still a Jew, but if a *ger* [a convert to Judaism] sins, the Jews will look at him as though he had become a goy again. If, God forbid, he were to cease performing the *mitzvot,* he would lose his sanctity—while my wife thinks, and quite rightly so, that even if she doesn't perform all the *mitzvot,* she's still a Jew."

David and Judith often told me that it was their background that made them so keen on bringing secular youth back to Judaism; "soul-snatching" was their way of repaying the rabbi for having led them back to the true path.

Until I started living in David and Judith's home, my feelings about the ultra-Orthodox were of the kind grown-ups might entertain toward a child whose idiosyncratic and at times exasperating behavior they humor because they think it only natural, and even somewhat charming, that children should act that way. In my own house, I had never heard religion referred to as anything else than *kalam farigh* (Arabic for "a lot of nonsense"). I recall listening, as a child, to the arguments between my father and his brother, a gentleman with a grave, ponderous manner. He would shake his head and say that at the root of all of Egypt's problems was the heritage of British colonialism, to which Father would retort, "Nonsense, our country's problem is religion!" What we needed, Father insisted, was a ruler like Atatürk, who would sweep away the vestiges of Islam and radically secularize the country.

Mother would have preferred to see more fear of God in our household. Her own attitude toward God was one of perfect correctness and impeccable courtesy. Sometimes when Father made a derogatory remark about religion at the table, and followed it by a burst of guffaws, she would lift her eyebrows and say: "Mahmoud, for God's sake, not in front of the children!" But my mind had already been subverted. By the time I was ten, I looked down my nose at anyone in religious garb, be it sheikh, priest, or rabbi—I thought they were all nincompoops and ignoramuses. Mother's quiet remonstrances that we should be ashamed of ourselves for eating during Ramadan while the servants fasted had little effect, nor did her view that all religions were equally good and the important thing was that everyone should have one. She herself valiantly clung to her Muslim faith despite our combined efforts to undermine it by ridicule. Every time I was expelled from school, she would demonstrate her piety by going to visit the Muslim shrine of Saidna Zeinab and, just to be on the safe side, following it up by a visit to the chapel of Saint Theresa, a Christian friend having avouched that the lady worked miracles.

But I could not dismiss David and Judith so easily. I was living with them—and the daily evidence of their kindness, generosity, and sincere faith made it impossible for me to maintain a pose of amused condescension. What's more, my immersion in their life was beginning to have its effect. In no time at all, it seemed I had come to feel that earlocks and *tzitzis* were no more ridiculous than the ponytails and earrings sported by the young men in Harvard Square. To sit up all night like David, studying Torah or reading Chasidic tales, was no more exotic to me now than studying the *I Ching* or the *Kama Sutra* were in my intellectual circle. Even the hypnotic trance dances of the Chasidim, which at first had startled me, now appeared as familiar as disco dancing. In fact the Orthodox Jews who surrounded me felt the same contemptuous superiority to the secular world as my with-it friends felt toward the "straight world."

It was clear that I would soon have to leave. I had originally planned on spending only a few days, but had ended up staying for almost four weeks. I felt increasingly awful for deceiving David and Judith. I worried every day that someone would recognize me when I went shopping in the morning, or would remember having seen the picture of the Egyptian celebrity in the papers. There was some comfort in the thought that the residents of this closed-in, ultra-Orthodox neighborhood had little contact with the rest of Israel—that they neither read secular papers nor listened to the radio—but I could never feel totally at ease. And now that I had won David's and Judith's trust, the shame I would suffer in the event of exposure would be all the greater.

On the other hand, the fear of exposure as an Arab was only part of my worries. I had told Ulpan Etzion that I would be gone for only a few days, and now I had been out of touch for far too long. Even more important, I had had no contact with Danny since I had started living with Judith and David; even if it hadn't been so difficult for me to slip in and out of their house without an excuse (Judith *never* went out), I had determined to immerse myself totally in the religious life. Finally, of course, there was the ever-increasing sense that I was indulging myself, straying further and further away from my mission. Was it really necessary for me to "become" an Orthodox Jew to understand Israel? I could hardly believe that I had stayed on as long as I had and had become so imbued with my role that I was hardly conscious of playing it. Nevertheless, I behaved true to character and kept putting off my date of departure until external events forced my hand.

One evening, David brought a young yeshiva friend home for dinner. His name was Adam, and he was a dark, slender fellow with deep black eyes. When I was left alone with him for a few minutes in the living room, I seized the opportunity to ask him about life at the yeshiva. Did he like it?

"Oh, wow, I love it," he cried. "What I like about it is the inspiration, the feeling that I'm special, that I'm better than most people in the world. You really become very pure. You get an education, you get everything for free, you don't pay a cent. The yeshiva is paid for by the contributions of rich people in the Diaspora—Americans mostly. So you don't have all the shit, you don't have to go to work nine to five, you don't have the Monday-morning problems—trying to cope with the world all by yourself, being lonely. You don't have to deal with the world at all. All you do is just sit around and try and be perfect."

I asked him what kinds of things he studied at the yeshiva.

"We learn the Talmud. It's logic, very hard logic. Like, say, it's the Sabbath and you're not allowed to carry anything, except a seed because that's very small. But what happens if while you're carrying it that seed grows into a tree? Then there are the laws, millions of laws, like if a girl of twelve is raped, the money goes to her parents, and if she is thirteen it goes to her. Now, suppose she died during the act of rape, and she was thirteen, who should get the money? She has the right to it, but she's dead."

I asked him whether he really believed Jews were superior beings. "Oh, I don't know." He considered. "The Lubavitcher rabbi teaches that there's a kind of chemical difference between the blood of Jews and the blood of other people. It's not something you can measure in the laboratory, but it is some spiritual thing that's part of the Jewish flesh."

"Do you believe that?"

"You know, it's hard to know what to believe in this world. Everyone naturally wants to be the guy on top, but God doesn't want everyone close to Him. You can believe that all human beings are basically equal, but still, within all of humanity, there are the chosen ones—Jewish people like you and me."

Adam then took me completely by surprise by announcing that "before" he was Jewish, he had been a Puerto Rican! His family had lived in Spanish Harlem; they had been very poor. Then, after the 1973 war, which he said had triggered his conversion, he studied the Torah and went for his circumcision under the auspices of a rabbi in New York. It was very painful, he said, because he had never been circumcised before, and he was sore for weeks afterward whenever he had to urinate or make love. But he knew that the pain was a necessary part of the purification; his spiritual change was going down into his body and becoming part of his flesh. "I saw a light come through my penis after they finished removing the foreskin, and my penis said, 'I was in Egypt, I was in Egypt!' I knew then that even before I was converted I was already a Jew and I had been in Egypt!"

I asked him why he had converted.

"Because I wanted to be one of the chosen people. I read the Torah and I was emotionally inspired. The Lord said, 'I will bless you above all other nations, and I have chosen you.' After my conversion, I really got high, like I was in another world. The program in the yeshiva in New York was fantastic. We got up at seven and studied till nine in the morning, then we had breakfast and studied the Talmud till one. After that I had only one hour of rest and we studied again till ten at night. When I went into the street it was a tremendous waste of time—even a thing like going to buy cigarettes, I felt, 'No, I'm too busy, I can't do it!' Only a few weeks earlier I couldn't live without cigarettes. It was the same with sex. I used to pick up whores a lot in New York, but one day when I was with one—inside her—I thought to myself, 'What the fuck is going on? What's this dark place I've slipped into? I can't live like this!'

"Two months later I came to Israel and enrolled at a yeshiva here. I had to give up a lot of things completely, like women and hash—when it comes to hash the rabbi's very strict, you know. I can't imagine what he thinks Moses was doing every time he went up that mountain!"

I was curious to find out where Adam stood politically.

"We should hold onto this land, by God, and not make any compromise with the Palestinians. They have no right to be here. They were in our home while we were away, being killed in Germany and settling America, but now we're back and they just can't stay. They didn't do a thing for this land, there were just sheep and rocks here when we got back. And besides, I don't trust them. If I were to tell you, 'Let's go to your house now and I'll take off your panties and I promise I won't do anything to you,' you wouldn't believe me, would you? Well, I don't believe that if we give them a little bit, they'll stop making trouble for us."

As I began to protest, he cut me off: "A Palestinian state here would be poison, pollution!" he cried, stamping his foot. "We're supposed to live here, and that's all there is to it. Because the Jews are pure whiteness."

The following evening, while we were having dinner, Judith began to ask David about Adam. His rather vague answers did not seem to satisfy her. She pursued the subject insistently, extolling his beauty at great length to David, who listened to her somewhat distractedly. This amused me, for Judith had always seemed to me so enamored of David that I had believed she had eyes only for him. I forgot about this conversation until a few days later, when I overheard her telling him that it would soon be time to arrange a match for me, and that he ought to start giving it some serious thought. It was only then that I grasped the nature of her sudden interest in Adam. I could not believe that she would think such an idiot would ever appeal to me, but I recognized her impulse: By making a match between us, she would be performing two *mitzvot* at once—bringing a newly Orthodox Jew into the religious community, and rewarding a new convert with a good wife. That night, I packed my suitcase.

Since I lacked the courage to confront them with either the truth of my identity or the fact of my departure, I stole away after they had gone to bed, leaving behind a tearful thank-you note. I knew they would misunderstand the motive for my departure; they would conclude that having found life with them too onerous and boring, I had slipped back into the licentious, secular world. It saddened me to think that I could never tell them the truth, that our friendship, even though compromised by my deceit, would have been impossible altogether if they had known who I really was.

It was past midnight when I reached the taxi station. The driver took one look at me and knew exactly what to make of me: After all, no decent Orthodox girl would be out walking the streets by herself at this hour of the night. "You're not one of them, are you?" he said, smiling insinuatingly. "No, I guess not," I answered coldly.

"Neither am I. It's a real pain in the ass working in this neighborhood. I can't even listen to my own radio when I'm driving. Any song that's the least bit romantic, they consider it bawdy and immediately ask me to turn it off. And if I ever let out a curse like *kus omak,* it's a whole story."

I was silent. The cabby took my silence for acquiescence, and as we drove toward the other world, he continued to treat me to recriminations I found particularly offensive now that I had Orthodox friends. "Dirty people, these religious guys. Their black coats reek with sweat. The minute one of them steps in here, the whole cab stinks. I have to ventilate it for hours after he leaves. They never wash, you know. They just run their palms under the tap and rub their fingers together. They think that's washing. . . ."

9

A New Vision

THE FIRST thing I did on returning to Ulpan Etzion was to check for messages from Danny. I had been certain he had bombarded the Ulpan officials with frantic telephone calls in my absence, and I was peeved to find that there were none. Nonetheless I decided to go see him. On the way to his house, I tried to picture the look of pleased surprise that would flash across his face, but it was Gila who came to the door. Danny, she informed me, was in South Africa. He had decided to resign from the army and had gone to check out a business opportunity in Johannesburg. How long would he be away? I asked, making an effort to assume an indifferent tone. "Don't know," she replied. "Maybe another week, maybe a few months." My heart froze. Afraid that Gila would notice my dismay, I mumbled something about not feeling well —sudden asthma attack—and quickly left.

To the disappointment of not finding Danny was added the shock of learning where he was. If there was one country that was, for me, beyond the pale, it was South Africa, and I believed that Jews, as victims of racism, had a special moral responsibility to boycott it.

Israel's foreign policy had more than once caused a battle between Danny and me. I had expressed my disturbance that even during the heyday of socialism in his country, the Labor government still had been willing to support French colonialism in Algeria in exchange for Mirage fighter planes. That the Israelis, who had themselves struggled against British imperialism in Palestine, should have cast their vote against the independence of Algeria at the U.N. seemed to me an indelible blemish on their record. It had also bothered me that Israel would loudly protest the suppression of the Kurdish minority in Iraq and then turn around and sell arms to Guatemala and El Salvador, two countries engaged in the extermination of the Indian and mestizo campesinos, or send an army to train the militia of Emperor Haile Selassie when he was at war against the liberation of the Eritrian people. And for all of Israel's agitation about the persecution of Jewish dissidents in the Soviet Union, it never raised a voice against the mass imprisonment, tortures, and executions carried out by the Shah of Iran as long as Iran was its main oil supplier.

Danny had always argued that a nation with so few friends in the world had to forge whatever alliances it could, and that questions of ethics consequently had to be subordinated to national interests. No matter how unsavory this logic struck me as being, I understood that it fell within the realm of realpolitik. But I drew the line at South Africa. I argued with Danny that all of Israel's efforts to keep alive the memory of the Holocaust among other nations were invalidated by its hypocritical "absence," year after year, when the program of the U.N. Special Committee Against Apartheid was voted on.

Why had Danny not told me of his plan to resign from the army? Had he really resigned? True, there was nothing unconventional in this, for high officers in the Israeli military often resigned their posts at a relatively young age; few people stayed on beyond their late forties, in fact. But why South Africa? What was this business of which Gila made such a mystery? A creeping suspicion that it had something to do with the export of Israeli arms to South Africa filled me with uneasiness. Could his presence in South Africa have something to do with the joint Israeli–South African development of a nuclear submarine that, much to my disgust, I had been reading about in the press? As in the past, my mistrust of Danny's role in the world quickly spilled over into our relationship. Was it possible that Danny was making a fool of me? Trying to use me?

My pitiless memory retraced for me every single step that had led from my first night with him to my present predicament. He had always seemed mysterious to me. His character would have been frightening enough for me in a "conventional" relationship with a married man, but this was so much harder. I thought of all the ways Danny might have implicated me. I had allowed myself to be seen in public with an Israeli officer—what claims could the Israeli army not make upon me now that I had compromised myself? Visions of wiretaps and hidden cameras assaulted me, images that perhaps were not all that fantastical given how heedlessly I had behaved with Danny.

My inflamed imagination let itself be carried away. While only moments before it had deployed itself in depicting for me the joys of this reunion with Danny, now it turned into my implacable enemy, portraying to me not only Danny but even Yoav as part of the Byzantine subtlety practiced by the army and aimed at involving me in their nefarious schemes. What else could have impelled Yoav to offer his apartment to me, a total stranger—and come to think of it, how else could he have gotten hold of my telephone number on the very first day of my arrival? Exaggerating the importance of this discovery, I began to credit Danny with even more Machiavellian duplicity. He did not love me, it was clear. What's more, he never had. My vanity was wounded, and I felt the keenest hatred for him.

When I got back to Rheines Street, I locked myself in my room, where I was free to wallow in the cruelty of my lot. The utter solitude I felt as an Egyptian traveler in Israel made the power of my dark imaginings all the greater. What would I not have given then to have one good friend to whom I could have turned for counsel! But the sad truth was that I had only Danny. The realization reduced me to tears.

I became more and more deeply depressed at the thought of the new disgrace my behavior would heap upon my family—my family, for whom even the idea of sleeping with a man was shocking, but a married man, an Israeli, and an army officer! Which of my mother's friends who came to see her in the salon hung with the crimson velvet drapes with the broad gold braids would dare to take my side? What tactful words could they possibly find to soften the blow inflicted by the frightful contempt of the Cairo drawing rooms?

I was furious at myself and angry at the whole world: Now I hated not only all Israelis but also all Egyptians.

But sentiments like these finally broke my mood. I thought of Danny shrieking with laughter at my melodrama, and with this my self-possession returned. Then I told myself that I would be even more of a fool than I was if I ever allowed myself to feel anything for this man again. When he came back, I'd tell him that I didn't love him. I determined that my judgment had deceived me. This consideration left me cool and calculating; I could think of nothing else for the rest of the evening but of ways to assure the triumph of my will over my passion. Now my chief aim would be to make myself as disagreeable as possible to Danny when he returned in order to punish both him and myself for the adoration I had felt for him.

But the next day it occurred to me that it would be even better if I simply left town, as he had, without telling him. When he came back and did not find me, he would realize that I had fooled him as he had hoped to make a fool of me. And if I was wrong, and Danny's interest in me was genuine, wouldn't my absence increase it a hundredfold? I decided to leave immediately for the distant kibbutz that I had been planning to visit. If Danny wanted to find me, surely he had the connections to track me down.

Since I had already lived at one of the oldest kibbutzim, I would now visit one of the youngest, Kibbutz Hazon Hadash ("New Vision"). It was an experimental venture by a group of kibbutz-raised young people who ranged in age from eighteen to thirty-five. In open revolt against the *embourgeoisement* of their parents' kibbutzim, they wanted to establish an agricultural commune that lived out the original egalitarian ideals of the founders.

My thought of working at Hazon Hadash had been inspired by a play I had seen with Danny, *Leil Haesrim* ("A Night in the 1920s") by Yehoshua Sobol. Based on the true story of a socialist commune in Palestine in the 1920s called Betania, the play explored every great problem that challenged Betania and continued to plague the modern kibbutz system: Could the community triumph over the primal power of the couple, and public interests over private ones? Would childbearing destroy sexual equality and push women back to nurseries and kitchens? Would a high level of work organization generate a caste of privileged specialists and thereby destroy the principle of the rotation of labor? After the play I had told Danny in a burst of enthusiasm that I regretted not being alive at a time when life was so exciting in Israel; what a pity it was, I said, that no such kibbutzim existed anymore. "But they do!" he had exclaimed. "You should visit Hazon Hadash."

Despite my fondness for many members of Kibbutz Vatik, I had hardly found kibbutz life an exciting expression of the socialist ideal. At Vatik, as at the other kibbutzim I had visited, prosperity had brought with it inequality and conspicuous consumption. People had become entrenched in positions of power, the powerful virtually always being men. Privileges had come to be attached to their jobs: private cars, trips abroad, secret bank accounts. As the family reasserted itself, children were increasingly taken out of their communal homes and lodged with their parents. The men preferred to settle down with their children in front of television in the evening rather than participate in the group activities and cultural events of the kibbutz, and the women were too busy cooking evening meals and baking cakes to bother attending kibbutz meetings.

The agricultural commune of Hazon Hadash, I had been told, harked back to the simple, frugal life of the pioneers, to their egalitarian ethos and political utopianism. In fact, the members were considered the enfants terribles of Israel because of their demonstrations against the government's retention of the occupied territories and its discrimination against "Arab-Israelis." I had been eager to get there even before I decided to distance myself from Danny.

As the overflowing bus groaned out of Central Station en route to Hazon Hadash, I became increasingly resentful of the soldier who was fast asleep to my right. While scores of us stood in the packed aisle, he stretched out across two seats, his muddy spiked shoes sticking out and rubbing against my skirt. As if in response to my dirty look, he opened his eyes and, to my surprise, said my name. In strongly accented Hebrew, he explained that he had seen my photo and read about me in an Argentinian newspaper, *La Opinión*. When I answered his question about my destination, he looked delighted. He introduced himself as Julio and said he was a member of Kibbutz Hazon Hadash, on furlough from his reserve duty in the army.

Accepting his offer of one of his seats, I sat down next to this skinny young man in the khaki jacket and baggy trousers. He had a long, bony face with thin whiskers that ran along the side of his mouth all the way down to his chin, where they tapered into a goatee. There was something very refined about him; his Israeli army outfit seemed incongruous, especially as he went on to explain to me that he was even more radical than most members of the kibbutz. Following his arrival from Argentina, he had joined Matzpen, the left-wing anti-Zionist group. He was harshly critical not only of the government of Israel for selling arms to the Argentinian military dictators despite their persecution of Jews, but also of the kibbutzim themselves. In his view, they were the spearhead of Israel's colonial expansion. "Not only have the kibbutzim shown no scruples about accepting land confiscated from Arab-Israeli villages after the '48 war, but they are currently building their own settlements on occupied land. Even Mapam [the left-wing Zionist Labor party], though it stated during the '67 war that it would never set foot in the conquered territories, has built kibbutzim on the Golan Heights! And now it's pressuring the government not to return the Golan to Syria," he added, his thin lips curling in disgust.

I asked Julio how he could hold such views *and* still wear the Israeli army uniform. I had heard that another member of Hazon Hadash had been imprisoned for refusing to serve in the 1973 war. He smiled at me conspiratorially and answered that the best way to subvert the enemy was from within.

As soon as we arrived at the kibbutz, Julio led me to the dining room, where, as he explained, "the comrades" spent practically all their leisure time together. Here they held their meetings and social gatherings: dances, concerts, and lectures. When we walked in, the members of Hazon Hadash—young men with long tousled hair, necklaces, and beards; barefoot young women without bras, a very un-Israeli look—. were squatting in a circle on the floor, in the middle of a heated discussion. A man who had entered the room right behind us, pushing a cart laden with pitchers of lemonade and enormous rounds of poppy-seed cake, called out my name. The group broke up; eager young faces gathered about me, and questions came from all directions: "Why did Sadat allow you to come here?" "Does Egypt want peace?" and the one question that never failed to embarrass me: "Do you like Israel?" I fended it off with my standard neutral answer, one of those well-worn phrases about its being most interesting and the like. And as I looked at their disappointed expressions, I felt how simple it should have been to say that I indeed liked Israel, but it was impossible for me to answer more openly. Years of indoctrination had created an inner censor in me; to this day I cannot give a straightforward, unequivocal answer to the question. Besides, if I could not admit to myself how much I had come to care about Israel, how could I admit it to strangers?

A ruddy, buxom girl with a mass of red curls and frayed shorts came to my rescue. "Leave her alone," she protested. "Can't you see she's dead tired?" She pulled me out into the cool night, introduced herself as Michelle, and asked me if I'd like to share her room, since her roommate had left to serve in the army. I would have preferred a room of my own, but I felt too embarrassed to say so.

While the older kibbutzim had come to resemble American suburbs, with handsome cottages framed by prim little gardens, this one looked ascetic by comparison, with its grim concrete shacks and mangy shrubs here and there.

Michelle's room was at once homey and primitive. Two cots sat astride sawed-off telephone poles, and all her possessions were heaped helter-skelter in a fishing net that was strung up by the bedside across two of the poles. These included a scraggly old hairbrush, a Che Guevara T-shirt, her battered sneakers, a Japanese fan, a photo album, and some novels and records.

Before my eyes had quite recovered from the bewildering assortment of plants, odd-shaped pebbles, and shells that graced the window ledge next to a spherical fish tank complete with coral sand, seaweed, eels, starfish, and sea urchins, she asked me if I liked the room. When I answered that I did, she told me that she had built the bed herself; her hobby was carpentry, and she wanted to know if I, too, enjoyed working with my hands. I was ashamed to admit that I was so mystified by anything manual that it had taken me a whole month to figure out how to ignite the pilot light of my oven when I first arrived in the United States, so I told her that I liked gardening. In reality I had not the foggiest notion about it, but it sounded more impressive than cooking —the only thing with which I was vaguely familiar because of my grotesque experiences at the King David Hotel. I remembered a present I had prepared for my mother's birthday when I was a little girl. I had stolen a daffodil bulb from our garden and had planted it in a pot, which I then laboriously hid way up in the attic of our villa in Alexandria. For two months, I carefully watered it in secret. One day, I saw to my great delight that a green stalk had sprouted, and soon a daffodil made its appearance. The eighth of August finally arrived, and I proudly offered it to Mother. She glanced at it somewhat absently and said, "Thank you, my love, but really you shouldn't go to all this trouble. After all, your father pays a gardener for this." That was when I first learned that manual labor doesn't pay.

Michelle tore me out of my reverie, saying that she knew I was tired but there was just one last thing she wanted to show me before we turned in. She led me to a little wooden hut adjoining her room, which she had built out of some leftover lumber she had found on one of the kibbutz construction sites. To my surprise, as we pushed the gate, a lame donkey with no ears and only one eye came limping toward us. Michelle had found her in a nearby field and had adopted her. "What do you think of Quasimodo?" she asked with pride. I was not mad about the donkey, but I was quite beguiled by Michelle's charm. With her red curls, impish freckled nose, and dimpled smile, she reminded me of Pippi Longstocking, the Swedish heroine of my childhood books, who could talk to horses and lift them up with only one hand.

The next morning, Michelle proposed that we go to the pool, since it was the Sabbath and she had the day off.

On our way she announced half-defiantly and half-triumphantly that practically everyone at Hazon Hadash swam naked. Seeing that I did not look unduly alarmed, she added, "We often go at night to make love in the pool. It's just lovely when there's a full moon. You can't imagine how wonderful one's naked breasts feel in the water!"

I was nonplussed by this, because at Kibbutz Vatik I had been struck by the repressive sexual morality of the young people, a quality they had inherited from the founders. Though popular lore often pictured the pioneers as free-spirited bohemians who went about barefoot and indulged in unrestrained sexual pleasure, nothing was further from the truth. Their contempt for the institution of marriage and for the cult of virginity did not include an ideology of free love. Quite the contrary: Shifting liaisons were considered a form of "bourgeois degeneracy," and sexual self-control was just as necessary to the stoical "new man" as the ability to withstand physical fatigue. The pioneers frowned on privacy of any sort—so much so that couples deliberately avoided sitting at the same table in the kibbutz dining room. They did encourage soul-baring conversations and confessions at kibbutz meetings, but they never allowed this spiritual intimacy to become a physical one. It was decreed that the relationships between couples were to remain monogamous, to be governed by the rules of fidelity.

Michelle confirmed that these codes still existed in even the most radical kibbutzim. "You wouldn't believe how puritanical our parents are!" she exclaimed. "You may have noticed that the girls here don't wear bras. One of the first things we did when we arrived was to make a big bonfire out of all the bras on the kibbutz!"

The pool was crowded. A scrawny young man with a freckled behind lay on a rubber dinghy, splashing water with his feet, while another one was getting ready for a dive. He straightened up, momentarily revealing an abundance of shockingly red hair around his genitals, then flashed past me and disappeared into the water. In the corner of the pool a few young girls were dunking each other, shrieking with laughter, while nearby a couple sat with their arms around each other, blissfully oblivious of the din; they had the plump, creamy white derrieres one sees in baby-powder ads.

Michelle, who had taken off her clothes, was unselfconsciously parading her voluptuous body. After strolling around idly for a while, she told me with a condescending smile, "You needn't if you don't want to." The smile annoyed me. I had no inhibitions about nudity—none, at any rate, that I was prepared to admit; I hesitated only because I felt I was intruding on an incestuous circle. Finally, just as I was about to take off my shirt, a skinny man in a bathing suit strode up to the pool, and I asked him how it was that he was not swimming naked like the others.

"I don't want to," he said. "I'm a very private person, and I don't uncover myself—not psychologically and not physically. A lot of people here would rather not swim naked, but they're not courageous enough to stand the pressure. As if exposing the pimples on their asses means they're not square!"

Michelle, who had been listening to him as she stood at the edge of the pool, holding her heavy breasts in her hands and testing the water with the tips of her toes, turned around and cried out to him: "We *should* expose our pimples, our fat buns, and our flabby bellies—everything! There's nothing to be ashamed of! Uncovering ourselves psychologically and physically is the only way we stand a chance of getting to know each other completely."

But he replied derisively: "What does it mean to know each other 'completely'? Do you know me? Do I really know you? All this talk, talk, talk, the endless philosophizing that goes on on this kibbutz. Maybe if we didn't talk so much and learned to think instead, we'd discover something about ourselves for a change."

As he walked away, Michelle called out after him, "What bullshit! You're afraid we'll see your puny cock if you take off your bathing suit. Why don't you admit it?" She giggled and jumped into the pool.

When we got to our little room that evening, Michelle bombarded me with questions about my past and my family. I resented this as an intrusion on my privacy, but I tried to fend her off jokingly, protesting, "Hey! Just a minute! I'm the one who's supposed to be doing the interviewing, remember?" I began to ask her about her family, and Michelle, who had made it clear she considered privacy a bourgeois notion, happily obliged by embarking on her family history.

She told me that her mother, Rachel, was a descendant of Isaac Luria, the sixteenth-century Kabbalist. Rachel had grown up in a Czech village with her friend Fritz, a little boy who spent all his pocket money on marzipan, which, being the most expensive item in her father's store, was kept in a blue jar on a high shelf well out of the reach of children with nimble fingers. At the age of seven, Fritz spotted Rachel sitting on the store counter, munching a poppy-seed cake. He instantly fell in love with her. She spurned him then and continued to snub him even after he grew up to be a devastatingly handsome young man and a hero among the Jewish partisans who led the resistance against the Nazis. He survived the Holocaust, and years later she ran into him accidentally in Israel and they became lovers. Fritz was Michelle's father.

Another important character in Rachel's life was Dakli, the family dachshund; her father had tried to leave the dog behind in the village when they moved to Prague, but he ran after them on his short legs all the way to the city and actually managed to find their house. Then there was the funny old aunt who lived with them and baked delicious fruitcakes for the holiday of Shavuot. The greatest influence on Rachel's early years, however, had been her older sister, Naomi, a radical feminist and militant Communist, whose childhood dream was to become a train conductor—a job she holds in Czechoslovakia to this day.

Czech was not spoken in the Jewish ghetto in which Rachel grew up. Its residents prided themselves on partaking of the *deutsche Kultur,* as opposed to the "barbaric" Slavic one that surrounded them. Having never forgotten that they were once a part of the glorious Austro-Hungarian Empire—most of the adults had in fact been born during the reign of the Hapsburg monarchy—they secretly nursed the same secessionist aspirations as did the Sudeten Germans. Some of the young men in Rachel's neighborhood even went so far as to dye their hair blond and wear swastikas, while others greeted the German invasion of Czechoslovakia with an ecstatic all-night celebration. But they were shortly to be rudely awakened. Rachel was fifteen when the Munich Pact was signed, and she remembered how soon after the agreement it was that she could no longer go to school, and how quickly the benches in the park where she played were marked "Not for Jews." Not long thereafter, in 1939, she left for Palestine. Her sister, Naomi, a committed anti-Zionist, refused to go; so did her parents, who had yet to be disabused about the greatness of German civilization. They and her aunt died in Auschwitz—a fate Naomi escaped by joining the partisan underground.

Rachel had brought only her mementos with her to Palestine. One was a stamp with the portrait of the Nazi leader Heydrich (smiling enigmatically as she showed it to Michelle, she had remarked on how handsome she had found him when she was a young girl), and the other was a snapshot that had been taken in the kitchen on the day she bade her family farewell; it showed her mother's ruddy, Slavic face bathed in tears. Rachel was one of the few Israelis who refused to accept reparations payments—blood money, she called it—from the German government.

Michelle herself had been raised on a Hashomer Hatzair kibbutz founded by her parents and some friends in 1949 in the Negev Desert. Hashomer Hatzair's exalted idealism and romanticism were largely inspired by a German youth movement, *Die Wandervögel* ("Migratory Birds"), so named because its recruits yearned to migrate out of the middle-class world of their parents to a new one that was more authentic and natural. Their rebellion against parental and school discipline, their hatred of militarism, their contempt for bourgeois norms, and their near-mystical worship of nature were compatible with a socialist creed based on a return to the land of Israel. Hashomer Hatzair's ideals were enshrined in a code of ethics laid down with the stern immutability of Mosaic law:

1. To be a truthful person.
2. To be loyal to one's people.
3. To be a brother to one's fellow member.
4. To be helpful and reliable.
5. To love nature.
6. To be obedient to one's leaders.
7. To be full of joy and gaiety.
8. To be thrifty and generous.
9. To be courageous.
10. To be pure in thoughts, words, and deeds.

(The last point was interpreted as an injunction against cigarettes, liquor, and promiscuous sex.)

Michelle sprang directly out of the Hashomer Hatzair movement. Her mother used to carry her on her shoulders to its marches and parades, proudly referring to Michelle's mass of carroty curls flying off in all directions like firecrackers as her very own red banner. Hashomer Hatzair's calendar of meetings and *sichot* (soulful discussions), its torchlit evenings devoted to the singing of the "Internationale" and other inspiring revolutionary ballads, shaped and dominated Michelle's whole childhood and adolescence. Many of her contemporaries—the children and grandchildren of revolutionaries—moved away from the kibbutz and the utopianism of their parents and toward a more materialistic and bourgeois ethic. "For my generation," Michelle said, "there was a war between our socialist education and the American pop culture. Elvis Presley was the hero of the rotten, spoiled, decadent Tel Aviv kids, and the enemy of 'good' Israelis. Well, the war is over. Elvis and his descendants have won it." But Michelle remained faithful to the movement. Throughout her high school years, until she was eighteen, she spent almost every night participating in the movement's activities. Each gathering would start with the Hashomer Hatzair salute, with everyone shouting in unison, *"Chazak ve ematz!"* ("Be brave and strong!"). Instead of saying "Shalom" when members of the movement met in the street, they called out to each other, *"Chazak!"* ("Be strong!").

Michelle's narrative was interrupted at that point by a knock on the door. It was Julio, my bus companion of the previous day. He had exchanged his army uniform for a white Arab *jellaba* and rubber thongs and had come to invite us to join him for a drink in his room. Michelle's reply was to pull her sheet over her face and pretend to snore, but I decided to go.

When I stepped inside Julio's room, I saw a long banner fashioned out of white cloth strung across the entire length of the wall with the slogan WE WANT PEACE—A PIECE OF EGYPT, A PIECE OF SYRIA, A PIECE OF JORDAN. It was one of the banners that he and other members of the kibbutz had displayed in a recent demonstration in Tel Aviv.

A scornful look suffused Julio's El Greco profile as he followed the direction of my gaze: "The only thing our demonstrations achieve," he explained, "is to maintain the system; they are part of the democratic charade. Then Golda, Rabin, Begin, or whoever is the figurehead can brag, 'We even have leftists, and we let them demonstrate.' "

"But what other way is there?" I asked.

He raised his serenely ironical eyes from his scotch and spelled it out for me: "R-E-V-O-L-U-T-I-O-N." Once the "bourgeois" regimes in Israel and the Arab world had been overthrown, he said, then it would be possible to unify the Middle East on the basis of socialism rather than nationalism. "The Israeli people should become Levantines, the very thing they consider at present the worst possible calamity. We in Matzpen consider ourselves Palestinians who happen to be of Hebrew culture. We are not Jews, we don't have much affection for the Jewish religion, and we are against all official connection between the state of Israel and the Jewish people in the Diaspora. Take the Soviet Jews today: By and large we feel that they should solve their problems by combatting anti-Semitism within their own country. This doesn't mean that individual Soviet Jews can't come here, but they have no more right to come than do the Palestinians—or any other people, for that matter."

"You don't think there's something unique about the centuries of persecution the Jews have suffered?" I ventured.

For a moment he wavered, fingering his reddish goatee, but then he resumed his defiant tone: "There is also something unique about the problem of the Biafrans and the Irish Catholics, and about the massacre of the Armenians. The Armenians could have said, 'Well, let's make a deal with the Americans and push American interests in the Middle East if they let us set up a state at the expense of the Syrian people'—as you know, there's a large Armenian community there. . . ."

We talked awhile longer, but the drink and my fatigue were setting in and I made ready to leave. Saying that he wanted to show me something first, Julio hauled out the shoebox that served as a drawer and said urgently, "You remember the story the Israeli propagandists spread during the '67 war, about the cowardly Egyptian soldiers who ran off, leaving their shoes behind, instead of standing their ground and fighting?" He whisked out a photo of Egyptian prisoners of war removing their shoes under pointed Israeli guns and announced: "I was there. It was my first war, and I can tell you a different story—about how, in killing heat, we ordered them to take off their shoes and made them march with their feet bleeding on the scorching sands and their hands raised up above their heads. When I told my commanding officer that they were moaning for water, he snapped back at me, 'Let them croak.' "

As I handed the picure back to him, Julio pulled me toward him and proposed that I spend the night. When I disengaged myself from his embrace, he invoked the practice of "free love" that prevailed at Hazon Hadash. I headed for the door without a word, but he called out after me that he wanted to give me something. He handed me the photograph and said, "Keep it, it's a small souvenir, I want you to take it back to Egypt with you."

The next morning Michelle took me to the *communa* (the communal wardrobe room) to pick out some work clothes, and told me: "Here, the way it works is that the jeans you see me wearing today will be worn by the next person after they're laundered. We're against the system of money allowances that the older kibbutzim are starting to use, because even though everyone there gets the same money, once they begin to buy things in the city, they give in to conspicuous consumption. Then they start taking money from their relatives in the cities to buy more and more things, and pretty soon the kibbutz as a whole becomes materialistic and inegalitarian. You know, our mothers may have wanted the revolution for themselves, but for us they want the same things bourgeois parents want for their children—designer dresses, good furniture, nifty kitchen gadgets."

After I had dressed, she told me to go to the dining room, where Jacob, the manager of the henhouse, was to pick me up. (It seemed to be my fate in Israel to get to know chickens inside out.) A slightly hunched figure was waiting for me at the entrance, and as he raised his head toward me I recognized the bearded profile of the young man who had refused to take off his bathing suit at the pool.

All the way down to the henhouse, Jacob grumbled about a co-worker, David, who had not shown up; the night before, he had hitch-hiked to a political rally in Tel Aviv and apparently had not been able to make it back in time for work. This was "catastrophic," Jacob explained to me, because the kibbutz had received a delivery of baby turkeys that very morning, and they had to be vaccinated immediately. If they were kept in the cartons for another three hours, they would suffocate from the heat. "We'll have six thousand dead chicks on our hands!" Then he went on to fulminate against this David: "If you count all the times David has missed work, you'll discover that out of the eight years he's been with us, he has spent about six outside the kibbutz. Even when he does show up, he's usually falling asleep on his feet because he's been up all night. It's simply not possible to work and make politics at the same time!"

I was curious and began to question him about David. To my surprise, he snapped at me angrily, saying with characteristic Sabra bluntness: "Listen, I have no time to gossip. If you want to find out more about David, go talk to the women!" As he opened the gate of the henhouse, he added with a sneer: "I'm sure they know him better than I do—in the biblical sense of the word, I mean!"

We entered a chick house that had been freshly prepared for the new delivery of baby turkeys. Dry, fluffy aromatic sawdust covered the floor, and the neatly aligned rows of bright-red plastic water containers that hung from the ceiling in perfectly straight columns, together with the automatic feeding devices of shiny aluminum, lent the place an air of order and efficiency. As I contemplated the frightened heads of the baby turkeys protruding from the holes of the stacked-up cartons, I could not help feeling some unease at the thought that this was just the first phase of an assembly line that would spit them out neatly plucked and packaged at a place like Off Meshek.

Jacob instructed me in the art of holding several chicks together at once by the legs and shooting vaccine into their thighs out of a pistollike injector. It was very hard work, because it required both speed and dexterity. As I held one of these tiny, velvety creatures in my hands, its forelegs, which were as brittle as matchsticks, snapped. Jacob told me to wring its neck, and when he saw me hesitate, he barked, "If you want to work here, you'd better get it into your head that this is a factory, not a little animal farm for children!" Then he grabbed hold of the chick and marched it off to the incinerator, muttering into his beard something about "hypocritical bourgeois types" who gorged themselves on fat steaks while spouting pious sentiments about suffering animals.

While I was trying to regain my composure, a handsome young man with long, soft brown hair and a luxuriant mustache burst through the door. Before he had a chance to open his mouth, Jacob cut him off curtly: "Don't bother coming up with an excuse, David, I had to get an Egyptian to do your share of the work."

David smiled at me. "So you've come to live with us! I wish you would stay; we need people like you, with ideals."

"But this kibbutz is full of idealistic people!" I exclaimed, somewhat embarrassed by the compliment.

"Ah!" he said, raising his eyebrows with the slightly affected air of someone anxious to show everyone present the superiority his cynicism afforded him. "When I first came to this kibbutz, I thought this was a group of people who really had the internal strength and the courage not to give a shit about the norms of society. But I was wrong: With us, the most important thing is to be *beseder* ["ok, regular"], to work hard and not cause any trouble."

When we had finished vaccinating the chicks, it was time for breakfast —an event that would become my favorite part of the day at Hazon Hadash. I delighted in the sight of throngs of young men and women in blue shorts and sturdy working shoes, the feel of the cool plastic chairs against my thighs, the soothing noise of the electric bread-slicer in the corridor, the rattle of spoons in the plastic teacups, and the huge pails of fresh yogurt and chunks of crisp rye bread set out on the tables. At the entrance, waiting for us on the floor, were piles of *Al Hamishmar,* the Mapam party's newspaper.

Now David stuck a copy in Jacob's face, asking, "Have you seen this? Our demonstration got front-page coverage!"

Jacob ignored him.

"Well, read it! Why don't you read it?" David shouted, his eyes flashing a fierce blue. "It's all there: the hassle with the police, the ones who got hauled off to jail, everything!"

"As far as I'm concerned, it's too bad they didn't put *you* in jail. It certainly would be no great loss for our work team, since you never even bother to show up!"

"So that's our politicized kibbutz!" David burst out indignantly. "Supposedly we came here because we cared enough to try to change reality. But people like you, who don't give a shit about the fate of the country, will wake up one day to find there's no kibbutz left. A communist enclave won't survive for long within a capitalist society! You can't just sit here and talk about socialism without being in touch with our proletariat in the factories, or about peace with the Arabs while you let our government put up settlements in the occupied territories!"

At the word "socialism," Jacob's eyes beamed ironically, and he said, "All this mumbo-jumbo about socialism is meaningless. Economics has its own laws: efficiency and productivity. They're the only criteria that measure the success of the kibbutz. If the kibbutz doesn't prosper, its children will leave. And besides, before you talk about changing *reality,* why don't you try changing yourself a little bit?" Then Jacob stalked off, leaving David, who had been chewing on his pipe, to nurse his resentments in a cloud of smoke.

David and I spent several more hours working together in the henhouse. He showed me how to stick my left forefinger into the turkeys' mouths below their nostrils and cut off their beaks—a bloody but necessary procedure to keep them from pecking each other to death when they got into fights. I too found David a little too smooth and clever, but sometimes in the midst of a conversation that was intended to be a display of his wit and verbal elegance to me, he would say something profound or genuinely moving. Perhaps it was only because he was so good-looking that I liked to imagine that a kind heart lay hidden beneath his arrogant exterior.

That night he stopped me on the way out of the dining room and asked, with his most seductive smile, if I'd like to meet him later by the pool for a short swim. I accepted.

When I turned up at the appointed time, we swam a few laps. It had been very hot, and we enjoyed splashing the water about; the cool currents felt silky against our naked bodies. As we rested on the tiles, still warm from the sun they had absorbed during the day, David confided: "Even though you're an Egyptian, I feel I have more in common with you, who talk about essential things, than I do with many of my so-called comrades here. All *they* ever talk about is their army service and their work. This hang-up about work that I was discussing with Jacob this morning, that's what damages the most essential part of kibbutz life. Work is so sacrosanct with everyone here that they're not even willing to discuss it, even though we live very comfortably now and can afford much more leisure time than our parents could. People say to me, 'What would I *do* if I didn't work?' To read, to think, to dream, would never occur to them as a fit occupation for a human being!

"The saddest thing," he added, "is that the people of this country have lost the capacity to dream." His tone had changed suddenly from cold superiority to despair, and I half-expected him to burst into tears.

What David had said certainly described Jacob perfectly. Hard-working, egalitarian, frugal, Jacob was the embodiment of the pioneering ethos—but without its imagination or inventiveness. I was not personally very fond of him, but still I felt compelled to come to his defense. How else *could* the kibbutz maintain itself? I asked David. Someone had to assume responsibility for getting the work done—and Jacob had sacrificed popularity and pleasure to that higher ideal.

But David would have none of it. "Don't tell me you let yourself be taken in by Jacob!" he burst out. "He's an idiot, an asshole! Don't you see? This little kulak *loves* work. He's inherited our parents' neuroses, their puritan need to show the world that the Jews are capable of manual work: ten hours a day, every day. Well, I think it's ridiculous!"

It did not require great discernment to grasp that the ideological feuds and bitter personal rivalries that had bedeviled the socialist communes from their very beginning in Palestine and had led by the mid-forties to the splitting up of several kibbutzim existed here too. The work ethic had been the very essence of the socialist-Zionist revolution, because the pioneers believed that anti-Semitism stemmed largely from the common perception of Jews as parasites who peddled wares, traded, banked, and were intellectuals, but did not engage in *productive* occupations. Hence the pioneers' scorn for "traditional" Jewish occupations and their glorification of manual work. The work ethic was the most important legacy they passed on to their children. Along with a reliance on automation and high technology, it resulted in great productivity and prosperity; paradoxically, some kibbutzim even became very rich. But whereas for the pioneers the work ethic was at the root of their psychological and social transformation, for their children it led only to material growth. By teaching their sons and daughters the work ethic as a sacrosanct doctrine, they raised a generation that was stolid, industrious, unimaginative. While the pioneers themselves had been innovative, their children were profoundly conservative.

Among the third generation, many left the kibbutz. Of those who remained, many stayed on merely because the kibbutz offered material well-being and security—it relieved them of the hassle of having to look for a job in the city and the problem of mortgage payments on apartments. The more idealistic ones, like the founders of Hazon Hadash, shared a desire to see the kibbutz return to the egalitarianism of their grandparents; they insisted that all work, including scut work, be done on a rotation basis and that no post be a source of privilege and monetary benefit. But while the conservatives, like Jacob, were content with correcting the "distortions" fifty years of prosperity had brought to their parents' kibbutzim, the radicals, like Michelle and David, went beyond that to question the value of work itself. By stripping work of its mythical dimensions and reducing it to a means for achieving more important human goals, they were embarking on the same revolutionary course their grandparents had charted when they placed manual work above intellectual and professional pursuits.

Fortunately, I was spared having to get more deeply involved in the battle between David and Jacob. Michelle recruited me to help her out in the toddlers' house instead, since her co-worker, Dahlia, had gone to Jerusalem for a week to visit her boyfriend.

The next morning I arrived late for work, having had to make a long-distance call. The toddlers' house was a bright yellow cottage with cheerful green blinds and a red roof, surrounded by a low wooden fence of alternating blue and pink slats. Toy trucks and balls lay scattered all over the yard, newly built sand castles stood intact in the playpens beside the pails and hoes, but there was silence everywhere and no one in sight.

I stepped onto the terrace, where five pairs of tiny hiking shoes, three brown and two red, had been lined up meticulously on top of a blue trunk. The door of the house was unlocked, so I went in. It was empty. The kitchenette-playroom area had been gaily decorated: Fish mobiles hung from the light fixture and children's paintings covered the walls. In the center stood a square red table of Lilliputian height surrounded by minuscule yellow chairs.

While I was examining my surroundings, I heard laughter, children's voices, and then the quick light steps of someone running up the stairs and onto the terrace. Then a tot, dripping water from head to foot, stood before me in rubber thongs and a green-and-yellow-striped bathing suit. "Shalom," I said, bending down with a smile, and tried to pick him up in order to plant a kiss on his cheek. But he let out a piercing shriek, wriggled out of my arms, and ran off hollering, *"Hamitzria kan! Hamitzria kan!"* ("The Egyptian is here! The Egyptian is here!"). Within moments I was surrounded by a throng of children, who looked up at me as indignantly as the three bears must have looked at Goldilocks when they discovered she had eaten their porridge and slept in their beds.

"Now, now, children, be nice to Sana, she's here to help while Dahlia is away" came the admonishing voice of Michelle. She apologized for not having waited for me, saying that the swimming pool was the one place in the kibbutz where the children were forbidden to go unaccompanied.

When Michelle went to fetch some towels and clothes for the children, they formed a circle around me, scrutinizing me avidly. This silent examination, which I found very embarrassing, was brought to an end by a mousy little fellow with large, soft brown eyes, who asked whether my father was a Pharaoh. When I told him that he wasn't, he looked greatly relieved, and the others became more relaxed about talking to me. One little girl wanted to know if I was married. Her question took me by surprise, and when I did not reply right away, she said, "You'd better get married quickly."

"Why?" I asked.

"Because you'll be a grandmother without any grandchildren, and you'll be lonely!"

Michelle asked me to give her a hand in bathing the children after their swim. The four-year-olds needed no help; they washed themselves in the communal shower, gossiping, joking, pinching each other, and having such fun that they had to be literally dragged out from under the water when their turns were up. But the smaller children, the two- and three-year-olds, had to be washed in huge zinc bathtubs, the only things in the toddlers' house that had been built to size so that we would not have to bend.

On that first day, I had just lifted two four-year-olds into the bathtub when one of them began splashing water with his feet and shouting, "Choo-choo-choo," in imitation of a locomotive. Intermittently, he called out, "Ding-dong, ding-dong," and wiggled his penis between his thumb and index finger to show me he was ringing a bell as the train pulled into the station. The other little boy, who was seated at the edge of the bathtub watching him enthralled, got up and tried to ring the bell but was pushed away. He fell backward and began to wail. Seemingly moved by this, the little train conductor kissed him on the head and obligingly handed him his penis. The boy immediately stopped crying and grabbed hold of it. After a while, the train conductor said, "*Dai*" ("Enough"). But the boy ignored him and went on flicking the penis back and forth with renewed vigor. A cry of "*Dai, dai*, you're hurting me!" finally made him desist. He removed his hand and contemplated his friend's reddened, stiff member with some astonishment, and then he knelt in the bathtub and kissed it.

Watching the exhilaration with which these children uninhibitedly played about in the nude reminded me darkly of my own upbringing. When I was in kindergarten at the Mère de Dieu, the sisters would, out of modesty, bathe us in our cotton undershirts and panties. How we hated the sensation of that sponge sliding underneath our clammy underwear! This was done to protect not only the sisters' virtue but our own as well. At no time during the bath were we permitted to set eyes on our own bodies. When we got out of the tub, one of the sisters would wrap a towel around us, under which, by a feat of superlative dexterity, we wriggled out of our wet underwear. She would then dry us chastely and, having completed her task, fasten the towel around our torsos and depart, drawing the curtains of the bathroom cubicle behind her. Moments later, the arm of the now invisible sister would slip in from behind the curtain with a little package containing the neatly folded laundry we were supposed to wear—clean underwear and a school uniform.

One day I discovered that the housekeeper had forgotten to put panties in my package. In a hurry to join my friends at play, I did not point this out to the sister, since I would have had to wait until she went upstairs to fetch me a pair; instead, I hastily slipped on my skirt and stepped out into the courtyard, where the children were playing a game called statues, in which everyone had to freeze suddenly in position and anyone surprised in motion was eliminated.

As I froze with one leg up in the air, a little girl noticed that I was wearing no panties and ran at once to tell the sister. For this "perversion" I was expelled. When I arrived home the next day, accompanied by a sister, I found my mother waiting for me with a riding crop in her hand. My aunt's chauffeur had brought it over early in the morning with her assurance that where all else had failed, this would surely tame me. Mother followed my aunt's recommendation, applying the crop liberally to the buttocks that had brought such shame on the family.

After Michelle and I had finished bathing the children, she sent me to fetch their lunch from the central kitchen while she dried and dressed them. I went and was handed eight large mess kits full of provisions. Michelle set the red plastic dishes out on the table, and at noon David arrived from the henhouse and we sat down to eat. It was part of the feminist convictions of Hazon Hadash to have a man participate in the children's care; he stayed with them until four in the afternoon, when they went to visit their parents.

I watched the kids, chuckling at the thought of my mother's shock if she could see their table manners. The first course was chicken soup, which some of them fell upon immediately while others dawdled. One, a plump, freckled four-year-old, guzzled all her soup and then leaned over to help herself again from the serving plate. Each time she brought the ladle over to her bowl, she poured soup all over the table. The other children immersed their fingers in these soup puddles and began to make "drawings."

The next course—meatballs with mashed peas—offered the children yet greater amusement. One of them, a scrawny boy with mischievous green eyes, began to push the meatballs with his tongue from one cheek to the other, yellling, "Look, I have a wart on my right cheek, now I have one on my left cheek." Soon a girl with golden curls called out, "I have green cheeks." She had smeared the pea puree on her face, and that set off a chorus of "Me too, me too" as each one of the children in turn imitated her.

When we left the table, it was dripping multicolored liquids from all sides, the lemonade jar had spilled onto the floor, and half-eaten meatballs were floating in the compote.

While Michelle cleared up, David and I placed those children who had opted for a siesta on the potties before tucking them into bed. Once more the scene was one of complete bedlam. Some of the children slid across the room on their potties, which, needless to say, resulted in their spilling half of the contents, while others got up to visit each other in the middle of the procedure. A boy and a girl were romping about the sodden floor, fondling each other and giggling madly. In the midst of this ruckus, a little girl sat imperturbably on her potty, masturbating. Suddenly, a triumphant cry hailed from one end of the room; a frizzy redhead was calling on her friends to come and see what she had done. All of them gathered around her, struck dumb with admiration. Then she snatched her "caca" and ran off to show it to David, who tweaked her ear approvingly, saying, "*Eze yoffi!*" ("What a beauty!").

David stayed with the children while they were napping, and Michelle took me over to the older children's house (ages five to ten) and introduced me to their *metapelet* ("caretaker"), Yael, a tall and rather glum young woman. No sooner had we sat down to a cup of coffee and begun to converse than we were interrupted by wails from the yard. We looked out the window and saw a group of children circling a small boy, chanting jeeringly:

> *Tu aleicha ve al paneicha,*
> *Hachatul hishtin aleicha.*
>
> (Tu! on you and on your face,
> The cat has pissed on you.)

The boy's tears, far from persuading his tormentors to desist, only excited them to new acts of aggression. Soon they got carried away by their nasty game, and two of the older boys rushed at him, pushing him onto the ground. I was about to go to his rescue when Yael grabbed me by the arm and said, "Let him fend for himself!" So I looked on impotently as one of them bit his arm in an effort to get him to release his water pistol while the other jumped on his chest. As he lay pinned to the ground, a little girl crawled up to him and pulled his penis. He let out a horrendous shriek, and at this point, unable to hold out any longer, I ran outside, picked him up, and carried him into the room.

I was sitting with him on my lap, consoling him and wiping his tears, when I noticed Yael's angry face. I looked at her in surprise, and before I had a chance to ask her what was the matter, she said icily, "You should not have interfered. Motti must learn to retaliate. We aren't trying to bring up Christians here, who will turn the other cheek. Israel needs strong men, not a bunch of sissies!" Michelle cast an ironic glance in my direction.

The next morning when I got to the toddlers' house, I found Michelle distributing canvases to the children. A little boy pulled me by the sleeve, saying, "Come and see my new crayons." But Michelle cut in reproachfully: "*Our* new crayons!" Then she asked me to mix the paints, telling the children that while they were waiting, she was going to teach them a little poem called "Etzlenu" ("At Our Place"), which she wanted them to commit to memory. It went as follows:

> At our place, there are no movies or theaters,
> And there are no skyscrapers either.
> But there is a tall silo that can be seen from far away.
> At our place, there are no cars,
> But there are tractors and horses we can ride,
> And a donkey each one of us can mount in turn. . . .
>
> At our place, nothing is *mine*,
> Everything is *ours*.
> Ours it is, Rami's and Dani's
> And anybody else's who will come and join us!

Later, as the class was drawing to a close, the little boy Michelle had chided beckoned me with his finger, and when I went up to his desk he shyly presented me with his painting: a man with a *kova tembel* (a folksy Israeli hat) standing beside a cannon aimed at a man in Arab headgear. The cannon was crossed out in red paint.

A few days later Michelle explained to me that in addition to drawing, finger painting, and clay molding, the children were taught by the "subject method." A certain period of time, generally a week, would be set aside for the study of a particular topic, like the frog, the Eskimos, or the Dead Sea. Dahlia was normally in charge of this program, but since she was away, Michelle proposed that I make Egypt the following week's topic.

I hadn't the foggiest notion of how to go about preparing the theme, though she had told me she would supply me with any materials I needed. I ruminated for a while without feeling in the least inspired. Then I remembered how the children had loved my bad drawings of the Pyramids and the models of Egyptian villages I had constructed out of clay, complete with buffalo, waterwheels, mud huts, and palm trees. And I had an idea.

There was an air-raid shelter with a peace sign painted across it just outside the toddlers' house. The kids referred to it as the dinosaur, since it lay hidden under the earth with only a long, snoutlike aperture emerging into the open. They would contemplate it endlessly, spellbound, because all kinds of animals came to sunbathe on its snout: Lazy cats, lizards, pigeons, and beetles liked to meet there for their midafternoon naps, and whole columns of big black ants marched on it all day. The children themselves often gathered there to peer down its dark staircase, and the dank, musty odor the snout exuded made their little bellies tremble with fear and excitement. I decided to convert it into an underground burial chamber for Pharaohs.

All week long Michelle and I worked on this with the children. The shelter had not been used in two years, not since the 1973 war, so we had to clean it out first. Then we built a sarcophagus out of old wooden boards, which I coated with gold paint, and constructed a gilded headdress for the Pharaoh out of wallpaper. He was to be accompanied by his consort; for her I made a wig of fine tresses, consisting of woolen strands dyed black and held together by a diadem in the shape of a snake. I also made clothes for the whole retinue of consuls, proconsuls, servants, and slaves who were to be interred alive with her. Finally, we prepared the provisions for the afterlife: large bread loaves that the children helped bake, earthenware jugs full of water, and baskets laden with fruit.

At the end of the week everything was ready, and each one of the children had a part to play—a role determined by the drawing of lots, since all of them wanted to be the mummy and no one wanted to be a slave. The funeral procession began at the animal farm. The queen led Quasimodo, Michelle's donkey, who bore the wooden casket with the mummy; she was followed by her ministers bearing the treasure chest filled with marbles. Last of all came the servants and slaves with the provisions, and a few live chickens, geese, and rabbits. As we proceeded slowly toward our final resting place, accompanied by the dirgelike rhythm of drums and flutes, the whole kibbutz turned out to watch us.

I never ceased to congratulate myself for this stroke of genius, and the subsequent need to keep up my reputation in the kibbutz as a miracle-worker with children so taxed my vanity that I would lie awake night after night racking my brains for a new "Egyptian game."

It was the thrill of my newly gained popularity that made me decide to stay on in the toddlers' house even after Dahlia, the other *metapelet*, returned from Tel Aviv. I offered to work as a *pkak* (literally a cork, meaning a floater), rotating as needed between the toddlers' house and the two children's houses.

It was clear to me from my first day in Yael's children's house that when it came to work and discipline, she belonged in the "conservative" camp. While Michelle's toddlers were never forced to eat, nap, or participate in activities they were not interested in, Yael maintained that the children needed a "structure" and that if they were not required to nap, they would become cranky and unmanageable by evening. To be sure, she did not rely on sanctions to enforce compliance with the rules; rather, she educated the children in kibbutz values from a very tender age, and substituted peer pressure for punishment. In this she followed the pedagogical line laid down by the pioneers, who, in revolt against the patriarchal authority of their "bourgeois" homes, ruled out all forms of punishment; they were great believers in talking things over with the children—a method that was also applied to adult deviants, who were often reduced to tears by relentless public criticism at a kibbutz meeting. And the system worked: There was no crime in the kibbutz; no one locked doors for fear of theft, or avoided walking through the fields at night for fear of rape. Yael claimed that her children were far happier and less neurotic than "Michelle's poor kids," who could not handle so many choices. To which Michelle replied with a shrug of the shoulders, saying that she'd rather raise neurotic children than square ones, or as she put it, "Jews rather than Israelis."

If the toddlers' house seemed to me a hedonistic paradise, the children's house, on the contrary, struck me with the stringency of its work ethic. At this young age, the children were expected to make their beds and shine their shoes every morning, and they were responsible for setting the table and clearing it after they ate (Yael had given up the idea of having them wash the dishes as well only because they invariably left them sticky). And any child caught loitering while performing these tasks would be sternly upbraided by Yael with "*Chaval al hazman*" ("It's a pity to waste time").

When I remarked on this to Michelle, she told me: "In my old kibbutz, we had a vegetable garden when we were children. We raised lettuce, radishes, scallions in neat little beds. Three tools were used for the gardening: a rake, a hoe, and a *turia* [an Arabic name for a big, heavy hoe for digging]. It was for me, as for everyone else in the children's house, a matter of great importance which one of these tools we were assigned for a task. We despised the rake. It was the lightest tool, a tool for a softy, a weakling, a female. The hoe was acceptable but not particularly desirable. And then there was the *turia*. It was glorious! It was the pride, the very emblem of the tough manual worker, the icon of our church—the Church of the Religion of Labor. Whenever we were shown pictures of the pioneers, they seemed to be carrying *turias* on their shoulders—the way Crusaders carried their crosses when they rode off to battle. And then if you worked long enough with a *turia*, you were sure to have blisters, and that was pure bliss! How much we scorned soft, white, clean, manicured hands! We loved to display these marvelous blisters. I was very proud of my father's horny hands. He worked in the kibbutz garage; his fingers were all chapped, and the tar had soaked into his skin and couldn't be washed off."

Though the children were not crazy about any of the chores Yael assigned to them, there was one job they all loved: taking care of their animal farm. They had some gray rabbits in a cage, as well as two goats and three sheep who wandered about a little fenced-in yard. There were also some ducks in a little pool the children had built themselves, a handsome peacock, three fat white geese, and a host of speckled black hens and roosters with metallic-blue necks that some Palestinian friends of David's from a village in the Galilee had given him as a gift. Fortunately, unlike their poor relations the kibbutz hens, who were confined to tiny cells, fed mechanically, and tricked by continuous artificial light into reproducing without respite, the children's hens were fed in the old-fashioned way: The children waited impatiently for their turn to scatter the grain for them and to search for the big brown eggs they laid every morning in the hay.

I do not know whether it was the result of seeing the animals copulate on their animal farm, but these children seemed unusually precocious when it came to sex. We were in the habit of taking them every morning on hikes in "Switzerland"—a name the children had given to the hills surrounding the kibbutz. These hikes were meant to instill in them both a love for nature and an intense attachment to the land of Israel. The biblical history of every mountain, ravine, lake, spring, well, rock, tree, and flower became an integral part of each child's personal experience as a result. If we happened to pass by a terebinth, Yael would tell them the story of Absalom, whose hair, which he wore long like a girl's, was caught in the branches of a similar tree as he rode by on his horse; if we came across poplars, she would describe how these same trees had adorned King David's courtyard. One day she stopped before a plot of pansies and asked the children if they knew the origin of their Hebrew name, *Amnon v' Tamar*. No one did, so she proceeded to explain that they were named after Amnon and Tamar, a brother and sister who, according to the Bible, had been lovers. The idea of incest was apparently totally new to the children; it excited them greatly, and they immediately asked her if a brother could impregnate his sister. Yael laughingly affirmed that he could and, pointing at me, said that the Pharaohs had been in the habit of marrying not only their sisters but even their mothers. At this the children's eyes grew huge, and they began to ask her all manner of graphic questions, which she answered with complete candor.

One day I became intrigued by a band of kids who skipped out every day after lunch while the others were napping or playing out in the yard. No one knew where they went, but when they returned they would huddle together whispering conspiratorially. Curious, I decided to spy on them. I trailed them at a distance, noticing how they scattered and how first one, then another, would bend over beside the communal showers, outside a hut's window, or by the bushes, apparently searching for something. Occasionally they would pick up an object from the ground. Was it a coin? An insect? Mushrooms? I was too far away to tell. Nor could I hang around to watch them return with their loot, since I had to be home before them so they would not suspect anything.

Finally I landed on a clue. Yael told me in a shocked tone that on the preceding morning she had discovered a bunch of condoms, all filled with water, dangling from the branches of the old oak tree in the school-yard. From this I guessed that the band had formed a secret society of condom-collectors, and I was not wrong. Kibbutz members, it seemed, discarded them rather carelessly, throwing them out their windows or leaving them on the lawn, by the trees, near the swimming pool, or wherever else they happened to be at night. The children had turned the hunt for used condoms into a great sport! They returned each day from their jaunt with pockets full of them and compared their finds to see who had amassed the most booty. In order to make condoms available to members at all times, the kibbutz had cut a slot in the facade of the health clinic so that anyone could slip his hand in and take one after the door was locked. Although the children had discovered the "secret" place, they disdained that source, regarding it as insufficiently challenging—it was no fun since it did not call for a search.

Two weeks after I unraveled the mystery, I was putting the towels I had folded into the little cubicles that lined the bathroom wall when I overheard two kids talking to each other in the toilet.

"Do you know why Amira got pregnant?" asked one.

"No," said the other. "Why?"

To which the little boy excitedly whispered that the condom storage facility had recently been invaded by ravenous white ants.

One morning Yael left me to fetch the children's lunch from the central kitchen. I was sitting in the playroom, where eight children were busy with a game of Monopoly, when one of them, a little boy, came up to me and patted my breasts. By then I was used to seeing children do this to the *metaplot*; they often caressed our breasts, kissed them, or climbed up on our laps and fell asleep with their heads nestled against them, so I did not flinch. A moment later he threw his arms around my neck and smothered me with embraces. I disengaged myself and sent him back to play with the others. Shortly thereafter he returned, began patting me again on the breasts, and said, "Your breasts are bigger than Yael's." I agreed they were, and he said point-blank, "Show them to me." A little girl who had been stringing beads on the floor beside me sprang up and began clamoring, "Yes, yes, show them to us!" The refrain was immediately picked up by the other children, who thronged around me, yelling excitedly. The suddenness of their attack took me completely by surprise, and I reacted in a quite conventional manner—with embarrassment. The children sensed this—kibbutz children have an uncanny talent for detecting weakness—and they instantly became bolder. One of them began shouting, "Let's take her clothes off!" Within moments they had clambered all over me. I began shouting, *"Ma ze po? Taf-siku!"* ("What's going on here? Stop it!"), but my voice sounded high-pitched and patently unauthoritative. Yael returned at this point and rescued me, but not before they had succeeded in tearing my bra strap.

Yael reacted to this incident with complete equanimity; she did not even scold the children. Like the other *metaplot*, she had been taught to look upon the manifestations of sexuality in children as natural. This pedagogical line was handed down to them by the pioneers, who, deeply under the influence of Freud, struggled to overcome the sexual taboos of their *shtetl* upbringings.

This permissive method of child rearing was applied to some other matters as well, particularly schoolwork, which the pioneers had little respect for because of their anti-intellectual bent. When I worked with Hazon Hadash's oldest group of children (aged twelve to thirteen), I found out they were allowed to choose their own courses. No one who didn't want to was forced to study math. One day I was asked to give a lecture on the Palestinian problem. I was to talk for ten minutes, after which the teacher would comment on points I had made; the students had been asked to write essays on the subject for their homework, which they were to hand in at the end of the class period.

When I arrived, the students, who clearly regarded my presence in class as a welcome novelty and diversion, began to clap their hands and stamp their feet. This lasted a few minutes, with the teacher adding to the general commotion by trying to shout, *"Sheket!"* ("Quiet!") over their applause. They ignored him and continued to carry on. When they finally quieted down, I began, only to be interrupted by the arrival of latecomers who continued to whisper and giggle among themselves despite the ongoing lecture.

After I finished, the teacher gave his commentary, stressing Israel's security situation and its reluctance to have a PLO-governed state in the West Bank. A student who disagreed with him cut in: "*Eze shtuyot ata medaber?*" ("What kind of nonsense are you saying?"). The teacher chose not to hear the remark and continued. When he finished, he asked one of the girls to step up to the desk and read her essay to the class, but she exclaimed, "*Ma, hishtagata?*" ("What, are you crazy?"), at which her classmates squealed with laughter. Finally, a boy volunteered to read his essay, but the students constantly interrupted him, blurting out whatever came into their heads without waiting to be called on. Others sat in back gossiping; one girl chewed gum and filed her nails while a boy read a review of a James Bond movie. The teacher called out to him, "Yossi, what are you doing?" to which he replied, without lifting his eyes from the magazine, "What d'you care?" This angered the teacher, who finally demanded, "Why aren't you paying attention?" The boy, looking defiantly at him, answered, "Because it doesn't interest me."

Noticing that the period was drawing to a close, the teacher said he would make some concluding remarks, but the students immediately pointed to me and began to chant, "Let *her* talk, let *her* talk!"

The enforcement of any discipline in the oldest children's house was left almost entirely to the peer group—the chief upholder and enforcer of kibbutz values. Peer pressure was the only form of punishment. If a child was thought not to conform, the punishment dealt out by classmates could range from something mild, like ostracism—the silent treatment at the dining table, or banishment from a group activity—to the much-dreaded *birur* ("hearing"), in which the student was judged before his or her entire age group and criticized.

One day, the head of the kibbutz Education Committee appeared in the oldest children's house. "Children," he said, "I am bringing you a new girl. She is an *ola chadasha* ["new immigrant"] from Rumania, and you must all help her integrate into our kibbutz and our country."

"Come in," said the teacher to the new girl, who stood huddled at the door, looking extremely ill at ease. "Take this empty seat in the third row." The girl moved awkwardly over to the designated chair without daring to lift her eyes. A burst of muffled giggles greeted her entrance. To these thirteen-year-olds, the newcomer must have seemed very funny indeed: She was the very opposite of the lean, muscular, suntanned

Sabra ideal. Her fat thighs bulged out from under her short skirt and her calves were thick and pale.

"What is your name, *chavera* ["comrade"]?" the teacher asked.

"Madeleine," faltered the timid voice.

There were titters from the class at such a "Christian" name. "Quiet!" yelled the teacher. But the whispering and giggling continued throughout the period as the students exchanged nasty cartoons of the unfortunate girl, with her *galuti* ("Diaspora-like") clothes: flounced dress with little round collar, black patent-leather Mary Janes, and pathetically neat braids tied with pink ribbons.

When the course was over, we went to the gym for physical education, where Madeleine's appearance in shorts was greeted with hoots. While her classmates ran nimbly about with the grace of young colts, she labored to keep up with them, red-faced and puffing.

Afterward, in the communal showers, Madeleine looked nervously about her. She was not used to undressing in public, and the prospect of having to shower in front of others was utterly humiliating to her. She waited until they had finished and then went in by herself, but they sneaked in and "surprised" her when she was naked, and jeered at her plump body. Madeleine ran off in tears to the head of the Education Committee and begged to be excused from gym, but that was simply unthinkable. Ironically, gym was the one subject that was mandatory at Hazon Hadash—indeed throughout Israel, even at the university level. How else was the new breed of tough young Sabras to be built?

In the weeks that followed, Madeleine tried hard to become integrated into the group of her peers. She changed her "Christian" name to an Israeli one, Carmela, and purchased a gilded Star of David of a size no one could miss, which she pinned over her heart. But that was not enough. Why did she have to go and choose such an awful, old-fashioned name, and an Oriental Jewish one to boot? So poor Madeleine changed her name a second time. This time she chose an "in" name, modern and more befitting a Sabra—Irit.

But there were just too many strikes against her. For one thing, she was an excellent student, her homework was always on time, and her notebooks were impeccably neat. So her classmates called her a *shwitzer* —a Yiddishism for someone who sweats, used to designate an arrogant person who tries to excel over others, an unforgivable breach of the egalitarian ethic of the kibbutz. And then the art teacher was always praising her for the "corny" European landscapes she drew, snow-capped chalets and ponds nestling in deep forests where deer grazed innocently. As though this were not enough, Madeleine was a dutiful daughter who went to visit her family every Sabbath instead of spending her time off in the youth movement. This evoked even nastier cartoons: caricatures of Madeleine strolling arm-in-arm with her "nice little family" in the park every Saturday.

In the end, despairing of ever being accepted, Madeleine found herself a boyfriend in the city. Her appearance changed completely: She cut off her braids, had her ears pierced, let her nails grow long, and even wore rouge. For this she was called before a *birur*, and her "sluttish" appearance was severely criticized; she was ordered to dress in a manner more befitting a kibbutznik. When she did not heed this warning, her classmates ganged up on her one night and wrenched off her earrings so savagely that one of her earlobes was torn. Then they soaped her face and dragged her to the swimming pool, where they proceeded to duck her head until she almost choked.

As usual when I was distressed or perplexed about things that happened at the kibbutz, I discussed the matter with Michelle. She told me: "You see, this is what comes of our forever ranting and raving about how we're kibbutzniks, we're special, we're really something! The kids naturally pick it up, and then they defend the insufferable parochialism that we think distinguishes us, the elite, from those strange, square 'others,' those dark ones, those *outsiders*. You should hear them say 'those city kids,' it's as though they were describing vomit! Even *within* the kibbutz there are outsiders, second-class citizens—the Oriental Jews. My parents' kibbutz used to adopt these children from the deprived neighborhoods, supposedly to give them a chance at a better education, but what a difference between their children's house and ours. They had a separate building, because our parents didn't want us to mix with them. Our children's house was nicely painted and had a pretty, well-tended garden, and theirs was an ugly concrete shack—it was like Harlem versus Fifth Avenue! We never played with them, and they attended separate courses, supposedly because they were not at our level. No one encouraged them to study in any case, since 'those people just aren't cut out for it.' Most of them dropped out of high school pretty fast and joined the kibbutz labor force, which of course was very advantageous for us. They even ate separately! The kitchen claimed it could not cope with so many people all at once, so the Oriental Jews and the Arab workers had dinner at six-thirty and the rest of the kibbutz at eight."

For all her criticism of the kibbutz, Michelle herself seemed to me the incarnation of its socialist ideals, a harmonious integration of commitment to work, politics, and personal freedom. I believed her to be one of the few successes in an otherwise flawed attempt to bring about a more just social order by creating a "new man." Had I told her this she would have laughed, yet there was about her a quality that was increasingly evident to me: a transparent honesty, a sort of pristine purity, a directness, an inability to tell a lie.

The more time we spent together, the greater became my admiration for Michelle. It was clear we were as unlike as any two people could be. I didn't know a daisy from a dahlia, a eucalyptus from a willow. I thought onions grew on trees and bananas on the ground, had no idea where leather came from or that fish laid eggs. If truth be told I found the landscapes that turned Michelle lyrical rather boring: What was the point of driving another thirty miles, I thought, to see yet more trees? Now if it were to drive to a city, that would be something else again—I could appreciate the beauty of cityscapes. All this amazed Michelle, who had never met someone quite like me before, and made her by turns irritable, contemptuous, or full of pity for me. My feeling toward her was too indefinite to be called by any one name, though it had something of awe in it and much of fascination.

Our differences of temperament and experience ran deep. As a child I had been an enfant terrible, while Michelle was a model citizen, helpful, obedient, and neat. My natural instinct was toward rebellion, hers toward compliance. But Michelle had a rooted inner strength. Though she could give in and accept a great deal even if she did not agree with it, she was yielding only up to a certain point: There was a barrier set by her honesty that nothing would have induced her to cross. Besides, her mother's determination not to be a *Yiddishe mama*—a determination typical of the pioneers—had inculcated in Michelle resilience and rugged independence. Sometimes her mother had carried this principle to extremes. When Michelle chipped her front tooth falling out of a tree at the age of seven, the *metapelet* went to break the news to Rachel, informing her that henceforth her daughter would no longer be allowed to climb trees. "Why?" Rachel had exclaimed. "Let her climb. When she's fallen enough times, she'll learn to be careful." How different from a mother like mine, who fretted deeply over my indigestion and followed me anxiously about the house with a sweater in hand. No wonder I was spoiled, self-indulgent, and egocentric—the very opposite of Michelle.

While I was effusive and verbose, Michelle was quiet and introverted. I had a way with people, and she was entirely without charm—in her eyes, charm was only hypocrisy and manipulation. I masked my jealously guarded privacy beneath a warm and ready smile; she rarely smiled, yet there was about her a genuine openness. Under her rough exterior lay a sensibility I thought made her one of the few members of her generation who deserved the name *Sabra*: a cactus whose fruit is unexpectedly sweet and juicy.

Michelle and I were becoming virtually inseparable. Every night after dinner, we would escape the stifling heat of her little shack by standing on the windowsill and hoisting ourselves onto the flat cement roof. There we would lie on top of an old mattress, smoking and chatting or just gazing up at the stars. Frequently we would fall asleep and be awakened at dawn by the dew that had covered us during the night like an invisible sheet.

One night, as we were lying up on the roof, I asked her why she did not have a boyfriend.

She laughed, saying, "You sound like the matchmakers in my parents' kibbutz. . . ." Then, more gravely, she added: "To be a single person in the old kibbutzim is the most horrible thing in the world. If you aren't seriously committed to getting married by the time you leave the army, everyone becomes absolutely hysterical. To meet the crisis, the kibbutz has devised a program known as bachelors' vacation. All the single girls and boys are sent together to a summer camp in Natanya for a ten-day visit. If nothing comes of this, the kibbutz throws itself into a flurry of matchmaking activities; the secretary might call you in for a 'serious' talk, the general assembly will meet to discuss your case, and they will probably decide to send you for a year of 'activity' in the city. The hope is that if a person has not been lucky enough to meet someone in the kibbutz, he or she will do it while working for the youth movement in the city. If nothing materializes by the end of that year, your case will be taken care of by the interkibbutz committee for matching. Each kibbutz movement has a list of all the single people within its kibbutzim, and it will try to match people with similar interests, as they do in computer dating, and arrange for them to meet suitable partners. If, after all this, the person still doesn't get married, they send him or her to the kibbutz psychiatrist. Naturally, a girl's case causes more panic, although men are definitely not exempted either."

That same night, Michelle and I stayed up for hours discussing the reasons for the return of the kibbutz to traditional Jewish attitudes toward the family. She announced to me that at any rate, *she* would never have children. This was a startlingly adamant statement, coming as it did from the mouth of a twenty-four-year-old. I asked her why, and she told me about Claudine.

Michelle had met Claudine when she was on a leave of absence from the kibbutz, studying at Hebrew University. She had taken on a part-time job in the evening as a telephone operator in Jerusalem. The only highlights of those dreary, uneventful months with the telephone company had been the visits of Secretary of State Kissinger; then the operators all tuned in to his private line. Otherwise the phone calls held little excitement until Michelle, who was working on the international telephone exchange, was put in charge of wrong numbers. If someone calling direct from overseas misdialed—that is, failed to omit the zero in front of the city code—he or she would automatically be connected to Michelle, whose task it was to explain the correct procedure.

One night she intercepted the call of a Parisian woman. They chatted for a while. Claudine told her that she had come to Israel from France with her husband after the '67 war. Both of them had always been fervent Jewish nationalists, she said, and their pride in Israel's victory had impelled them to decide to settle there. Because they were Orthodox Jews, they went to live in a religious neighborhood in Tel Aviv. But once in Israel, Claudine became gradually disenchanted with her husband and with religion. She came under the influence of Matzpen, Israel's extreme left-wing political movement, and became critical of Israel's refusal to vacate the land it occupied in '67. Eventually she decided to leave her husband and return to France.

For months after that call, whenever Claudine was bored she would misdial deliberately and she and Michelle would have hour-long toll-free conversations. Then came an invitation from Claudine to visit Paris. Michelle accepted. With her savings and some money borrowed from her mother, she purchased a youth ticket on El Al and was off.

Claudine was waiting for her at the airport, waving a bright green scarf as had been agreed. They embraced and took off for Claudine's tiny studio on the Boulevard St. Michel. The whole place was no bigger than a bathroom, but in Michelle's rapturous state of mind, it had seemed palatial. After all, it was her first real trip abroad.

Shortly after Michelle had unpacked, Claudine confided to her that she was bisexual. Michelle gagged on the Chinese noodles: The idea of being alone with such a bizarre woman in a strange city made her uneasy at best. But when in time it became clear to her that Claudine was not about to make an advance, she relaxed.

Claudine sought to attract Michelle by maintaining an aloof front with her while going out every night with other women. Michelle, all alone in the little studio, began to romanticize Claudine's very indifference. She would lie awake night after night in her sleeping bag on the floor, yearning for Claudine to call her to her bed. But Claudine deliberately bided her time. A few months went by before they began to be intimate together.

Claudine, a petite blonde, was a typical Parisian bourgeoise, spoiled, clever, witty, elegant, coquettish, and with more charm than real beauty. She held equal sway over men and women; for her, the affair with Michelle was just one of many flirtations. One day Michelle received a postcard "explaining" that Claudine had caught sight of a slender young woman with delicate features who was standing, "as pale and immobile as a statue, in the Jardin du Luxembourg." She had fallen instantly in love with her, she wrote, and had gone to live with her and her young son in Nantes. Brokenhearted, Michelle left Paris and returned to Israel.

As Michelle ended her story, I groped in vain for the appropriate words, but I was too agitated to sort out my confusion. My only contact with homosexuality had been through a pornographic book my older brother had kept hidden under his mattress when I was a child. What images I had of lesbians were linked mostly to grotesque pictures of dildos and toothbrushes sandwiched between chapters on the aberrations of women who had obtained sexual gratification with dogs, eunuchs, and other such exotic partners.

I was not about to show Michelle the revulsion her tale inspired in me. But try as I did, I could not push her story out of my mind. I walked about in a state of feverish excitement for the next couple of days, like a child who had inadvertently stumbled on some grown-up secret and was burning to tell it to someone. And whenever Michelle's eye caught mine I would blush as though I were her accomplice in some crime.

One night I went to see *The Lady from Shanghai*. (The kibbutz showed old Hollywood movies every Tuesday night, which Michelle, who referred to them as the "American garbage series," would not deign to watch.) When I returned home, she lay fast asleep with her back toward me. I stepped up to her bedside, overcome by vague feelings of virginal bashfulness. Only her arms—pale, plump, and fragrant with soap—were visible against the dark blue sheets.

She's asleep, I thought, at once disappointed and relieved. As I was tiptoeing away, she turned and held her hand out to me without a word.

"Show me what to do," I said.

"Just do whatever you feel like."

I lay next to her, stiff, tense, hardly daring to breathe as she unbuttoned my blouse and gently eased out my breasts. I could feel her tongue and lips pressing against my nipples. Then she slipped her hand under my skirt and moved it lightly up my thighs. So this is it—this is all there is to it, I thought, overcome by a flood of relief. During all those days since she had told me her story, I had lain awake at night conjuring up a world of images without substance. And now it had happened. The rite of passage had been remarkably easy.

A long time passed before Michelle came near me again. We went on sleeping in separate beds. Having satisfied my curiosity and having found nothing particularly arousing about making love with a woman, I was not eager to repeat the experiment. Sensing that, Michelle did not press her attentions on me.

One morning I got up especially early because I had to go into the city to give a talk before a group of Israeli university professors from the Shiloah Middle East Center. I had prepared an impasssioned plea for Palestinian self-determination, which I rehearsed in silence as I was dressing. Michelle was in a playful mood, and as I reached for my shirt, she teasingly pinched my breast. I chased her away and went to sit down on the floor, with my back leaning against the bed. While I awaited the arrival of the kibbutz supply man, who was supposed to drive me to Tel Aviv, I flipped through a magazine with nervous trepidation. Michelle sat on the chair opposite me, eating *café matzot* (matzoh flakes in coffee, a Jewish version of cornflakes).

Then she stretched her leg out and slipped her bare foot between my thighs. Out of sheer inertia, I let it pass. Responding half-absentmindedly to the pressure of her sole, I lent my body to the rocking motion. The tingling sensation was not unpleasurable.

My fear that my ride might arrive at any moment only heightened my arousal, as did the distant sound of footsteps on the gravel path, the loud knocking on the door, the folly of it all. Responding to the soft, insistent tread of her foot, I could feel the tiny kernel inside me gradually come to life, grow, and finally burst.

From then on, we made love every night, over and over again until, at five in the morning, we said to ourselves that we really must try to get some sleep now. But since we had to be at work in the children's house by seven, this was hardly a realistic proposition. So we resolved to exercise more self-control the next night. But we never kept to our resolution.

During that phase of my life with Michelle, I felt I could have been content to go on living at Kibbutz Hazon Hadash forever. It was therefore quite a shock when she returned one night furious from a kibbutz meeting and announced that she was leaving. The meeting had been called to discuss the case of Roni, one of the members, who had refused to be drafted during the '73 war and so had been imprisoned for six months. When he returned to Hazon Hadash, the issue had been put on the agenda of the kibbutz meetings, but then it had been quietly dropped; several clashes between Roni and other members of the kibbutz had finally forced it to a crisis. Roni's enemies were numerous; in their view, it was precisely because of Hazon Hadash's public image as a radical kibbutz that they could not afford to get into trouble with the army by sheltering someone who refused to fight, especially in the increasingly right-wing climate.

Once again, David and Jacob exemplified the split in the two approaches of the kibbutz. Michelle described the meeting to me; though she and David had stuck up for Roni, the majority, led by Jacob—who had threatened to quit if Roni were allowed to stay—had voted for his expulsion. "I find the mystification and worship of the army that goes on in this country revolting, and the hypocrisy of this kibbutz even worse," she told me. "I was patriotic once—I was proud of being called to the army after I finished school. But a year later, when I went back to school to attend a friend's graduation ceremony, the headmaster gave a speech and said, 'More graduates of this school have fallen in the wars than those of any other school.' And he was proud of it! That's when I had an insight. I thought to myself: They love all this—reading poems and eulogies and playing the Mozart funeral dirge in the background. They *love* to have a tombstone with a lot of names in our schoolyard. I've been a pacifist ever since."

That night hardly anyone on the kibbutz slept. For a few days after Roni left, Michelle seemed very depressed, but she didn't mention her resolution to leave the kibbutz again, and I concluded that it was just something she had said in the heat of the moment. But one afternoon she came to look for me at the dining room and told me, "You know, I've been doing a lot of thinking since Roni was kicked out. Maybe a genuine pacifist can't live in Israel at all. If you live in Israel, you're unwittingly taking part in the situation, and I can't help feeling there's something dirty about letting other people do the fighting for you. I'm going to France."

"But how will you live?" I asked her. "You have no money." She shrugged, saying she'd find some kind of a job. And a few days later she packed her meager belongings in a knapsack and was gone.

Hazon Hadash was in an uproar. Michelle's departure had thrown the conflicts within the kibbutz into sharp relief. The polarization over the Roni issue mirrored that of the country at large, and perhaps for that reason the debates that followed his expulsion had the quality of a mortal combat. The 1973 war had left in its wake not only a huge death toll but also widespread charges that the war could have been avoided, which resulted in the resignation of the Golda Meir cabinet—and irrevocably altered the unquestioning commitment of young Israelis to take up the call to arms that had characterized Israel in '48 and '67. While some voices could be heard saying that Israel had no choice, had to toughen her armor, others argued that they were prepared to fight for Israel's existence but not for her conquests.

As the debates raged around me, I felt lonelier than ever. Michelle's departure left a big gap in my life. Before meeting her, I had had the greatest difficulty making friends with people my age, because in reaction to the emotionality of the European-born generation, the young people were very cold. And kibbutzniks were colder still. As children they had had to share everything in the children's house, and so they soon learned to hoard the only thing left to them—their thoughts and feelings. It was ironic that the kibbutz, which grew out of idealistic youth movements in which all were expected to bare their souls to their comrades, should produce some of the most introverted Sabras.

But it was not only Michelle's openness that had caused me to seek out her friendship; she was also one of the few people I had met in Israel who had made me feel genuinely liked for myself. Right from the outset, she had exhibited none of the typical fuss that usually greeted my introduction as an Egyptian in Israel, and she was one of the only Israelis I'd met who did not seem to feel compelled to tell me how much she liked Arabs.

The effusion that greeted the news of my being Egyptian was for the most part sincere, and even moving, yet I had never felt more alone than I did in Israel. I would be standing in line with a Dutch girl, trying to get my visa for temporary residence renewed, and my friend would ask the official if he could do it for me that same day because we had to catch the bus back to the kibbutz, at which point one of the clerks would mumble under his breath, "*Al tikra et hatachat shelcha beshvilla, he lo mishelanu*" ("Don't rip your ass for her, she's not one of us"). I would be praising a friend's wife to my neighbor, and she would answer, "*Ken, aval at yodaat, he lo Yehudia*" ("Yes, but you know, she's not Jewish"). Or I would be yelling at a woman in Tel Aviv's *sherut* station for cutting in front of me, and the driver would step between us to make peace, saying, "*Lo, lo, ze lo yaffe, kulanu Yehudim*" ("No, no, this isn't nice, we are all Jews"). In time, I accepted my limitations and learned to keep my place—that of a goy. I understood that Jewish history—that long, awesome chronicle of persecution—stood between me and any possibility of true acceptance.

The weeks passed, yet I felt no better. I often had whole days of depression at the thought that although I now had met hundreds of people in Israel, I had not a single friend, and while everyone invited me to their homes, it was only to display me as an item of curiosity. Even for Danny, I was little more than an exotic Egyptian, and my decision to put distance between us had only served to confuse my feelings about him further. I had had no contact with him now for months. Whether he was in South Africa or Tel Aviv I had no idea, and though I sometimes thought about him, he was becoming an increasingly blurry figure.

When Michelle wrote that she had found a job in Paris, I decided to visit her. The visit had another purpose: to see my parents, who were spending the New Year's holiday there. Since I could not risk traveling to Egypt to see them, this was a rare opportunity to meet. With Michelle nearby, I felt more courageous about what was likely to be an upsetting encounter. I had not seen my mother and father since that stopover in Geneva on the way to Israel almost a year and a half before, when I had been planning to stay for only six weeks.

10

A Vacation in Paris

HUDDLED IN the back seat of an old Parisian cab, which was all too swiftly driving me toward the place where my parents were staying, I felt at once eager, hopeful, and very apprehensive. It was probably foolish of me to be harboring any expectations. Perhaps because of the acute loneliness and sense of isolation I had felt during my last weeks in Israel, I looked forward with longing to touching base with my family, my past, my world. Despite my better judgment, I could not help hoping that the passage of eighteen months would have laid my parents' recriminations to rest.

There was no concierge in sight and no elevator, so I grabbed hold of the suitcase, which the cabbie had deposited by the doorway, and began slowly to climb the stairs. They too were deserted. A big window overlooking a courtyard with potted plants had been left open on the first-floor landing. An identical window greeted me on the second. And here was the third floor, here was the apartment my cousin had lent my parents. My heart beat violently. Drawing a breath, I rang the bell. There was no answer. I rang again more insistently.

The door flew open, and a cry of joy greeted my appearance. Both my parents rushed at me simultaneously and clasped me in their arms, crying, laughing. They had been sitting there glued to the couch for over an hour, waiting for me. I stood locked in their embrace, my knees shaking. Then I took a step forward and sank into the armchair.

We dried our tears. I asked how they had been, and about my sister and brother and things at home. They told me about friends and family in Cairo, and said I looked well, healthy. And then a constrained silence settled upon us, the kind of silence that takes hold of three strangers who meet for the first time. My parents sat on the couch opposite me, studying my face avidly. At last Mother broke the silence:

"Tell us why," she said. "Why did you do it?"

Again a moment of silence.

"Why do you think I did it?" I asked cautiously.

"I don't know," she answered in a tone of complete bewilderment. "Your father and I often wondered about this. Was it just to get attention?"

I was stunned. Was that what they thought? I would not answer and sat in sullen silence.

"What was it then?" she pursued. "Was it the money?"

"The money?" I repeated incredulously. I looked to Father for some sign of sympathy, but he too was eyeing me uneasily. There was no doubt that he did not understand either.

Mother then got up and began to lecture me about the recklessness of my conduct. Her voice had become very stern. I gazed at those perfectly regular, classical features I had always admired as a child and the soft gray eyes that could flash with such fury. Why was she so angry at me? I wondered as I watched her frail body shake with indignation. After all, no harm had come to my family as a result of my trip to Israel; they had not been hustled off to prison as they undoubtedly would have been if Nasser were still alive.

"You must write to Sadat!" she concluded in a tone that left no room for argument.

"Yes, of course! You must!" agreed my father emphatically.

"Why should I?" I exclaimed. "What wrong have I done to Sadat? How can you ask me to go crawling on my knees to a man who sends thousands of people to their death and looks on it as a virtue, while if someone dares to stand up to him and say 'enough!' he looks on it as a crime?"

"Don't be a child!" he said softly. "Do you want your passport to be revoked?"

"I don't care, let him revoke it!" I shouted. "I will not be one of those cowards who sit back home whispering that these wars must stop, that they are insane, but don't dare say so publicly. That's why I went to Israel, if you want to know, not for money or fame, or even to benefit mankind, but—"

"Ach, shush!" Mother interrupted irritably. "You *will* write to Sadat. You must ask his pardon and God's."

At this I could not help laughing. "Really, this is absurd! God's pardon?"

Her face suddenly changed; a tremor passed over it. She looked up at me reproachfully, and tried to say something but couldn't; her eyes filled with tears.

My heart softened. I went up to her and put my arms around her. But she drew away from me and, gazing up at me with a mournful smile, said, "You are a strange girl, Sonia [Mother called me that in her affectionate moments]. You kiss and hug me—but you don't realize the consequences of your actions! There is no one in the world as alone as you are now, my poor girl." She began weeping bitterly. Many of Father's high-ranking friends, she told me, now shunned them, afraid of being implicated by association, and even old family friends pretended not to see them when they turned up at the Guezira Sporting Club or in some café.

I could not laugh at that. I understood only too well how terrible such humiliations were for her. I looked at my father and saw the anguish in his eyes. I could feel his great love for me, and strange to say I felt it suddenly burdensome and painful to be loved. By coming to Paris, I had hoped to rid myself of my guilt feelings toward my parents; now I suddenly felt more unhappy than ever before.

I told my parents I was sorry to have caused them pain. But I could not think what else to say. All at once exhausted, I excused myself and left the room.

As I pulled the door shut behind me, I heard Father say, "Don't worry. I am sure she'll come around to writing this letter," and Mother answer, "Oh, Mahmoud, you are such a fool! Don't you see she is not to be trusted? She is *batala* ["evil"]." I tiptoed to my room and sank onto the bed. For the first time I realized how irremediably Mother and I had drifted apart. The fear that I might have lost her forever preyed on me.

For a long time I lay still, feeling chilled all over. Images without any order or coherence flitted through my mind, faces I would not normally have recalled, fragments of scenes from long ago. I remembered the frequent attempts my mother made to curb my willfulness, the occasional indications my father gave of his pride in me.

When I was a little girl, everyone in the family was always telling me, "*Inti talaa le abouki*" ("You take after your father"), which meant only that my own headstrong qualities were a smaller and more wayward version of his; in other words, my rebelliousness was to his independence of mind as my stubbornness was to his personal integrity. But the comparison was there, and that's what mattered to me—so much so that, from the youngest age, I used to spend hours observing his every gesture, waiting for the word, the repartee, the observation that would make my heart swell with pride or my eyes fill with tears.

Mother idolized my father and recounted endless tales of his valor. One in particular made a lasting impression on me. Father's uncle,

Roushdi Pasha, who had been prime minister during World War I, had appointed Father to be the director of his office when he was still a very young man. One day there were demonstrations outside the ministerial headquarters, and Father came to inform his uncle that the people were clamoring for his resignation because they considered him pro-British. Roushdi Pasha stepped up to the window and, looking down his imperious Turkish nose at the mob gathered by the gate, scoffed, "The people—what people? These are animals!" (He used the Arabic word *bahayim*, which refers to beasts of burden.) To which my father replied with trepidation—for he revered this man, who had raised him since his father had died when he was a little boy—"Uncle, beware—even donkeys sometimes overthrow their yoke when it weighs on them!"

My father's aura had surrounded me from the time I was a very small child. One day, as I slept, Mother came to my room, parted the mosquito net, and lifted me out of bed gently in order not to alarm me. Then she carried me up to the glass-enclosed veranda. As I lay in her arms, I saw a column of flames advancing toward our little island as if to engulf it. Terrified, I burst into tears.

The year was 1952, the eve of the Egyptian revolution, and an angry mob had just set fire to the boutiques, cafés, opera houses, and other haunts of the privileged classes. Mother was alone in the house with me. Suddenly, the bell rang. When Mother did not answer, loud knocks followed. Mother stepped up to the door, trembling, and a short man with a long nose and a huge moustache entered, doffing a red fez. It was the king's prime minister, Ali Maher. "Pasha, what on earth are you doing here?" Mother exclaimed. He said he had come to see Father. "Excuse me for asking," my mother said, "but are you here about the new cabinet posts?" He nodded. "Pasha, please stay away from my husband. You know that he has just resigned his ambassadorship because he's disgusted with the political scene." To which Ali Maher replied, "Madame, the country is burning today because our leaders are corrupt and self-serving. Your husband is one of the few men who are above the favors of political parties and the king. We need him in the cabinet. His duty to his country must take precedence over his personal sentiments."

Although my father was persuaded to accept a post in the cabinet, he had not been in the government for more than two months before he resigned in protest. Shortly thereafter, the revolution broke out. In the late 1960s, Nasser passed a law aimed at accelerating the weeding-out of the privileged classes from influential posts, which compelled the members of corporate boards to resign when they reached the age of sixty. Since my father had recently passed that limit, he was forced to relinquish his positions on the boards of several top-ranking firms. One evening, we were visited by Vice President Hussein el Shafii. When the servant came to announce him, Mother turned to Father and whispered, "Only a few years ago, this man would have been admitted to our presence only by way of the service stairs!"

I followed him and my parents down the long corridor that led to the salon with the Aubusson tapestries and overheard Shafii tell my father that he had been sent by Abdel Nasser. Aware that Father had been affected by the law, the president wanted to offer him a consolation prize—an important post on the administrative board of the Suez Canal. "We respect you," the vice president told him, "because unlike so many others of the ancien régime, you are a man of integrity. We think it would be a shame for the country to be deprived of your talents, and we urge you to accept our offer."

"Thank you, sir," my father replied. "You will tell President Nasser on my behalf that if he esteems my integrity today, it is because I never accepted special favors from the king. I am sure he will understand that I cannot accept favors from him either."

The meaning of these words became evident to me only some time later. I was sitting with my father in the lobby of the Hôtel du Rhône in Geneva, where he was working as an international arbitrator, when the deposed King Farouk entered. He walked past us as though he had not seen us and went up to the hotel desk. Father followed him, saying, "Don't you recognize me anymore?"

"Of course I recognize you, Mahmoud Pasha!" the king answered. "But I was not sure you would want to shake hands with me in public. All the Egyptians who used to kiss my hand before now pretend they don't see me."

To which my father replied, "But Majesty, I never kissed your hand, and therefore I am not afraid to greet you in public."

After the king left, I asked Father why he had said that, and he described to me his first meeting with Farouk. It seems that when the head of the royal cabinet died, the crown councilor mentioned Father to the king as the most suitable replacement. The post was a fairly important one, as the person occupying it became the chief mediator between the king and the cabinet ministers.

The king agreed to look my father over but stipulated that he did not want him to be informed of the purpose of this visit. Accordingly, Father was told that the king wanted to see him to discuss American policy toward Egypt. My father did not get the job; the king had apparently been angered by his informal manner of address and considered it a mark of disrespect. "What is this man you bring me?" he had berated his adviser after Father had left the room. "He did not even have the decency to stand during the audience. He dared sit cross-legged in my presence and talked to me with one hand in his pocket and a cigarette dangling from his lips. And instead of backing out of the room, he had the gall to turn his back on me as he made for the door!"

(Mother had fared considerably better with the king than Father. One day, they were invited to the palace. It was then the custom for women and men to congregate in separate chambers, but the king, who had a weakness for women, would slip away unnoticed by his male guests and conceal himself behind a screen that had been specially set up for him in a little alcove overlooking the ladies' reception room. He would amuse himself in this fashion, observing them and eavesdropping on their gossip. From this hiding place he overheard Mother say that the women in the United States found him quite dashing (it was during his younger days, before he had put on so much weight). This so flattered the king's vanity that the next day he sent a messenger to our house to offer Mother the post of chief lady-in-waiting to the queen. Father instructed her to decline the offer. But it was not until much later that she found out why she had been selected by the king.)

Although my father would not have admitted it, I suspected that he had a certain degree of pride in a daughter who in many ways was as pigheaded as he. And indeed, in the days that followed, as things gradually returned to "normal," I could see that behind his front of reproof his reaction to my trip was not altogether hostile. We carefully avoided the troublesome subject; the letter to Sadat was not mentioned again, and I for my part did not bring up the details of my life in Israel. On the other hand, my mother continued with innumerable recriminations —not the least of which concerned the treatment of "*ton pauvre mari.*" Tahsin had paid a visit to my parents in Paris a few weeks before my arrival, during which he had complained about having been "kicked downstairs" to a purely honorific position on my account (he had been appointed Egyptian delegate to the Arab League) and thereby further incensed my mother against me.

In truth, Mother had always been leery of my marriage to Tahsin. "It would be all right if you were a solid person like your sister, but with a nut like you, this marriage will not last more than a year," she had stated to make clear her misgivings about our age difference. And the fact that I insisted on leaving for Harvard after the honeymoon, since Tahsin, as a career diplomat, had to go wherever he was sent, seemed to her yet another example of my immaturity. "You'll lose him this way, my dear, you'll see," she had said. And now in Paris, she could not resist reminding me that her prediction had turned out to be right.

I argued that it was unfair to blame me for the failure of a marriage which I had not in fact sought. I had met Tashin during the student demonstrations of 1972. The students were clamoring for war to regain the territories captured by Israel, calling Sadat a fool and a coward for his inaction. As one of the few opposed to war and in favor of direct negotiations, I went to canvass the opinions of political leaders and intellectuals. I interviewed Prime Minister Aziz Sidky and a number of other notables, including Tahsin, who was then Sadat's spokesman. I was greatly impressed by him, and he ended up asking me to marry him. But I had never held the notion of conjugality in high regard. I answered with all kinds of objections to marriage. It was conventional, bourgeois. I proposed instead that we live together, but he countered that this would virtually ensure his exclusion from an ambassadorial post in the future; in no country, let alone an Islamic one, could a diplomat turn up at an official reception with his mistress, he said. He called my holding out on principle against an official wedding "infantile" and "egotistical." In the end I let myself be influenced by concern for his diplomatic career, which, ironically, this very marriage was to jeopardize.

And had I not also subconsciously been impelled to marry him as a way of pleasing Father? It had been drummed into me from earliest childhood that my vocation was to advance the brilliance of the family by making an aristocratic marriage. While my parents had always stated that they did not attach the least importance to the wealth of the man I married, and that his religious persuasion was a matter of total indifference to them, the question of class was very much an issue. I could see that Father fancied the idea of his daughter marrying this ambassador-to-be, even if he did not say so in so many words. Was it not my duty to follow thus in his footsteps, since my sister had chosen not to marry—much as I had taken up the study of politics in order to make up for my brother's choice, finance? Finance! It was all right to have money, a lot of it, even quite proper, but to pursue it like some common businessman? No, I had never forgotten how crushed poor Father had looked the day my brother announced his admission to Harvard Business School, even though I was only a little girl then. And while I was not like my sister, whose strong sense of family obligation made her instinctively hostile to my concepts of free will and self-development, I nonetheless was aware of my family responsibilities and proud of them. I was saturated with my family history. So when Tahsin had tried to talk me into the marriage, I had been seized by a familiar feeling of self-importance. Even as I objected on grounds of conventionality, I found myself dwelling on all the notable particularities of our family chronicle: on my paternal great-great-great-grandfather, a general in the Ottoman army sent by the sultan to subjugate Egypt, who had defeated the British troops at Rosetta in 1807; on my father's father, the dean of the medical faculty of Cairo University, who had been the private physician of the khedive; on my paternal great-uncle, Prime Minister Roushdi Pasha, who had brought Father up; on my maternal great-great-uncle Minshawi Pasha, who had greatly increased our family's fortune by introducing mango plantations into Egypt. No, there was no doubt at all that I, Sana Hasan, Mahmoud Pasha Hasan's daughter, who, even as a child, had had my hand kissed by the servants, was charged with sharing in this glorious family history through my marriage.

Still, whatever the reasons, I had married Tahsin and brought him much trouble in the bargain. If I did not feel as remorseful as I should have on hearing the news of his demotion, it was because I was still furious that he had not stood up for me to the foreign minister who ordered our divorce, that he had not stood by me from the start. I was angry too at the whole class that had banded together to reprimand me and punish him, and at my mother for her lack of respect, not to mention support, for my choices.

When Mother was not reproaching me, she was terrified about the consequences of my activities. She worried greatly that I would be barred from reentry to Egypt. She never tired of telling me how sad it was for my father, in his old age (he was in his seventies at the time), to know that he could not count on his daughter's returning home if he became sick and was bedridden. Why, I would not even be able to be present at his funeral! What she said frightened me; I preferred not to think about it, and pushed it out of my mind.

Her anxiety attached to everything. She invariably suspected that the mail I received contained threats or worse, and she trembled every time I took a stroll down the street from our place—which, as luck would have it, was in the vicinity of the Egyptian embassy. When I scoffed at her fears, she reminded me of the attempt that had been made by Egyptian secret service agents during the Nasser era to kidnap an Egyptian who worked as an Israeli agent and ship him back drugged and packed in a box. The plan, which had received much publicity in the European press, had been foiled by the customs officials at the Rome airport. But the same method was used successfully to abduct an Egyptian opposition figure living in self-imposed exile in Europe. Much as I tried to shrug off my mother's warnings, in the end I began to walk in fear.

My respite from the scoldings, the fear, the disappointment at finding my parents' company so much less affirming than I had hoped for, came in the time I spent with Michelle. Throughout my month in Paris, there was a tacit agreement between Mother and me that I would not go along whenever my parents were invited by Arab friends for tea or dinner. This suited me well, for it was during those times that I slipped away to see Michelle, about whom I had kept my parents in total ignorance.

When I had first gone to meet Michelle in Paris, I had hardly recognized my kibbutz friend in the sophisticated woman who stood waiting for me outside a bistro. Her unruly locks had been fashionably bobbed, and she had traded her jeans for a well-cut suit. Most extraordinary, she wore make-up. As I came up behind her, she turned, saw me, and before I could quite rejoice at the flush of excitement that had suddenly colored her face with more familiar hues, threw her arms around me. I was relieved to find out that beneath her mascara, her gaze was as candid and open as ever.

In the bistro, I told Michelle about my trials with my parents and she regaled me with stories about her job as a security guard at El Al Airlines. She had passed the test of detecting the one forged ticket among the twenty-two for a tour group, and she had discovered the tiny revolver secreted in the bosom of an El Al agent masquerading as a potential hijacker. As we came out, she pointed at an old beat-up Vespa. "This is Quasimodo Two," she announced with a proud smile, and then explained that she had just bought it from a soldier. I studied it with some alarm: I had never been on one before. "Come on," Michelle said, propelling me forward. "What are you afraid of?" And she stalked up to it with the strong, confident strides of a young man. I closed my eyes and clutched onto my shoulder bag for dear life as she stormed down the streets of Paris, narrowly missing a van headed in our direction and scattering pedestrians like so many chickens on a country road.

Whenever I could get away, we explored the city together. Paris had a certain romantic aura for me because Father had confided to me the passionate love affair he had had there during his student days. I took Michelle to see the little studio on the Bois de Boulogne where he had met secretly with his French mistress, a married woman, during the 1920s. Michelle in turn took me to the *chambre de bonne* overlooking the Hôtel de Ville in which her mother had lived when she was pregnant with her. This was where Rachel had spent those hot, damp August days during the last week of her pregnancy, lying on a hard cot amid the clatter of dishes and the smell of cigars and cheap food that poured into her tiny window from the restaurant below.

Michelle told me how her mother had ended up alone and pregnant in Paris. Upon arriving in Palestine, Rachel had joined a Communist commune whose members, when they were not talking revolution, were communicating in more intimate ways. They were all adolescents without parents, and they lived off oranges, the cheapest form of nourishment available. There Rachel met up again with Fritz, the marzipan boy, and together they went off to the Negev and founded a Hashomer Hatzair kibbutz. Fritz was also very active in the movement: He edited the Hashomer Hatzair newspaper and made frequent trips to Tel Aviv. But the role of the dutiful mate who waited for her husband's return home twice a week, ready to lend him comfort and support, did not suit Rachel: When she realized she was pregnant, she found herself a job on a ship and said good-bye to him. By giving birth abroad, she would put a maximum distance between herself and Fritz, and thereby establish her sole claim to their child. For five months, while she cleaned the cabins on the ship, her pregnancy went undetected, but by the sixth it was no longer possible to hide it. The captain sent the steward round to inquire why she had gotten so fat, and on receiving her answer—Rachel had never known how to lie—declared that he could no longer keep her on board, because if she gave birth on the ship and the baby died, he would be criminally liable. She left the ship when they reached Marseilles and traveled to Paris.

Knowing no one, speaking not a word of French, and having almost no money, Rachel managed nonetheless to rent the small *chambre de bonne* Michelle had taken me to see.

After Michelle was born, Rachel had survived on the little money she made mending the clothes and darning the socks of a few neighbors and others to whom she had obtained referrals. Michelle snoozed the first three months of her life away, rocked by the capable arms of the old concierge while her mother was out picking up and delivering the clothes to her clients and looking for work. The old man would warble the "Marseillaise" over and over again. His voice was none too good, nor was his repertoire vast, but Michelle liked his singing, and he surely liked the baby. When he died of a stroke, Rachel, unable to cope on her own with Michelle, picked her up and left to return to the kibbutz, where she could obtain communal care for Michelle.

Shuttling back and forth between my parents and Michelle, I inevitably compared the two worlds and reflected on my place in them. I was struck by the fact that Michelle, whose life had seemed beset by insecurity from the very start, whose mother had no family, no country, and not even enough money to take the métro, was perfectly secure and happy. While I, born to plenty, was at odds with myself.

Michelle's basic trust allowed her a spontaneity I particularly admired. I had grown up in a family that had spent years cultivating an image of the proper way to dress, eat, talk; as a child I had been forced to walk with books under my armpits to correct my posture. Michelle was utterly oblivious to the need to keep up appearances. Her direct manner of speech sometimes epitomized the bluntness of the Sabras, whose pioneering parents had seen in politeness and refinement, in neckties and makeup, in the manners and fashions of bourgeois Europe, only hypocrisy and artifice. But even as I was shocked and embarrassed by what appeared to me at times her sheer tactlessness, I could not help being drawn to it, coming as I did from a class in which the refinement of speech was carried to such great lengths as to verge on deception. Often in my parents' salons I had had the feeling that the admirable external correctness of their friends was little more than a veneer of good breeding, disguising a callousness that would surface the moment they were called upon to show a genuine concern for each other. The boredom of this mode of life, the sole purpose of which was to impress the outside world, had become intolerable to me since I had come to know Michelle.

But if I was beguiled by Michelle'e life, she for her part was awed by mine. She, for whom the pioneering ditty "Banu Bli Kol Vachol" ("We Came with Nothing at All") had so often served as lullaby, whose whole childhood was governed by this idealization of frugality, was dazzled by my money and connections, by the way I dined with heads of state and flew back and forth between the United States, Europe, and the Middle East as though it were nothing. She too began to dream of living in grand style; she pictured to herself the lavish establishment my parents kept, and compared it with the modest, somewhat dull comfort of her mother's cottage. She was impressed also by my ambition: She knew that I aspired to a brilliant career, a *career*—the very word that was never to be mentioned in her house, for her mother believed that the wish to excel over others was a serious violation of the egalitarian ethic. Michelle had studied in a kibbutz school, where there were no grades and no exams precisely in order to root out competitiveness in the children. Above all, her mother, like other pioneers, frowned on intellectuality; the very quality that was considered a particular strength of Jews in the Diaspora was seen as debilitating to the nation. It was through manual labor that her country had achieved salvation, through the backbreaking work in the fields of Eretz-Israel. But Michelle was no longer as sure as she once had been. As she watched my life run its privileged course, she was amazed by the way I went about as if I owned the whole world, as if everything were due to me, as if I had "rights," an attitude that came naturally to someone born into a family that had always had high status and power. Her mother's warnings notwithstanding, Michelle was completely fascinated by this Egyptian who had so audaciously come to Israel, who seemed to her so assertive, so unconventional.

Our differences gave each of us an additional perspective when we were together that we lacked when alone and added to our enjoyment of Paris. As we tore around Paris, meeting friends, talking to everyone from the café owner to the concierge, as we drank endless cups of café au lait in Michelle's studio—a simple, pretty, sunny room that brought back memories of another room—I felt I had found a bit of Hazon Hadash, of Israel, direct and warm, here in the heart of the sophisticated city.

It was curious how much my attention gravitated toward Israel. One day, when I was roaming about the streets of Paris with Michelle, an ad on one of the billboards along the Boulevard St. Michel practically jumped out at me. It was for a lecture by the well-known Israeli novelist A. B. Yehoshua at the Centre Broca, a Jewish cultural center in Paris. I wanted to go to it because I had been struck by one of Yehoshua's stories, "Facing the Forest," which explored the delicate issue of Israel's repressed guilt vis-à-vis the Palestinians.

When Michelle and I arrived at the Centre Broca, we found a hall full of Frenchmen, some of them in skullcaps, listening with rapt attention to a pale-faced young man with blazing dark eyes. He was berating a heckler for objecting that no Israeli had the right to come to France and advocate the surrender of Judea and Samaria to the Palestinians because it was the patrimony of the Jewish people the world over. "I have plenty to say about the so-called attachment of Diaspora Jews to their land," Yehoshua was saying. "I think it's a lot of hypocrisy! We always speak of the Diaspora as something that was forced on us by circumstances, but the fact is that throughout the centuries only a small number of Jews have chosen to return to the Holy Land. In 1917, when the Balfour Declaration was issued, only thirty thousand Jews out of fifteen and a half million came to Israel—while the millions who were leaving their homes in Russia and Eastern Europe went to the West.

"Now, more than three decades after the establishment of the state, the percentage of those who came of their own free will is minute. Most of those in Israel today are either Holocaust refugees who didn't have anywhere to go, or Oriental Jews—and among these, it's only the poorest ones who came. Look at the Jews who have gone to such incredible lengths to be allowed to leave the Soviet Union. We're waiting for them with open arms, dying to have them, and where do they go? To Belgium, to Germany, to America. . . ."

"Why?" sounded from the audience.

"Why? Because we are a sick people, that's why!" Yehoshua answered bitterly. "We seem to have a love of exile deeply rooted in our culture. Our very nation was formed in the Diaspora—in Egypt. Abraham, the father of our people, was the first *yored* [a pejorative Israeli term for someone who emigrates out of Israel, literally someone who descends]. He left the Holy Land in difficult times, when there was a famine, and went to Egypt; Jacob died in Egypt. Already, after the destruction of the First Temple, when the time came for the Jews to return to Israel from Babel, a number chose to stay on in the Diaspora. And by the time the Second Temple was destroyed, nearly one-third of our people were living in the Diaspora. They sat in Alexandria, and in Rome, and some of them—probably out of guilt—lent their support to our extremists, the Zealots, who brought about a terrible catastrophe by revolting against the Romans. Yes, we worship Masada—but I tell you, it was a terrible catastrophe. We are the only people who were not able to reach a modus vivendi with the Romans—had it not been for that senseless revolt, we might have been today a nation of many millions. So when I hear some of the Jewish leaders who live overseas come to Israel and tell our rulers not to give in to American pressures to return the West Bank, it reminds me of the Jews of old who were so eager to participate, from Alexandria and Rome, in the dangerous adventures of our Zealots—without having to take the consequences, of course! It's not their sons who will die in the wars!"

No applause greeted the end of Yehoshua's speech. The stunned audience sat for a few moments in wrathful silence. I took advantage of this to rush up to the podium and introduce us, pressing on him an invitation for coffee, which he accepted, before others had a chance to swoop down on him.

At the café, Yehoshua asked Michelle and me what we had thought of his talk. I replied that the audience had seemed a little shaken.

He slapped his thigh exultantly. "Good! Excellent! That's precisely what I wanted to do. As a Zionist I cannot help looking upon the

Diaspora as a mortal danger to Israel. I think there's too much harmony between us and the Diaspora Jews these days. At the time of Ben-Gurion, we despised the Jews abroad as weak and parasitic. We still affect an air of superiority in talking about them, but it's clear that we've been forced to turn to them more and more for help over the years. This is a very bad situation, because it makes it easier and easier for Israelis to take up residence overseas—one out of every ten young Israelis is now living abroad. And of course it takes the onus off Diaspora Jews who choose not to come to Israel."

For a few moments Yehoshua mulled over what he had said, tapping his unlit cigarette on the table; then, turning to me, he asked if I accepted the concept of Zionism. Somewhat taken aback, I answered that I had nothing against it, even though I believed there was less place in today's world for Zionism—or for any other form of nationalist identification—than there had been in the forties, when the state of Israel was created. I was not, I said, against the existence of a Jewish state.

Yehoshua looked at me in obvious disbelief, and said, "Are you sure? I know Zionism has always been anathema to the Arabs; do you realize the implications of what you are saying?"

I nodded.

He leaned back in his chair and, crossing his legs, asked me pedagogically, "If I tell you I am a Zionist, what does that mean to you?"

Annoyed at being cross-examined like a schoolgirl, I told him curtly that I understood it to mean that he favored the creation of a Jewish state and looked upon Israel as the homeland of all the Jewish people throughout the world. I accepted this, I said, and had nothing against the Law of Return, though I believed it should also be extended to the Palestinian refugees who wished to return.

He was not satisfied: "Does that mean you would accept Israel's right to exist unconditionally, no matter what it did, even if it were to oppress the Palestinian people and refused to return the West Bank?"

"Certainly not!" I retorted.

"Aha! You see! Then you are hypocritical when you say you have nothing against Zionism."

My first sensation was surprise, but almost immediately I was angry. How dare he call me a hypocrite—I who had jeopardized my citizenship for my convictions! I opened my mouth to tell him just what I thought of him, but he interrupted: "I can prove to you that you are a hypocrite," he said. "You will agree that your own definition of a Zionist as someone who favors the creation of a Jewish state implies nothing about the nature of that state, right?"

I nodded a reluctant agreement.

"Well then, don't you see? Even if Israel had been set up on the basis of fascism or apartheid, it would still be a Zionist state, as long as it was a Jewish state based on the Law of Return!"

Now I could see what he was driving at, but I feigned incomprehension.

"It's so obvious!" he exclaimed. "Take the case of Germany. Would it ever occur to you to say that Germany has no right to exist because it was ruled by Nazis? No, you would say that everything possible should have been done to topple the people in power. Well, if in your heart of hearts you accepted Israel as fully as you do Germany, and Begin were in power—as you know, many Israelis consider him little better than a fascist—you would seek his overthrow, but you would never dream of saying that the state itself had no right to exist because of him!"

The mortifying thought suddenly occurred to me that my longtime idealization of the Jewish people was in itself a form of anti-Semitism. By endowing the Jews with a heroic sensitivity and conscience, I had in effect imposed on them a terrible burden. Lurking just underneath my admiration was a tolerance no less tenuous than the anti-Semite's: I had made it their moral duty to salvage for me all the qualities I found lacking elsewhere and had in effect warned them that they would violate this ethical code only at their own risk and peril.

Yehoshua was too sensitive not to notice how troubled I was. He said, in a tone that had recovered its former delicacy, "Don't feel bad, you're not the only one who thinks that Israel has to justify its existence by being an exemplary society. Even the founders of our state, for all their talk about normalizing the Jewish condition, couldn't free themselves from believing that Israel had to be a truly exceptional country, a place in which greater justice would reign than anywhere else in the word—a 'light to the goyim,' as Ben-Gurion put it. But I think these pretensions are very dangerous, because the world takes us at our word. Like you, they expect too much of us and make our acceptance conditional on our good behavior."

Hard as it was to swallow, I had to admit to myself that he was right. For me Israel had long ago ceased to be "enemy territory." It had become familiar, endearing; I had developed an almost proprietary feeling about it. But even as I became more attached to individual Israelis, I certainly relished finding fault with the country itself. I had watched with a kind of horrible satisfaction the way the Israeli right grew in power and seemed, to the rest of the world, to represent Israel itself. The more fanatically I saw it behave, the better I felt: Was this not a complete validation of what we Arabs had always believed to be the true character of Israel and Zionism? This recognition—that despite the many pronouncements I made to others and the things I told myself, part of me still held out against fully accepting the Jewish state—was very unsettling.

The conversation with Yehoshua was nothing short of a revolution in awareness for me. It was true, there were whole areas I knew nothing about and aspects of the country that I had never dared to confront. I had been a tourist, I realized, indulging myself in the company that attracted me, even flattered me—curious politicians, pioneers, colorful religious folk. But I had never risked meeting up close any of the Palestinians who had remained in Israel, nor the expansionists determined to drive them out and willing to risk any consequence in pursuing the mission that possessed them—any of the figures, in short, who might challenge my acceptance of the Israel I had chosen to see. But if my acceptance of Israel was conditional, a product of selective vision, what would happen if I took off my blinders? If I sought out experiences I had so far avoided, would I end up condemning Zionism?

All too quickly, the time came for me to leave Paris. I had already spent much more time in Israel that I had initially planned, but my trip was clearly far from over.

Although my parents knew I was going back, they had always hoped I would change my mind. When I announced my departure, Mother cried out in exasperation, "Why don't you just go and settle there once and for all, since you love the Jews so much!" Father looked pained but embraced me warmly. Michelle poked fun at my "confounded Zionism" but said I should go back if I felt I must, even though she would miss me. Still furious about the kibbutz's expulsion of Roni, and still uncertain about her own ability to live in Israel without letting her hate for its chauvinism overwhelm her, she was staying on in Paris.

My sorrow at having to leave was temporarily dispelled by Michelle's impromptu proposal that we spend my last weekend in France on the Côte d'Azur. I told my parents I was going south to visit a childhood friend in Monaco, and early the next morning I was sitting behind Michelle on Quasimodo II, heading for Menton. I had chosen the place for more or less nostalgic reasons, since I had often been there as a child; my parents thought it quainter and less touristy than neighboring Cannes and St. Tropez.

Once in Menton, I took Michelle around to visit all the places I had known as a child. In the ice cream parlor the old proprietress, who claimed I had not changed a bit since the last time she had seen me (when I was ten!), was so beguiled by Michelle that she bounced out of her chair and, flipping the lapels of Michelle's blazer open, exclaimed, "You are marvelous! Are you a boy or a girl?" Then, with no further ceremony, she began to whirl her around the floor to the sentimental tune of "Ce n'est qu'un au-revoir," which was playing on the ancient jukebox.

The rest of the day we strolled around from boutique to boutique like an elderly provincial couple looking for souvenirs. At night we picked our way through huge bowls of bouillabaisse, and then, after dancing in Jeux des Dames, a little disco with kaleidoscopic lights, we walked along the beach, waiting for the sun to rise behind the hills.

But just below the surface of those frothy, carefree days on the Riviera there was a sense of unease at the thought that I was about to return to a place where I would once more be on my own—the Egyptian in Israel, entertained and patronized as the object of curiosity and suspicion, but quite alone.

PART THREE

↗ 11 ↖

Strangers in Our Own Land

W HEN I arrived at Ben-Gurion Airport, I heard a newspaper vendor
just outside the automatic door calling out, "Idiot . . . idiot . . .
Sadat says no peace in our generation. . . ." * I picked up a paper from
the stand and, taking hold of his palm, pressed his fingers down over a
lira note, telling him to keep the change, for his jacket was ragged. He
threw back his skullcapped head in thanks; his eyes were holes.

On the way to town in the *sherut* I read the lead article, an acerbic
commentary about an interview with President Sadat in which he had
said that a complete peace with Israel, with open borders and a free
flow of tourists, would have to wait for another generation; the current
one was too scarred by the wars. The extraordinary journey Sadat would
make to Israel less than two years later was impossible to imagine then,
and I read the words with despair.

I was headed for the Grand Beach Hotel, where I was about to take
advantage of the hospitality that had been extended to me "anytime you
wish" by the charming, debonaire mayor of Tel Aviv, former general
Shlomo Lahat. When I checked in, the receptionist recognized me and
was very kind. He led me to my room himself and shortly afterward
brought me a magnificent basket of fruit with a card that read: *"Brucha
habaa la orachat Hamizriah!"* ("Welcome to our Egyptian guest!"). I
was back.

For a while I stood listlessly by the open window, missing my family
and Michelle. Gradually, however, my sadness gave way to a kind of
jittery exuberance. For, though the Grand Beach was a first-class hotel,
it happened to be located on Hayarkon Street, Tel Aviv's main hangout

---

· * The name of Israel's best-selling newspaper is *Yediot Achronot* ("The Latest
News"), referred to as *Yediot*, which vendors often pronounce as "idiot."

for prostitutes—a site full of associations for me because it was there that Leila had been initiated into her trade by Ali. Even as I thought about her, my restless gaze kept returning, again and again, to the Shalom Tower. I remembered how I had observed it from the veranda of my Jaffa apartment on the day I first arrived in Israel, standing like a beacon gracefuly silhouetted against the seashore, so rosy in the rising sun. Now, in the harsh light of day, it loomed disconcertingly close and ugly.

As I lay down for a short midafternoon rest, I remembered a story told to me by Moshe, a Libyan Labor party official in the governmental bureau in charge of "Arab-Israeli" affairs. While he was working as a translator for the military governor of the occupied territories after the '67 war, he had become friends with the son of the Gaza mayor. "One day I brought him to Tel Aviv and showed him our skyscraper, the Shalom Tower," Moshe said. "He'd never seen anything like it. His eyes popped! He couldn't believe that it was thirty-four floors high!"

I thought it was ironic that this tacky pile of brick and steel—Israel's truncated version of the Empire State Building—should be held up to the "primitive" Arab as a triumph of modernity, the culmination of Western civilization.

The next day I took the bus to Jerusalem to get the key to Yoav's Tel Aviv apartment and seized the opportunity to look up Leila. She had moved out of her place, so I went over to her sister's house in Nachlaot to find out how to reach her. A surly Aziza met me at the door. Leila, she informed me, had died a month ago. I attributed her curtness to grief and pressed her for details, but my frantic questions received only apathetic replies: She did not know exactly how it had happened; Leila had been sick, some sort of kidney disease, she thought. Aziza had a strange way of systematically avoiding my gaze as she repeated laconically, "Chaval ["A pity"], such a young girl!" But I could not elicit another scrap of information from her.

Stunned, I returned to Tel Aviv. Leila had been only twenty-one, and she had never said a word to me about a kidney disease. The next day I woke up marveling at my hard-heartedness: I had not shed a single tear. For a while I thought about going back to ask Aziza where Leila was buried, but then I dismissed the idea as sentimental and pointless.

I kept very busy that week. First, I had to find a job, for I had run through the funds I had brought from the States by then. Following my arrival in Israel, my parents had transferred all the assets in my Egyptian bank account into their own for fear that the Egyptian government would attach it, as had often happened to those who were blacklisted.

When I had told them in Paris that I was returning to Israel, they had refused to let me have any money, in the hope that my financial duress would drive me back to school. The only alternative to working would have been to ask my ex-husband for money, and that I was not prepared to do—precisely because I knew he would have acted the *grand seigneur* and given it to me.

When I was not hunting for jobs, I was running after the mail. One day, after I had discovered one of Michelle's letters to me lying in the yard and badly mangled by a dog, I decided to have a talk with the mailman, whose manner of delivery was to toss our building's mail vaguely toward the doorway.

I positioned myself on the balcony of my apartment and waited. At around noon, a bald, sparsely whiskered fellow biked by.

"Shalom," I called out. "How are you today?"

He grunted suspiciously.

"Look here," I said, "there's a problem with your way of delivering the mail."

"*Ma pitom!*" he exclaimed (roughly, "What are you talking about!"). "I do my work very well."

"Of course, of course, I don't doubt it. I merely wanted to tell you that it would be better to put the letters in the mailboxes. You see, when you throw them, the wind scatters—"

"Listen, lady! I don't have time for that, I can't get off my bicycle at each and every one of these buildings. Do you realize how many houses I deliver to?"

"What kind of bullshit is this! Mailmen all over the world have hundreds of letters to deliver. It doesn't prevent them from doing their work properly! If you don't put my letters in my mailbox, I'll complain to the postmaster!"

At this threat the mailman's face flushed and the veins in his wrinkled neck swelled. "You can complain to the postmaster," he yelled. "You can even complain to the prime minister if you like! I am a war invalid, no one has the right to say anything to me!" Then he jumped back onto his bicycle and added, "I have ten children to support; I have to ride around for hours every day. And you have the *chutzpah* to sit there on your balcony and give *me* instructions on how to do my work! You should be grateful to me for bringing you your mail every day. I could hold it back for a whole week, and you wouldn't even know about it!" And he rode off with a haughty flourish.

I burst out laughing. Those were the times I really enjoyed being in Israel.

For weeks on end I canvassed the town—this time with some desperation—looking for a job, without any luck. Then a friend told me she might be able to arrange something for me with her brother, who was, she said, a big industrialist. This surprised me, because my friend belonged to the extreme left and hardly lived like a person of means. Yet as it turned out, by one of those ironies not uncommon in Israel, her brother was a millionaire. Thanks to her intercession, I was hired to work at Rotex, one of Israel's most important textile factories. It was a low-paying packing job, but I was relieved to get it. As earlier, my real identity was kept hidden by agreement with my friend's brother.

Rotex was not an unpleasant place to work, partly because the supervision was lax. The workers—most of whom were Oriental Jews—always seemed to find a way to *lehistader* (in the Hebrew vernacular, to "get by," a euphemism for "bend the rules"). There was, for example, a regulation that we were not to eat on the job, in order to avoid soiling the garments we were packaging, but the women got around this by excusing themselves on the grounds that they had not had time for breakfast, felt dizzy, had a headache, were pregnant, and the like. Similarly, there were always "urgent" reasons for defying the prohibition against making phone calls—a quarrel with one's husband had to be resolved; or for arriving late—a sick child needed attention; or for not showing up at all—a daughter had just gotten married and needed help moving into her new house. If a woman was absentminded and did sloppy work, it was because she was suffering a bad case of *azabim* ("nerves") as a result of some conflict with her mother-in-law. Everyone demanded special treatment, and a foreman's refusal to grant it would be countered with a tone of high outrage, arguments rich in gesticulations, and where all else failed, tears. By then I was so familiar with the way Israelis were able to circumvent municipal ordinances and regulations regarding customs duties, taxes, and licenses that I was not at all surprised to see that the management of factories was neither more nor less lenient than that of public bureaucracies. And since I came from Egypt, it all seemed perfectly normal.

The women from the different departments took advantage of the frequent absences of their supervisors to visit each other and exchange bits of gossip. In this way I made many friends. One of these was an Egyptian Jew by the name of Gaby. She was stocky, short, and generally ill favored by nature. All day long she sat at her sewing machine in the department across the hall from where we packagers worked, hating her job. Unlike the daughters of the middle classes, these young women did not view work outside the home as a woman's independence; quite the contrary—they dreamed of being housewives and spoke endlessly of the golden days before their families had come to Israel, "when Mother sat at home like a queen." Though Gaby was only eighteen, she lived in the continuing dread of not finding a husband and of having to keep her job for the rest of her life. Nor was her situation at home an enviable one: She complained that her father beat her, her mother picked on her, and her sisters and brothers jeered at her appearance.

After we had worked together for some time, Gaby confided to me that she had a twenty-two-year-old Christian Arab boyfriend by the name of Eisa (the Arabic equivalent of "Jesus"). He was a metallurgy worker she had met in the café across the street from Rotex where the workers from the various factories in the area congregated. Gaby made me swear on the Torah that I would not breathe a word of this to anyone, claiming that if her father were ever to find out, he would kill her.

I was curious to meet Eisa because I wanted to know more about the life of Arab-Israelis, as they were officially called. While I had been at Kibbutz Vatik, I had begun to piece together their complex history of oppression. I learned that even after the '48 war, they had continued to be robbed of their lands throughout the fifties, and that under the military administration during that time, they lived by the six o'clock curfew and were unable to go to a "Jewish" city without a special permit. Nikolai had told me that within the neighboring complex of Arab villages known as the Triangle, the military governor had declared an area off-limits for "security reasons," denying the peasants access to the fields on which their livelihood depended. Then the government, in order to obtain those lands for the surrounding Jewish settlements, had availed itself of the Law of Uncultivated Land, which entitled it to claim any plot that lay fallow and assign it to someone who would work it. More recently, in the 1960s, the government had again taken lands from the Palestinian peasants in its intensive drive to Judaize the Galilee. In order to preempt any attempt of the Galilee to secede and to link up with an independent Palestinian state in the West Bank, the government had set up a series of Jewish settlements like Karmiel, which sat astride the hills in much the same way as the Jewish settlements in the West Bank did. I myself had just witnessed in March of '76 the demonstrations of Palestinians in the Galilee against a government plan to confiscate yet more land for "development purposes"; five Palestinians had been killed during the protests.

One of the most wounding things for these Arab citizens of Israel to see was the way that as soon as a Jewish settlement was erected on their lands, the new settlers were given electricity, telephone lines, industrial plants, decent hospitals and schools, and other basic services, most of which were still missing in their own villages. The failure of the government to build industries in the Arab townships and villages was particularly resented since it meant that the "Arab-Israelis" had either to commute long distances to work or to live all week separated from their families in the "Jewish" towns and farms. The discrimination in the granting of building licenses and in the allocation of funds for development was another stinging issue, particularly the matter of constructing the buildings that were to house schools in the Arab villages. The current schools were often dilapidated and badly overcrowded, with inadequate library and laboratory facilities. Because the inferior high school preparation of Palestinian children as compared with Jewish children made it difficult for them to gain admission to universities, they often found that if they did not wish to be farmers or industrial workers, the only vocation open to them was teaching Arabic. Even those few Palestinians who managed to overcome these obstacles were confronted by the discrimination that pervaded the various professions. Sometimes they did not even get as far as the interview. "Looking for a young man who has completed his army service," some ads read. Since Palestinians were not allowed to serve in the army, it did not take great discernment to grasp that they need not apply.

The only "Arab-Israelis" I had met were those I had seen from a distance when Michelle took me for rides at the kibbutz.

Often, after work, we would harness Quasimodo to a light two-wheeled cart and drive down the dirt road past the silo and the sheep-house to the mango plantations. Beyond them lay the living quarters of the Palestinian construction workers. The five-minute ride alongside their dilapidated shacks always seemed interminable, and in the hope of slipping by unnoticed I would urge Quasimodo on, embarrassed by the relative comfort of my own accommodations and the solicitude of which I was the object. They stared at me with resentment, I thought. To them I was just another Arab, and they probably wondered why such a fuss was made over an Egyptian while hundreds of thousands of "Arab-Israelis" were subjected to daily indignities and cruel indifference.

The Palestinians would come to do our kibbutz construction work, living in our midst from Sunday through Friday and returning every Sabbath to their villages in the Galilee to visit their families. They stayed on the kibbutz for months, until the new buildings had been completed, then moved on to another kibbutz. In theory, the Histadrut (labor union), to which they belonged by virtue of being Palestinians from within Israel proper, protected their interests, guaranteeing them equal pay with Jews. In practice, however, laying bricks was one of the menial occupations in which there were virtually no Jews, a fact that enabled employers to pay them very low wages.

The Palestinians lived for as long as a year at a time on the kibbutz, but they might as well have been ants for all the difference it made to the members of Hazon Hadash—in spite of their insistently progressive position on almost every other issue. As far as they were concerned, the less they saw of the construction workers, the better. The Palestinians were aware of this attitude and rarely left their huts after working hours except to go to the dining room. Even there they never ventured forth by themselves but only in pairs or as a group. In the morning, when we served them their fried eggs, they stood in line awkwardly shuffling their feet, their eyes lowered. They ate in silence, hurriedly swallowing what was before them, and left, too timid ever to ask for seconds. In the evening, they never felt they had the right to watch the television in the room adjoining the dining hall. And although there were always kibbutz members sitting out on the lawn after dinner, the Palestinians knew that it would be considered almost indecent for them to lie out on the grass. So they stayed inside their shacks, playing cards or listening to Arab songs on their transistor radios. When the kibbutz held celebrations or dances, no one invited them.

My attempts to broach this sensitive issue with the kibbutz members had met with no success. Any allusion I made to it evoked shocked indignation. "*Ma pitom!* ["Come on!"] *Our* Arabs are a hundred times better off than their brethren in the Arab world. Israel is a paradise for them," the kibbutz secretary once told me, echoing what Begin and Golda Meir had said to me. Without going quite that far, the other kibbutzniks would insist that there was absolutely no difference between themselves and the Arabs on the kibbutz, that all of them were workers. The children, however, wore no such blinders. One day, when Jacob was describing to me the celebrations his committee was planning for May Day, his four-year-old son asked him why the kibbutz put up red flags on that day. Jacob explained that while the blue-and-white flag belonged to the whole nation, the red flag was the workers' flag. "*Nu*, do you understand?" he asked him. The little boy nodded and, smiling with self-satisfaction, replied, "The blue flag is ours; the red flag belongs to the Arabs."

After Gaby and I had become quite close, I asked her to introduce me to her boyfriend. She was reluctant until, in an effort to persuade her, I revealed to her my own nationality. Then she consented.

Eisa was a skinny lad with a pale, drawn face and solemn eyes. He told me Gaby was the first Jewish girl he had gone out with who knew he was an Arab and accepted it. "The only Jewish girls who are willing to go out with Arabs in this country are the prostitutes. If I meet a nice girl in a movie or a café, even if I'm an angel, she rejects me. It's very difficult for them to go out with us, and they know it can't lead anywhere marriagewise—it's a great *busha* ["shame"] in Israel to be married to an Arab.

"Before I knew Gaby," Eisa told me, "I was in love with a girl from Bukhara in the Soviet Union. She assumed I was Jewish, and I didn't tell her I wasn't. She was pretty, with everything a man could want in a woman. I met her when I was on vacation, in a workers' hostel in Zichron Yaacov. She was very much in love with me, and after she invited me to her place a couple of times, she began to talk about getting married. I would have liked to marry her, too, but I had to tell her the truth first. So I said to her, 'I'm sorry, but there's something I have to tell you that I've kept from you all along.' She got pale, thinking I was going to tell her I was already married. She just never dreamed I'd say I was an Arab. Well, I told her. She said, 'What? You must be joking!' So I took out my ID and showed her. She was quiet for a minute or two; she just sat there with a dead face. Then she started to cry and asked me, 'Why is there something called Jew and something called Arab? Aren't we just human beings?' What could I say?

"Well, she cried a lot, and then she said, 'I wish you good luck for the future; try not to be angry with me for leaving you. But if you ever meet me in the street, please don't say hello.' And believe me, I'm not the first Palestinian this has happened to."

One morning, I went with Eisa to Hamashbir, a store in the shopping mall at the base of the Shalom Tower. We were walking under the bridge that connects the tower to the neighboring building when a very loud voice sounded behind us: "Hey! You! Are you an Arab?" The passersby stopped and stared. Wincing, I turned around and caught sight of a fat, dark policeman with a crafty, ill-natured face, who was standing at the entrance to one of the shops. (In Israel, security guards are routinely stationed in all the big department stores to check the shoppers' handbags for explosives.) "Are you talking to me?" I asked smoothly, inwardly shaking with anger.

"No, him," he said, jerking his chin in Eisa's direction.

"Me?" replied Eisa with a trembling smile.

"Yes, you," the policeman snapped, and without another word he grabbed Eisa and pulled him inside the shop. I stood outside, nervously gnawing my fingernails as I watched their silhouettes behind the glass panel and wondered what he could possibly want from Eisa.

A minute later Eisa reappeared looking very pale, followed by the policeman, who resumed his post by the entrance. "Let's get out of here," Eisa muttered, and he began walking very fast down the side street. I had to scuttle to keep up with him. "What's the matter?" I called out after him. "Why are you so upset? What did he say to you?" Eisa told me that he had ordered him to show him his ID.

"And what did you say?"

"I said to him, 'Why do you humiliate me like this in front of my friend? Don't you think I'm a human being with feelings? I'm an Israeli citizen, just like you. Why should I have to show you my ID?' But he yelled back, 'Shut up, *ya munhat* [Arabic for "scum"]. Either you show me your ID or I'll take you to the police station!'"

We had reached the corner. Eisa leaned against the wall and pulled out a cigarette. I noticed that his hands were shaking. "For heaven's sake!" I said. "Pull yourself together. There is nothing that man can do to you."

"I can't help it," he replied. "The feeling is stronger than I am. I've been taught since I was a child to be afraid of Jews—especially Jews in uniform!"

"Has this ever happened to you before?" I asked.

"Of course! Something like this happened just a few months ago, before I met Gaby. I was so ashamed, I wanted the earth to open up and swallow me. I was taking a Yemenite girl to the movies, and I hadn't told her I was an Arab because I knew she would have refused to go out with me. So when the policeman stopped me at the entrance and asked me for my ID, I decided to lie, and even though it was in my pocket I said I didn't have it. I figured that if I told the truth, not only would I be humiliated in front of her, but the policeman would be angry at me for going out with a Jewish girl; if I lied, I knew the worst thing that would happen to me was I'd be hauled to a police station and given a few slaps on my face when they found out I was an Arab. And that wouldn't matter so much to me anymore, since the girl wouldn't be around to see it. Actually, I was lucky that time, because the policeman just asked the girl, 'Is this your boyfriend?' and she said, 'Yes.' Then he said, 'Jewish?' and she said, 'Of course!' and he left. You know, here the police can stop anyone on the street and ask to see their ID. The only Arab I know that it doesn't happen to is my brother's friend Wahib. Maybe his way is the only solution."

"What do you mean?" I asked.

"Well, Wahib is by now not an Arab anymore. He's a Jew. If you see him, you'll know what I mean. He even looks like a Jew: He wears sunglasses and khaki shorts and has braces on his teeth. If you talk to him in Arabic, he'll answer in Hebrew. He's actually not a Jew *or* an Arab. He reminds me of the fable about the crow who tried to walk like a partridge and couldn't, but later, when he tried to return to his crow's walk, he realized that he couldn't do that either."

I had never met an assimilated Palestinian, and I asked Eisa to put me in touch with Wahib. I called him one day and set out for Lod (previously Lydda), where he lived—a town on the outskirts of Tel Aviv whose population had been entirely Palestinian until the '48 war.

I got off the bus and walked toward a compound of *shikunim*—standardized, middle-class, jerry-built housing. When I could not find the name of Wahib's family on any of the nameplates on the door, I asked a man I saw leaving one of the buildings if he knew where the Eliases, a Palestinian family, lived.

"What are you talking about? Arabs living here?" he exclaimed. Then he went on to tell me that I must be looking for the "Arab ghetto"—a district of Lod where the Palestinians who had remained behind after the '48 war had regrouped and now resided.

"No, no," I insisted, "I have the street right, and they told me to look for number twenty-two."

The man opened his eyes a little wider. "Really! Arabs living here! They must be spies!" When he got over his amazement, he told me that all of these buildings had two entrances and that I should try the "B" entrance on the other side.

A slim, stoop-shouldered boy with fashionably long hair came to the door, wearing jeans and a black turtleneck. He introduced himself as Wahib and led me into a spacious, imaginatively furnished living room decorated with art posters, glass bookcases, and a great variety of beautiful plants. When he excused himself and went to turn off the rock music that was blasting from the stereo in a bedroom, his older brother, Joseph, a muscular six-footer in a denim vest, tight pants, and expensive leather boots, stomped into the room. For one giddy moment I forgot where I was, conjuring up the hip café in Cambridge where I often went with other students.

We sat down and Wahib asked why I had wanted to meet him. I came directly to the point, telling him what I had heard about him, and asked him if it was true that he was torn between being Arab and Jew.

Unruffled, he replied: "I know where I stand, I'm completely together —I don't feel torn. I'm a Palestinian first, then a Christian, and last an Israeli—or, if you prefer, I'm an Arab national of the Christian faith who happens to hold Israeli citizenship." (All the Palestinians who stayed behind after the '48 war were given Israeli citizenship.)

"But how much weight do you place on the Israeli part of your identity?"

"I don't know, I've never thought about it."

"You see!" his brother exclaimed, butting in. "He can't answer you."

Wahib protested, insisting that he felt himself to be a Palestinian by nationality, even though he was Israeli by culture. He boasted that he was more fluent in Hebrew than he was in Arabic, telling me that he even dreamed in Hebrew. Most of his friends, he added, were Jews, since he went to a Jewish school, but he did have some Palestinian friends.

"What Palestinian friends?" Joseph scoffed. "They're all your cousins!"

We were interrupted by the arrival of the rest of the family: Wahib's father, looking sleek and prosperous in his stylish English tweed suit; his mother, a robust woman of around forty-five, attractive despite her matronly figure, in a peach-colored angora sweater that smelled strongly of perfume and cigarettes; Rose, his adolescent sister, a girl with handsome Mediterranean looks, wearing an elegant narrow slit skirt; and his youngest brother, a little boy of twelve who wore his curly blond hair long, like his brothers.

In their dress and manner this family was indistinguishable from any upper-middle-class Jewish family in Tel Aviv. Nor was there anything patriarchal about them: Wahib's mother sat with us and was, if anything, even more vocal and opinionated than her husband, a well-to-do bakery owner; the little boy was as ill mannered as any Israeli child; and the girl was free of the affectations that normally characterize Arab girls of "good" families, who have been taught to sit cross-legged in salons, one hand resting gracefully in the palm of the other, a smile glued to their lips and a beatific expression glazing their eyes. Also absent here was the warmth and the legendary hospitality of Arab homes. The hosts were reserved, and nothing was offered to eat or drink during the entire length of my four-hour visit.

After everyone had settled down, Wahib went on: "It's hard for me to have Palestinian friends, because as soon as they notice that my Arabic isn't very good, that's already a mark against me. They also think I'm superior to them because I have another mentality. For instance, I'm used to going dancing every Friday and Saturday night. They don't know what dancing is! If they see a couple kissing in the street, they watch with seven eyes and let their mouths hang open."

At this his father laughed, telling me that the Palestinians still have a "primitive" mentality, with no idea what it meant for boys and girls to go on trips together. His children, he said, went on such excursions all the time—even his daughter, who, he said in the falsely negligent tone of someone who is name-dropping, was now studying at Hebrew University—while most Palestinian girls were not allowed to do so because their parents did not want them to be alone with boys for an entire week. So his son was forced to seek his girlfriends among Jewish girls: "Some look upon my boy as an Arab and won't go out with him, but others don't mind, because they've been together with him for twelve years at school."

I asked Wahib if the fact that he was a Palestinian ever caused him problems at school.

"No, but if there's ever a discussion in class about the Arab-Israeli conflict, I keep quiet. I don't allow myself to take sides. If I forget my place and butt in, then they'll start to abuse me. It's not worth it. Better to stay quiet and keep your dignity. If I let out a word by mistake, they'll start to say, 'You Arab, get out of here,' and other things I don't want to hear. Everything I've worked to build up over the past twelve years would just fall apart. It happened to me once. Mordechai, my best friend, called me a dirty Arab in public, in front of the whole class. And what do I need that for?"

Turning to Mr. Elias, I said I wondered whether it might have been less problematic for the children if they had been sent to Arab schools. He smiled, a strained, sour smile.

"Generally speaking, this isn't really an option, because there are no Arab high schools in this area. So they'll have to hear a few words of insult; it won't kill them."

"A Palestinian can't afford to be too sensitive if he wants to live in this country," Wahib told me. "Just the other day in the bus, there was an announcement over the radio that some children had drowned in the Sea of Galilee; then they read their names. A woman with a strong German accent turned around and asked me if these were Oriental Jewish names. When I told her they were Arab names, she said, 'Bah! She'yelchu l'azazel!' ["Let them go to hell!"]. You can imagine how good I felt to hear this. But there was no point getting into a fight with her. I know we're a minority here, so we have to learn to put up with it and keep quiet."

Joseph cut in indignantly, "I wouldn't have shut up! When I was in high school, I always spoke my mind, and the Jews spoke theirs. We had arguments all the time. I don't think it spoiled our relationship." After a moment of reflection he went on: "Of course, when the time

256

came to go into the army, it was more of a problem to keep up the friendships, and with the war everything fell apart. I had a few very good friends in high school and I saw them all the time, but when we finished school we went our separate ways—they were called up for army duty, and I went to Hebrew University. Then the Yom Kippur War broke out; some of them were narrow-minded and started saying to the other ones, 'What's Joseph doing with us? He's an Arab!' And our friendship was shattered."

"It's not fair that they don't take us into the army!" Wahib exclaimed. "A person can't be fully equal here without participating in the army, because wars are such an important part of the life of this country. Besides, I really enjoyed the *gadna* [military training] at school. I like using weapons and learning army discipline and roughing it."

But his father told him, "Even if you had been allowed to volunteer for the army, all you would need would be one Palestinian to spot you in an Israeli army uniform, and the next day all the Palestinians of Lydda would know about it and you'd be a dead man." And turning to me, he added, "Besides, I don't want him in the army. He has a cousin in Jordan; does he want to end up killing him?"

His own family had been split at random, Mr. Elias said, during the course of the house-by-house expulsions that had taken place in Lydda during the '48 war. One night he was awakened by the sound of shouts, and when he ran to the corner of his street, he saw soldiers pummeling on doors with their rifle butts and yelling, "Go to Abdullah!" (the king of Jordan at the time). Families were being hauled out of their beds in the middle of the night and sent marching across the hills without food or water. His relatives lived in one of the houses the armed men were surrounding. He pleaded with the officer in charge to allow his sick aunt to remain behind, but the officer retorted, "Let her walk, the fresh air will do her good!" Three days later the old woman was found lying dead on the road.

He had been spared by sheer luck. The eviction operation had been halted in mid-course, and the officer in charge told him that they would come for the remaining families the next morning. He had gone home and told his wife to pack her bags. But no one came the next morning, or the one after. The operation had been inexplicably halted, and those Arabs who had not yet been forced to leave began to take heart; they unpacked their belongings, and slowly life returned to normal.

But he had not forgotten. He knew a family who had been expelled from their village and then turned away by Israeli soldiers wherever they went in search of shelter; they had walked for days. He had watched people from his town hugging their miserable belongings: men with mattresses or heavy sacks of flour on their backs; women with lambs or chickens, their only worldly possessions, under their arms; mothers with babies; lost children wandering about crying; senile old women who passed him with vacant stares, mumbling to themselves as they went; grandfathers who had to be supported because they could barely walk. And he remembered the soldiers who had shot over the heads of these pathetic human columns to keep them moving to Jordan, and the faces and the screams of the ones who fell.

It was these memories that had led him to the conclusion that the only way for his sons to survive in the land of the Jews was to assimilate, and that meant, above all, keeping out of trouble.

I wondered how successfully Joseph, his older son, had assimilated, and asked him if he felt accepted at the university.

"I myself," he said, "never had any problems being accepted at Hebrew University, but with other Arabs it's a different story. As soon as the Arab student puts his foot into the university, he gets his first shock. To begin with, he has to get used to the language, since he comes from an Arab high school and isn't used to Hebrew. Often he comes from a small village, and he has no idea about life in a town—and even less about campus life. He's only eighteen; the Jewish students are three years older than he is, because they've completed their army service, so the Arab student has to make up for his lack of maturity. He's intimidated and scared, so he immediately looks to other Arab students for comfort. The Arab students generally stick together, which I think is a big mistake because it makes them conspicuous. You can't help noticing them: As soon as a lecture is over, they all gather and leave the classroom together. They live in a kind of ghetto, they don't even try to make connections with the Jews around them."

"Why do you blame the Palestinians? Why don't the Jewish students help them feel more at home?" I asked. But instead of replying to my question, he embarked on a long litany of the failings of the Arab students.

"First of all, they should talk to Jews in their own language, and I don't mean just speaking Hebrew, but learning their jargon, the slang, learning to think the way Jews think, which is different from the way Arabs think. Then they should try to change their appearance by dressing the way Jews do—you know, wearing mod clothes instead of the small-town things they wear, and combing their hair with style, the way the Jews do. They also have to change the way they act. They're very insecure; they have an inferiority complex. Just to give you an example, the other day I was sitting in the cafeteria with a Jewish friend of mine, and a guy came and sat across from us. He was a nice-looking young boy who didn't look Arab at all. We were watching him when all of a sudden he turned around and said, 'Are you staring at me like that because I'm an Arab?' "

Joseph then went on to tell me that the Arab students didn't like him; they attacked him for hanging out with only Jewish friends and for refusing to take part in their demonstrations. They demonstrated, he said, because they wanted the university to give them more dormitory space; it was very hard for them to find people in the city who were willing to rent them rooms. They also wanted the police to stop coming to their dormitory to check their IDs in the middle of the night.

"By why *don't* you join them?" I asked, letting my disapproval slip out.

"The status of the Arab student is very precarious," he lectured me. "The moment he starts to express political opinions, he gets blacklisted. He can be kicked out of the university because of his political ideas, or he can have serious trouble later on when he goes to look for a job or needs a government license to open a business or build a house. So usually the students who demonstrate are the ones who have nothing to lose, because they're already in the government's black book for something or other."

Mr. Elias interrupted: "You know, as a Palestinian father I have to make many sacrifices to send my children to the university. The Russian immigrants who come here can go to the Jewish Agency for scholarships, and even the Oriental Jews have access to special development funds, but we have to pay for everything ourselves. Now, I own a bakery, and I don't complain. I make good money. I can afford the tuition fees, but it's a horrible problem for me to pay for Joseph's housing as well. This is a problem Jews don't have, because any Israeli who completes his army service has the right to a housing loan. If I make all these sacrifices, it's for my sons to *study* while they are at the university, not to make politics. Joseph goes there to get a degree so that when he finishes he can help support his younger brother. It's important he stay out of trouble. Politics can be very hard on us. We are strangers in our own land."

Though I had met many friends of Eisa's and invited him many times for lunch or dinner at my apartment, he had never invited me to his place. The one time I had tried to find out where he lived, he had answered vaguely that he rented a room in a house in Jaffa that had belonged to Palestinians till '48 and was now owned by Moroccan Jews. When I asked him to describe his room to me, he replied, "Oh, it's just a room." So I assumed it was shabby and poorly furnished and he was ashamed to invite me over; I never brought up the subject again. But one day I had to get in touch with him to cancel an appointment we had. Since Eisa had no telephone, I found out his address from Gaby and went to Jaffa to tell him.

When he came to the door, the color drained from his face, and he whispered, "How did you get my address?" I opened my mouth to answer him, but he put a finger to his lips and, grabbing me by the arm, hurried me inside his bedroom. There was no chair, so I sat down on his bed. Noticing that he had remained standing, I felt uncomfortable and stood up again. "You must never come here," he said curtly. And before my surprised silence, he added, "I can't explain now, I'll tell you tomorrow. You have to leave right away." He half-opened the bedroom door and glanced quickly down the corridor. "Okay, you can go now," he said. And seeing that I was hesitating, he snatched my blazer off the bed, thrust it at me, and pushing me toward the vestibule, snapped, "I told you to go, now go!"

The next day he came to see me and explained his bizarre behavior. He had, it seemed, not told his landlady that he was an Arab, and he was afraid that I might unwittingly expose him in front of her.

"If I say I'm an Arab, no one will want to rent me a room," he said. "When I first started going to a vocational school in Tel Aviv, I wanted to live in the city because it was too exhausting for me to commute every day from the village. I would go to ask about a room for rent, and after I had said I was an Arab, the owner would always say, 'Leave your number and I'll call you,' and he'd never call back. I had this experience dozens of times, and so did some friends of mine, so I started to lie and say I was a Jew. If they asked for my ID, I'd say I'd bring it in the morning, and I would just disappear. But often they didn't ask.

"Recently I had a little luck. I changed jobs, so I went to rent an apartment that was closer to my work from a Moroccan Jewish lady who lived with her mother. We hit it off real well. She asked me where I worked and what I studied, and she was so nice to me that I felt bad about deceiving her. So I told her, 'You know, I lied to you. I'm an Arab, not a Jew.' And she said, 'Well, never mind, but when my mother comes don't tell her, because she's religious and she wouldn't like it. You'll have to change your name to a Jewish one for her because she'll know if I call you Eisa. So I'll call you Esav.'

"The old mother liked me because I was clean and tidy. I helped them around the house, and I ran errands for her. If she was sick, I would go to get the doctor, and when she fought with her daughter, which was almost every day, I'd try to make peace between them. So one day she bought me a present, a *mezuzah*. And she said, 'You're a nice young man, and I want you to put this on your bedroom door.' Well, what could I say? I thanked her, and ever since, whenever I go into my room, if she's around I kiss the *mezuzah*."

What Eisa said moved me. Now I understood the reason for his rudeness toward me, and I empathized with his plight. Yet the silence he had kept about his living arrangements seemed to me a kind of deception that I could not accept from a friend. At the very least, it showed me that he hadn't trusted me. Why hadn't he told me? The question kept gnawing at me, and in spite of myself I began to grow cool toward him. At some point he must have sensed it even though I myself was not yet aware of withdrawing, because one day he looked me in the eyes and said, "You're still mad at me, aren't you?" I denied it. "Yes, yes, I know you are," he countered. "You shouldn't be, you know. It's not that I didn't trust you. . . . It's . . . it's . . . how can I explain? I was ashamed."

Then he added with a rueful smile: "You're not the only one I've had to keep away. One day I was in bed with the flu. I woke up because there was a loud argument going on outside, in the vestibule. I recognized my father's voice, and my heart began to beat like crazy. I hadn't found a way to tell him either, because I knew he would feel humiliated at the thought of his son passing himself off as a Jew. Well, it seems my uncle had had to come to Tel Aviv to buy a blade for his electric shearer, and my father had decided to go along. He passed by my factory, and they told him that I was out sick and gave him my address, so he came to see me.

"He asked for me, and the landlady's mother said, 'There is no Eisa here.' But because he insisted, and because she was not too pleased in the first place at being visited by an Arab in a *kaffiyeh*, she told him, '*Lech meepo terach, ein Aravim kahn!*' ["Go away, you dumb old man, there are no Arabs here!"].

"It wrenched my heart to hear my father being spoken to in this way, but there was nothing I could do. If I had come out of my bedroom, she would have discovered my real identity and would have thrown me out. Then the whole nightmare of impossible apartment-hunting would have started all over again for me. So I just lay there, and listened, and when my father left, I cried."

12

From the Nile to the Euphrates

AFTER MY return from Paris, I fell back into the habit of seeing Danny. I had run into him one day on my way back from work, in Dizengoff Circle, and he had acted as though we had parted only five minutes before, proposing to me jauntily that we stop off at Kassit's for coffee. When I brought up his abrupt departure, he was evasive. He turned my question into a joke about his interests in South Africa, saying that as long as Egypt refused to have relations with Israel, he was forced to do business in other African countries. And as I tried to impress upon him how very abhorrent his attitude was to me, he told me in all earnestness that South Africa was being unfairly maligned. After all, he said, things there simply were not as bad as I thought: The whites had greatly improved the living standards of the blacks, and in any case, large tracts of South African land had been empty when the European settlers first arrived, the blacks having come only later, when they were attracted by the economic opportunities created by white entrepreneurs. The uncanny resemblance of these arguments to what Israelis had to say about the Palestinians was not lost on him; he even defended the Bantustan puppet states created by South Africa as similar to "the autonomy we have granted the West Bank." In essence, Danny, like many Israelis, thought South Africa suffered from an image problem because "like Israel, it is the scapegoat of the world." He even favored the joint South African–Israeli economic and military aid to Latin American dictatorships, seeing in it an exercise of their common responsibility as the "bastions of the free world."

He rattled on at great length and with great animation, as though he felt that as long as he went on speaking, all could not possibly be at an end between us. And I looked at him then with new eyes, filled with cool detachment. But in no time at all, the memories of our past happiness together again took possession of my mind and destroyed all the work of reason.

The sight of Shimon Peres warmly welcoming Prime Minister Vorster to Israel in April of 1976 and invoking the great friendship between the two countries was once more the occasion of wrangling between Danny and me. The fact that Vorster, a man who had been imprisoned as a Nazi sympathizer during World War II, was being paraded around Yad Vashem, the memorial to the Holocaust victims, seemed to me a desecration of the memory of the dead. I barraged Danny with my indignation.

In the end, however, I abandoned my efforts; I no longer asked him about his work, which he refused to discuss. We tacitly agreed not to bring up the subject of South Africa because of the terrible animosity it generated between us. Yet the constant strain of this hypocrisy and my inability to let him know what I really thought began to erode our friendship. I kept to myself my suspicion that I had been misled by our past intimate conversations into believing that he trusted me when in fact he saw me as *the Egyptian* who would divulge his secrets. When my earlier thoughts about espionage, subversion, and manipulation resurfaced, I suppressed them, as I did the fear that my sense of closeness had been illusory all along. Every so often I would remind myself of his high rank, his real work, and so discipline my yearning for him.

But there were times when I could feel nothing but tenderness for him. Sometimes Danny laid his head against my naked body and wept. My caresses drew tears when I rubbed my cheek against the inexpressible softness of his skin. His body seemed even thinner without his clothes, utterly lacking in strength, in muscle. There was no hair on his chest, nothing "masculine" about him outside of his sex, which gave such powerful pleasure. I wondered how he ever got through all those army drills and the many tests of physical endurance, which had sounded like horror tales when my kibbutz friends had recounted them to me.

He never told me why he wept—memories of his son? Another, earlier hurt? It was as if he loved his pain as intensely as he loved me, perhaps preferred it to me. For he had changed since he had resigned from the army. I realized now that there had been a visionary side to his military calling. But those years were over, and now he was just a businessman in South Africa. He had begun to feel his age. Like a mask, the look of youthful vigor and amiability, which for some time now had been preserved only by constant effort, fell from his face when he came to bed, betraying instead a jaded weariness. Could it be that he too was filled with distaste at the hateful dealings in which he was engaged? I asked him that many times, but he answered me one way in his strong, purposeful moods and another in his weak, discouraged moments. And sometimes he did not answer me at all. Sometimes an overpowering need to possess me took hold of him, to lay his head upon my breasts, to close his eyes in my arms.

I too would have liked to stay like this, silent, safe in his warmth, but I knew he must return to his wife. Occasionally when I fell asleep, he woke me up with kisses, whispering that he had to leave. Other times I would lie awake as he slept, waiting for his inevitable departure. Through the blinds I would watch the coming of dusk. As in Egypt, the light of day persisted until very late into the night, and one recognized the approach of evening first by the timbre of the noise. The noise that came up to my little Rheines Street apartment from the streets of Tel Aviv would become deafening: earsplitting guttural cries, car horns, screeching brakes. When the walls could no longer muffle the sounds of evening, I knew there was no privacy left to us, nothing solid to separate us from the city.

Of course, we were not always sad, Danny and I. Sometimes we played and laughed together like children, crouching and splashing under the hot-water boiler with the Pharaonic eyes in the shower of my tiny bathroom. Danny would do hilarious imitations of Israeli political figures, and we would laugh at that too. Then we would dress and go out to a little restaurant by the sea for a simple meal of fish broiled in grape leaves over the open fire and watermelon with salty white cheese. Nothing was ever so good.

Still, the boundaries of our happiness were never beyond view. Once Danny told me I was the only person who had been able to make him laugh since his son had been killed. I knew he meant it and liked to flatter myself that I was also the only woman who had ever made him happy. But we never spoke about the future; we had both known from the very first moment that we could not possibly have a future together. In the frozen time that we created for ourselves, we simply abandoned ourselves to pleasure.

And so my life with Danny continued in this fashion. Even after I left Tel Aviv, I would commute by *sherut* from Jerusalem and pick my way through the swarming streets of the city, oblivious to the crowds who pushed and blundered into me, so full was my mind of our forthcoming meeting. I would climb up to my Rheines Street apartment, relishing the excitement of waiting for him. My uncertainty about exactly when he would knock on my door only heightened the romantic intensity of that moment. I would picture him walking up to me with that slow, bashful gait that was peculiarly his own and taking me in his arms. South Africa had receded into the distance. And my love for him, far from dying out, was making rapid progress since my return from Paris.

In between working, seeing Danny, and worrying about not seeing him, I tried not to forget the purpose I had imposed on myself after my conversation with Yehoshua—to explore what I had not wanted to know, and to meet those I had excluded from my approved version of Israel. I decided to meet one right-wing politician whose activities had attracted special virulence from my socialist friends. She was later to become the leader of the parliamentary opposition to peace with Egypt, achieving notoriety by tearing up a copy of the Camp David agreement in the Knesset and flinging it in Begin's face.

I had first heard about Knesset member Geula Cohen during my stay at Kibbutz Hazon Hadash. One night, to punish her for having participated in a march in favor of the new religious settlement of Sebastia, the comrades decided to pay her an impromptu visit at home. Having filled the kibbutz van with sand and rocks from the desert, they set out for Tel Aviv and on arrival proceeded to unload it in front of her ground-floor apartment, jamming the front door as well as the windows. On top of these mounds they planted placards reading YOU WANT LAND—HAVE SOME! To make their message clearer, before they returned to the kibbutz they pasted up WANTED posters bearing her picture all over town.

When I telephoned her at her Tel Aviv residence, she seemed suspicious and asked who had told me about her; and when I mentioned Kibbutz Hazon Hadash, she sneered. In her view, Hazon Hadash was a perfect example of the Labor government's failure to inculcate a Jewish consciousness into Israel's youth, she said, a mistake she had made sure to correct in the education of her own son. Why, that very morning, in the Knesset, she had criticized the minister of education for removing all sense of Zionism from the curriculum and teaching the children only to love the state. She asked him, "Am I a citizen of a country thirty-eight years old or four thousand years old?" There was a conspiracy, she told me, to keep all mention of the ancient Hebrew kingdoms out of the textbooks and to give children the history of the state of Israel instead. "Because if you talk about the whole of biblical Palestine, the student will say, 'Well, if it was ours, why don't we have it anymore?' He must be taught the ancient history of the Jews in Palestine, instead of just the Holocaust, the Holocaust, the Holocaust—that's the only thing students are taught here! He should be told the truth—that we are here not because of the Holocaust but because of our biblical rights to this land." When I was able to get a word in edgewise, I made an appointment to see her.

After this introduction, I had imagined someone very different from the person who came to the door. Having developed a great antipathy for her in advance, I had conjured up an elderly woman in a dowdy suit, with sharp features and short-cropped gray hair. These qualities, which I had assigned to her quite arbitrarily, were drawn from the Knesset women I had met, who, perhaps because there were only 8 of them out of 120 members, felt compelled to eschew more feminine attire in order to win the respect of their male colleagues.

Instead, there stood before me a gorgeous creature with long black hair that fell in unruly curls over her amaranth robe. Her eyes were dark and sensual.

"Shalom," she said in a husky voice.

She led me to an oriental-style living room decked out with hand-woven Bedouin rugs and embroidered Palestinian cushions. Tones of red and gold shone in the modest circle of light cast by an iron lantern. The corner table, a large tray of inlaid brass resting on a low stand, sported an incense holder with a minuscule earthenware oil lamp. This was the lamp she lit for the Chanukah celebration that commemorates the Jewish victory over the Greeks in biblical times, she explained to me.

Still amazed at her appearance, I sat down on an octagonal stool of delicate arabesque woodwork as Geula Cohen placed herself opposite me on the rocking chair. She smiled at me languidly, leaning back and shifting her long legs with nonchalance. A cigarette hung loosely from her lips. Framing her was a handsome oil canvas that depicted Jerusalem. When I admired it, she replied, "I don't like it that much, but it's the only painting of Jerusalem I could find without the Mosque of Omar that's stuck in the middle of every picture of the city today."

"That's true, but the Mosque of Omar is superb, don't you think?"

"It's all right, I suppose," she conceded with a pout, "but I don't want to be reminded that our Temple is gone every time I look at my painting. Jerusalem will be beautiful the day the Temple is rebuilt."

I suggested that the Mosque of Omar probably reminded her of an Arab presence, and that she should realize by now that the Palestinians were here to stay; there was no point in sticking one's head in the sand like an ostrich, I said, for didn't Jews and Arabs have to learn to live together?

No, she did not believe that they were meant to live together. If the story of Abraham had any significance, the opposite was true. Why else would God have ordered Abraham to throw out his first wife, Hagar, and their son, Ishmael? Clearly, He did not want Sarah's son mixing with an Arab!

She took a deep drag on her cigarette and let the smoke curl from her crimsoned lips. Then she went on to assure me that she was not sticking her head in the sand. She did not deny the existence of Palestinian nationalism, the way Golda Meir had done, she said. But she felt the trouble "these people" were creating for Israel was the fault of the Labor leaders. Why hadn't they listened to Jabotinsky when he told them that no peace anywhere in the world was ever obtained by giving up? "Back in the twenties, when the first Arab disturbances started, he had said we should bring an army here made up of Diaspora Jews and nip their movement in the bud."

"What do you mean?" I asked, shocked at her callousness. "Are you suggesting that they should have thrown the Palestinians out?"

"Not all of them," she replied airily, "just the nationalists. The others don't count. They were just a handful of fellahin, coming and going. This land was empty—politically and physically empty. No nation existed here! The place was ruled by the Turks."

"But even if there were only a handful of fellahin here, as you claim, aren't they human beings with rights?"

"No," she said quickly. "The fact that a few Arabs lived here doesn't give them any right over Palestine any more than those Jews who lived in Poland had a right over Poland."

"If you can't even admit that the Palestinians have a right to a state, there will never be peace!"

"Peace! You make me laugh! You sound like our ministers. Every time they go abroad to America or Europe, they say we want peace, instead of telling the world what our rights are in this land. The result is that when the Western nations hear the Palestinians say, 'This is our land,' and then hear our leaders snivel about peace, they tell themselves that the weak person who whines apologetically must have a guilty conscience, that the land isn't really his. And I must say I can't blame them for coming to this conclusion!"

She brooded silently for a moment. Then, turning to me with a contemptuous gaze, she said, "You see, I don't believe in compromises. If you read the story of Solomon, you'll see that the real mother refused to compromise; she was the one who could not let her baby be cut in two. *We*, Israel, are the true mother, and we will never agree to have this land repartitioned."

Her cheeks flushed with pleasure, and she began to rock back and forth triumphantly on the chair. At that moment I hated her. "Don't you have any sympathy for a refugee people who have suffered so much?" I asked.

"For me, morality is not a word that is relevant to the suffering of individuals," she said, looking at me steadily. "The morality of a nation is superior to individual morality. I can't regard the moral rights of Arabs as equal to those of Jews! The Arabs have moral rights here only as individuals, not as we do, as a nation. God selected this country for us; He told Abraham to leave Iraq and come to take possession of this land. He told him to go and plant his seed throughout the land between the Nile and the Euphrates. So it's just too bad for the Arabs!"

"Aren't you ever afraid that one day you may lose the war, and the Palestinians will turn the tables and say, 'Now it's too bad for you'?"

She snickered. "You forget that our name is Israel! It was given to Jacob after he fought the angel God sent against him and won. The name Israel means you can fight even God and win."

Having satisfied herself that my moral education was now complete, Geula Cohen got up and crossed to the back of the room toward a cluster of Yemenite tambours that resembled long-necked jars. Flopping down on the floor beside them, she asked me whether we had musical instruments like these in Egypt, and without waiting for my answer she clasped one of the tambours between her knees and started drumming it with her slender fingers.

For a long time she played in this manner, sitting upright, her back perfectly motionless, her neck swinging furiously from side to side, her hair cascading over her face and shoulders. Then she leapt up and with a light bound sank breathless onto the couch next to me. I complimented her on her performance. She laughed and told me that she had inherited the tambours from her father, who had come to Palestine from Yemen in 1905 at the age of five. He married a Moroccan woman and fathered ten children, all of whom were born at home with the help of a midwife. While his wife was in labor, he would sit outside her bedroom reading the Bible. When the birth of the baby was announced to him, he would run his finger along the paragraph he had been perusing and select a name for the child. In this way, all his sons were named after biblical characters. The girls, being of inferior rank, were not so honored, but even their names were selected from Jewish history. Thus, one girl was called Esther, after the Jewish queen of Persia, and another Judith, after the heroine who cut off Holofernes's head. Geula was born on the day when, according to tradition, the Roman siege of Jerusalem began; her name means "redemption."

The name made a deep imprint on Geula. When she was little, her mother used to sing her a lullaby about how she would grow up to be a heroine and bring redemption to Israel. And she would tell her stories about her grandfather, who, though he was a vizier in the court of the Moroccan sultan, never ceased to yearn for Zion. One night the prophet Elijah had come to him in a dream and said, "How long are you going to stay here while Jerusalem is in anguish?" It was like an order. Four days later he had packed and led his wife and daughter (Geula's mother) out of the city on camelback. They had to journey for six months across the desert to Jerusalem, and whenever they felt tired and began to lose heart, he would sing them this song:

> Mother, I want to go to Jerusalem.
> I will go to its meadows,
> I will feed on its grass.
> When I see Jerusalem from afar,
> I will even forget my father and all my family.

Geula's family had been very religious. As part of the blessing before every meal, her father would beseech God to bring His people back to Palestine and rebuild the Temple. Each time one of her brothers or sisters was married—and there were many such weddings in the course of her childhood—the glass was broken in commemoration of the destruction of the Temple. Geula came to see her life as inseparable from the life of her people.

While she was telling me her story, a heavy iron key nailed to the wall opposite us caught my attention. I interrupted her to ask about it, and she told me that this was the key to the cell in which she had been imprisoned while Palestine was under British occupation.

How had it happened? When she was sixteen, her father found her a husband, but instead of marrying him, she ran off and joined the Irgun, the Jewish underground under Begin's command. After a short time she left, for she believed it was too moderate: Begin had agreed to put a stop to attacks on the British stationed in Palestine for the duration of the war so that England could concentrate its efforts on defeating Hitler. The majority of his followers supported this decision, but a minority of dissenters, Geula among them, seceded. Under the leadership of Abraham Stern, they formed a more militant cadre, Lechi. Stern was also more uncompromising than Begin in his territorial aspirations: The Irgun claimed only both sides of the Jordan, while Lechi's platform called for the reestablishment of the region's biblical borders, extending "from the Nile to the Euphrates." In Geula's eyes, Abraham Stern far eclipsed Begin as a leader. "Some men are born to be magnets," she explained, "others, just iron filings. Stern was the magnet, and Begin the iron filing; if Stern had lived, it is he who would have been the leader of the right today." (Stern was captured and shot by British police in 1942.)

Pulling a volume from her bookshelf, she read me one of Stern's verses:

> We will wrestle with God and with Death,
> We will welcome the redeemer to Zion.
> We will welcome him.
> Let our blood be a red carpet in the street.
> And on this carpet,
> Our brains will blossom like lilies.

"Isn't that a lovely image!" she cried. I stared at her in astonishment. Her face was pale with emotion, her lips quivered with a kind of morbid delight.

The highlight of Geula's life as a young "freedom fighter" was the trial she underwent after she was captured. When the British judge announced the sentence—a nine-year prison term—her mother, who had sat in court day in and day out, sprang up and in a frenzy of patriotic fervor began to sing "Hatikva." Geula herself scoffed at the sentence. She told the judge defiantly that the British would not be in Palestine long enough to enforce her prison sentence, and that in any case no one could keep *her* in prison.

Within a year, she had escaped. She was the only woman who succeeded in freeing herself from the heavily guarded prison in Bethlehem. "When I jumped over the wall, I landed on barbed wire, and it tore at my skin and flesh. I had to clamber over thickets of thistles and thorns, so I forced into my mind the image of our Maccabean freedom fighters who had once fled across these same hills and hidden in these same caves and crevices. My face and palms were scorched, but I no longer felt the pain."

She was caught and brought back to prison. This time she was put in solitary confinement. Since she was never let out of her cell, she realized that the only way to escape was to make herself sick so that she could be hospitalized. For weeks she worked toward this, eating cigarette butts and plaster scraped off the cell walls, drinking her own urine— but in vain. Finally, she said, God came to her aid. She became ill with tuberculosis and was sent to a carefully guarded hospital ward.

It was Palestinians from the village of Abu Gosh who, prompted by hatred for the common British enemy, let themselves be convinced to help her escape. They pretended to be coming to the ward to visit an old Palestinian woman who lay in a coma and, after slipping Geula an Arab dress with a veil, started a fistfight to divert the nurses. In this disguise, Geula slipped past the unsuspecting hospital guards to freedom.

When I left that first night, I did not expect to see Geula again. But I did, again and again.

Though I found her political views noxious, I had a sneaking admiration for her outrageous candor; she dared to express things others would never have admitted. And perhaps I felt a certain ease with her that I did not feel in the company of liberal and left-wing Israelis, whose relentless self-criticism embarrassed me: The harder they condemned the flaws in their own society, the more I had to admit those in ours. And this feeling of unease was accompanied by a crushing sense of my own impotence to change things. Geula presented me with no such pangs of conscience. By comparison with her, I could, without the slightest moral effort, bask in the gratifying role of the great humanitarian.

I was also charmed by her personality. Hers was a generous nature that many others far more open-minded politically might well have envied, for Geula knew how to give. Her phone rang day and night, her house was always accessible, and though she worked eighteen hours a day, she was never too tired to hear a friend's problem.

Most of all, I was fascinated by her relentless dedication in the service of "the cause." For her, politics was nothing short of an obsession, and I never ceased to be amazed by the way it governed every aspect of her life, from the most banal incident or conversation, to the most important.

Once I invited her for dinner at Casa Mia, a cozy little Italian restaurant around the corner from my apartment, run by Italian-speaking Jews from Libya. She arrived wearing an ankle-length blood-red skirt that set off her dark complexion and her long, black curls. In her jingling gold earrings and the profusion of turquoise and sapphire charms dangling from her wrists, she resembled a beautiful gypsy. We enjoyed a good meal, drank, and gossiped quite a bit; by that time I had largely given up discussing politics with her, for the extravagance of her views was beyond both my comprehension and my patience. That night, I spoke of places I hoped to visit: India, Russia. She said she did not care to travel, because "whenever I'm abroad, I feel myself less attractive, less intelligent, less good, less everything. I remember the first time I stepped on board a ship. I asked myself, 'What! Am I going to leave my own country to go somewhere else? Is it right that there are other countries all over the world?' Of course, I knew in my head that there were other countries—I'm as intelligent as anyone else who's studied geography— but deep down in my soul, I was so childish as to not want any other countries to exist outside of Israel. And when I returned home, I read in a book of our sages that to go out of Israel is considered a crime if it's not to work or for some other essential purpose!"

A few moments later she had an afterthought: There *was* one place she would like to visit—Egypt! I was surprised. Although it was not unusual to hear an Israeli say she wanted to visit Egypt—at the time, practically every Israeli I met asked me if I could somehow arrange a visa for Egypt, a request that always embarrassed me because of my inability to gratify it—there was something about the way Geula said it that I found puzzling. A dreamy, hopeful look had come over her face, the romantic look of a young idealist. When I asked her why she wanted to go to Egypt, she confided to me that she wished to visit the graves of two fellow freedom fighters from Lechi, who had been condemned to death at the time of England's mandate over Palestine for their part in the assassination of the British high commissioner in Egypt, Lord Moyne. They were buried in Cairo.

For a while she stared at me with spirited eyes, and then she bent forward, lowered her voice to a whisper, and, after swearing me to secrecy, elaborated a plan she had hatched for smuggling the bodies— which the Egyptian government at the time still refused to turn over to Israel—out of the country. The only problem with her scheme was that it entailed my cooperation. When I declined to participate in this folly, unwittingly betraying the sort of repugnance her ecstatic fantasies some- times inspired in me, her mood changed to sullen anger. For the rest of the meal, she was irritable and rude.

Geula perceived my refusal as an act of disloyalty to her, and she cooled considerably toward me. Some time later I tried to call her, but she hung up on me, so I sent her a postcard from Nazareth to patch things up between us.

When I next ran into her, I asked if she had received my card. She had but was not going to mention it because it made her very angry, she said. "How could you have been so tactless as to send *me* a postcard of the Church of the Annunciation?" she demanded.

I stared at her, uncomprehending.

"I can't stand the sight of a church!" she exclaimed. "I remember when I was imprisoned in Bethlehem and I looked out the cell window and saw all those churches. How I hated them! In my eyes they weren't blue or white, as they were in reality, but red—because I saw only blood. In 1952, when I was sent to Paris with a group of Hebrew University students, our whole delegation went inside Notre Dame, even the Orthodox students. I couldn't. I just stood outside and cried. One of our leaders came looking for me and said, 'Why don't you join us? There are such beautiful paintings and statues to see!' I told him, 'I can't. For you it's just a museum, but I see corpses everywhere. I hear the shouts of all the Jews this church has put to death!'"

Despite my gaffe, shortly thereafter she invited me for a picnic. It was a lovely warm spring day. The birds sang and the grass seemed alive with the chirping of crickets. Geula's beauty stood out more than ever surrounded by the pink and white blossoms of the almond trees and jasmine bushes. Pulling up the large wicker basket she had brought along, she took out a checkered tablecloth and spread it on the grass. Then she laid down a crisp loaf of bread, a cold chicken, a bottle of fine red wine, some plums, and a few oranges.

The good smell of that freshly baked bread made my mouth water. I helped myself without waiting to be asked, and Geula tackled a leg of the chicken with the same voracious appetite she had for all things, now and then taking a swig of the dark wine. Then she dug into an orange with her long vermilion nails.

We were both in excellent spirits and talked and joked a good deal. Never before had I known anyone who seemed so at ease with all her contradictions. She made a joke of logic and turned consistency into boredom. Nowhere was she more contradictory than vis-à-vis men. Although Geula's lifetime achievements would have been hard for most men to match and fully established her as an independent national figure, she still hankered for male domination. This explained the ferocity with which she attacked the civil rights platform of the secularists who worked to free women from the disabilities imposed on them by religious laws. She herself was in no way religiously observant; she ate nonkosher meat, she drove on Saturday, and she did not even partake in the lighting of candles on the Sabbath—a tradition honored by many Israelis, even those who were atheists. But still she fought for the preservation of the power of the Orthodox Jewish rabbinate.

She actively crusaded against the efforts of Israeli feminists to liberalize the abortion laws (a bill that aroused such vehement opposition in religious circles that its opponents later threatened to bring down Begin's cabinet if it was passed; it wasn't). Likewise, though Geula had nearly become a victim of the divorce laws by having the custody of her own children denied—because according to Jewish law, boys over the age of six belong to the father—she adamantly opposed the efforts of the civil rights leader Shulamit Aloni to extend the right of divorce to women. Planting her wine bottle firmly on the ground, she proclaimed: "Man should have the sole right of divorce because this is decreed by the Jewish tradition. A woman was created for only one man; if she gets the right of divorce, she will live with more than one, and she will not fulfill herself as a mother and do the tasks nature assigned to her."

While Geula had always had a great deal of success with men, she believed that women were not created to have sexual pleasure as men were. God gave women their organs for procreation only, while men, on the other hand, could go with more than one woman because they had no such responsibilities: It was the woman who remained "with the full stomach."

Then, between one plum and the next, she added: "I don't believe in equality. I don't want to be a man, and I don't want a man to be a woman. I want a man to love and protect me, and I want to be good to him and fulfill my biological task. I believe in the same political rights, but not in the same jobs and education for men and women. I want to educate a girl to be a good mother, a good wife, a good lover, and to learn to use cosmetics so she can take care of her appearance. And I don't want a man to have to baby-sit."

As for her own political career: "Women make better leaders than men because they are less adventuresome, have better organizational talents than men, and are more concerned with the preservation of human life." That she, who spoke so recklessly about going to war, should say this seemed to me the height of irony, but I refrained from comment.

As I was savoring the late-afternoon light and my wine, Geula unexpectedly threw herself at me and kissed me resonantly on the cheek. With her arms still about my neck, she asked me if I liked her. Embarrassed by this sudden show of affection, I shrugged and answered obliquely that I had never given the matter much thought. It was just as though she were asking me if I liked Israel, I told her. But almost immediately I regretted having spoken so coldly. To my surprise, instead of being offended, Geula was positively delighted. "Why, that's the nicest thing you could have said to me!" she exclaimed, and in all innocence she added, "I feel I *am* Israel."

How presumptuous, how ridiculous! I had thought to myself then. But in time I came to see that there was some truth to this statement. My friendship with Geula would not have been possible before my discussion with Yehoshua in Paris. In finding room for Geula, I had also found room for an Israel that was not an enclave of angels, but an exasperatingly normal country with weaknesses and strengths.

Driving every day from Tel Aviv to Jerusalem to attend Knesset sessions, writing articles for newspapers, taking care of her son and her house— all this was not enough to use up Geula's inexhaustible supply of energy. In addition, she ran an educational center every evening. It was funded by Begin's Herut party and catered to the political education of "these poor children" who had been "cheated of the truth." It taught them the "authentic version" of what happened in Palestine from biblical times to the present and gave them the "bald facts" about Arab demography at the turn of the century, when the pioneers had begun to arrive in Palestine. It also offered an enthusiastic history of the underground movement, which Geula claimed the Labor governments had deliberately dropped out of the school curriculum. Occasionally, it featured distinguished guest speakers who attracted a large audience.

Geula always insisted that I come along to her center—she said it was good for my education—and often after the lecture there we would have dinner with the guest speaker.

The main teacher was Geula's friend Israel Scheib, or Eldad, his *nom de guerre* in the Jewish underground movement. At the time I met him, he was the most notorious right-wing intellectual in Israel, and believed to be the author of the famous, or perhaps infamous, map of Israel extending from the Nile to the Euphrates, which had haunted the Arabs.

I went to meet him at his house to please Geula, for he was her intellectual mentor. She revered him and had often spoken to me of his fine qualities. As soon as I arrived, Eldad offered me a seat in his musky study, which boasted the complete works of Nietzsche translated by Eldad into Hebrew, and proceeded without further ado to tell me—as if to set me straight right from the start—that there was no love lost between him and the Arabs. When I made no reply, he went on to say that there was only one way to settle the conflict with the Arabs—force.

According to Eldad, the name Zahal, the Israeli Defense Army, was a misnomer. For Israelis, the question at hand was not, as in the past, how to defend themselves against pogroms, but how to liberate the *whole* of Eretz-Israel, their rightful patrimony. As for the Arabs, they had better not "interfere" with the return of the Jews to their homeland.

Eldad had parted company with Begin when the Herut party ceased to give more than lip service to the goal of restoring Israel's historic borders. He had joined an extraparliamentary group that opposed the existing parties, convinced that the map of the Middle East needed to be revised and that the Israeli leaders should not just sit idly by and watch it happen but should give the process a helping hand. The way to do this, Eldad asserted, was to break up Arab states, and the disintegration of their borders could be accelerated by Israel's alliance with all the minorities within these countries—Druzes, Kurds, Circassians, and Maronites.

When I mentioned the Palestinians, Eldad pointed his finger threateningly at me. How dare I call this fictitious entity a nation, and compare their aspirations to those of the Jews, a nation of geniuses whose right to the land was firmly established by prophetic tradition! Besides, what kind of nation was this that was so cowardly as to run away in time of war, abandoning whole cities without fighting for them tooth and nail?

I listened to him in silent disgust, my brain seething with arguments.

As if determined to push me to the point of no return, he added, "Their only claim to civilization is the murder of women and children. Their Arab *mentality*, which combines delusions of grandeur with a deeply rooted sense of impotence, works itself out in acts of criminal aggression. Where the Romans left behind them aqueducts, and the Crusaders castles, the Arabs' legacy has been miserable, filthy hovels and Maalot" (the school that was taken hostage by the Palestinian guerrillas in 1974).

By then, I was so furious that for the first time in my life, I felt capable of committing murder without moral compunction. Unable to contain myself any longer, I reminded him that in the days leading up to Maalot, the Israeli air force had kept up a continuous bombardment of the Palestinian refugee camps in southern Lebanon, killing well over two hundred civilians and making thousands homeless. "I'll tell you what Israel's contribution to civilization is," I cried. "It's the devastation of Lebanon, the charred bodies of thousands of women and children!"

I had screamed so loudly that my voice cracked into a pitiful squeak. Then my anger snapped like a thread, and I began to feel thoroughly depressed instead.

I stepped outside into the night. The misshapen moon, barely visible now through the dark clouds, shed a cold, mournful light over Jerusalem.

Among the most frequent guest speakers at Geula's center was General Ariel Sharon, well known to me as the chief villain of the Kibya massacre in Jordan and numerous other punitive raids—which seemed to have turned him overnight into a military hero for young Israelis with right-wing sentiments.

But even Sharon's reputation for flexing his muscles at Arabs was not always enough for the kind of audience that attended the center's lectures. On one of the evenings, the students, already incensed because Sharon had suggested Israel give up part of the Sinai to Egypt in return for peace, were not in the least mollified by what he said next: "We have heard a lot of talk since '67 about withdrawing from the West Bank so that Israel will not be stuck with a large Arab minority in the midst. But I say we shall never live in Eretz-Israel without a big Arab minority; the Arabs are here, and whether we like it or not, there's nothing we can do about it." This seemingly innocent statement infuriated listeners. One of them howled, "Yes there is! We can kick them out!"

There were a few moments of silence as the entire audience sat gloating over this image of revenge, and then a young man called out: "When you said that the Arabs of Judea and Samaria have to learn to live with the Jewish settlers, just as we had to learn to live with the Arabs within our borders at the end of the '48 war, you made an incorrect analogy. It's the Jews who are having to put up with the Arabs in the West Bank, not the other way around! The true parallel would have been for you to call on Jordan to accept our settlements." This response drew a thunder of applause from the house.

As soon as Sharon had finished his talk, a withered old man who had sat next to me, growling ferociously all the while, tottered up to the podium and began to scold him as though he were a little boy. He was chastising Sharon for viewing the state of Israel as an end in itself rather than as an instrument for recovering Israeli sovereignty over the rest of the Promised Land. "You represent only the state of Israel," the old man snorted, "while I represent the *land* of Israel." Sharon smiled back at him, a timid smile. The old man was the famous poet Uri Zvi Greenberg, a friend of Eldad's and another great believer, I had been told, in an Israel that extended from the Nile to the Euphrates.

Geula had skipped out early to prepare dinner for Sharon, but before leaving she had whispered in my ear that I should get a ride with him to her house after the talk. When we arrived, she greeted us, looking lovelier than ever in a dress the color of a peacock's tail; it gave her eyes a brilliant sheen and her body a sensual vitality. I noticed that Sharon's roving eye was not insensible to Geula's charms.

He slumped into an armchair, which groaned under his massive frame. A delicious smell of meat wafted in from the kitchen, making his nostrils quiver with pleasure. Soon Geula brought in a Yemenite specialty, a boned leg of lamb stuffed with barley, pistachios, pine nuts, and raisins. It arrived smoking, golden brown, and diffusing a warm aroma of spices and gravy. The moment Sharon dug into the food, it seemed to disappear: meat, rice, nuts, everything. Then he scoured his plate with a piece of bread until it shone.

After dinner he slouched once more in the armchair. Stretching his legs out on the seat opposite him and loosening his belt, he said to me: "You know, I'm known in Israel only for my military prowess, which isn't really fair, because I'm first and foremost an expert on good food. I'm an excellent farmer; I grow the biggest, sweetest watermelons in this country." And at the thought of the watermelons, his plump, boyish face lit up.

Before leaving that night, he told me to come and visit him at his house in Rechovot, an invitation I promptly accepted.

Apparently concerned that his friendliness at Geula's might have led me to draw the wrong conclusions, Sharon undertook to set me straight when I arrived at his house. He warned that I should make it clear to Sadat that there would be no negotiations over the West Bank, not with the king of Jordan, not with the Palestinians, not with anybody. (I found it ironic that so many Israelis assumed I was an emissary from the Egyptian government when the reality was that I was considered a traitor.) Eretz-Israel was and would remain a country extending from the Mediterranean to the banks of the river Jordan, Sharon continued, "and between us, let it be said, it would not surprise me one bit if Israel were one day to include Jordan as well, because the Arabs will undoubtedly continue with their usual monkey business, so we'll have no choice but to take over the land to the east of the river—and *that* will be the end of the Palestinian problem!"

"Oh yes? And what about the Palestinian guerrillas?" I retorted.

"We'll kill them," he answered with his brassy voice, his face as expressionless as a wax mask.

"And do you plan to go about it the same way you did in Kibya?" I asked acidly.

"Kibya is not the only place in Jordan where civilians were killed," he said, in a cheerful tone that shocked me. "I'm not one of those Israelis who claim we never harm civilians. My view is quite simply that if there's cancer in a body, you have to remove it; if the terrorists nestle amid the populations of the towns and villages, then the civilians sheltering them must be punished."

278

"Does your view of punishment include the killing of innocent children?" I asked.

"There is no war in which children don't get killed," he retorted matter-of-factly. Then, changing the subject, he told me that the Bible was the best guide to the West Bank and that I should read it because there I would see that all the Arab villages had once been Jewish. "Just go to their cemeteries and look at the names on the gravestones," he said. "You'll see for youself that these Arab peasants are nothing but converts from Judaism."

A woman wearing a skintight black pullover stood in the doorway preparing her smiles just in case one was called for. She entered bearing a tray of beer and appetizers. Tall, with a long dark ponytail, artificial lashes, and heavily rouged cheeks, she turned out to be Sharon's wife, Lily.

Sitting down opposite me, she questioned me about what I had done in Israel so far, assuming a look of great interest. Sharon wandered off and presently returned armed with an album of pictures taken during different battles and featuring Egyptian prisoners of war. He accompanied this display with many anecdotes about the victorious Israeli army. His tone was meant to be hearty, but in fact it was highly insulting.

On the way out, I saw an unusual gun on a corner table. I wondered if this was part of his collection of antique guns, for I remembered having been told that by a cruel irony, this collection had cost him the life of a son. One day, he had heard a shot, followed by a ghastly cry. Rushing into the room where his boy had been playing with friends, he found him crumpled on the floor, covered with blood. One of the antique rifles had been loaded and had gone off in his hands. Sharon picked him up and ran out with him in his arms, howling with grief, but it was too late.

As he led me to the door, he noticed a camera lens protruding from my shoulder bag and stopped dead in his tracks. He demanded, "You didn't take any pictures of my house, did you?"

"No, why?"

"Well, I don't know, you're like those American spy satellites—you travel here, you travel there, you take photos, and who knows, you may decide later on to show them to some of your Palestinian friends. . . ."

Of all the men I met in Israel, no one exemplified the mystique of machismo better than Ariel Sharon. He was the prototype of the new Jew with muscle—virile, aggressive, arrogant, with that lack of sensitivity so characteristic of the generation of the sons of the pioneers. Every time I set eyes on him, I thanked heaven there were still some Jews left in Israel whom Zionism had not yet succeeded in curing of vulnerability and ambivalence as it had intended to.

But for Geula it was otherwise. Sharon—tall and blond, with the barrel chest of a prizefighter and that strange combination of lush sensuality and martial discipline—was her idea of the ideal male. Unfortunately, it was an image to which her husband had failed to conform, and her son now seemed to be departing from it as well.

Geula often told me she missed the discipline her father had imposed on their household. Although she had broken free from his authoritarian yoke by running away from home, she had never quite rid herself of the guilt that this rebellion had cost her, and she coped with it by idealizing patriarchal authority. When she first joined the underground at the age of sixteen, the man she eventually married had seemed a hero to her. He was much older than she and was in charge of the entire department that directed Jewish underground activities against the British. He had been imprisoned many times and had twice succeeded in breaking out of his cell.

"He was like a god to me," Geula said, "because he was prepared to suffer and die for his ideals. But though he was a revolutionary, when he came out of the underground he became very conservative. He wanted to lead a 'normal' life—too normal: to sit at home, have his tea with his wife in the afternoon after work, have children. For him the revolution was over, the past was something to put away in the drawer, dead—as dead as the memorial he wanted to build for the boys who were hanged in Egypt for killing Lord Moyne. But for me, the revolution wasn't over. How could it be, when we still didn't have Jerusalem, Hebron, Jericho, Shechem, and so many other places? I didn't want to come home in the evening and sit with him. I wanted to meet my friends from the underground in cafés, to talk about our political problems. I didn't want to have children, at least not right away. I wanted to go on with our struggle, to spread our beliefs. That's why I started working with Eldad on the publication of the monthly *Sulam* and wrote articles for newspapers and ran for the Knesset."

Geula's marriage slowly disintegrated. They had come out of the underground with nothing but the clothes on their backs, with no work, no money, not even a roof over their heads. But they had their reputations. She started to sell her articles to newspapers, went on to the university, and from there embarked on a political career. But he drifted from one job to another, working first as a truck driver, then as a low-paid clerk in the Jerusalem municipality. He withdrew to his private sphere and nursed his memories of life in the underground, giving up all political involvement. In civilian life he was a quiet man, reserved, timid, rather sweet. In time Geula tired of him and left him, but not before they had had two sons.

One son had died as a child, and the other, Tzachi, she brought up to fulfill the heroic ideal she believed his father had betrayed—to be strong, fearless, ready to sacrifice all for the nation. Unfortunately, Tzachi was asthmatic. He could not meet the army's criteria for physical fitness and was rejected. But when I met him he was in the process of trying again for Geula's sake, because she considered it a shame she could not live down. Although he was shy and withdrawn, more given to listening to music and reading than to physical activities, he had lined the small alcove of the bedroom he shared with his mother with posters of karate heroes, boxers, wrestlers, and hefty Mr. Universes. On getting up every morning, he would lift weights, and in the evening he would run twice around the block. He lived for one thing only: to raise his military profile so that he would be accepted by the army. One day Geula invited me to meet him.

The boy who came to the door when I rang was slender and graceful. His gaze beneath long eyelashes was gentle, his movements lithe.

Geula fetched us a Yemenite dinner from the kitchen—spiced chicken hearts with chick peas—and we went to sit in the living room with the oriental furnishings, settling on poufs around a low table. The flames of the old-fashioned paraffin lamp buzzed softly in the milky glass funnel, casting a subdued glow.

We talked a great deal, and the evening unfolded pleasantly enough until I broached the topic of the Palestinians. Then Tzachi revealed himself: "I don't accept what you say about the Jews and Palestinians having equal moral rights. I don't believe the so-called legitimate rights of the Palestinians exist. They're not legitimate and they're not rights. But I just want peace. I don't want to die in a war. I would give back the Golan and the Sinai both if I thought for one moment that would bring peace. Especially the Sinai. I hate the place: I hate the sand, the heat, the wind."

"And what about the West Bank?" I asked.

"I don't think we have the right to give up Hebron and Shechem [Nablus]," Tzachi retorted. "But I would give them up for one hundred percent security. I think the Palestinians should be allowed to live in their own state if they don't threaten us."

At this Geula's face began to change color. "What do you mean, give it up? Hebron is yours!"

The boy answered her boldly: "I don't think that Hebron is mine any more than it belongs to the Arabs who live there. So I don't know what to say—maybe Hebron and Shechem could be in an Arab state, but the citizens of Israel who live there would be under Israeli jurisdiction."

Geula, whose patience with her son was rapidly eroding, was drumming nervously on the table with her long fingernails. "But you have to decide something!" she blurted.

Looking at her defiantly, the boy said, "I don't have to decide anything. I'm thinking, and I'm allowed to be confused."

And Geula, who was struggling hard to banish the irritation from her voice, probably because she felt it would not do to lose her temper with her son in my presence, asked him, "What's the difference for you between the Sinai and the West Bank?"

"I don't think I have the right to be in the Sinai, because nobody in Israel wants to live there. Nobody wants it," he repeated with emphasis.

"I do!" cried Geula.

Tzachi shot a look of complicity in my direction. "Okay, I think you're wrong, Mother, because I don't think the Jews have any historical ties to the Sinai."

I had never seen Geula discomfited before and I stifled a laugh. Now openly aghast at her son's opinions, she asked him, "What about the West Bank?"

"I told you, we have a moral right to live there," he replied, but in the manner of someone who is grasping at straws.

"What about politically?" Geula went on implacably.

"Politically, I want the Arabs to stay there," the boy replied, exasperated.

"So make them stay there! Who wants to throw them out? Do I?" she burst out.

"But they want to live under their own government. I don't see why we should deprive them of that."

"Deprive whom?" she asked, glaring at him savagely now.

At the sight of her eyes, the well-meaning boy froze and began to stammer: "The citizens of the West Bank . . . provided there is peace, of course," he hastened to add, in an attempt to mollify his mother, for her face had turned scarlet.

I was moved with pity for the boy and tried to make peace between them. "Tzachi may be trying to say—" I ventured, but she cut me off: "Wait a minute. I want to understand my son. Tzachi, are you for a Palestinian state? I know he's not," she added, turning to me.

"No, I'm not for a Palestinian state," he replied, smiling at me apologetically.

"But Tzachi, you just said that provided they didn't threaten your security . . ." I started to protest.

Now Tzachi was really foundering: "I mean . . . I don't mean I'm against a Palestinian state."

"How can you say such a thing?" Geula hollered. "Why, when we conquered Judea and Samaria, you were as joyful as any of us, you sang and danced!"

He smiled thinly. "Yes, Mother, but what if, for the sake of peace, I'm prepared to give up this part of my land?"

After Tzachi left us, Geula, still visibly upset, told me not to take him too seriously. He was too young to know what he really wanted. Then she returned to her favorite topic of conversation: the flaws in Israel's educational system. Her own son was a victim of brainwashing by the Labor party! It was appalling. And God knows she had tried to educate him to know his rights. Above all, she had always taught him to be prepared to sacrifice his blood for the nation. From his earliest childhood on, she had given him inspiring examples: "I would read him stories from the book of our sages about men whose devotion to Israel was extraordinary. Like the story of a false Messiah, an Arab Jew who was in his own way our first hippie. He was thin, with long flowing white hair and bare feet, and he went to a community of Jews and told them, 'Follow me, I will lead you across the river into Eretz-Israel. The river will open for us as the Red Sea did for Moses.' They followed him, and all of them drowned!" She concluded triumphantly, pausing to see if I had been properly impressed with her story.

I tried to look dumbstruck with admiration, and she seemed satisfied. She continued: "I also read him the story of another Jew, who, after reading in the Bible that we would be carried to Eretz-Israel on the wings of an eagle, went to his community and told them, 'I will tell you when the right time comes for our dream to be realized.' Then one day, he took them all to a roof and said, 'Now, jump.' They jumped and were killed instantly," she exulted.

Before leaving that night, I said to her—and not without feeling a trifle remorseful even as I relished my wickedness, "Geula, I must ask you a very cruel question. Suppose one could guarantee you that if the Palestinians had a state of their own, there would be no more wars; which would you choose, the life of your son, or the West Bank?"

She was not in the least put out by the question: "Sana," she said, with an indulgent smile, "when one speaks of war, one must never see it only from a private point of view. I tried very hard to explain to you many times that for us Jews, national life and private life are one. The model for me is—as it should be for every Jewish mother—Hannah. She had seven sons, and her sons were killed one by one before her eyes because she refused to embrace the idolatrous faith of an alien emperor. And finally, when her last son was killed, she went to the roof and jumped to her death."

13

The Unending War

GEULA'S GREAT magnetism and generosity—and the friendship she extended to me—sometimes made it possible to think of her politics as something separate from her, an obsessive mission I could choose not to take too seriously even though she was devoting her life to it. But as weeks turned into months, I was keenly aware of taking the comfortable way out again, of enjoying the pleasures of her company while still insulating myself from the far less exotic lives of those actively involved in the bitter drive to expand Israel's borders. It was one thing to be around Geula, to bask in the luxurious warmth of her house, and quite another, I was sure, to confront the reality of the West Bank. I determined to visit a settlement as soon as possible.

The mayor of Jerusalem, Teddy Kollek, had sent me an invitation to come and reside in Mishkenot Sha'ananim—the elegant guest house for renowned foreign artists, musicians, and writers. Aside from entry to a glamorous world, a stay at Mishkenot would allow me to be close to the West Bank. I was sorry to leave Tel Aviv, a city where I had been able to see Danny almost daily. But I reasoned that Jerusalem was after all only an hour's drive away.

So I quit my job at Rotex and called up the novelist Yoram Kaniuk, whom I had once met when he came to talk at Hazon Hadash, asking him to take me along the next time he went to Jerusalem. He was in the habit of driving across the country to give political talks, and he often let me hitch rides with him.

We left Tel Aviv by way of a road that led to the peaceful meadows and apple orchards of Mikve Yisrael, an agricultural school that had been founded in 1870 on land leased from the Ottoman sultan to attract and train the first wave of immigrants to Palestine from Russia. It was here that Theodor Herzl had tried to talk the kaiser into establishing a

Jewish settlement in Palestine, under a German protectorate. The famous photograph of their meeting flashed into my mind: Herzl standing on the school's fields, his white pith helmet in hand, and the kaiser on horseback, wearing Arab headgear.

Next we drove past the Israeli town of Yazur, formerly an Arab village. This was where the first skirmishes had taken place in 1948 between the Israeli convoys, on their way to relieve a besieged Jerusalem, and the Palestinian peasants, who blocked the road with barbed wire, nails, and bits of broken glass. Among the typically drab Israeli buildings, the tomb of a sheikh stood out. Dwarfed by the newly built highway, which almost reached its windows, it had lost some of its prominence. From the perspective of a speeding car, its tiny white cupolas, shimmering under the fierce glare of the sun, had a tremulous quality that made them resemble seething foam. Israeli respect for this sacred Muslim shrine was not great: Above the central cupola stood a huge red and blue billboard advertising shaving cream.

We drove past fields of red gladioli spread out like a fiery carpet across the golden plains. Suddenly we came upon what looked like a whole armored division lined up behind a barbed wire fence. I stared, confounded by the Arab lettering on the trucks. Yoram noticed my startled expression and, laughing, explained that these were the spoils of the '67 war—Russian military hardware captured from the Egyptian troops.

A little farther down stood the maximum security prison of Maasiyahu, where Koso Okamoto, one of the men who carried out the Lod airport massacre, was incarcerated. And hidden from view behind it was Lod (Lydda), the home of Eisa's assimilated Palestinian friends. Just past the ubiquitous cluster of hitchhiking soldiers another Arab town, Ramleh, was clearly visible. It was from this area that tens of thousands of Palestinians had fled during the 1948 war—not out of fear in this instance, but because of a calculated Israeli policy to expel them. Moshe Dayan's commando unit played a major role in the capture of Lydda, Ramleh, and the surrounding countryside, and Israel's current prime minister, Yitzhak Rabin, was the commander who worked out the plans for the conquest of those two Arab cities.

On the outskirts of Ramleh, in front of the train station, the old Muslim cemetery dating back to Ottoman times rested under the eucalyptus trees with their smooth yellowish trunks. Moss had formed over the irregular tombstones, and here and there tall squills, their white petals aligned around perfectly straight stalks, stood solitary and immobile as if gathered in prayer.

Down the road, a bizarre old building with a fresh coat of loud cherry paint over its pocked walls hid among thick thistles. I pointed it out to Yoram, who told me it was an abandoned Arab house that the Israelis had renovated and turned into a Wimpy stand. The drive between Tel Aviv and Jerusalem proved too short to make it worthwhile for customers to stop for snacks, so the venture had been given up.

Right around the bend was the Latrun Valley, with the fringe of purple-peaked mountains. There Joshua, after his stunning victory over the five kings of the Amorites, had made the sun and the moon stand together in the sky to light the battlefield all through the night. In his wake had come the Babylonians, Persians, Greeks, Romans, Arabs, Crusaders, Turks, British, and Israelis. Perhaps no single plot of earth in history had drunk so much blood.

After the '48 war, this whole area had been left as a kind of no-man's-land between Israel and Jordan because the Rhodes Conciliation Commission could not decide whom to allot it to. But every so often, one or the other of the parties would try to bite into it on the sly. At the start of each agricultural season, they would engage in a ferocious competition over who would succeed in plowing up more land, thus temporarily establishing de facto jurisdiction. Attired like medieval warriors, the kibbutzniks would sneak off to the fields in the dark, steel shields around their tractors and bayonets in hand, and work feverishly through the night. These expeditions often resulted in casualties, when Palestinian peasants took shots at them from across the Jordanian border.

During the '67 war, Egypt sent some of its best commando units to the Latrun Valley to lead the advance to Tel Aviv. When they found themselves surrounded on all sides by the enemy, they hid among the wheat stalks of Michelle's kibbutz, but the fields were set on fire and most of them were either burned alive or shot down as they tried to escape the flames.

On the heights ahead of us lay a piece of scenery lifted out of the French countryside—a Trappist monastery. Bathed in the soft light of the approaching sunset, it rose on top of a hill speckled with waves of tiny silver bells. They turned out to be the leaves of olive trees, planted symmetrically all the way down to the valley.

Below the monastery stood the deserted police station of Latrun, the tenacious Arab outpost that had effectively blocked the Israeli fighters from the road to Jerusalem during the '48 war. With its grim, khaki-colored walls and smashed windowpanes staring down blindly at the valley, it suggested a corpse left to rot in the sun.

When the Israelis finally succeeded in capturing Latrun during the

'67 war, they repeated what they had done in '48. To assure Israel's security, as they put it, they razed every Arab village in the area stone by stone, down to the very tombstones, and redistributed the lands among the neighboring kibbutzim.

I mentioned this to Yoram, and he said sarcastically: "That's why it's called the Israeli Defense Army! We always defend, we never attack, you understand. We bomb Lebanon, killing hundreds of civilians, and call it 'cleaning out the area.' We destroy the village of Shubath in southern Lebanon and call it 'creating a protective curtain.' It makes things simpler for us so we can live with ourselves without guilt feelings. I fight it all the time, because I can't forget that the Germans created a whole language and a whole world of images before they did away with the Jews. Otherwise, it would not have been so simple for them to kill six million of us."

As we drove on, leaving the Latrun Valley behind us, Yoram told me a joke about a Frenchman, an Englishman, and an Israeli who were caught by cannibals. While the cannibals heated a big pot of steaming water to boil them in, they told the prisoners that each one of them could have a last wish. The Englishman asked for a cup of tea, the Frenchman for a glass of wine, and the Israeli for a kick in the rear. After the cannibals had complied, the Israeli said, "Ah, so you kicked me! You scoundrels! You'll have to pay for that!" and he took out his gun and shot them. The Englishman and Frenchman looked at him in amazement and exclaimed, "Well, if you had a gun all along, why the hell didn't you use it earlier?" To which the Israeli replied, "Because our army is called the Israeli Defense Army."

We had reached Shaar Ha'Gai ("The Gate of the Valley"), or as the Arabs call it, Bab el Wadi. It was this narrow gorge with twisting curves and steep rocky slopes that the Israeli convoys had had to climb in '48 to bring desperately needed food and medical supplies to a besieged Jerusalem. To get past Bab el Wadi they had to fight every inch of the way, for the heights belonged to the Palestinians. Two Palestinian villages guarded them: Kastel, situated beside the ruins of a Crusader castle, which had itself taken the place of a Roman stronghold that stood watch over the entrance to Jerusalem at the time of Christ, and Colonia, where Titus's soldiers had been stationed during the siege of Jerusalem.

Today a modern Israeli highway has been cut through the once inaccessible rocky slopes to prevent any such ambush in the future. Old armored vehicles the color of rust appear to be tumbling down the mountain. This piece of staging is an attempt to commemorate the Jewish soldiers who gave their lives to capture these heights.

I strained my eyes but could see not a single trace of Kastel and Colonia; only thorns and thistles remained. Yoram had been wounded during the first, unsuccessful attempt to take these mountains: "I remember lying not far from here, among thirty corpses, with a bullet in my leg, pretending to be dead and waiting for a chance to escape. I was only eighteen. My entire platoon had been wiped out, and some of their heads had been cut off and stuck on sticks, which the Arabs planted on the hilltops as a warning to the Jews."

My mind wandered off to the village of Deir Yassin, which lay within gunshot of Kastel on the western approach to Jerusalem. Its inhabitants, who had the reputation among Jews of being a peaceful community, had not taken part in the fighting. This, however, did not prevent the soldiers, members of the Irgun, the Israeli underground headed by Begin, from massacring 250 of its people. According to the testimony of the British medical staff that was filed at the time, old women and babies had been battered, pregnant wives had been gutted, adolescent girls had been raped, and women's earlobes had been ripped off for their earrings. How could either side be proud of the carnage, and how many more generations of it would it take for peace to come?

We descended the steep rib of Kastel and drove up the spiraling terraces again, as if on a roller coaster. The peaks ahead of us lay buried in black clouds so low we could almost touch them. Small Arab cottages veiled by fog looked as if they had been carved into the ridges of the mountains. Below them, a big yellow quarry gashed the foothills. In the distance, concrete cubes clashed with the soft undulating slopes—the tract houses of Offra, a new Jewish settlement. Above it all on the heights stood Mont Joie, an old church built on the site from which the Crusaders supposedly first spotted Jerusalem and Richard the Lion-Hearted wept with joy.

And suddenly, Jerusalem.

We drove past houses lost in mire, past cold, wet stones, past closed rusty iron shutters, past a mass of twisting alleys. Only silhouettes hinted at the silent presences in the interstices of the city—a barrel here, a table there, a solitary tree, stairs leading to hidden cellars. A thin, freezing wind flashed through the open car window, stinging my face. The fog crept into my eyes and nostrils. The lane turned and wound, and abruptly closed in on us: Dead end. We had invaded the privacy of Jerusalem. The adjacent alley was even darker. The small houses huddled on either side of the curb in bizarre disarray, casting heavy shadows against each other. Bleak lights loomed through the gauze curtains of barred windows. In the courtyard, behind the buildings, was a spiral staircase. Very white, it brightened the dark afternoon.

The austerity of the Jerusalemite stones lent elegance to this city, but already I had begun to miss Tel Aviv. Shabby and vulgar though it might be, it hummed and whirred with warm life.

Mishkenot Sha'ananim ("Peaceful Habitation") owes its name to Isaiah: "My people will abide in a peaceful habitation, in secure dwellings, and in quiet resting places." But this mansion straddles the rocky slopes overlooking the Valley of Hinom—two Hebrew words which taken together read gehinom ("hell"). Across the valley lies the Jordanian border, and Mishkenot's own pockmarked walls bear testimony to the Arab sharpshooters who manned the walls of the Old City until the '67 war.

A low, long building with stone walls three feet thick rising up like mountain ramparts, Mishkenot is reinforced with battlements and iron grilles implanted in the Moorish arches of its windows. But its massiveness is relieved by fine cornices, gracefully wrought iron arches, and the ornate metalwork of the gates.

Now, the dull noise of pneumatic drills rent the air as submachine guns once did. Giant yellow caterpillars seemed to have overrun the hills surrounding Mishkenot, gnashing the stubborn rocks with steel jaws like mythical monsters.

At the reception desk, a beautiful Moroccan Jew named Annie seemed genuinely moved at the prospect of an Egyptian guest. She called the director, who was equally enthusiastic, and he in turn introduced me to the rest of the staff, all of whom outdid themselves to be cordial. This promised to be very different indeed from my last stay in Jerusalem, when I had the honor to labor in the scullery of the King David Hotel, just a step away.

Rebecca, the housekeeper, was summoned to lead me to my apartment. I could tell she felt the hosting of an Arab to be quite beneath her, not so much by the haughtiness of her tone as by her affectation of humility. She greeted me like an aristocrat who wants to show a commoner that nobility is not merely in one's title. Then she told me peremptorily to leave my suitcase in the lobby—the "Arab boy" would bring it—and led the way, her body so rigidly erect it appeared to be mounted on wires. The gray hair that framed her dry, angular face was pulled back tight, not a single strand escaping the clutch of her barrette. Beneath her penciled eyebrows, her eyes stared opaquely ahead. Her black shirt, buttoned all the way up to her chin. had been neatly tucked into a tweed skirt with sharply creased pleats. As we walked along, she rattled a set of heavy iron keys, which, she explained to me, were as old as the building itself and, as such, irreplaceable. Modern keys, she said, were not nearly as secure.

Small greenhouses with exotic cacti and birds of paradise framed the entrance to each apartment, and the luxury inside was beyond belief. The tiles in the bathroom were inlaid with the daintiest blue and gold designs. A marble staircase led up to the bedrooms decorated with opulent red drapery and white sheepskin rugs. In the living room an antique mirror with an ivory frame stood against the wall between two fine etchings of Jerusalem in the nineteenth century. A white leather couch had been placed under a giant canvas whose blazing red sun rays contrasted with the pale stone walls and dark iron grillwork of the doors and windows. On the ledge, beneath the Moorish arches of the window, was an assortment of Roman oil lamps and a medieval Islamic bowl of finely engraved silver. The window overlooked a terraced garden.

As I took stock of the apartment, the housekeeper wiped imaginary dust from the edge of the table and frantically rubbed a spot her sharp eyes had detected on one of the glasses in the kitchenette. She apologized, saying that the Moroccan maids did not know how to clean; she had to keep after them all the time. They were lazy, it was part of their culture. Their fathers played backgammon and drank *arak* all day, and they passed these habits on to their children. Other ethnic groups had also started out with nothing when they first arrived in Israel, but at least *they* were willing to work. Take her, for example. In Germany her family had lived very comfortably. Her father was a lawyer in a small provincial town, and they had had a beautiful villa and a maid. The family left everything behind when they emigrated to Palestine. Times were very hard at first. She had gone from house to house looking for laundry to do and floors to mop. But slowly things had improved. She had worked her way up to the position of housekeeper in the household of Foreign Minister Abba Eban, and now she had this job. And she had saved enough money to give her sons a university education. "That's the difference between us and them," she concluded. "We work ourselves to the bone so our children may have a better future, while they sit at home and send their children out to work for them."

She paused on the way out to center the pot of poinsettias more exactly in the middle of the table, as though this act of ordering could give her back some measure of control over a life that had been so subjected to the whims of fate.

A few minutes after Rebecca had left, the "Arab boy" arrived. Omar was one of those characters of indeterminable age whose worn appearance might have been the result of either time or toil. As it was, he looked around sixty. His height too was ambiguous: He could have shriveled up either with the years or with labor. He wore a threadbare jacket of doubtful color, trousers that flapped about his bowlegs, and a pair of shoes that seemed twice his size.

He shuffled as he dragged my heavy suitcase to the center of the room. Having completed his task, he steadied himself and stood looking at me. I thanked him. He smiled a ghastly smile; all his teeth were gone except for the four up front and a long pointed canine rising tenuously out of his lower jaw like a yellow tusk. He made a few sounds in my direction and, as I did not catch on, drew closer and said, in Arabic, "You and I are the same." I was unable to respond immediately. Thinking I had not understood, he pointed his finger at me, then back to himself, and repeated, "You and I are the same." This time I managed a feeble smile. "You mean we're both Arabs," I said. "No, we're both traitors!" he lisped, with a certain satisfaction. He added that he never ventured past the walls of the Old City because he knew he was on the list of those marked for death. His job at Mishkenot Sha'ananim consisted of guarding the guests against Palestinian guerrillas, and to that end he toured the premises every half hour. Then, half-boastfully, half-apologetically, he lifted his jacket, displaying his gun. "Allah forgive me," he said. "A man has to make a living."

After Omar left, I tried to read a novel, but I couldn't concentrate. Even the exquisite strains of the Brahms Violin Concerto floating into my bedroom—Isaac Stern was practicing next door—failed to calm me.

I set aside my book and walked to the window. Night had fallen. The rain had begun a meager, dismal drizzle. Between us and Arab Jerusalem, which hunched menacingly behind its city walls, the valley stretched like a dark abyss.

For as long as I can remember, those walls had always represented for me the end of Jerusalem—indeed, the end of the civilized world. The Arabs who had lived within the safety of this massive structure until the '67 war would no more have conceived of letting the Israelis in than they would have imagined leaving unbolted the gates that had kept the roving bands of marauders and wild animals out of the Old City earlier in the century.

In our textbooks this boundary was represented by a heavy black line beyond which hovered sinister black shadows. It was not until I had come to Israel that I learned that for the Jews, this same wall had all along been nothing more than a symbol, a metaphor for the Temple to be rebuilt. On their road maps of Israel before '67, our thick dividing line was replaced by a delicate green band, hardly distinguishable from the maze of other colored bands specifying highways, asphalt roads, unpaved roads, and railway lines. As an Arab, I was surprised to discover that *the wall* that existed with such concrete finality in my own mind, and that I had always considered an unalterable state boundary, was euphemistically referred to as the municipal town boundary on the Israeli map.

I went back to my bed and lay down, losing myself in the rain's monotonous trickle and the strains of Stern's violin. Just before falling asleep, I heard Omar's heavy tread outside on the porch and thought how easy it would be to break into our street-level apartments.

The mournful howls of jackals from the nearby hills pierced my sleep and gradually roused me as they merged with human voices: "Kiiiissingerrr! Kiiiissingerrr!" droned the loudspeakers. "Wake up, Kiiissingerrr! Go home, Kiiissingerrr, do you hear us? Go home!"

I looked at my watch. It was three in the morning. Next door, at the King David Hotel, Henry Kissinger must have been trying to get some sleep.

The scene outside my window was out of Boito's *Mefistofele*. By the misty halo of the street lamps I could barely make out a frenetic dance. Spectral figures emitted eerie incantations: *"Am Yisrael chai, am Yisrael chai!"* ("The Jewish nation lives!"). The hills were being exorcised in a supernatural nocturnal visitation from the militant religious activists known as Gush Emunim ("The Bloc of the Faithful"), who were responsible for Israel's West Bank settlements.

I returned to my bed, but for a long time I could not sleep, torn between fear and curiosity. The next morning, after paying a thank-you call on Teddy Kollek, I decided to visit one of their settlements.

A few hours later, I took an Arab bus to Hebron. It was a melancholy winter day, and the trees shivered with the cold. Among the motley crew of passengers, I noticed a veiled woman with a baby, and a few young men with drawn, hard faces, threadbare jackets, and flashy ties. They installed themselves opposite me and began to size me up until I felt so uncomfortable I had to change seats. I moved to the back of the bus next to the veiled woman, who was carrying her baby and a bread basket.

Her doelike eyes—the only visible part of her face—were velvety black. Suddenly she slipped her hand into an invisible slit at the side of her flowery dress and pulled out a large breast with a nipple so dark it was almost purple. I felt myself blush. Then she bent foward and pushed the tip of her breast into her baby's mouth with the greatest composure. The sleepy infant rejected it. She held the heavy breast in both her hands, squeezed a drop of milk onto the nipple, and placed it once more within range of her child's mouth. He licked it, and then he gripped her bosom and began to suck slowly and regularly. She moaned.

I was sitting with my eyes glued to her, wondering, as I had whenever I sighted the poor nursing in the public gardens of Egypt, how this was possible in a milieu where men placed their wives in virtual purdah, when an Israeli military jeep waved us off to the side of the road. A poker-faced soldier with large stony eyes clambered aboard. He did not greet anyone or even look at the passengers; he was a perfect specimen of the boorishness that seems to come naturally to the soldiers of an occupying army. "You," he called out to the driver, "get up!" The driver stared at this intruder with a mixture of fear and resentment, then rose to his feet and submitted apathetically to the body search. The soldier stalked past the rows of scared faces toward the men in the back seats and, snapping his fingers impatiently, motioned them without a word to get up. They looked at him for a moment, mouths open with surprise and terror, and then complied. After he was done with them, he turned to the woman and jerked his chin in the direction of her bread basket. She did not understand what he wanted and asked him in halting Hebrew. Without answering, he pried her basket open with his rifle butt. She began to whimper, and one of them men protested. "*Iskut!*" ("Shut up!") the soldier snapped in Arabic. His task completed, he strutted past me, casting a "Shalom" in my direction, dismounted, and whacked the back of the bus to signal that it could leave. Obviously he had assumed I was Jewish. I sat through the rest of the journey with downcast eyes, ashamed to look the others in the face.

A quarter of an hour later we were making our entry into the West Bank town of Hebron, where the religious settlement of Kiryat Arba was located.

Curved like a pale crescent, Hebron nestled at the foot of the hill. In the center of the town a charming mosque with stained windows raised its blue dome. Its sight caused me a pang of homesickness.

I caught a taxi at the station, and it wended its way up a narrow alley, past mules straining under loads of olive twigs, past veiled women in gaily embroidered dresses balancing big urns on their heads, past open-air cafés where wizened, bleary-eyed old men sat twirling beads, past the mosque containing the Tomb of the Patriarchs.

Fewer and fewer houses. And abruptly, it was as though I had come to a frontier—the border between occupier and occupied. Here, the gate was bolted and bales of barbed wire stretched as far as the eye could see. Farther up at the crest of the hill, the squat new cement towers of Kiryat Arba cast long shadows in the late afternoon. Down below, in the valley, the old Arab town of Hebron lay waiting.

The guard came over to peer suspiciously into the taxi. My explanation about being an Egyptian on a visit to Israel and wishing merely to look the settlement over did little to allay his suspicions. He insisted politely but firmly that because of security considerations, he was not authorized to let uninvited strangers in. Then, to find a way out of this impasse, I mentioned Elyakim Haezni, a lawyer I had met in Tel Aviv who had told me that even though he himself was not religious, he had moved his family to Kiryat Arba because he believed it was his duty as a Jew to help populate "Judea and Samaria." The guard telephoned, and when he was told I would be received, he raised the gate. I asked the driver to come back for me at eleven that night and climbed down the stairs toward a broad courtyard around which crowded a dozen or so hideous tract buildings. Some were still under construction, and Palestinian workers could be seen hammering away at the scaffolding. On one of them a poster read in Hebrew: ARAB. DO NOT EVEN DARE THINK OF A JEWESS. And another: DAUGHTER OF ISRAEL, DO NOT GO OUT WITH AN ARAB OR ANY OTHER KIND OF GOY.

These West Bank Palestinians were even worse off than their "Arab-Israeli" neighbors. I remembered the first time I had seen such workers. I had had a heated argument with a kibbutznik who was in charge of recruiting Palestinians from the West Bank to do the manual field work during harvest time. He had told me he wanted to take me along the next time he went so I could see for myself "how happy they are to get the work we give them." I agreed to go.

We drove up to the village in a Peugeot pickup truck. The *rais* (Arab work manager) had already been instructed to assemble the prospective workers in the marketplace at seven that morning. His relationship to them was that of pimp to prostitutes; he pocketed the money and paid them a trifle. Though the kibbutz was aware of this abuse, it chose to look the other way because working through an intermediary who guaranteed them a regular supply of labor was far more practical than hiring individuals one by one.

When we reached the village, we circled very slowly around the marketplace. A small melee ensued as the Palestinian women and children, pushing and yelling, clambered into the rear of the truck, which kept on going. Once it was full, it picked up speed in order to prevent additional people from jumping in. Some of the children, more agile than the others, managed to get a hold on the outside of the truck and hang on. At that point, the *rais* intervened: Using a big stick, he hit them on the knuckles to force them to let go. But the most desperate ones clung on despite the blows that continued to rain on their hands and heads. All the while, my kibbutz escort looked on impassively.

In this fashion, packed like cattle, the Palestinians were driven straight to the cotton fields. When the time came for their lunch break, they were not even invited into the dining room. The only thing the kibbutz provided was water. My escort commented, "Look at them, they have no spirit of solidarity; see how they push each other to get at the water first! A nation like this will never amount to much."

Kiryat Arba resembled a military barracks far more than it did a residential neighborhood. Machine guns were everywhere—slung across the shoulders of the young men strolling with their wives in the Sabbath dusk; sticking out of the straw baskets of giggling teenage girls; strapped to baby carriages that matrons in wigs pushed down the lanes; tucked away under the prayer shawl of the shy adolescent on his way to the synagogue.

I walked past a jumble of seesaws and swings. A toddler with blond earlocks and a skullcap embroidered with the words "Soldier of G–d" hung onto the railing and looked me over as he picked his nose. Beside one of the doorways, two young men excitedly discussed some obscure liturgical problem, one of them twirling and untwirling his earlocks around his finger while the other listened nervously, plucking at his beard. Nearby, a pudgy old gentleman listened to his Bible partner with a smile of gentle irony on his face, as if he were surveying his young friend's vast arsenal of folly and had made up his mind not to be too hard on him. Occasionally he would nod silently, but the agitated motion of the chubby, dimpled fingers clasped behind his back hinted that he was carrying on a lively private monologue.

As the daylight faded, mothers called their children home and whole families drifted back to their apartments. It was getting colder, and the stiffening breeze sent up swirls of dust. The courtyard emptied. The flickering candles made the windows squint. I heard a chant, perhaps from the synagogue, but now I could no longer make out the building.

I asked a young man who stood in front of a door calmly combing his beard whether he knew which block Elyakim lived on. He turned out to be a visitor himself from the neighboring religious settlement of Kfar Etzion, but he knew Elyakim and offered to show me to his apartment. On the way over he introduced himself as Yochanan and asked me my name and where I was from. I told him. He froze in his tracks, looking at me with an air of indignant surprise. He did not understand how Elyakim could receive me, he said, for he himself could never let an Arab past his threshold.

I asked him what he had against Arabs. He gave me a long look.

"I can't forget that because of one of them my father is dead and my whole life was twisted."

Kfar Etzion, where he lived, had been overrun by the Jordanian army during the '48 war. Its men were taken prisoner and told they were going to be photographed, but instead they were lined up against a wall and shot. "Every year since '48, all of us, orphans and widows, have been meeting at the Jerusalem cemetery where our fathers are buried. We, the children, would climb to the top of the hill overlooking Kfar Etzion and vow that one day we would return. Now we have almost fulfilled our promise. Of the sixty sons whose fathers were killed, forty have come back since the '67 war.

"When we first came back, the Arabs were afraid to return to their fields because they feared our revenge would be terrible. Only one of them, a stubborn old man, continued working on the land where we wanted to plant trees. We told him this was our land, so he retreated a little with his donkey. As we kept advancing, he kept moving back the stones marking his field, and every time he would mumble, 'You are like nettle. If it's not entirely eliminated from the fields, it grows right back. We remove you, and you come back, we remove you, and you come back.'

"Today there is only one Arab family left, Abdullah and his three children. Many times we have tried to buy the land from him, but he says his father and grandfather lived there and he does not care for the money. I understand him, but I know that sooner or later he will be squeezed out. He's already surrounded by five new religious settlements. They have roads, electricity, telegraph lines, water; he lives the way his grandfathers and great-grandfathers lived. He cannot hold out much longer—one day the government will confiscate his land to make a road that connects the different settlements. So even though I understand him, I have no answer for him other than the answer of the Bible. When it comes to Judea and Samaria, we have a religious law that says a war of conquest is a *mitzvah*, and there is a commandment to give up your life to keep the land of Israel."

I trudged up the concrete stairs to the second-floor landing and rang the bell. Elyakim threw open the door and addressed me as though we were old friends. "Sana!" he exclaimed. "We were wondering what had become of you."

A shock of frizzy hair topped his broad forehead, and thick glasses sat halfway down his nose. But the most remarkable thing about his appearance were the ears that flapped on either side of his head, so large they almost doubled over.

Elyakim introduced me to Rabbi Waldman, a middle-aged, black-frocked man with a round, childish face and a timid, almost fearful look who was sitting in his living room. He was the head rabbi of the settlement's yeshiva, and while he did not seem particularly pleased to meet me, he was willing to spare a few minutes to explain to me God's master plan for the liberation of Palestine and its return to the Jews. In a soft, flat voice, he informed me that God's orders had begun to unfold almost a century ago with the arousal of nationalist sentiments among Jews who had previously been content to live in the Diaspora. If Zionism was the first stage, he said, the next "progressive stage" in Jewish history was the Holocaust. The concentration camps were a necessary tool for compelling the Jews—the vast majority of whom were opposed to Zionism until Hitler came on the scene—to return to the Holy Land.

Horrified by this, I asked him how he could believe in such a cruel God. "My dear," he replied with a benign serenity, "if I understood God fully, I would not believe in Him, because then I too would be God. All I can tell you is that if the redemption could not be brought about in a good way, it had to be brought about in a difficult way." Then he went on to unravel to me God's design for the '67 war: "At first we thought we were going to war only against Egypt, but at the very last minute King Hussein flew to Cairo and signed the pact which brought Jordan into the war. God arranged this agreement between them in order for us to liberate Judea and Samaria. So, the Six-Day War was another great step forward for our people."

As he left, I wondered whether the conquest of Jordan would be the next "great step forward" in Rabbi Waldman's divine plan.

Elyakim offered to show me around Kiryat Arba. We drove farther up the hill along a twisting dirt road, and he told me about the settlement.

Ever since Israel had captured the West Bank in '67, he and his friends from the Gush Emunim had wanted to move out here, because they believed it was important to fragment the West Bank into a grid of militarily fortified Israeli settlements so that it would no longer be a unified area that could support an independent Palestinian existence. But the Labor government, "a bunch of weaklings and traitors who deserve to be shot," was opposed.

His eyes lit with mischievous pleasure as he related how his group

298

had forced the government's hand. After their initial attempts to purchase land and houses in Hebron were foiled by the Israeli cabinet, they resorted to a ploy. They offered to rent an entire Hebron hotel over Passover. Tourism had been sluggish in Hebron since the '67 war, because rich clients no longer came from neighboring Arab states. The owner of the hotel was therefore unable to resist such a tempting offer —the Jews were prepared to pay not only for every bed in the hotel, but also for all floor space that could be turned into overnight accommodations for additional persons. After the deal was concluded, the settlers made the hotel kitchen kosher and moved in truckloads of school desks and chairs, washing machines, and refrigerators. By that time, the worried owner began to suspect that this was to be more than just a short visit and begged them to leave, but they refused.

Moshe Dayan was furious with the settlers for ruining the good relations he had striven to cultivate with the West Bank Arabs. Thinking that where the cabinet had been able to remove them by force he would succeed by guile, he persuaded them that it would be unsafe to continue living in the hotel; they should move to the military compound for their own protection. He counted on the crowded, uncomfortable living conditions of the barracks to dissuade them from their pursuit, Elyakim said, but he underestimated his opponents. Within a matter of weeks, they had succeeded in embarrassing the government by calling in reporters and displaying their "deplorable living conditions." The cabinet was once more under heavy pressure to compromise, and they agreed to build a limited number of accommodations for the settlers within the compound, provided no more settlers would move in. Now Elyakim laughed and tapped his forehead at the thought of the government's stupidity: "You know how it is with religious Jews. Within a year, they had the first child, within two years, the second, pretty soon they had eight, ten children, and so in each room we had the nucleus of another Jewish family. The birth rate in Kiryat Arba is the highest in the country. Every day of my life I savor the idea of how we tricked the Israeli government."

At last we had reached the peak. Elyakim stopped the car and we got out. It was night. Almost directly below us stood Kiryat Arba, the candles in its windows flickering like eyes in the dark. Looking harder, I could just barely make out the shadowy outlines of the concrete apartments. Better lit at the base of the hill was Hebron, and across, on the opposite slopes, the bright lights of the homes that belonged to wealthy Palestinian notables. The air was much colder here and the wind steady. Elyakim gestured downward, toward the settlements. "We will build many more apartments here," he said, stretching out his arms as if to encompass the entire Fertile Crescent. "We are two hundred and fifty families now, but soon we will be fifteen hundred families." He then explained to me the development plan for the religious settlement of Kiryat Arba. It was to be in the form of a horseshoe, with Arab Hebron in the center, nearly surrounded by Jewish settlers, who would control the heights. They had patterned their growth after the Arab towns of Nazareth and St. Jean d'Acre, two cities within Israel proper that had been allotted to the Palestinians in the U.N. partition plan of '47 but had subsequently been captured by Israeli forces in the '48 war. There large Jewish residential sections were built on the heights to preclude the possibility that the heavily Arab-populated Galilee should try to secede if a Palestinian state were ever to come into existence on the West Bank.

I shivered from the cold and hugged my cape more tightly around me, but Elyakim, though dressed only in a shirt and light sweater, was oblivious to the chill. His shock of hair blowing in the wind, he stood in the dim light like a king surveying his realm, gesturing toward his people, whose religious beliefs he respected but did not share. For Elyakim was a fanatic without a faith.

He talked on and on about the benefits of the plan. He stressed the economic progress that the hillside industry would bring the local Arabs, explaining to me that seventeen factories were already in existence and four more under construction. He chuckled and added that the most prosperous were the souvenir factories, where Arab boys fashioned *mezuzah*s and Stars of David under the vigilant supervison of a rabbi.

If the plan succeeded, the Palestinians would live at the bottom of the hill, in a ghetto, commuting daily to the all-Jewish sections of town to do the manual labor, while the Jews did the skilled work and controlled the industry. I said this to Elyakim, pointing out that even some Israelis recognized that unless the West Bank was returned to the Palestinians, what he called "economic opportunities" for the resident Palestinians would be nothing more than the exploitation by one ethnic group of another's cheap labor.

My remarks set him off on a tirade: "All those fine Israeli liberals and socialists of yours who complain that the Arabs do the menial jobs are hypocrites. Five years ago it was the Oriental Jews who had these jobs, but they didn't seem to mind *that* so much. Now the Oriental Jews have moved up, and it's the Arabs who have them, but that somehow bothers these great moralists. Now let me tell you about an Arab I know, and judge for youself. His name is Guma, and he used to live in a refugee camp in Gaza where the Egyptians kept him at the level of a beast. Now he lives in Hebron, he has bought a taxi, and every morning at five-thirty he brings six Arabs to our settlement to work. He collects his fare, parks the taxi, and works on the construction of these buildings. When he finishes, he returns home, eats quickly, and begins to work as a taxi driver between Hebron and Jerusalem. This man makes hundreds and hundreds of liras. Soon his sons will also be working, and his family will pull in two, three, four, five times as much. This is the kind of 'exploitation' you hear about from the left! Besides, they have a lot of nerve talking about exploitation when from the very beginning the Labor government not only robbed the Arabs of their land but stole their water rights too!"

We were unexpectedly blinded by the full beam of a spotlight that lingered on us. I froze. "It's only a patrol," said Elyakim. "They'll recognize me and leave."

Without letting the interruption get in the way of his argument, Elyakim continued: "These so-called liberals and leftists, they're hypocrites and dreamers—more hypocrites than dreamers, because right at the outset, when they first came to Palestine, they knew they wanted a Jewish state, but they told the Arabs they had come to cure their trachoma. Our leader, Jabotinsky, used to say: 'We must tell the Arabs the truth, because if we say we have come to look after their eyes, they will say thank you very much, we want to keep our disease. They will then invite us in for coffee, but if we insist on staying, there will be wars.' "

Abruptly, although only a few minutes could have passed, we were again flooded by a patrol spotlight. Elyakim hardly noticed. For him, it was part of daily life—the security of the insecure.

On the way back to his apartment, he told me, "You say this land belongs to the Palestinians, but how long have the Arabs been here? Thirteen hundred years. And how did they acquire it? Through conquest. Well, this land once belonged to me, and I was chased from it by the Romans, so I will do unto the Palestinians as was done unto me."

In his living room, Elyakim pulled a thick volume from the bookshelf and thrust it into my hands. It was in German and was entitled *Macht ohne Moral* ("Power without Morals"). While I thumbed through the photographs of the grotesque savagery of the Nazi concentration camps, he admonished me severely: "Take a good look at these pictures. This is what happened to my family, and that's why I'm not afraid of going to war to keep Judea and Samaria. The casualties from all our wars put together don't amount to one day's death toll in Auschwitz! Just before you came, I had another visitor, an Israeli—one of these crazy left-wingers—who said to me that because of settlements like ours, Israel has lost many supporters. And I told him, 'What else is new? Do you imagine that just because the Jews have come to Palestine, the goyim are any less anti-Semitic, or the Jewish destiny has changed?' "

"But surely," I protested, "you're not saying that all of us who are opposed to the settlements are anti-Semites!"

This was precisely what he meant, Elyakim said.

When we stepped out into the courtyard, I noticed that the candles on the windowsills had burned out and that the guards had been reinforced for the night. Elyakim walked me over to the gate, where I was relieved to find my taxi waiting. His handshake, as we said good-bye, was resolute and unyielding.

As the taxi pulled out, I looked once more at the bales of barbed wire —the sharp, harsh borders of this new community. The settlers' closed logic seemed to find its physical expression in this fortress, with its metal moat. I remembered the myriad Israeli towns I had seen on my way to Jerusalem, all of which had supplanted Palestinian villages, and realized with alarm that what had happened there in '48 was happening here now. Down below, Hebron was slumbering. When would it wake up? And if it did, how long would Kiryat Arba hold out? A decade? Centuries? I wondered. I remembered Yoram Kaniuk, my Israeli novelist friend, telling me, "The Jews have not known dramas, they know only tragedy. There is a solution to drama, never to tragedy."

We drove on. For a long time I remained wrapped in my thoughts, oblivious to my surroundings. My view of the settlers of Kiryat Arba would have been less disturbing if I had been able simply to hate them. But I couldn't. I could see all too clearly how the terrible cost in bloodshed and wars—the horrors of Auschwitz, the raw wounds of '48—far from breaching their implacable logic, had just confirmed them in their beliefs. I found these people, so warped by their tragic memories, unutterably sad.

That night marked a turning point for me. I shed my optimistic faith in the infinite power of rational discourse to bring about concord between Jews and Arabs—the faith that had impelled me to make the trip to Israel.

The taxi started the difficult climb back up to Jerusalem, past narrow winding gullies and twisted gorges. I was keenly aware of the night all around me. The road was deserted, and there was silence everywhere save for the creaking of branches and the sound of the wind moaning in the bushes. A cold, damp breeze came through the open window. As I tried to peer into the murky outlines of the hills, I thought, not without some unease, that this wilderness was a perfect setting for a murder. Since the driver mistook me for a Jewish visitor to the hated settlements, might he not try to take his revenge? I lived through all the gory details of the crime—death by strangulation, followed by dismemberment and disposal of the body in the surrounding pits and ravines. No, he would not do me any harm once I told him I was an Egyptian. Having come to this comforting conclusion, I breathed more easily for the next few moments. But soon my fears began to reassert themselves. Wouldn't the sudden revelation of my real identity render me all the more suspect?

I had already begun to feel sorry for my poor parents, who would naturally blame my death on the Israelis.

"You're scared of me, aren't you?" The voice rang out very loudly through the still air. I fairly jumped with fright.

"Well, are you?"

My denial sounded unconvincing.

"Then come and sit next to me."

He stopped the car. I froze in my seat, my heart beating furiously. Then he started up again.

"You see, I knew you were afraid. You've been told Arabs do bad things to Israeli girls, haven't you?"

I didn't answer. We drove on in silence. All the way home the only thing I could hear was the thumping inside my chest. My false identity was no longer something I could wear with any ease, and the longer I stayed in Israel, the more elusive my true one was becoming.

14

Crossing Over

I RETURNED TO Mishkenot Sha'ananim in a state of anxiety that stayed with me over the next days and weeks. Although Mishkenot offered diversions—concerts nearly every evening, an endless stream of artists, writers, and musicians I was eager to meet—my peace of mind failed to return. I began seeing in everything around me a mirror of my own agitation, a warning of the dangers of trying to live in two worlds.

There was, for example, Moshe Ben-Yacob, the other porter at Mishkenot and Omar's Jewish equivalent. A tiny, shriveled hunchback with cavernous cheeks and the narrow chest of a consumptive, Moshe always walked with his head hanging obliquely forward, giving him the look of a beaten dog. I passed Moshe once or twice a day in the hallway, but he always sucked himself in with such haste when I went by and looked at me in such a timid, apologetic way—as though he reproached himself for the tiny amount of space he took up—that I felt tongue-tied. So a fairly long time elapsed before I spoke to him.

One day I ran out of matches and went over to the housekeeper's office to ask her for some. It was ten in the morning, and the help were gathered in the service quarters for their coffee break. I overheard one of the Oriental Jewish maids and the Arab domestic, who was otherwise soft-spoken and polite, jeering at Moshe in the cruelest way. Unable to believe that a shy, self-denigrating person like Moshe could arouse such strong passions, I entered the kitchenette and asked why they were ganging up on him. No one would say a word, so I asked Moshe to come to my flat.

To my great embarrassment, he burst out crying as soon as he crossed my threshold. For a long time he stood by the door, sobs racking his frail chest, unable to speak. When he finally calmed down and I managed to persuade him to take a seat and have some coffee, he told me that everyone picked on him because his father was an Arab.

I learned that his father, a Palestinian peasant, had been kicked out of his village, together with other residents, by Israeli troops in '48. When he took to the road, he was sighted by a Jewish woman who took pity on him and, after giving him something to eat, offered him shelter overnight. He never left her house. Later he married her, though she was quite a bit older than he; at the time they met, he was only a boy of eighteen and she was thirty-six. Moshe was born of this union.

According to Jewish law, Moshe was Jewish because he was born of a Jewish mother, but Islamic law held him to be a Muslim, because in Islam it is paternity that determines a child's religion. Moshe's father at first gave him a Muslim name, Musa ibn-Yacoub. Having later realized that there would be no future for his son in Israel as an Arab, he Hebraized his name to Moshe Ben-Yacob. But as a child Moshe was accepted by neither Jews nor Arabs. The Arabs considered him a traitor for trying to pass as a Jew, and the Jews ridiculed him for having an Arab father.

When the opportunity arose, I told the help to leave Moshe alone. But it was to no avail. Everyone continued to bully and tease him, and somehow it seemed that in his own pathetic way he enjoyed being a laughingstock. There were times when he responded to their mockery not with anger but by clowning about and laughing at himself with them. The more they insulted him, the more ingratiating he became, as though he sensed that if it weren't for these insults, his flimsy presence would go completely unnoticed.

If I could see Moshe as the grotesque byproduct of two clashing worlds—and perhaps a warning of sorts to me—I was also aware that I could no longer keep my distance from either. And as I became more receptive to dissonant views, the experiences put before me seemed to become ever more extreme.

On one of my trips to visit Danny in Tel Aviv, we went to see Hannah Maron, Israel's most celebrated actress, in Chekhov's *Seagull*. When the play was over, the manager offered to take us backstage. Since Danny did not want to get home too late for fear of arousing his wife's suspicions, he declined. But I went, and Hannah Maron invited me to visit her at home the following morning.

Her house was in the posh northern suburb of Herzliah Pituach, and the room I was shown into was decorated with wanton extravagance. Hannah Maron reclined on a velour couch, flanked by a crystal vase of red roses. Amber, jade, and bluish liqueurs sparkled like gems on an end table. The Tiffany lamp that hung from the ceiling suffused the room with a golden light, softening its colors and adding an extra touch of opulence to the furniture.

"My dear," a mellifluous voice called out to me, "come sit here next to me." The faint German accent added to its appeal.

Smiling, Hannah patted the chair by her side and stretched out a perfumed hand to me without getting up. I went and sat down beside a console stacked with several oversized art books. As I examined her from close up, I could not help thinking that she was hardly beautiful: She had prominent blue eyes, her face was puffy, and too much rouge lent her cheeks a waxen bloom. Yet when one watched the sensual languor of her movements, or heard her giddy, light-headed laughter, one could understand the fascination she exerted.

The maid brought up some strongly scented jasmine tea and a cake oozing syrup. Hannah chatted away, occasionally flashing one of her dazzling smiles at me or laughing immoderately, with a handkerchief to her eyes, over a joke she had made.

The heat, the carefully arranged lights, the food, the musty odors of the walls, the fragrance of the blossoms, and her strong perfume all combined to dull my sense of discrimination. Like a cat snugly settled in an armchair, I gave myself up to the delights of well-being.

I asked her to tell me about her career, and she said that she had begun acting at the age of four in Berlin. Her mother, whose artistic aspirations had been frustrated, had decided right from the start that instead of going to school her daughter was to be coached for the stage.

Hannah's first role, as Red Riding Hood, was an immediate success. By the early 1930s, she was winning critical acclaim in the Nazi newspapers, which referred to her as *unsere liebe Hannale* ("our dear little Hannah"). But for all her fame, Hannah led an unhappy life: She was not allowed to play with other children and was subjected to the most Spartan of work disciplines.

She was totally unaware of her Jewish identity. Neither she nor any member of her family looked Jewish; her father, with his burly physique, blond hair, and blue eyes, was indistinguishable from any one of the Aryan workers with whom he went bowling on Saturday night after boozing in the local pub. Nor were any of the Jewish traditions observed in Hannah's house. They celebrated Christmas and ate pork.

One day, on her way home from the theater, Hannah heard a blind old vender huckstering his wares by the entrance to her building. She drew close, goggling at the treasures spread out on the table. A curious little thing caught her fancy—a glittering red-and-black pin in the shape of angled bars. It was attractive, so she bought it. As the vendor handed it to her, he winked and said, *"Raus mit den Juden nach Palestina!"* ("Out with the Jews to Palestine!"). She did not understand what he was saying, and she repeated it innocently after him while she fastened the pin to her coat.

But as soon as her father saw her, he threw a violent fit and, tearing it off her lapel, warned her never to wear it again. "Why can't I?" she demanded. "It's pretty!"

"Because I say so!" he thundered.

The first time Hannah learned that she was Jewish was in 1933, when she was ten. She had been participating in radio plays for some time, and one day her employers sent her a poem that she was to read for Hitler's birthday. When her mother opened the envelope, she became very pale, and taking Hannah by the hand, she told her they must go to the broadcasting station at once.

With her plump red cheeks and golden locks, Hannah was considered the station's little darling, and as she made her way toward the director's office, many of the employees stopped to give her a hug or chuck her under the chin.

Hannah's mother went up to the director and informed him that her daughter could not read the poem. When the director, loath to lose his child prodigy, asked why, she looked him straight in the face and, pronouncing every word with utmost clarity, said, "My daughter is Jewish."

"My God! I didn't know. . . ." The poor man snatched the poem from her mother's hand and, trembling, thanked her a thousand times for "saving my life." Then, very courteously, he escorted them to the door, apologizing profusely for "this inconvenience." It was then that Hannah's father decided the time had come for them to leave for Palestine.

Here, Hannah was able to go to school and live a normal life. Her new freedom was exhilarating, and she assimilated rapidly. She enjoyed her Bible studies and was relieved to find out that her Jewish heritage was no disgrace. In no time at all, she became very patriotic and joined a group of young zealots from school who roamed the streets in search of shops without Hebrew lettering on their signs. When they found them, they would smash their windowpanes and scrawl the message: "Jews, speak Hebrew!"

Once she had mastered the language, she said, she was ready for an acting career in Israel.

At this point Hannah sprang up and began to pace the floor excitedly, remembering her Israeli debut. The pleasure of her reminiscences brought a spendid natural color to her cheeks: Now she looked beautiful.

"I was very lucky, I really became very popular. I was a sort of symbol for everybody. I was *marvelously* successful!" she said.

Having established her reputation in Israel, she began to long for an offer to perform abroad. "Let's face it, Israeli theater isn't great; we are a small, provincial country in the Middle East, cut off from the mainstream of Western creation. I mean, there is no getting away from it—the reason the Jews are so creative in the Diaspora is that they are connected with the culture of the particular countries in which they live. But I must say that the one time I got a chance to work abroad, I lived to regret it."

When I asked her why, she gazed at me with a strange smile, half ironic and half indulgent, and said, "Because of this."

She hitched up her skirt, disclosing a patch of bare thigh, very white against the sumptuous purple of her silk slip. I was astonished and a trifle embarrassed by this bold gesture, but in a moment I understood. With indescribable effort, I compelled myself to look at the prosthesis.

I blurted out something about being sorry and not having known, and then asked her with pretended casualness what had happened.

Chaim Topol, an Israeli actor who lived abroad, had called to offer her the part of Tevye's wife in the movie production of *Fiddler on the Roof*. Her plane had stopped off in Munich on its way to London; it was the tenth of February, 1970.

"I knew the pilot, and he invited me to have coffee with him in the lounge at the airport. We chatted and joked—you know how it is between old friends—when all of a sudden I heard someone running up to me. I turned around and saw a young man standing very close to me, holding something in his hands; it looked like large egg. He said, 'This is an attack, we're going to kill you.' At first it sounded like complete gibberish—unreal. Then I realized that the thing in his hand was a grenade, and I knew he meant it.

"I remember him well. He was a very good-looking young man with beautiful dark eyes. I'll never forget those eyes. There was such hatred in them. I had never really met anybody who hated me before. I mean, you think very quickly in such moments, but it all seemed like slow motion to me. I remember thinking, 'Why does he want to kill me, why does he hate me?' Then there was shooting, and I thought, 'This is like war, I should lie down.'

"When I came to, I saw another young man standing in front of me with a gun. There was a scuffle as some of the Israelis tried to disarm him, and then I fainted. The second time I regained consciousness I heard a man's voice hollering, *'Da liegt ja noch eine Frau!'* ["But there is still a woman lying here!"]. It seems the grenade that had hit me had also shattered the radiator next to me, so I was lying there buried in the debris, and apparently the rescue squad hadn't seen me. If that young waiter hadn't spotted me, I could easily have died, because an artery was severed and I was losing blood very rapidly. But as it was, they called the ambulance back and took me to the hospital."

The event was one of several attacks by Palestinian commandos on Israelis. Shortly thereafter, these Palestinians hijacked a plane, held the passengers hostage, and traded them for their captured comrades who had attacked her: "The German government released them before they had even stood trial, and I guess they lived happily ever after."

A growing uneasiness compounded my shock at her words. Had she read in one of the Israeli newspapers about my support for the Palestine Liberation Organization? Could she possibly be making an allusion to that? Embarrassed, I tried to explain the desperate circumstances motivating the actions of the people who had attacked her. The line between an explanation and a justification being a dim one, though, I soon found myself on dangerous terrain. I cast a furtive look in her direction.

The eyes that met mine were indulgent, and she kept nodding encouragingly while listening to my little speech, as if to say, "Go on, that's all right. Be frank."

When I finished, she picked up the narrative where she had left off: "Well, what can I tell you about the hospital? At the beginning there was the desperate hope that the leg would be saved, followed by some doubts. Then the doctor's decision, this time irrevocable, that it had to be amputated for fear of gangrene. There were four interminable months in the hospital ward, two more operations . . . You get those awful sensations called phantom pains; you feel your leg is hurting even though you have no leg. And there's that other kind of pain I still get because my nerve endings are alive and the whole weight of my body is pressing down on this short stump. But worst of all was the psychological part, the despair that came from thinking that I would never be able to act again.

"I don't believe I could have ever pulled through if it weren't for my husband. I want to tell you that I really have a most unusual husband. It's not just that he stood by me in those difficult times, which was the natural thing to do, but it's the way he did it, he was really marvelous. As soon as he heard about it, he left everything—the children and his work—and he came over. He was there, in the room with me, from the moment I opened my eyes to the moment I left the hospital four months later. And since he understands me so well, he knew just how to deal with me, when to sympathize with me and when not to pamper me—he could be very harsh. When I started walking again, which was incredibly difficult, he would push me to do it by myself even at the risk of my falling. And he kept repeating that if I really wanted to act badly enough, and if I worked hard enough on myself, I could do it, until I finally believed it myself.

"And then there was this flow of love that came to me from my country all the way to Munich. I got all sorts of letters from people I didn't know, but one in particular I remember. It was from a young soldier. He said, 'I'm writing to you even though you don't know me, because I had a leg amputated in the last war. I know that many people are telling you right now how sorry they feel for you, and others are saying, don't worry, you'll learn to walk again and everything will be like before. I want to tell you, don't believe them: Nothing will ever be the same again. So you have two choices. You can either wallow in self-pity or you can say to yourself, "All right, this happened to me, I have to find a new frame for my life, I can do almost everything I did before, only differently." And I would suggest that's what you do. And do it slowly. Don't try to accomplish too much right away. Set yourself a small challenge every day, and work toward it. You must get back to the stage. Don't ever forget who you are. You are Hannah Maron. If you fail, you will not only be letting yourself down, you will be letting us all down.' "

Then she told me that when she made her return to the stage, he showed up on opening night. And later on, when he got married, she danced with him at the wedding.

I fought back the tears that were rising to my eyes and tried to think of something to say. Perhaps sensing my discomfort, she assured me that she bore the Palestinians no grudge for what had happened to her; her chief concern was that her children should grow up not knowing what hate is: "When I came back, my son said he wanted to kill them, and it took me a long time to teach him not to hate everything that's Arab. I knew that the way of violence was the wrong way, because I had been a victim of it myself. I'll tell you something. Before I left for London, I had been offered the role of Medea by a young director who thought it was dangerous for me to get typed as a comedienne. He wanted me to be more versatile. But I felt somehow that the role was too big for me, I couldn't fill it. When I came back from the hospital, it was the first part I took on. *Now* I could really understand Medea. I had faced violence, and I knew what revenge and blood were about. Medea incarnated for me the Palestinian revenge, their abysmal hatred, their violence. Because she too talks about lost kingdoms, about how she had once been an important person, the daughter of the king, and how all her lands had been taken from her. And I thought maybe I, who had been a victim of violence, could interpret the role in such a way as to show that using violence is wrong."

The maid appeared at the doorway and announced that dinner was served. Hannah asked me to share their meal, but I felt it would be good form to refuse.

As we went down to the vestibule, she cast a coquettish glance at her reflection in the large gilt-framed mirror and smoothed her hair. This gesture, which I would have thought vain only hours before, now appeared to me charming. There was a certain courage to this woman, even nobility, that I had come to admire.

A sudden urge to hug her overtook me at the door. I stepped forward, but my hand reached out toward hers instead. Was it my embarrassment at this sentimental impulse which had checked me? Or was it the knowledge that this would be too facile an expiation?

I said good-bye to her in a tone I endeavored to make sound natural and almost staggered out into the garden, trembling with emotion. I heard the dull, metallic sound of the latch behind me. And that was that.

Much as I wanted to, I could not bring myself to get in touch with her again. The sharp edges of all my convictions were being eroded, but I could not yet see what would take their place. It was new for me to feel humility, and I wore it uneasily.

When I returned that evening to Mishkenot Sha'ananim, even more unsettled than usual, I received a long-distance call from Danny inviting me to join him for Passover at the army base in Gaza, where he was on reserve duty teaching a course in what he referred to cryptically as his "specialty." I was elated at the opportunity to see him and have some respite from my agitation; if anyone could cheer me up, he could. Besides, a visit to Gaza would give me a chance to interview General David Maimon, now the military governor of Gaza, who had become famous as the only Yemenite to achieve the rank of general in the Israeli army.

So I got in touch with the army spokesman who was in charge of issuing permits to enter military bases. Fortunately, I knew him because he was married to Moshe Dayan's daughter, who had interviewed me for *Maariv*—at the time Israel's leading daily newspaper. He was very gracious and promised to notify the Gaza authorities about my visit.

I was glad to meet Danny away from Tel Aviv. For whatever intimacy my flat on Rheines Street could afford us, Gila's proximity always lent it a furtive, clandestine flavor that had long ago lost its appeal. It would be a luxury to spend time with Danny in a different atmosphere.

When I awoke the next morning, I thought of asking Rebecca whether I could get a *sherut* for Gaza at the Old City. But I hesitated; our relationship had been somewhat strained of late because I had inadvertently mixed up the kosher cutlery in my kitchenette, half of which was designed for the consumption of dairy and the other half for meat. This oversight on my part had stemmed from my inability to grasp the occult nature of the tiny blue and red dots on the back of each utensil to distinguish the two categories from each other. The housekeeper, who had not taken the trouble to explain this code to me at the outset, nonetheless held me responsible for the error, insisting it was common knowledge. She alleged that on my account, Mishkenot Sha'ananim would have to incur an enormous expense after my departure because the defiled set had to be discarded—though Rabbi Hirsh had assured me that it could be saved if it were simply buried in the earth for three days.

The convenience of having such an accessible source of information, however, overcame my prudence; I stuck my head out the door and called to her, "Rebecca, do I have to go to Arab Jerusalem to catch a *sherut* for Gaza, or does it stop here by the railway station?"

"What do you mean?" she retorted indignantly.

I repeated my question.

Her face grew pale, and with a voice trembling with exasperation she said, "There is no Arab Jerusalem, there is only *one* Jerusalem, and it is the capital of the state of Israel."

I told her coldly that while this might well be the case for her, for me there were two Jerusalems.

My anger must have frightened her, for she lost the look of exasperation and put on an air of tragic calm instead. "Since you *are* staying here," she said in a manner that made it clear how much happier she would have been if I weren't, "it's my duty to inform you that we caution our guests against taking Arab taxis."

"Why?" I asked.

"I think you know why."

On this happy note we parted, and I set out in search of a cab for Gaza.

The *sherut* was packed to the roof with Palestinians, many of them on their way back home to Gaza after a day's construction work. Some of the men showed the marks of the hard, laborious tasks they performed. One was bandy-legged, with a slightly twisted spine, and another had a left shoulder noticeably higher than his right. All of them had hands so calloused they resembled crabs' claws. I examined the man next to me from the corner of my eye. He sat with his hands clasped tightly around a howling radio. From time to time he took a large white handkerchief out of his pocket, folded it neatly, and, removing his *kaffiyeh,* dabbed the drops of perspiration that glistened like tiny white beads on his balding forehead. I wanted to talk to him, but no sooner had we pulled away from the curb than he fell asleep, oblivious to the tinny wails emanating from his lap.

And so I leaned back in my seat, admiring the landscape. The taxi jostled up a bumpy road, and my neighbor's lolling head listed onto my shoulder. He woke up and said, *"Slicha"* ("Sorry," in Hebrew). I told him not to worry about it, I had been happy to oblige, and his jaw dropped in surprise at my Arabic.

He began to laugh and said, "You're Egyptian, aren't you? I'd recognize that accent anywhere. You people have such a funny way of speaking."

"We think it's *you* who have a funny dialect!" I quipped.

He wanted to know what on earth an Egyptian was doing in Israel. I told him, in turn learning that he did construction work in Jewish Jerusalem. And did he earn a lot of money? I asked him.

"Yes, a great deal." He told me that before the war, he had made the equivalent of fifty liras a month as a salesman in a small soda stand in the refugee camp; today he brought home two thousand liras.

When I asked him what he planned to do with all that he earned, he told me that he was saving it to buy land in a village, because he wanted to move out of the Gaza refugee camp where he lived with his extended family. An uncle of his had succeeded in doing so after earning money as an oil driller in Saudi Arabia. He added that a landless refugee wasn't worth a thing—no matter how much money he made, he could not hope to make a good match because people looked down on him. He himself had had his eye on a girl for a long time, but her father, a carpenter, refused to give her to him because he was a refugee, even though he earned twice as much as the father.

I expressed surprise at this, but the worker assured me that the Palestinians of Jerusalem jeered at him, saying, "You ran away and left your land to Jews." He said that he was often followed by boys who threw stones at him and called him a trespasser.

A young soldier was waiting for me at the taxi station in Gaza. Danny sent his apologies for not being able to meet me on arrival, he told me, but he had been called away from the base on an "urgent mission." He should be back within the hour and would come to pick me up at the army headquarters.

We drove through the town of Gaza, with its eight refugee camps. Into their squalid shacks nearly a quarter of a million Palestinian refugees had been herded. They brought to mind a story told me by Cathy, the wife of my friend Yoav. I was visiting them in the beautiful old Arab house where they lived, in Ein-Kerem, a suburb of Jerusalem that had once been a Palestinian village.

"One day, shortly after the Six-Day War, I was working on this veranda. In place of the stairs you see here, there was only a ladder at the time, leading to the garden. Suddenly, I saw two hands, two very wrinkled brown hands, at the edge of the veranda. An old woman—she must have been more than eighty—all in black, was coming slowly up the ladder, followed by two middle-aged men who turned out to be her sons. She started to explain that she used to be the owner of our house, when all of a sudden her eyes darted to the wall and she began to stutter. A huge black cast-iron frying pan hung there—I had found it when we first moved in and had put it up as a decoration. She ran over, grabbed the frying pan, hugged it to her breast, and started crying. I understood that it had been hers and said she could keep it. You should have seen how grateful she was. She kissed me and told me, 'When there is peace, I'll come back and we'll live here together.' "

"Two weeks later, she was back with some more of her relatives; she wanted to show them the house and asked for my permission to pick some almonds from the almond trees in the garden, which she said her grandfather had planted. Well, of course, I had to let her.

"My neighbors, who are Moroccan and Tunisian Jews, told me I should be much firmer with her. They were sure the old woman was lying and taking advantage of my credulity to steal the almonds. But I knew she was telling the truth, because she had said that her grandfather had built the house a hundred years ago over an artesian well, and I later discovered two cisterns in the exact spot she had indicated. And when I led her past our darkroom, she remarked, with a look of reproach on her face, that this door hadn't been here before, we must have put it in. She couldn't possibly have known that without having lived here.

"Well, there's just no way you can handle this sort of thing nicely. I mean, you can be kind to them, but they feel terrible all the same, and you feel terrible after they leave. I don't know how Yoav really feels, but I know that for a week after they leave I'm depressed, and they keep coming back every summer. It's like living in a house with ghosts."

Did she feel guilty?

"It's not that I feel guilty, but I feel very, very uncomfortable. I mean, I look at these thick stone walls and think of someone building them with the idea that he and his children and his grandchildren would live here. We've also carried stones and laid cement here, you know. I feel we've put a lot of work into it. I thought that this old Arab woman would see all the improvements we had made, the fact that we put in the plumbing and the electrical wires and all the rest. Maybe you think it's naive of me, but I sort of expected her to say, 'Gee, what a nice job you've done on the bathroom,' or something like that. But she just stood there looking glum. And I could tell she felt I had ruined her house."

Then Yoav, who had been quiet till then, said that maybe the neighbors had been right after all. It wasn't the sort of situation in which being hospitable helps: "You know, my mother always had this dream about going back to visit her parents' house in Poland. Well, for a long time it was impossible to get a visa because Israel didn't have relations with most of the Communist countries. But then she finally managed to get one, and she went back to the village where she had lived as a little child. The family who live in her house now let her in and were nice to her, but they were apprehensive and looked quite unhappy that she had reappeared from the past. And after all those years of planning and waiting for this visit, she just walked around for fifteen minutes and then went away. There was nothing to say, nothing to do."

As I left them that day, I could not resist asking them how they would have felt if they had been in the old Palestinian woman's shoes.

Yoav replied, "You know, I've often imagined what would happen if the Arabs broke through the border and we had to run away. When the Arabs came back here, they'd probably get rid of all our things. They'd say, 'Ugh! How ugly, let's throw out this and this'—just the way we did when we first moved in. I think I'd blow up the house first before I'd let them have it!"

The old Palestinian woman we were talking about was one of the many refugees of the '48 war, and, sadly, I had learned from Israel

315

Shahak, a professor at Hebrew University, that new refugees had been created in much the same manner during the '67 war. "I saw with my own eyes," he had told me, "how, during the Six-Day War, we used to load the Palestinians on trucks like animals and send them across the Allenby Bridge to Jordan. It happened, among other places, right here in the vicinity of Jerusalem, in the village of Beit-Sachur. We would bring a couple of buses to a village, and then a loudspeaker would announce that whoever wanted to leave the area was invited to come to the station and we would provide them with water, food, and transportation to Jordan. But no one showed up; the peasants were so frightened that they locked themselves into their houses. So then our army jeeps would start crisscrossing the villages, shooting in the air to scare them for about half an hour. Then the loudspeaker would repeat the announcement. Imagine such a thing going on every two or three hours for twenty-four hours! Well, after twenty-four hours, the buses finally started to fill up. These people were driven to the Allenby Bridge, where they were dropped off, and the Israeli soldiers would shout 'Udrub!' [Arabic for "March!"] at them—that's how we sent them into Jordan. Half a million Palestinians were expelled from the conquered areas in this way in '67. And then their houses were razed. Even their cemeteries."

Not surprisingly, Shahak's views were very unpopular at the university. In 1970, he had signed a petition drawn up by Israelis and addressed to the U.N. about the atrocities committed by Israeli soldiers in the occupied territories—expulsions, demolition of houses, arrests, torture—and it was published in *Maariv*. The next day, when he entered the lecture hall, he was greeted with shouts of "Traitor, traitor!" For a long time after that, students would follow him down the university corridors and call him pig and Arab-lover.

Gaza's central lanes were crowded with donkeys, horse-drawn carts, and ramshackle vehicles, while alongside the curbs clustered a multitude of tiny stores overflowing with dates, nuts, spices, straw wares, and various knickknacks. We reached the periphery, where the sea crawled lazily toward the shore.

I felt uneasy driving around an occupied territory in a military vehicle, but all around me men in Arab headgear plodded about their business, unheeding. The sight of Israeli soldiers had long since ceased to attract their attention.

The low profile of the Israeli occupation here made the Star of David that fluttered over the base headquarters appear all the more startling. We drove past the checkpoint undisturbed and pulled up inside the quadrangle. A man in a *kaffiyeh* stood in one of the doorways, speaking with an Israeli officer. Pointing him out to me, the soldier said he was a "stinker"—a pejorative term Israelis use to refer to those Palestinians who are paid to spy on their compatriots.

My escort offered to introduce me to General Maimon while I waited for Danny to return, and I eagerly accepted. Having climbed two flights of stairs, we entered an oblong reception room at the end of which was the general's office. I stood outside his door while the soldier went to speak to him. A bosomy receptionist in army uniform was sitting behind a desk typing a letter. Maimon's young bodyguard lounged nearby, looking surreptitiously down her neckline.

Suddenly, I heard a roar. A fierce, fuzzy head peered through the doorway, then vanished. From the thundering that went on in the office, I gathered that General Maimon had not been notified of my visit and was beside himself with rage at the idea that an Egyptian had been admitted to an Israeli military base. I overheard the soldier telling Maimon that I had obtained permission to visit the base from the military spokesman and that I wanted to meet him. He insisted on verifying this, and to judge from the rising inflection of his voice, his first effort to reach the military spokesman must have failed.

General Maimon was relentless and unflinching in his determination to clarify "the matter of this Egyptian visitor" and called in what must have been every senior officer on the base. The thought that my mere presence could cause such a headache to the formidable Israeli army gave me no small amount of pleasure. I sat down and for the next half hour let myself be entertained by the parade of officialdom that passed in and out of Maimon's office.

Then the door flew open, and the fuzzy head of this illustrious personage was fully revealed to me. He stood tall and proudly erect, with bushy eyebrows that extended all the way across the bridge of his nose and an enormous, upward-curling moustache that would have been the envy of a British imperial officer. There was not a trace of anger on his face; he was positively beaming. He stretched out his hand and, feigning surprise, exclaimed, "You here! What an honor! Why didn't anyone tell me? I would have invited you in for a cup of coffee. Please, do come in." And affecting his most reproachful air, he turned to the driver, who stood contritely by, and upbraided him: "How could you not tell me that you brought an Egyptian visitor along? Shame on you for keeping her waiting all this time!"

I followed him into the office, where, addressing me once again, he said, "But let us speak Arabic." Had Ben-Gurion not said he would consider Zionism a success the day he was shown the first Yemenite soldier who had made it to the grade of officer? Maimon's command of Arabic had undoubtedly been an important asset in his appointment as military governor of Gaza.

But his enthusiasm cooled considerably when I asked him about the Palestinian refugees of Gaza, some of whom had been forcibly resettled in another town, El Arish, after their homes were demolished by the Israeli soldiers. Without erasing the grin from his face, he answered me: "Of course they didn't like it! But it wasn't *that* bad. We have nothing against these people personally, but the camps have to be controlled, and to control them effectively we had to create a *cordon sanitaire*, which meant that all the houses that fell between certain boundaries had to be razed."

Then, unprompted, he riffled among his papers and said: "Unfortunately, I don't seem to find the figures for the houses of the refugees in the Gaza Strip that were torn down, but there couldn't have been more than five hundred. We relocated most of their residents in Gaza, but those we could not find empty houses for—approximately ninety families—had to be sent off to El Arish. What's the big deal anyway? What difference does it make if these refugees exchange one camp that's in a shambles for another place that's equally in a shambles?"

For Maimon, a refugee was a negligible entity incapable of forming an attachment to any place. "We have no responsibility toward the refugees," he decreed. "We didn't create this problem; it's the Arab countries that created it. As long as we're at war, I don't see why I should bend over backward to solve the problems of the refugees while the other side isn't willing to solve my problems."

For the next few minutes he wore a look of resigned weariness as he listened to my questions about young men who had been picked up by soldiers for interrogation and flogged so savagely they had had to be hospitalized.

Then he answered, shrugging, "If five or six guys are rounded up, they might get beaten up. Don't forget that the soldiers are on duty in an area where they're in constant danger of being shot at; they have to be on the lookout for saboteurs."

When I brought up a well-publicized incident of soldiers firing at a group of women who were demonstrating outside the prison of Rafiah, where their husbands were being held, killing one of them and injuring several others, he did not evince the least sympathy; it was as though he felt they had gotten just what they deserved. "The soldiers panicked and opened fire," he said airily. "Anyhow, I assure you this happens only in exceptional cases, it's not the rule."

I could not help smiling ironically as he conveyed these sincere reassurances. He noticed this and sneered with fury, "If the soldiers were all Ph.D.'s like you, maybe they wouldn't have shot at them, I don't know!" His anger seemed to have spent itself with this comment, so I asked if I might take a look around the base. The unctuous smile reappeared once more under the moustache as he told me that he was at my service. Then he darted a significant glance at the driver and, returning to Hebrew, grunted between his teeth, "You're to show her the *usual* places, you understand?"

Just as we were about to drive off, Danny arrived, wearing a khaki uniform with an ornate cluster of green leaves embroidered onto his shoulder boards. It was the first time I had seen him dressed in this fashion. I could not suppress a start.

After we had bidden the driver good-bye, Danny and I went for a walk. We passed barefoot Palestinian children going through the garbage cans of the barracks in search of food, and a seated Israeli officer who was having his shoes polished by one of them. Farther up, some soldiers were leaning against a fence drinking beer. A little Arab boy was entertaining them by singing a popular Israeli football cheer in hilariously accented Hebrew. Everybody laughed, and one of the soldiers tossed him a lira. Another soldier beckoned the boy to come nearer and gave him a sip of beer: "Do you like it?" The boy nodded, so the soldier let him have the bottle and the boy guzzled it down, to everyone's amusement. "How old are you?" a soldier asked.

"Seven, sir."

"Can you smoke, too?"

"You bet, sir."

"Show us," the soldier challenged, and threw him a cigarette. He picked it up from the ground and puffed away like a little old man. Everybody clapped.

We walked on in silence. Somebody called out Danny's name. It was an officer in an army jeep, who offered us a lift. By way of conversation, I asked him how he liked being stationed in Gaza. "To tell you the truth I never liked it here, though it's no longer as horrible as it was. Danny's lucky, he only has to stick it out for another three weeks. I'm stationed here permanently—they wanted me here because I know Arabic. At the beginning we organized patrols and went after the fedayeen, and we had to comb out suspects and send them off to prison. It was a dirty job.

We'd load the men onto the buses, and their women were hysterical. They'd cry and kiss our hands and beg us to take pity on them, saying that if we took their husbands there would be nobody to suport them and their children would die of hunger. It was awful; I couldn't do anything for them, I had my orders. But at the same time I didn't have the heart to push the women away, so I would just stand there like an ass and let them clutch onto me until one of the other soldiers came to shoo them off. Later I went to my commanding officer and said, 'Get me out of here, I'm not cut out for this job. It's horrible, I wasn't brought up to do these kinds of things.' But he said, 'This is part of war, and war is horrible—someone has to do it.' So I stayed."

We got out, and after walking for a while about the town we went into a small café for a glass of tamarindi. I did not tell Danny what had happened in General Maimon's office; I felt it would be indelicate to bring the subject up. Nor did I ask him about his "mission" out of fear he would say that he could not tell me "for security reasons." Trying to avoid politics altogether, I began to talk about life at Mishkenot. Pretty soon we were carried away in converstion and forgot all about our surroundings.

We talked about many subjects that afternoon, and in the course of our conversation I happened to mention that I would have to start giving some serious thought to returning to the States, having absented myself from Harvard for almost three years.

Danny averted his gaze. He sat for a full minute in silence, his forehead resting on his hand. I could see only the stiffened nape of his neck and the sun faintly touching his hair with gold. Abruptly, he turned to me and said, in a tone so distraught that it surprised me, "What are we going to do?"

I did not know how to answer him and was about to cover up my emotions in the usual manner, by making a joke, when a rush of tears welled up in my eyes.

Then he began to talk about our living together in South Africa. If he was ever to find the courage to leave his wife, he would have to put distance between Israel and himself, he said. South Africa would be a chance for us to build a new life together as husband and wife. There was a community of some twenty thousand Israelis who now resided permanently in South Africa, as well as a constant stream of visitors from Israel—tourists, academicians on leave, businessmen. So he would not feel uprooted. He had already established a circle of friends down there, and his business was doing well.

I looked up at him. We had never before talked of a future together;

it had always been a foregone conclusion that I would leave someday and that he was committed to Gila. Yet the intensity in his voice left no doubt about his sincerity. Why, then, did I find his offer, which should have made me radiant with happiness, so singularly depressing?

I must have known the answer even then. I would never have considered even visiting South Africa as a tourist; I simply could not picture us joining the growing numbers of Israeli couples who set out for South Africa, their new homeland, in search of villas with swimming pools and plentiful black servants! What's more, I simply could not picture *us*. But I kept that knowledge at bay, mumbling something about it all being too sudden and having to think things over.

Danny gazed at me in disbelief and then astonishment, for he no doubt had expected me to jump at his proposal. I felt myself turn pale under his searching look and was terrified lest he should guess what I was thinking.

Engrossed as we were by our conversation, we had forgotten the passage of time. As we were rushing back to the base for the seder, Danny spotted a military jeep and flagged it down. The soldier at the wheel was afraid of being late for the ceremony and drove like a maniac. "Slow down a little," his friend cautioned him. "There are lots of kids in these lanes." He shrugged his shoulders and said, "*Laharog otam ktanim*" (Hebrew for "Kill them while they are little"). Danny's face colored, and I pretended I hadn't heard in order not to embarrass him.

When we arrived at the mess hall, it was already packed. It was clear from the sudden silence that greeted our entrance, from the stares and nudges the soldiers exchanged, that they had been told they were having an Egyptian guest. I felt all eyes on me as Danny escorted me to the seats that awaited us at the head table. The atmosphere of the room was so charged with supressed excitement that the poor yeshiva student who had been sent from Jerusalem to officiate at the seder had a hard time competing for attention.

"Why is this night different from every other night?" the student asked, and muffled titters answered from around the room. As the ritual commemorating the Jewish exodus from Egypt continued, the traditional words took on new meaning that escaped no one, least of all me. When the time came to enumerate the ten plagues that "the Holy One, blessed be He, brought upon the Egyptians in Egypt," the soldier whose turn it was to spill a drop of wine to celebrate each of the plagues, as custom required, looked over at me and intoned, "Blood . . . frogs . . .

vermin . . . beasts . . . cattle disease . . . b-b-b—'' Afflicted by a fit of giggles, he had to stop at "boils."

Shortly thereafter we stood up to sing "Dayenu," the cheerful ode of praise to the Lord for His gory decimation of the Egyptians:

> How thankful must we be to God, the All-Present,
> For all the good He did us.
>
> Had He brought us out of Egypt,
> And not executed judgment against them,
> It would have been enough for us.
>
> Had He done justice to their idols,
> And not slain their firstborn,
> It would have been enough for us.

I tried to sing along, but the meaning of the words overshadowed the merry tune, and my voice trailed off.

> Had He slain their firstborn,
> And not given us their property,
> It would have been enough for us.

At this point the soldiers all began to laugh till they were gasping for breath and tears were rolling down their faces. The laughter was contagious: At the sight of these fellows writhing as if in pain, I too joined in. Soon the student, a scrubby, sallow-faced young man, clearly no match for this uproarious bunch, abandoned all pretense of conducting the service. Leaving their seats and pressing around me, the soldiers barraged me with questions, exchanging jokes among themselves about hosting an Egyptian in Gaza, a town that, only a few years ago, had been ruled by Egypt.

But even though I was charmed by them, a mood of depression and despair began to settle in on me as the evening drew to a close. Perhaps it was the ceremony of the seder that highlighted for me the irony of a once homeless people now making others homeless. Or perhaps it was Danny's proposal that weighed me down and intensified my confusion. The noise the soldiers were making, the buzz of their voices, the sight of their exhilaration, shook my nerves, and Gaza's proximity to the Egyptian border flooded me with memories of home. Here I could hardly escape ironies that were more personal. What was *I* doing here in Gaza, celebrating the Jewish people's ancient liberation from their

Egyptian oppressors with a group of jolly Israeli soldiers who were the official occupying presence in Egyptian territory? I felt like a mass of broken fragments without a center. No matter what else I might have become, I was an Egyptian—but what was that? Again and again I sought to pull myself together and to look bright when Danny's eyes rested on my face, to tell myself that this day was the greatest of my life. But all I succeeded in doing was brooding over the feelings the whole celebration aroused in me, and still more over those I would have liked to feel but could not.

As we walked back from the base toward the taxi station, we had to push our way once more past throngs of screeching, barefoot Palestinian children playing football out in the middle of the street. They called "Shalom, shalom" to us, and a fat boy with lackluster eyes—the standard little bully who must show off in front of Israeli soldiers—cleared a swath ahead of us by thrashing his arms about in every direction and pushing the others roughly aside. Then he waddled up to Danny, smiled, and invited him to proceed, saying, "Please, sir, pass, please." Danny shot a side-glance at me but said nothing.

When we left the children behind, he told me, "Every time these refugee kids smile at me it hurts me deeper than an insult. I feel myself in the skin of a conqueror. I would prefer jeers to those terrible smiles —smiling lips, eyes filled with hatred."

And I found myself thinking of my converstaion with Professor Shahak. He'd said that he was very sensitive to injustice because he believed that what had been done to him and his family in the Warsaw ghetto and Bergen-Belsen was now being done to others by his own people. I told Danny the story Shahak had told me about a friend of his: "We had been in the same school for Holocaust orphans in Palestine. He was part of a battalion that had been ordered to raze a village on the Golan Heights during the '67 war. He was opposed to doing it and tried to find others who would join him in resisting the order, but he could find only one other soldier. Since there was no chance they could make their wills prevail against an entire battalion, they decided that at the very least they would protect the family assigned to them from maltreatment. They told this family that they had orders to see to it that their house was evacuated within half an hour, but they would make sure that the family was not subjected to harassment or looting by the soldiers. Then they went out to allow the family their privacy.

"While they were waiting, my friend told the other soldier, a Sabra, 'You'll see, the first person to come out will be a child, a little girl or boy, seven or nine years old maybe, carrying a bag that contains the family's money and jewels.' 'How can you know this?' the Sabra asked. My friend answered, 'I just know, you'll see.' And they bet a certain sum. And half an hour later the front door opened and a little girl emerged hesitantly looking to the right and the left, and then stepped out. She was holding a paper shopping bag. The Sabra asked my friend, 'But how could you possibly have known?' And my friend answered him: 'I know because in 1944, when my family was expelled from our house in Europe, I was that child.' "

15

Going Home

Back at Mishkenot Sha'ananim, I remained for some time in a state of wretched indecision. In my aimless wanderings about my room I caught sight of my own face in the ivory-framed mirror, and it brought me to a stop. The eyes that returned my stare were the most unhappy eyes I had ever seen. For the first time, I felt in disinct danger, for I saw with terror that I had come far beyond the point of knowing "the enemy" and had become vulnerable to identifying myself with Israel—that I was in jeopardy of losing myself. I could not cross over, but there seemed no way back.

It was time to leave.

For someone who had come to Israel on a six-week trip, I had clearly overstayed my time. As the summers had succeeded each other, I had warned myself repeatedly that if I did not show up in time for registration in the fall, I might be expelled from Harvard. But notwithstanding this fear, I kept on drawing up lists of things I *had* to do in Israel and people I *had* to meet if I were to justify the length of my stay. Half-consciously, I was aware that the reason I kept putting off my return to the United States was that I had grown deeply attached to Israel in spite of myself. I could no longer look casually upon leaving it the way I might have if it had been any other country. I was afraid that once I left, I might never be allowed to return. What if there were still another war and the Israeli government, disillusioned about the possibility of achieving peace with the Arabs, denied me an entry visa? Or what if the Egyptian consulate confiscated my passport once I was back in the States, making it altogether impossible for me to travel? The thought that I might not be able to return at will to this country where I now felt so strangely at home, that Israel might once again become a forbidden land for me, caused me tremendous anguish.

And then there was Danny. I knew that leaving the country was the only way of severing my emotional ties with him, since I did not have the willpower to be near him without seeing him. But if I finally summoned up enough courage to leave, it was because I realized that my attachment to Danny was symptomatic of the chilling isolation in which my broadened sympathy for Israel had placed me. I needed to return to the safety of my known identity as a Harvard student; I needed the comfortable distance that separated me, the political activist for peace, from Israel. Above all, I needed to go home, to Egypt, to find myself again.

The day of departure arrived. I drove out of Jerusalem one last time, past the legendary mountain where the Arab ghost village of Kastel had once formed part of a fortified promontory. The setting sun stained the clouds crimson, and the trees that crowned the mountaintop were turning russet with here and there a touch of gold.

The slopes had been entirely reforested after the '48 war with the help of money collected overseas by "selling" saplings to individual Jewish donors. And, indeed, when Jewish tourists reached the entrance to Jerusalem, their hearts surged with pride at the sight of these fine young Jerusalem pines—the symbol of Israel's rebirth and of its triumph over the boulders and thorns that for millennia had defined the harsh landscape of these hills. But the new verdure was deceptive, for on closer inspection the trunks of the pines appeared ashen. A mysterious disease had beeen ravaging the forest. No one knew its cause; it had first been noticed after the '73 war. It was as though the trees contained within themselves the seeds of their own decay: The disease first attacked the core of the pines, then gradually spread outward from the trunk into the branches, finally choking the trees to death. Expert after expert had been brought in for consultation, but none was able to understand the cause of the malady or to find the cure. The eerie thing was that the disease seemed to affect only the Jerusalem pines whose seedlings the Israelis had imported from Europe, shunning all the humbler, indigenous species.

On arriving in Tel Aviv, I checked into the Grand Beach Hotel and asked the receptionist to reserve me a cab for the airport at five o'clock the following afternoon.

In the evening, as I was having dinner in a small restaurant on

Hayarkon Street, my eyes fell on a broad-faced, carroty-haired man sitting at a table across the room from me. It took me a while to recompose the features of that stranger into those of Ali, Leila's pimp, but when I did, the cocky grin on his face told me that he had already recognized me. I immediately went up to him and asked him about Leila. How had she died? When? Why? He told me she had committed suicide by jumping off the Shalom Tower. When he saw my eyes scanning him suspiciously, he asked, "You don't believe me?" I didn't answer. He jerked his chair back, calling out, *"Tikfetzi li!"* ("You can jump on my penis!"), and stalked off angrily.

That night I dreamed that someone had given me Leila's new address, indicating its exact location by a cross on a road map. I followed the directions and reached the bank of a vast swamp full of wild plants and animal life. I could see Leila standing in the middle of it, painting a large, closed shell. By her side was a pile of drawings, already completed, with identical figures. All of them featured a nightingale outlined in blue —the inky blue used in Delft porcelain work. I could not reach Leila because she was surrounded on all sides by water and I was afraid I'd sink if I stepped into the swamp, so I called out to ask her how I might cross over. But my voice had that hoarse, indistinct quality of someone trying to talk while asleep, and she could not hear me. I woke up crying.

At five P.M. sharp the next day, the taxi arrived at the hotel to pick me up. As the images of the outside world rushed by the window on that drive to the airport, they appeared blurred, gray, meaningless. I was thinking of Danny.

The cabby was a freckled man with twinkling blue eyes and a clownish nose. He wore a violet ascot around his neck and a large sombrero. Halfway downtown, he asked in a thick Polish accent where I was going, and when I told him I was leaving for America, he asked whether I'd be coming back. I said I hoped to one day but wasn't sure. *"Chaval!"* ("A pity!"), he exclaimed. "We need intelligent young roots like you in this country."

"Oh, come off it," I said jokingly. "There are plenty of intelligent young Sabras in Israel. Besides, what makes you think I'm so intelligent?"

"No, I'm serious," he replied. "Just look at what's happening in Israel. We have all these Oriental Jews—a lot of garbage! And now, because of the territories we captured in '67, we're stuck with a million and a half Arabs to boot! We need Westerners to come and settle here and act as a civilizing influence on this country."

I was too depressed to get into an argument with him, so I held my

peace. For the next twenty minutes or so I listened somewhat distractedly to the spicy anecdotes to which he treated me. Occasionally I even
threw in a laugh. When we got to the airport, I took out my wallet.
"Listen, *chamuda* ["sweetie pie"], you're cute, so forget about the fare."
I insisted, but he would not be prevailed on. "Don't worry, it's my own
cab. I do as I please." He stretched his arm out the window, chucked
me under the chin, and was off.

Inside the terminal, I looked furtively for the telephone and walked
over to the booth. A man had just finished phoning, and he placed the
receiver in my hand. I hung it up and walked away. No, I would not call
Danny.

The announcement over the loudspeaker jolted me out of my reverie:
"All passengers headed for Paris and New York are requested to present
themselves at the El Al check-in point." Once again the El Al agent
looked suspiciously at my passport, and once again the security guard
turned my suitcases inside out as he put me through the by now familiar
repertoire: Why had I gone to Israel? Whom had I visited here? Had
anyone handed me a gift to take to friends or relatives overseas? Once
again my tape recorder elicited great attention and its batteries were
confiscated. Once again my boarding pass featured a mysterious roman
numeral III scrawled in Magic Marker. When I was forced to take off
my underwear inside the booth this time, I flushed not with shame but
with anger. I knew a body search was to be expected, but I could not
help feeling insulted at the thought that after living for nearly three years
in Israel, I was still suspect.

The roar builds. Outside, the blue sparks of Tel Aviv's runway gather
speed. My heart sinks as we lift into the sky; I am going to miss that
wretched little town that I have so often surprised myself thinking of
with affection. The plane skims once more over the sand dunes—they
look like purple waves in the failing light—then soars up into the air,
banking over the Shalom Tower.

Sunset. The reddened cloud flakes form a brilliant trail against the
dark sky. I think of Leila. We had often visited the tower together. On
its ground floor was a wax museum that featured many of Israel's war
heroes: Ariel Sharon, with a bandaged head, valiantly staving off the
Egyptian offense along the Bar-Lev line during the 1973 war; a triumphant Dayan entering Arab Jerusalem with Rabin after the '67 victory;
men like Trumpeldor, a much-decorated soldier of the Czarist army
who had lost his arm in the Russo-Japanese War and had later died in

battle defending the Jewish settlement of Tel Chai in Palestine against an Arab attack. His last words were *"Tov lamut be ad artzenu"* ("It is good to die for our country").

But it was especially the ride to the top of the tower that Leila had loved. From there one had a view of the whole city. Each time we took the tour she would listen spellbound to the sullen guide saying, "We really never had suicides before in this country. Of course, occasionally someone might take his life by quietly drowning himself in the sea, but for years and years we didn't even know what suicide was. Yet it seems that lately people have been coming here from all over the country just to jump off this building. . . ."

Outside my window, the sky had deepened to vermilion and the desert to india ink. Throughout the flight, my thoughts and emotions raced back and forth from Leila to Danny, from the pain of one loss to the pain of another.

By the time we landed at Orly, I felt as if I had fought a thousand battles and lost them all. Aware of my disheartened look, the El Al attendant who escorted me and two other Arab passengers to the security section before we were to board the plane for New York treated me kindly and even offered to carry my hand luggage.

Of course both my luggage and my body had to be searched once again to make sure that I had not managed, in the course of the two hours I spent in the departure area, to acquire a bomb, a gun, or God knows what else. I was asked to wait outside the search booths until I was finally summoned by a security matron. It was not Michelle.

I thought of her with a pang of longing. How far I had traveled since the days of Kibbutz Hazon Hadash—and not necessarily in the best direction. As my feelings for Israel had become both stronger and more contradictory, so my ambivalent love affair with Danny had become all-consuming. While I always had enough energy to arrange the most convoluted ways of seeing him, I never seemed to find time to answer Michelle's letters, and my neglect eventually discouraged her from writing at all.

In the plane again, frantically searching for my passport—my last token of identity—I accidentally fished out a map of Tel Aviv. Of all my Israeli guides and city maps I had kept only this, because it contained the suburb with Danny's street. The sensation of this piece of paper between my fingers brought back the memory of our last encounter— our sad acceptance of a future apart, our tender good-bye—and with it warm waves of comfort mingled with pain.

I congratulated myself on my "sacrifice" and took pride in the thought that I had been able to make the final break. Only now was I beginning to wonder whether it was Danny I had been in love with or his pain. Why else would all the associations I had carefully elaborated around that melancholy gaze cease to be compelling the moment I was forced to come to terms with the prosaic image of Danny, happily married—to me! I had previously thought myself to possess a kind of subtle knowledge that enabled me to understand him merely by his looks and gestures, by the cadence of his voice, even by the timbre of his silence. But now, I thought, I knew very little about Danny beyond his delicacy, his gentleness, and the peculiar sadness that surrounded him. It was to these traits—and to his inaccessibility—more than anything else that my mind had attached something profound and romantic.

If Danny represented, in a sense, everything that had been romanticized in my attraction to Israel (and particularly my attraction to its pain), Michelle, in her simplicity, forthrightness, and fundamental decency, embodied all that I considered positive and genuine about the country. I missed her vividly. I had lost her, lost myself. If I had known then that the future was to bring us together again, I would not have been able to grasp it.

At Kennedy Airport, I went through a moment of panic. U.S. law requires of certain nationals a passport with a validity of six months beyond one's date of entrance. Mine was less than two weeks from expiration; would they deny me entry? And if so, where was I to go? I remembered the sea I used to watch as a child from the balcony of our Alexandria villa, which was located within arm's reach of a tram station named Roushdi Pasha, after my great-uncle, on Sharia Toufoula el Saida ("Happy Childhood Street"). Whenever I felt despondent because I had been unjustly punished, I would stand on the balcony looking out at the ships and dream of escaping to America—my birthplace—by stowing away on one of them. I had first conceived this idea the day I heard some relatives whisper about Mother's cousin, Muhammad Menshawi, a wealthy landlord who had been imprisoned for his opposition to Nasser. They spoke of arranging his escape from prison and of smuggling him out of the country in a cargo crate. Nothing came of this plan; he died in his cell of maltreatment. But I had begun to set aside money for my own escape by emptying the coins Father kept for the golf caddies out of his waistcoat every morning while he was in the shower. My plans aborted when the maid discovered the money, which I had sewn into the mattress, and stole it, knowing full well that I would never dare tell on her since it would prove to be my own undoing. But the concept of America as a haven had remained with me throughout childhood, though I had been too small when I left that country, with my family, to remember it afterwards. This vision was now actually to materialize in the form of political asylum, the kind of haven that I had never foreseen I would need.

The name Harvard worked miracles for me at the airport. They let me in with the proviso that I report to my consulate first thing in the morning to get my "passport problem" straightened out. I obeyed, gave them my passport, and never saw it again. The long wait began.

Shortly after my return to the United States, in November of 1977, the State Department granted me political asylum. The passport I had given the Egyptian consulate for renewal had been withdrawn because I had used it to travel to Israel. Two weeks later, Sadat himself went to Jerusalem, but when I mentioned this fact in requesting the revalidation of my passport, I learned that there was one law for presidents and another for ordinary citizens.

Two years later the first good portent appeared. The Egyptian journalist Anis Mansour, who was generally considered the president's spokesman and who had previously attacked me for going to Israel, now defended my trip. The man who had once called me *sazga* ("naive and stupid") for falling into the "Zionist trap" referred to me as a "gift of heaven" in the May 20, 1979, issue of *October* magazine.

The same magazine featured this headline on its front page the following year: "A passport for Sana Hasan, the first Egyptian to have gone to Israel!" The article introduced me as "Mrs. Sana Hasan, the daughter of former Ambassador Mahmoud Hasan and the ex-wife of Ambassador Tahsin Basheer" (my ex-husband had just been appointed ambassador to Canada). It went on to explain why I had been forbidden to reenter the country, ending with the words "A new passport will be issued to her in accordance with President Sadat's order so she may return to her country and her father whensoever she pleases!"

"Whensoever" turned out to be a somewhat optimistic forecast. The president had indeed issued a pardon, but it took a year for it to filter through the labyrinthine corridors of the Ministry of the Interior down to the Egyptian embassy in Washington.

In 1981 I returned to Egypt after eight years of absence, five of which I had spent in exile. I received the red-carpet treatment at the airport: A representative from the Ministry of Foreign Affairs met my flight and ushered me into the reception room for "honored guests" while he saw to my passport and customs clearance. But after that ceremony I was on

331

my own. My parents were to arrive that evening, having cut short their vacation to welcome me.

It was only a few weeks after Sadat's assassination, and as my cab was leaving the airport and making its way through the maze of Cairene lanes leading to Zamalek, we passed a banner depicting Sadat as "The Martyred Hero of Peace." The portrait of the *rais* ("leader") showed a colossal, solemn, absolutely hieratic figure. Sadat was dressed in his admiral's uniform and bore a golden scepter in lieu of his field marshal's baton. The arm holding the scepter was rigid—almost mummified—like the ones in the Pharaonic burial chambers of the Valley of the Kings. And underneath was the inscription "Why peace? Well, what did we get from war?"

This rather flippant slogan, offered to the Egyptian people as a rationale for peace after a conflict that had lasted a century and had cost the lives of a hundred thousand Egyptian soldiers (not to mention the countless other Arab and Jewish dead), reminded me of an anecdote I had once heard. The Schleswig-Holstein wars had plagued Europe for decades. When a peace was finally signed, Prince Albert of England is reported to have said: "Only three persons ever understood what these wars were all about. The king of Prussia—but he is dead; the king of Sweden—but he is in a madhouse; and myself—but I have forgotten."

It was midmorning, and the busy intersection of Tahrir Square was choked with traffic. As the cab crawled through the streets, I tried to digest what had just happened. The cab driver I'd flagged down at the airport had pulled over reluctantly and, when I told him my destination, said, "Oh, shit! Are you Egyptian?" He had picked me up, he explained, only because he'd thought I was an American whom he could inveigle into paying in dollars. And then there had been the police officer at the airport: when I went up to him to ask where I might find a telephone, he cut me off before I'd uttered two words, inquiring with a smile: "Israeli?" I was nonplussed, and asked him what in Allah's name could have put such a strange notion into his head. He apologized profusely, blushing to the tips of his ears, and said: "The only tourists I ever meet who speak Arabic are Israelis."

There was something uncanny about returning home after eight years only to find that my own people mistook me for a foreigner, as though my inner changes were somehow reflected in my physical appearance. I noticed that the town too had changed: It seemed smaller—or was it simply that there were more people in Cairo, masses of people wedged in at the crossings? There seemed to be no forward movement to them; even the air felt stale, all but exhausted. Finally we reached the bridge, and the imposing buildings that carried the comforting names of my childhood: Park Lane, Dorchester, Nile View. These venerable buildings were the Cairo I knew; they were my past. They had stood there, immovable and dignified, during all those years when I had scorned them as bourgeois artifacts and relics of a colonial past best forgotten. Now they brought tears to my eyes. But any hopes I had of recapturing the past and my place in it were soon dashed. I had returned to a different world.

I hardly recognized my own neighborhood. What two decades of Nasser's "socialist" revolution had not succeded in accomplishing, Sadat had brought about in a few years with his "Open-Door" policy. The old, impoverished aristocracy had been run out of Zamalek by hordes of Egyptian nouveaux riches and Japanese and Western businessmen. This once exclusive island now resembled any downtown area, with the same congested streets and the same rubbish-strewn sidewalks.

Even my home seemed foreign to me. Gone were the Louis XV brocade chairs. In their place had come modern furniture. Since the salons were seldom used these days, the settees and armchairs were covered with sheets of linen meant to keep the dust off the pale, raw silk upholstery. These lent the rooms the lugubrious look of an apartment in which someone had just died. I went back and forth between the marble stand with the statuette of Cupid and the little round table that supported porcelain bonbonières, enameled cigarette boxes, and ashtrays of solid silver, as well as a bouquet of flowers fashioned of delicate bits of irregular colored glass, and the Sèvres hunting dog in black and white. I had always made fun of these useless objects; now I found comfort in their presence.

How many times had I come furtively to this salon, which had been strictly out of bounds to me if I was unaccompanied by an adult, because Mother feared I would knock over one of these fragile pieces? I would push the tall, ponderous doors open and slip silently into the room. It kept very still at my passage. Then I would make my way to the next room with the big oil painting of the half-naked Abyssinian slave girl, which had been in my great-grandfather's house. I would stare at her beautiful bare breasts, the color of coffee, and at our exquisite Persian carpet with the tiger hunt that had fascinated me as a child. But most of all I would look at myself in the long, narrow mirror framed by coils of twisted gold. This mirror knew a great deal about me. I had stood beside it on tiptoe in the early mornings when I was no more than a toddler, happy in my bonnet, on my way to play at the Guezira Sporting Club. And I had stood there as a child, in the afternoons when Mother was out, my face zigzagged with her lipstick Indian-style or my eye blackened pirate-style with the cosmetics she had forbidden me to use. Years later, all dressed up, before sneaking out of the house at night to meet my boyfriend in secret, I approached it trembling, ecstatic to see emerging gradually out of the dimness that ravishing apparition that was myself.

In those days my imagination had sided with me. But now the mirror threatened me with its knowledge. Who was I now? What had I become? I did not want to give up my childhood as forever lost; I tried to conjure it back in the mirror. I recalled all the tiresome, interminable tea parties I had endured in this room with the sleek-haired, distinguished-looking gentlemen and their elegant wives into whose presence I had been summoned by my parents. I do not know which I had hated more, to be asked to speak in German, much to the amusement of these fine people, who laughed at my embarrassment, or to have to listen to them calling my father Pasha and Excellency, and to Mother recounting and embellishing the episodes of his career. Father seemed so distant and awesome to me when he was invested with all his dignities that I had to force myself not to pull away from him when he held out his arms to me from the armchair that, having always been reserved for him, bore the imprint of his head. Yet his tone was tender and playful; he was proud of his daughter. And when I finally nestled in his lap, I had a view of the Nile out of the corner window with the Nile-green satin draperies, and I could dream of our lovely walks together.

I went to the window now; perhaps there was still something out there that belonged to me. The quiet, palm-lined lanes were all but buried under the new Mercedes Benzes and BMWs triple-parked right on top of our curb. There too, things were changing in the same indifferent way; there too, nothing was left but my loneliness—the loneliness that I had brought on myself. And I could not understand how I had forsaken Egypt and the people I cared for.

I recalled my very earliest childhood memory. One night I had set out on my first exploratory venture into the Promised Land, which was located—so I had made believe—in the darkest and deepest recesses of my bed. Suddenly finding myself trapped beneath the bedcovers, unable to find my way out again, I was seized with panic as I tried to thrash myself free, my screams muffled by the suffocating mass of blankets and sheets. Now this childhood terror had become a reality. Having crossed so many boundaries, having invented so many Promised Lands, I could no longer find my way back home.

Like Michelle, I would have to make peace with an identity that did not depend on being part of a group, or a country. I would return to Egypt many times, but the world I had come to be most familiar with was that of the outsider, the stranger, the exile. And though I would continue to long for a tangible homeland, I realized that for me its site would henceforth be no more than a place of memory or imagination, occasionally recaptured, only to be lost again.

Books of Related Interest

THE BIRTH OF ISRAEL: MYTHS AND REALITIES
by Simha Flapan

A ground-breaking and controversial history of the founding of Israel, which gives the reader the first true account of one of the most momentous political events of the century.

"A contribution of great value, with far-ranging implications concerning recent history and current policy."—Noam Chomsky

0-394-55588-X $18.95 cloth

THE ISRAELI CONNECTION: WHO ISRAEL ARMS AND WHY
by Benjamin Beit-Hallahmi

A powerful story of intrigue and covert action, this is a masterful account by an Israeli of the way his nation's struggle to survive aligns it with some of the most reactionary and brutal regimes of our time.

0-394-55922-3 $18.95 cloth

AFTER THE LAST SKY: PALESTINIAN LIVES
by Edward W. Said

with photographs by Jean Mohr

Through text and photographs, distinguished cultural critic Said uses the successive dispossessions Palestinians have suffered in the past as a point of departure for a moving portrait of the Palestinian people.

"I would urge everyone to read this unique book."
—Amos Elon, author of *Israelis: Founders and Sons*

0-394-74469-1 $14.95 paperback

THE MANTLE OF THE PROPHET:
RELIGION AND POLITICS IN IRAN
by Roy Mottahedeh

A highly intelligent and successful novel on the culture and politics of modern-day Islam as told through the story of a young cleric.

"An exquisite book."—*New York Times Book Review*

0-394-74865-4 $9.95

About the Author

Sana Hasan was born in the United States, where her father was Ambassador from Egypt for ten years. She was raised in Egypt, but returned to the United States to attend university. In 1984 she received a Ph.D. in political science at Harvard. Sana Hasan was co-author, with Amos Elon, of *Between Enemies,* and she has also written on the Middle East for the *New York Times* and the *New York Review of Books*. She is currently a visiting scholar at the Hebrew University's Institute for Advanced Studies, in Jerusalem.